Death, Property, and the Ancestors

DEATH, PROPERTY
and the
ANCESTORS

A STUDY OF THE MORTUARY CUSTOMS
OF THE LODAGAA OF WEST AFRICA

Jack Goody

STANFORD UNIVERSITY PRESS

STANFORD, CALIFORNIA

Permission of Faber and Faber, Ltd., London, to quote from T. S. Eliot's "The Hollow Men," from *Collected Poems 1909–1935*, is hereby gratefully acknowledged.

Stanford University Press
Stanford, California
© 1962 by John R. Goody
Printed in the United States of America
ISBN 0-8047-0068-0
Original edition 1962
Last figure below indicates year of this printing:
89 88 87 86 85 84 83 82 81 80

Preface

Field work apart, the development of a sociology that is not simply limited to Western Europe requires three things: first, hypotheses, second, the comparative analysis to test them, and, third, the conceptual tools to build them.

In their attempts to avoid the errors of nineteenth-century writers, most social anthropologists over the last few decades have concentrated upon presenting the results of their own particular researches. Although their work has often been guided by theoretical considerations, on the whole they have treated such issues implicitly rather than explicitly; and while they have frequently been interested in questions that involve comparative research, they have given little attention to the methods of investigation that such problems entail.

In this study I have made a deliberate attempt to consider the relevant theories put forward by earlier writers and to look at these hypotheses in the light of my own material. This I believe to be one important way of building up the basis of comparative sociology; otherwise each generation stands in danger of spending its energies in proposing "new" theories that have been suggested long since, without bothering to test what already exists. The question of validation is not easy to solve, but it is one that must be squarely faced, if we are to escape from mere assertion.

My own techniques in this respect are rudimentary, but I have made use of certain types of comparative method. To some extent this approach was thrust upon me by the nature of the material I was dealing with; for I was forced to compare the variations as well as the similarities between nearby communities and to ask questions about the correlates and causes of these differences. In addition I have referred to material from other societies where this seemed appropriate to my theme. I would have preferred to make such reference more systematic and to have examined certain hypotheses by means of a cross-cultural sample. For example, it would be interesting to test by such a method the idea that variations in the attitude to the ancestors and the degree of elaboration given to funeral ceremonies depend upon whether property and other relatively exclusive rights are handed on during the holder's lifetime or after his death. But the only instrument I know of that might have helped here is the Human Relations Area File, which was not available to me during my research.

Comparative sociology also needs analytic tools. Some sociologists think it adequate that each writer should develop his own vocabulary to deal with his own field work material. For those who are interested in more than particular reports from particular societies, this procedure has its disadvantages. In earlier papers, I have tried to clarify certain usages (e.g., "double descent," "ritual," and "lineal" and "lateral" relationships) in order to increase their usefulness for comparative work; the reasons for what some people may consider an arid exercise will be more apparent after reading this book. My aim has been to produce tools to be used in analysis rather than concepts to be defended in polemic.

Let me add a word about the way the material was collected. I worked in Ghana (then the Gold Coast), the Upper Volta, and the Ivory Coast for two periods, from August 1950 to September 1951, and from March to December of 1952. My first tour was spent mainly among the LoWiili, my second mainly among the LoDagaba. Although I spent less time in the second community, the discrepancy was partly balanced by my better knowledge of the language and of the culture. Whichever community I was in, I had on my staff (for most of the time) members of the other. By this means I was able to check on similarities and variations, and though I have undoubtedly missed some, questions of this sort were always in the minds of the persons with whom I was working most closely.

I spent some hundred days attending funeral ceremonies and even longer inquiring about them; I attended about twenty-five burial services. But the material I collected is not evenly distributed over the various ceremonies. It is better distributed for the LoWiili than the LoDagaba, better for the burial than for the later ceremonies, better for the exoteric than the esoteric rites. However, while further fieldwork would show the account to be inadequate in certain details, I do not think this additional knowledge would affect my general analysis of the main differences between the two communities.

I would conclude by saying that I do not look upon comparative sociology as a closed discipline, and if I could have found other techniques to deal with the problems in which I was interested I would have used them. Much comparative work in the field of kinship inevitably raises questions about the "strength" or "weakness" of the various relationships, and this is a problem with which I have been concerned in the present study. I do not believe we are likely to make a great deal of progress here until adequate tests are devised that give us some more accurate measurements than our present impressionistic techniques are capable of.

No one can carry out an extended piece of research of this kind without incurring many debts to many people. Mine are numerous:

To the providers of funds: the Colonial Social Science Research Council and the electors to the Anthony Wilkin Studentship at Cambridge University for help during the period I was working in Ghana (1950–52); the electors to the Allen Scholarship and the Behavioral Sciences Division of the Ford Foundation, when I was working through my material in Cambridge (1953–54), and the Center for Advanced Studies in the Behavioral Sciences, for a stimulating year at Stanford (1959–60).

To many people in government service, especially the late Gerard Charles, Mr. and Mrs. D. Dyer Ball, and Mrs. Chilver of the C.S.S.R.C.

To those who have helped to see this manuscript through the press, especially H. E. Goody for reading the proofs and Miss Pauline Wickham (of Stanford University Press) for her many useful suggestions.

To other social scientists, to members of the graduate seminars in social anthropology held by Meyer Fortes at Cambridge and by Max Gluckman at Manchester, to the Fellows at the Center for Advanced Studies in 1959–60, to the many people with whom I have discussed certain of the problems, to Kathleen Gough, David Schneider, and especially to Esther Newcomb Goody. And finally to the three visiting Professors of Social Theory at Cambridge in 1953–56, Talcott Parsons, Lloyd Warner, and George Homans, notable practitioners in a field to which I should like to think this study made some contribution, that of comparative sociology.

But of course my heaviest debt of all is to the LoDagaa themselves, to my own staff, and to the inhabitants of Birifu and Tom.

JACK GOODY

St. John's College, Cambridge
December 1961

A Note on Orthography

Where two forms of a particular word directly follow one another, the first is the LoWiili version, and the second is the LoDagaba; alternatives in a single dialect are separated by the conjunction "or." When only one form is given, this belongs to the LoWiili dialect unless preceded by the letters LD, i.e., LoDagaba.

In order to avoid typesetting difficulties I have not used the phonetic script recommended by the International African Institute as in some of my earlier publications. I have therefore not distinguished between the open and closed forms of vowels; the voiceless velar fricative is printed *gh*; the voiceless palato-alveolar fricative is represented by *sh*, the voiced post-alveolar fricative by *j*, and the velar nasal consonant by *ng*.

Contents

PART FOUR: THE ANCESTORS

List of Plates

(BETWEEN PAGES 100 AND 101)

List of Figures

PART ONE

General Background

CHAPTER I

The People and the Problem

Social anthropologists working in an unfamiliar society are rarely in a position to select in advance, with any degree of accuracy, the problems with which they eventually deal. These problems arise out of a conjunction of the theoretical interests of the field worker and the particular situation in which he finds himself, a situation that may turn out very differently from what the sketchy reports of missionaries, traders, and administrators had led him to expect. I therefore want to begin by saying something about the people among whom I worked in Northern Ghana and explain how the choice of the problems and institutions treated in this book arose in the course of the field work itself.

I am primarily concerned with the social life of the inhabitants of two settlements in the northwest corner of Ghana that are known as Birifu and Tom. Situated near the Black Volta River, which at that point forms the boundary with the newly formed Republics of the Ivory Coast and the Upper Volta, these villages have a population, according to the 1948 Census, of 2,939 and 1,135, respectively. The inhabitants speak dialects of Dagari, a Mossi language, and so form part of the Voltaic- or Gur-speaking peoples, who occupy much of the savannah country within the Niger bend.

The people with whom I am dealing have no centralized political system, and settlements do not automatically group themselves into larger territorially defined units that one can call a society or a tribe. There is of course a certain homogeneity of culture over the whole area, but it is only relative; for customs change gradually from settlement to settlement like the dialects of a language. The people themselves are more aware of the differences than the similarities. Normally they call themselves by the name of the settlement in which they live, and more inclusive tribal names either for themselves or for their neighbors are ill-defined, except where linguistic differences are more than dialectal. However, it does happen that a person may wish to compare or contrast the customs of his own settlement, in whole or in part, with those of other nearby groups. This he will do by means of a pair of "directional" terms, Lo and Dagaa, which indicate both spatial and cultural position, rather as Eastern and Western in Europe today often imply more than merely geographical location.

Since group nomenclature usually operates only in this relative way beyond the boundaries of the settlement, or named local unit, I have had to introduce my own classification of the peoples living in the area. To do this on the basis of differences of custom and artifact raises the difficulty that faces those who attempt to establish "culture areas," namely the problem of which differences and similarities to select as criteria. However, in this instance, the question is answered by the people themselves. By observing the actual way in which they employ the terms Lo and Dagaa, one sees consistencies of usage over particular areas. For example, not only the inhabitants of Tom, but also those of many nearby settlements use the terms in identical ways to refer to aspects of the culture of neighboring peoples. Similar usage with regard to outsiders implies a relative homogeneity of custom in those employing the terms. And although a number of cultural differences may be referred to in this way, such as the types of xylophone played or the sort of lip ornament worn, the central reference always appears to be to the degree of emphasis placed upon relationships traced through men (agnatic) or through women (uterine). The distribution of peoples who use the terms Lo and Dagaa in broadly similar ways is given in Figure 1, and the letters A to G indicate relative position on the Lo-Dagaa axis.

When I write of the inhabitants of the settlement of Birifu as members of the larger community that displays relative homogeneity of culture, I refer to them as the LoWiili, whereas the people of Tom I include among the LoDagaba. The LoDagaba are further subdivided into the LoSaala and the LoPiel; in this case, the names are ones employed by these peoples to refer to each other. More often, even when specific names exist, they are used mainly by outsiders, whereas the actors define their own position only in contraposition to that of other people.

For these peoples as a whole, the LoWiili and the LoDagaba together, there is no accepted name, although some writers refer to them as Lobi; technically they are a "phyle" (Hogbin and Wedgwood [1953]; Goody [1957]), a people without a specific tribal designation, but, from the standpoint of their culture, relatively uniform. I speak of them collectively as the LoDagaa. Figures 1 and 2 will help to clarify this situation, which is summarized in the table below.

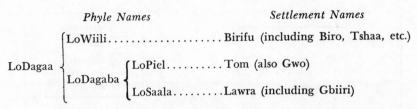

It is important to be clear about this classification at the outset, since the problem with which we shall be concerned has to do with the differences between these communities rather than with their similarities. However, the resemblances are certainly the more numerous, and my account of the social system of the LoWiili (Goody [1956a]) applies in most respects to the LoDagaba. Let me briefly summarize the general situation.

The area inhabited by the LoDagaa, astride the banks of the Black Volta River, is the typical savannah country of West Africa. It is a land of low trees, whose numbers vary inversely with the human population, but are nowhere more dense than the average orchard. The year is abruptly divided into dry and wet seasons, the latter lasting from April

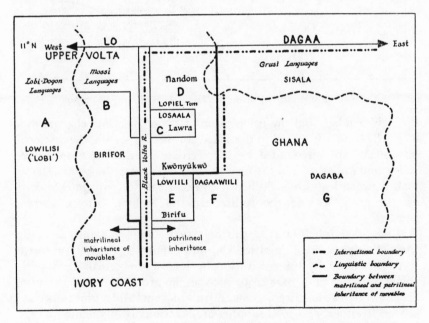

Fig. 1.—The use of the directional names Lo and Dagaa for external reference.

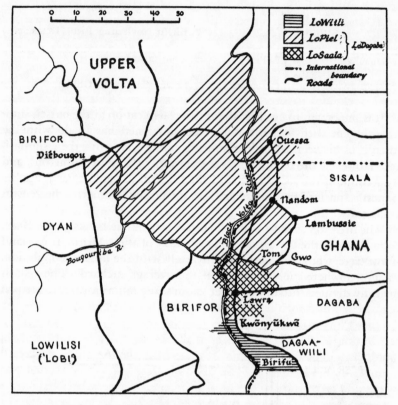

FIG. 2.—The distribution of the LoDagaa (LoWiili and LoDagaba).

through October, and the complexion of the countryside changes dramatically from one season to the other. In the wet season, the scattered homesteads are surrounded by tall, verdant patches of guinea-corn, maize, and millet, and in the uncultivated bush areas thick grass shoots high between leafy trees. When the rains cease, the sun quickly dries up the grass, leaving the rolling country looking brown, barren, and bare.

Like other inhabitants of this belt, such as the Tallensi, a people with whom they share linguistic and other affinities, the LoDagaa gain their livelihood by the cultivation by hoe of the cereals mentioned above, together with root crops such as the groundnut and the yam. Shorthorned cattle, sheep, goats, dogs, chickens, and guinea-fowl are kept as livestock, and food supplies are occasionally augmented by the flesh of wild animals, by fish, oysters, and turtles from the rivers and pools, and by wild leaves and fruits, especially those of the dawa-dawa, the baobab, and the shea, the last being noted for its oil-bearing nut.

Until very recently all the inhabitants were farmers and hunters. In addition, some men specialized in smithying, others in playing and making xylophones, still others in divination and other activities of a magico-religious nature. The only full-time specialists, mostly traders, are to be found in the villages or the quarters of foreigners that are distributed along the main trade routes. The inhabitants of these are mainly Moslem, and their relationships with the indigenous peoples are virtually limited to the market place.

The compact villages of foreigners stand in great contrast to the dispersed settlements of the LoDagaa, whose houses are scattered unevenly over the arable land, fifty to a hundred yards apart. But although there are in most places no obvious boundaries, in fact the whole countryside is divided into parishes or ritual areas, the extent of which is usually coterminous with a named settlement. The persons who owe allegiance to a particular Earth shrine are in effect a local congregation, bound together by the observance of certain prohibitions, the most important of which forbids the shedding of the blood of a fellow member. To break any of these avoidances is to lay oneself open to the mystical retribution of the Earth, on whom the fertility of the crops and the inhabitants depends. Such misfortune, which may be visited not merely upon the sinner himself but also upon his close kin, can be averted only by making an offering at the local shrine. Such occasional sacrifices, as well as the regular offerings made at harvest-time, are made by the custodian or priest of the Earth shrine, who is selected from the patrilineal clan recognized as the first to settle in the area.

Traditionally, there are no other officeholders in the community. There are of course some positions of authority within the patriclans, but the jurisdiction of any one of these extends only to a very limited number of persons.

The inhabitants of a parish belong to a number of different patriclans, the members of which are generally found living near their fellow clansmen. The patriclans themselves are named, exogamous groups, claiming common descent, and are widely dispersed throughout the whole region. Their subdivisions, the localized groups of members found within one parish, I speak of as clan sectors (Hogbin and Wedgwood [1953]).

The area inhabited by a clan sector tends to correspond to a subdivision of the parish, the minor ritual area that has its own sacred grove. However, these territorial units are of peripheral importance in everyday life.

Within the clan sectors are found genealogically defined lineages of shallow depth. Here the two communities differ somewhat one from another. Among the LoWiili, the clan sector is visualized as divided into a known number of patrilineages, varying between two and four and having an over-all depth of about five generations.[1] Each lineage has a recognized elder, the genealogically senior male, and the elders from the same clan sector consult together informally when matters of common interest require. Among the LoDagaba, the internal organization of the clan sectors is looser, and there is no division into a recognized number of lineages. Both the clan sectors and the lineages are smaller in size. This difference in the internal organization of the clan sectors appears to be related to other features of the social organization, as the subsequent discussion will show.

The patriclans are grouped together into more inclusive units in two ways, by joking partnerships and by legends of common origin; those associated in this latter way I call linked clans, and they have a greater part to play among the LoDagaba, among whom the lineages are of less importance.

In addition to the agnatic groups, there is a further series defined by uterine descent. These matriclans also spread over a wide area; but, as distinct from the patriclans, they can have no localized subdivisions apart from the children of one woman, since marriage is virilocal. To differentiate these various types of clan in respect of their spatial distribution, I speak of the matriclans as non-localized and the patriclans as dispersed, both being distinguished from compact descent groups.

As in the case of the patriclans, the matriclans found among both the communities are recognized as the same groups. They are four in number, and these again are paired in joking partnerships. It is in respect of the matriclans that the central difference between the two communities lies, a difference that is constantly discussed among the inhabitants themselves and, as I have remarked, that is the central reference in establishing cultural direction by means of the terms Lo and Dagaa. The LoWiili inherit all property in the agnatic line. The LoDagaba transmit immovable property, rights in land and houses, in this way; but movable wealth, cattle, money, and the produce of the land, all pass in the uterine line. Thus, although the same four matriclans, bearing the

---

[1] By over-all depth, I mean the inclusive count from the junior living generation. For this purpose I assume the number of living generations to be three.

same names, extend throughout both communities, only among the LoDagaba are they property-holding corporations (Fig. 3). To this fact the inhabitants themselves attribute a number of differences between their two societies, especially in the relationships between close kin.

It is the validity of this assumed correlation that I wish to examine. And to do this means comparing the standardized modes of acting in the two communities, in order to see where the differences lie. Having established the covariations, we have then to try to determine which are the dependent, which the independent, variables; that is, we have to ascertain which of these differences are functionally related, in the mathematical sense, to what the actors take to be the independent variable, the system of property relations.

One way of doing this would be to analyze changes in property relations over time and then isolate the concomitants. Although evidence concerning changes in the past is not lacking (indeed the process of change still goes on), I do not intend to present such material here except in summary form. I am avoiding a detailed account, partly because it would involve an elaborate exposition of population movements and personal histories, which are only meaningful if the framework of the social system has been analyzed beforehand, and partly

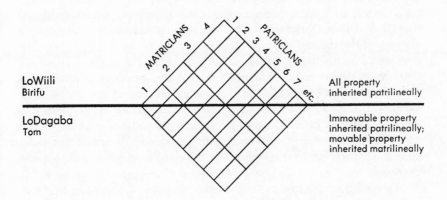

FIG. 3.—Double clanship and double inheritance among the LoDagaa. The same-named patriclans and matriclans exist in both communities, but only among the LoDagaba are the matriclans property-holding. Every person belongs to a clan of each sort, so that these groups are cross-cutting from the standpoint both of the individual and of the community. The diagram should not be interpreted to mean that any particular clans are more numerous in one community than in another.

because it would raise some general problems about the change from one type of "descent" system to another, problems that require consideration in the context of earlier hypotheses on the subject.

Instead, I shall examine the differences between the communities in order to discover, first, which of these are attributed by the actors to differences in property relations and, second, which can be logically accounted for in this way from the observer's point of view. Third, by looking at developments that occurred during the short space of time covered by the field research and the personal histories of informants, an attempt will be made to outline the operation of specific mechanisms of social interaction related to these variables in situations both of continuity and of change. And insofar as this last endeavor is successful, I will in effect be not only assigning direction to the differences between the two communities, but also eliciting a causal sequence.

Nadel ([1951] chap. 8) maintains that any such enterprise necessarily entails the introduction of psycho-physical factors.[2] It is certainly true that the present analysis involves a consideration of such factors as the hostility to which systems of property and authority give rise and that this hostility is seen as the intervening condition, the necessary link, between the dependent and independent variables. In this sense, I have to deal with "psychological" constituents, such as sentiments. Those who object to the intermingling of what they see as distinct levels of analysis should recall that even the most "sociological" anthropologists have been forced to similar procedures in the past (e.g., Radcliffe-Brown [1922]), and that Durkheim's criticisms, which have formed the source of much of the subsequent thinking on the subject, were directed against the sort of instinctual psychologizing that prevailed at the turn of the century. A different position from that of the sociological purists has been put forward by Nadel [1951], and a recognition of the interlocking nature of the social and personality systems forms one of the main theoretical premises behind the work of Parsons and his associates. But whatever our stand, it should be remembered that it is always the social aspects of such sentiments that are of significance for our present purposes.

To return to the question of establishing the important differences between the two communities, it is clear that within the limited compass of this book, we can make no detailed comparison of the whole gamut of social behavior among the LoDagaa. What, then, is the most profitable area to investigate?

The crucial features of any system of relatively exclusive rights, the

[2] Newcomb ([1950] chap. 1) and Spiro [1953] make a similar point in discussing "intervening variables."

general category into which property falls, seem most likely to be displayed when these rights are transmitted from one individual to the next, a process that is made inevitable by the inescapable fact of death. In most societies this transfer occurs between close kin, and it occurs at death. It has an importance that those brought up in industrialized societies, with their greater emphasis upon alternative methods of access to property and to restricted statuses, find difficult to appreciate.

This comparison, therefore, will concentrate upon examining the mortuary institutions of the LoDagaa; in this phrase I include the funeral ceremonies, ideas of the afterlife, the worship of the ancestors, and, closely bound up with these practices and beliefs, the way in which relatively exclusive rights are handed down from one generation to the next, especially the system of inheritance.

The mortuary institutions of the LoDagaa will be analyzed not only for the purpose of comparing these two communities, but also in order to throw light on some of the more general problems involved. Methods of inheritance, for example, have received little systematic treatment, and we shall be particularly concerned with them from the standpoint of the relationship between persons of adjacent generations, the hostile element in which is seen to derive from a number of situations, of which the distribution of exclusive sexual rights is but one. Funeral ceremonies and ancestor worship have had more attention from those concerned with the comparative study of society, and the contributions of these writers will be discussed in the following chapter.

My own general interest in these institutions derives from two sources. In the first place, funeral ceremonies are the most elaborate of the ceremonial occasions of the LoDagaa, whether this be measured in terms of numbers attending, time taken, or emotion generated. Equally, ancestor worship can be considered the most significant of their relationships with supernatural agencies. Owing to the importance of funeral ceremonies in the social life of the LoDagaa, examination of these institutions raises, in acute form, methodological questions relating to the analysis of rite and ceremony, and these I discuss in the third chapter. In the second place, funeral ceremonies are inevitably involved with the problem of mortality, how to avoid and how to accept it, which is central to every set of religious beliefs. Although the belief in survival after death requires the existence of another world, the reverse is not necessarily true; however, in practice the two beliefs are invariably linked together. Ancestor worship involves one form of this belief in an afterlife, and funeral ceremonies are the means by which the actual passage of a human being from the Land of the Living to the Land of the Dead is effected.

The significance of mortuary institutions for the sociology of religion was recognized by nineteenth-century writers, who developed conjectural schemata by which they tried to show that here lay the source of religious activities. The rejection of this kind of untestable conjecture about the origin of things, combined with the shift in emphasis in defining religion from "spiritual beings" to "the sacred," has led in recent years to a declining interest in these phenomena. But whatever the changes of emphasis among sociologists, the problem of mortality remains a major focus of all systems of religious practices and beliefs, just as the distribution of property continues to be a central concern of secular activities.

CHAPTER II

Approaches to the Study of Mortuary Institutions

Of all sources of religion, the supreme and final crisis of life—
death—is of the greatest importance. Death is the gateway to the
other world in more than the literal sense.

MALINOWSKI

Many of the early contributors to the comparative sociology of religion, especially Edward Tylor and Herbert Spencer, saw in the institutions that center upon death—funeral ceremonies, cults of the dead, and beliefs in an afterlife—the kernel of their studies. Sir William Ridgeway, for example, not only found in the performances surrounding death the source of all religion, but also discerned the origin of Greek tragedy and of the Olympic games in the commemoration and propitiation of the dead.[1] Recent trends have led to a discounting of the validity of speculations about the origin of social phenomena and to a concentration upon the synchronic studies of particular societies. There can be little doubt that this change has greatly contributed to the development of field anthropology; on the other hand, it has also perhaps tended to encourage a degree of ethnographic myopia.

In this chapter, I want briefly to review the part that the study of funeral ceremonies and ancestor worship has played in the various social sciences over the past hundred years. My purpose is not only to explain the background against which this study is written, but also to suggest that the problems raised by writers of an earlier period, or by those in neighboring disciplines, cannot always be dismissed as easily as recent anthropologists have sometimes supposed. Since nineteenth-century writers were mainly occupied with ancestor worship and beliefs

---

[1] "The Tragedy . . . was the lineal descendant of the tragic dance and solemn hymn round the tomb of the old hero" ([1910] p. 55).

in an afterlife rather than with funeral ceremonies, I shall begin by considering the discussions that centered upon the first of these institutions.

ANCESTOR WORSHIP

The examination of the religious beliefs of primitive peoples received a great stimulus from Darwin's formulation of the doctrine of evolution in 1859. The year 1865 saw the publication of Tylor's *Researches into the Early History of Mankind* and Lubbock's *Pre-historic Times, as Illustrated by Ancient Remains, and the Manners and Customs of Modern Savages,* in which evidence from the "inferior races" was adduced to illustrate the development of human institutions, and the method applied to stone tools was used to trace the sequence of beliefs in supernatural agencies.

Of all the concomitants of Darwin's work, it was perhaps the reexamination of accepted beliefs in the supernatural that caused most stir in contemporary intellectual circles. In their earliest works, neither Tylor nor Lubbock had given much space to the study of religion. But in the year following the publication of *The Early History of Mankind,* Tylor contributed an article to the *Fortnightly Review* on "The Religion of Savages." This interest was subsequently elaborated in his *Primitive Culture* (1871), as well as by Lubbock in *The Origin of Civilization,* published in the same year.

Although on the ethnological side the approach of these two writers owes much to the German anthropologist Bastian,[2] each made contributions of his own to the study of the phenomena we are considering here. Lubbock maintained that dreams were the basis of beliefs in the other life ([1902] pp. 226–27), and Tylor emphasized the association of these beliefs with the body-soul dichotomy. This association led to a concentration of interest upon ancestor worship. Particular attention was given to beliefs in the metamorphosis of soul into ghost. Offerings to the dead body were regarded as the prototype of sacrifices to the ancestors. Ancestor worship, associated as it is with the universal fact of death, became the archetypal form of primitive religion.

Tylor's whole discussion of animism, the belief in Spiritual Beings, a phrase that he offers as his "minimum definition of religion," centers on the idea that spiritual beings are projections of human ones. "The doctrines of the lower races fully justify us in classing their spiritual

---

[2] *Der Mensch in der Geschichte* [1860], Vol. II, "Psychologie und Mythologie," especially the section entitled "Die Seele," pp. 304–79.

beings in general as similar in nature to the souls of men" ([1920] II, 110). Manes or ancestor worship became the focus of attention as

> one of the great branches of the religion of mankind. Its principles are not difficult to understand, for they plainly keep up the social relations of the living world. The dead ancestor, now passed into a deity, simply goes on protecting his own family and receiving suit and service from them as of old; the dead chief still watches over his own tribe, still holds his authority by helping friends and harming enemies, still rewards the right and sharply punishes the wrong ([1920] II, 113).

The schema used by Tylor and Lubbock defined the range of discourse of many subsequent writers on comparative religion, and controversy developed around two main points: first, the antiquity of ancestor worship, and, second, the friendliness or hostility of the ancestors.

The first of these discussions centered upon the position taken by Herbert Spencer in *The Principles of Sociology* (1875–76), which, even taking into account its debt to Tylor on the anthropological side and Comte on the sociological side, was a truly remarkable survey. Although Tylor vigorously promoted the idea of an evolutionary sequence of human institutions, his analysis of religious beliefs tends to be typological rather than sequential. Evans-Pritchard ([1933] p. 298) has pointed out how Frazer took Tylor's analysis of magic, religion, and science and transformed the categories into stages of a unilineal evolutionary schema, with an Age of Religion following an Age of Magic and being succeeded in turn by an Age of Science. In a similar way, Spencer incorporates Tylor's discussion of religion, develops its evolutionary aspects, and proposes a single historical sequence for beliefs in supernatural beings. He writes, for example, of the "transformation of ancestors into deities," and "the growth of funeral rites into worship of the dead, and eventually into religious worship" ([1896] I, 294). He traces the genesis of supernatural beings through a number of stages: (1) the belief in the continued existence of the soul; (2) offerings at funerals; (3) ghost-propitiation, "for a subsequent interval"; (4) "persistent ancestor-worship"; (5) the "worship of distinguished ancestors" subordinating that of the undistinguished; and (6) the worship of deities ([1896] I, 303–5). And finally, as in Tylor's discussion, the worship of idols, fetishes, animals, plants, and Nature is traced to one and the same source.

Criticism of Spencer's schema arose on the grounds that since ancestor worship was a "family cult," and since the family was considered to be absent in the early stages of human society, this cult could not have served as the progenitor of other types of religious institution. Jevons writes in his *Introduction to the History of Religion*: "Like all other private cults, the worship of ancestors was modelled on the public worship of the community; and as the family is an institution of later growth than the tribe or clan, the worship of family ancestors is a later institution than the worship of the tribal god" ([1902] p. 13). Hence it was totemism, "the cult of the clan," that was singled out as the most primitive form of the religious life in the works of Frazer, Robertson Smith, Durkheim, and others of the period. And this assumption was given some encouragement and support by the excellent reports of Australian peoples that were becoming available at that time.

Westermarck's disposal of "primitive promiscuity" and establishment of the universality of marital institutions automatically put an end to this objection to the Spencerian schema. The primacy of the family and the primacy of ancestor worship then dovetailed together in a manner that particularly appealed to the predilection of some psychologists for identifying ontogenetical and phylogenetical sequences. For Freud, for example, the feelings developed toward the parents are projected onto supernatural beings. It is not surprising, therefore, to find that psychoanalytic writers have displayed a special interest in ancestor worship. Flügel, indeed, writing in 1921, went a long way toward accepting Spencer when he wrote: "There can be no doubt that the most important aspects of the theory and practice of religion are very largely derived from, and influenced by, ancestor worship, even though they may not, as Herbert Spencer has contended, have entirely originated from this source" ([1948] p. 135).

In *The Elementary Forms of the Religious Life,* published in 1912, Durkheim also criticizes the Tylor-Spencer approach (which he treats as one),[3] but from a very different point of view. However, his argument against Tylor's position is somewhat involved because he tries to deal with at least three questions at the same time: namely, the "minimal" definition of religion as the belief in spiritual beings, the derivation of the body-soul dichotomy from dream experiences, and the question of ancestor worship as the elementary form of religion.

These are logically separable problems upon which Durkheim makes a rather blunderbuss attack, offering some nine arguments in quick-fire

[3] Durkheim maintains that Tylor thought of ancestor worship as the earliest religion, summarizing him as saying that it is "to the dead, to the souls of ancestors, that the first cult known to humanity was addressed. Thus the first rites were funeral rites; the first sacrifices were food offerings destined to satisfy the needs of the departed; the first altars were tombs" ([1947] p. 52).

succession in an attempt to demolish Tylor's position. But this was not so easy as it appeared. Tylor's first problem had to do with the definition of religious institutions, which I do not intend to discuss at this juncture. But it is noteworthy that recently at least one major contribution to the study of non-European societies, Evans-Pritchard's notable study of Nuer religion [1956], has reverted to Tylor's usage.

With regard to the second question, we may reject the claim that all religious institutions are ultimately founded upon dream experiences, but something of value yet emerges from Tylor's discussion. For the body-soul dichotomy does appear to be a universal feature of human society, and this suggests that some common element in man's experience may possibly be associated with the existence of these concepts. Some mammalian species act as if they were dreaming (de Haan [n.d.], p. 142). The development of speech in humans would lead to the need to communicate two forms of human experience, the perception of images while awake and during sleep, which though broadly similar in respect to content, are radically different in terms of relationship to the world outside. The dualistic view of man, the distinction between the flesh on the one hand and the spirit, soul, double, or shadow on the other, is an economical way of meeting some of the difficulties involved in giving verbal expression to these experiences, and one that opens the way both to beliefs in an afterlife and in the mystical activities of witches. However this may be, it is certainly true that, as Lubbock declared, dreams are intimately associated with the "lower" forms of religion ([1902] p. 225), and it is difficult to deny the *functional* association between the body-soul dichotomy and the explanation of dreams, beliefs in witchcraft, and beliefs in an afterlife, even though it is quite impossible, as Durkheim rightly insisted, to test the *causal* association.[4]

On the third question, Durkheim asserts that "The ancestral cult is not greatly developed . . . except in advanced societies like those of China, Egypt, or the Greek or Latin cities; on the other hand, it is completely lacking in the Australian societies, which . . . represent the lowest and simplest form of social organization which we know" ([1947] p. 63). And he goes on to conclude that if "the cult of the dead is shown not to be primitive, animism lacks a basis" ([1947] p. 65). Durkheim's position here is far from sound. To begin with, there was ample evidence, even at the time he wrote, to show a much wider distribution of ancestor worship. Crooke's contribution to *Hastings' Encyclopaedia of Religion and Ethics* [1908], for example, mentions the existence of such

---

[4] Forde [1958] has recently defended Tylor's position on this subject in his Frazer Lecture for 1957.

cults in India, Africa, Polynesia, Melanesia, and Malaysia. Moreover, even as far as Australia is concerned, it is possible to regard this form of totemism as a kind of ancestor worship, the totemic spirits and the ancestor spirits being closely associated both in the totemic well and in cult objects (Warner [1937], chap. 13). Finally, Durkheim goes far beyond the assertion that the Australians have no ancestor worship, for he even denies them a cult of the dead, the basis for animism.

In view of my later argument, it should be understood that this phrase of Durkheim's, the cult of the dead, is used in a special sense. He admits that there are funeral rites and rites of mourning, but denies that these constitute a cult, which he says "is not a simple group of ritual precautions which a man is held to take in certain circumstances; it is a system of diverse rites, festivals and ceremonies which *all have this characteristic, that they reappear periodically*" ([1947] p. 63). Thus he would speak of marriage rites and not a marriage cult. "There is no cult of the ancestors except where sacrifices are made on the tombs from time to time, when libations are poured there on certain more or less specific dates, or when festivals are regularly celebrated in honor of the dead" (*ibid.*). In this passage Durkheim fails to distinguish between ancestor worship and the cult of the dead, a distinction of some importance in the analysis of these institutions. For although the worship of ancestral spirits is not universal, one of Durkheim's group, Robert Hertz, had already maintained, with good reason, that cults of the dead were to be found in all societies.

In Durkheim, the historical and morphological meanings of the term "primitive" are at times somewhat confused (though less so than in many writers of the period), so that he was still partly concerned with the antiquity of ancestor worship. Today, anthropologists are no longer greatly interested in this problem, since there is little evidence that can be brought to bear one way or the other. The importance of the institution for the comparative study of social phenomena is sufficiently attested by its widespread occurrence. Indeed, taking the term in the morphological rather than the "evolutionary" sense, ancestor worship has been partially re-established as the elementary form of the religious life, despite Durkheim's opposition and his counter-promotion of totemism. Radcliffe-Brown, for instance, declared that: "In my own experience it is in ancestor-worship that we can most easily discover and demonstrate the social function of a religious cult" ([1952d] p. 163).

But this revival of interest in ancestor worship, though not unconnected with the study of kinship, no longer rests upon the question of whether or not the family is a universal institution. It will be remembered that the grounds upon which Spencer's Euhemerism had first been rejected, and then partially rehabilitated, depended upon an assumption that ancestor worship was a "family" cult. Further study brought to light the fact that the typical congregation of the ancestral cult is not the cognatically constituted family, but the unilineal descent group, the clan or the lineage. Indeed, this point was explicit in Fustel de Coulanges's analysis of Greek and Roman religion [1864], was later discussed by Bertha Phillpotts in *Kindred and Clan*,[5] and was subsequently formulated by Radcliffe-Brown in much the same words as those used by Coulanges: "The cult group in this religion consists solely of persons related to one another by descent in one line from the same ancestor or ancestors" ([1952d] p. 163). It was not accidental, therefore, that this renewal of interest arose in conjunction with the analysis of societies in which unilineal descent groups played an important part. Especially was this the case in the study of lineage systems, in which the genealogy that serves as a reference for social relationships may also act as the framework for a developed cult of the ancestors, as is the case among the Tallensi of Northern Ghana (Fortes [1945]).

One other feature of the controversy about the antiquity of ancestor worship is relevant to the intellectual history of the comparative study of religion. The reaction against the approach of Tylor and Spencer took several forms. There were attempts at a more inclusive definition of religious phenomena, by Marett and Durkheim for example, which tended to undermine the basis of the temporal sequences. There was Durkheim's insistence on the analysis of interrelationships, rather than the elaboration of highly speculative evolutionary schemata that were susceptible neither to proof nor to disproof. And, finally, there was an increased emphasis on the study of "High Gods." Indeed, the establishment of the universality of the High God became a matter of some weight to the divines, who now entered the field of comparative religion in the wake of the anthropologists. For if all men could be shown to have worshiped the One God, this could be taken as in indirect justification of their own beliefs. With High Gods as the fixed point of reference—the truly elementary form of religion—the dead were seen as "achieving divinity."

This is the position of Andrew Lang, and it is implicitly accepted by Radin when, in his article on the subject in the *Encyclopaedia of the Social Sciences* [1930], he defines ancestor worship as "the equation of

---

[5] "It is obvious that ancestor-worship, so frequently found in connection with a clan system, must segregate the kinsfolk into organizations either on patrilinear or on matrilinear lines" ([1913] p. 271).

one's ancestors . . . with spirits and gods, and the transference to them
of all specifically religious acts and attitudes which are usually associated with the worship of the spirits and gods." More recently Eliade,
in his *Patterns in Comparative Religion,* reverses the order of Spencer's
stages and speaks of the "history" of Supreme Beings and sky gods who
tend to disappear from the cult to be replaced by other religious forces,
"by ancestor-worship, worship of the spirits and gods of nature, spirits
of fertility, Great Goddesses and so forth" ([1958] p. 109).

Radin's suggestion that religious behavior toward the ancestors is
modeled upon behavior toward the gods and spirits avoids the more
general question of the model for the acts and attitudes of humans toward supernatural beings, and of supernatural beings toward men. Of
course, from the standpoint of the member of any particular society,
the appropriate modes of behavior, as well as the supernatural beings
themselves, are, as Durkheim insisted, given. Nevertheless, the sociologist must assume that religious relationships, those between men and
spiritual beings, are patterned upon interpersonal relationships, those
between men. For the one premise on which he can begin such an investigation is that the unknowable can be conceptualized only in terms
of the known. The observer sees both ancestors and deities as standardized social projections, behavior toward which is based upon that obtaining among the living. Such an assumption is implicit in the work
of Tylor and of other writers both before and since; in 1889, Robertson
Smith wrote, in *The Religion of the Semites*: "The feelings called forth
when the deity was conceived as a father were on the whole of an
austerer kind, for the distinctive note of fatherhood, as distinguished
from kinship in general, lay mainly in the parental authority, in the
father's claim to be honored and served by his son" ([1927] p. 59). This
approach was later made quite explicit by Freud, for whom supernatural beings were the apotheosis of parental figures.

A discussion of this point leads directly to the second main aspect
of the nineteenth-century controversy over ancestor worship, the question of the attitude of the ancestors to their living descendants. Robertson Smith regarded the relationship as being essentially positive in character: "It is not with a vague fear of unknown powers but with a loving
reverence for known gods who are knit to their worshippers by strong
bonds of kinship, that religion in the true sense begins" ([1927] pp. 54–
55). Here he refers to supernatural beings in general, but a little later
ancestor worship is more specifically treated by Jevons in very much the
same way.

A different line of thought, represented by Tylor and Frazer, perceived the ancestors not as friendly but as hostile to humanity, as a threat rather than a help to their descendants. In two lengthy works, *The Belief in Immortality and the Worship of the Dead* [1913–24] and *The Fear of the Dead in Primitive Religion* [1933–36], Frazer produced a formidable mass of evidence to support the claim that a man is thought to be more hostile to his descendants after his death than during his lifetime. For example, he examines the very widespread precautions taken to prevent the return of the dead to this world, and the actions adopted to protect the survivors from the hostility of the departed should they succeed in their efforts to come back. He also observes that the greatest danger is felt to lie with those of the bereaved who had been closest to the dead man. But having remarked upon these general features, Frazer confesses he is uncertain what to do. In the introduction to his last volume he writes:

> The only lesson we can safely draw from the survey of facts here submitted to the reader is a lesson of humility and hope: a lesson of humility, because it reminds us how little we know on the subject, which, of all others, concerns us most nearly; a lesson of hope, because it suggests the possibility that others may hereafter solve the problem which has baffled us ([1936] Vol. V).[6]

However, instead of leaving matters at the point of hopeful humility, his final words suggest a more specific solution: ". . . we may surmise that the same fear [of the dead] has gone far to shape the moulds into which religious thought has run ever since feeble man began to meditate on the great mysteries by which our little life on earth is encompassed" ([1936] p. 311). Thus his conclusion seems to suggest that the fear of the ancestors, and indeed much of religious thought, is an extension of an instinctive fear of the corpse.

Malinowski, developing his thesis about the importance of the reactions to death as a source of religion, was also concerned with the fear of the corpse, which like Frazer he considered instinctive. In his study *Magic, Science and Religions* (1925), Malinowski maintains that the assumption of most anthropologists that the dominant feeling among the survivors is one of horror at the corpse and of fear of the ghost is only a half-truth ("which means no truth at all"). The emotions aroused, he claims, are extremely complex and even contradictory; this results from an intermingling of two elements, love of the dead and fear of the

[6] A similar dilemma is reached by Miss Bendann in her book *Death Customs*, in which she writes: "As Jochelson suggests, the question why dead persons are supposed to radiate such danger especially upon those to whom they have been most attached and dearest in life, is one of the most difficult problems for the ethnologist to attempt to solve" ([1930] p. 80).

corpse. The fear of the corpse he sees as fear of annihilation, against which man has erected funeral customs and the belief in life after death ([1954] pp. 47–53). He concludes: "The saving belief in spiritual continuity after death is already contained in the individual mind; it is not created by society. The sum total of innate tendencies, known usually as 'the instinct of self-preservation', is at the root of this belief" ([1954] p. 62).

The conclusion has not gone unchallenged. On the sociological side, Radcliffe-Brown denies that Andaman burial customs are due to an instinctual fear of the corpse, pointing to the way in which treatment of the deceased varies according to his social position. He also notes the hostility believed to exist between the living and the dead, and at one point speaks of this as "ambivalent, compounded of affection and fear" ([1948] p. 299). But his explanation differs from Malinowski's in stressing the social elements: "The fear of the dead man . . . is a collective feeling induced in the society by the fact that by death he has become the object of a dysphoric condition of the collective consciousness" ([1948] p. 298).

On the psychological side, Anthony has maintained that the reactions of children to death are remarkably matter-of-fact and devoid of anxiety. She claims that it is only at a later stage that the "idea of death is invested with affect . . . through linking with (a) birth anxiety and (b) aggressive impulses" ([1940] p. 134). Attitudes toward death appear to be learned rather than instinctive, a conclusion that is supported by the work of Nagy in Budapest (Murphy [1959]).

In *Totem and Taboo*, originally published in 1913, Freud had already pointed to the inadequacy of those writers who had explained the institutionalized treatment of death in terms of an instinctive fear of the corpse ([1952] p. 57). In this work he related both mourning customs and the ruthlessness of the ancestors to a third factor, namely the guilt that the survivors experience as a reaction against the hostile element inevitably present in all close relationships.

> . . . after death *has* occurred, it is against this unconscious wish that the reproaches are a reaction. In almost every case where there is an intense emotional attachment to a particular person we find that behind the tender love there is a concealed hostility in the unconscious. This is the classical example, the prototype, of the ambivalence of human emotions (*ibid.*, p. 60).

Whereas Malinowski treated the relationships to the dead as contradictory and associated this with the conflict between the positive feelings for the living and the negative feelings for the corpse, and while

Radcliffe-Brown ascribes these same phenomena to the hostility existing between the world of the living and the world of the dead, Freud pointed out that the relationships among the living were themselves ambivalent, and it is in terms of this that he explains attitudes to the dead. At times, Freud appears to regard this ambivalence as a biological given. For although he attributes the hostility of the sons to jealousy of their father's sexual rights, he also assumes "that the psychical impulses of primitive peoples were characterized by a higher amount of ambivalence than is to be found in modern civilized man" ([1952] p. 66). In other words, the situation is seen rooted in the organism, the assumed changes in the degree of ambivalence being assigned to phylogenetic factors, to the slow maturation of civilized man from his savage childhood.

Freud's work has had a considerable influence on the study of funeral ceremonies and ancestor worship, but the differences that exist between societies have forced the sociologist engaged in comparative work to make certain modifications. For example, the variations in relationships between members of adjacent generations cannot be satisfactorily explained in terms of the operation of hereditarily derived instincts. Indeed Freud himself was not altogether consistent in this matter; although he did not always appreciate the extent to which personality formation is a matter of learning within a specific social system, his conception of the Oedipus complex by no means precludes the influence of social factors.

The demonstration of differences in the crucial social relationships from one society to another led to various attempts at further refinement. Margaret Mead, in "An Ethnologist's Footnote to *Totem and Taboo*," pointed out that cultures emphasize different aspects of the ambivalent attitude, and went on to maintain that the choice of which aspect "is culturally stressed will depend upon historical causes" ([1930] p. 304). However, few social scientists working in non-literate societies are in a position to adopt such an approach, even if it were shown to be the most profitable, since they inevitably lack information about past events of this kind. But it has proved possible to say more about the factors involved by approaching from another angle.

An alternative to the search for specific antecedents is the search for correlative factors with which to associate the ambivalence, that is, for relations of interdependence. This approach was adopted by Opler [1936] in his paper on the fear of the dead among certain Apache groups, among whom he considers the hostility of the dead to be a manifestation of the ambivalent attitude toward relatives resulting from matrilocal residence and the authority vested in kin. Fortes's study of Tallensi ancestor worship, which is seen as a social projection of filial ties in a patrilineal society [1949 and 1959], represents a more refined and more detailed treatment in the same general tradition.

This approach has resulted, both in this field and in much recent work on witchcraft, in further attempts to link hostile supernatural relationships with the stereotypical conflict situations in the social system. Particularly valuable in this respect is Gough's comparison of Nayar and Brahman cults of the dead [1958]. Discussing the differences in the expression of ambivalence in various social systems, she raises the following question: "Why . . . do some societies express ambivalence in mixed attitudes to the dead, others in predominantly hostile attitudes with the benevolent suppressed, and still others in predominantly benevolent attitudes with the hostile aspects suppressed?" ([1958] p. 453). The matrilineal Nayar have a cult that is punitive in type, whereas the Brahman ancestors are in general more lenient to their descendants. In trying to reconcile these differences, Gough takes a hint from Whiting and Child, who attempted to correlate "the fear of others" with socialization anxiety, on the hypothesis that such fears represent an overgeneralization of the reaction to parents ([1953] pp. 265–69). She suggests that in the Brahmans' case socialization may in fact so repress aggression against the parents as to inhibit the expression of intergenerational hostility, even after death; whereas cults of predominantly punitive ancestors, such as she finds among the Nayar, "are likely to be accompanied by kinship relationships in which the senior generation retains control over the junior until late in life, but in which major figures of the senior generation are not highly idealized" ([1958] p. 457).

This approach represents a merging of certain psychological and sociological methods of handling the institutionalized treatment of death and is similar to the kind of analysis attempted in the chapters that follow. In these, an examination will be made of the conflicts within the social system that give rise to what Freud called ambivalent feelings in the personality. These conflict situations will be looked at within the context of the ritual and religious institutions that mark the two neighboring communities, a comparison that will assist the isolation of the particular variables involved. Specifically, I shall try to relate differences in the mourning customs and ancestor worship of the two neighboring peoples to differences in their nuclear social relationships, and these in turn to differences in the mode of inheritance and locus of domestic authority: that is, in the location of what may be called the holder-heir and socialization situations.

There is one danger in using the concept of ambivalence that must be mentioned at the outset. Freud's usage derives from Bleuler, who wrote: "Even the normal individual feels, as it were, two souls in his breast, he fears an event and wishes it to come, as in the case of an operation, or the acceptance of a new position. Such a double feeling tone exists most frequently and is particularly drastic when it concerns persons, whom one hates or fears and at the same time loves."[7] Hence, to say of a particular social relationship that it is ambivalent is often to say very little, since all relationships are surely characterized both by a positive and by a negative component. The same point has recently been made by Gough ([1958] p. 453). Instead, then, of looking for the presence of ambivalent attitudes as such, I shall try to examine the differential distribution of the hostile and friendly components of social relationships; an attempt can then be made to relate these to the type of conflicts that a particular set of social institutions might be expected to engender.

FUNERAL CEREMONIES

Despite the remarkable analysis made by his teacher Fustel de Coulanges of the relationship between lineage structure and ancestor worship and its relevance to the wider problem of the connection between social groups and ritual institutions, Durkheim followed the prevailing trend and relegated ancestor worship to a less important place in the study of religion than it had held for earlier writers. Little attention was paid to these particular practices and beliefs by other members of his circle. But in the study of funeral ceremonies, his associates made some notable contributions, particularly Hertz in an article entitled "Contribution à une étude sur la représentation collective de la mort" (1907; Eng. trans. 1960) and Van Gennep in *Les Rites de passage* (1909; Eng. trans. 1960).

In the field of comparative religion, one of the points of common orientation of the *Année sociologique* school was their criticism of the "animist" interpretations of religious phenomena. The positive implication of this criticism was that magico-religious practices were no longer only, or even mainly, analyzed in terms of their associated beliefs, but were related to other institutions of the social system. Van Gennep comments that the whole *folkloriste* approach attempts to isolate single ritual acts from their contexts. It is for this reason, he argues, that Frazer fails to see that seasonal ceremonials form part of a wider constellation of social acts, *rites de passage,* which leads him to restrict his attention to the magical and religious aspects of such performances in

[7] Bleuler [1930], cited in L. E. Hinsie and J. Shatzky, *Psychiatric Dictionary* (New York, 1940), p. 24.

the limited sense (Van Gennep [1960], pp. 92, 180; Hertz [1960], p. 121, n.56).

Accepting the same general approach, Hertz begins his essay on death by referring to an observation made by Lafitau in 1724 about the wide distribution of the double funeral among savage peoples, and asks what the significance of this virtually universal custom is ([1960] p. 28). In answering this question, he observes first of all that the horror of the corpse cannot be explained on a physical basis alone, but is also of a social kind. Societies regard themselves as on-going systems, and consequently the death of any member threatens their very existence. "Thus, when a man dies, society loses in him much more than a unit; it is stricken in the very principle of its life, in the faith it has in itself" (*ibid.*, p. 78). Death is therefore perceived as something contra-social and in this sense unnatural. Moreover, the refusal to accept death as an inevitable occurrence opens the way for its attribution to anti-social causes of a mystical nature, to the hostility of present members of the community (witchcraft and sorcery), of past members (the ancestors), or of other supernatural beings.

But whereas the *conscience collective* cannot reconcile itself to the necessity for mortality, it also refuses to consider death irrevocable. Death is not simply an end to life, it is also the beginning of a new existence in another world: "the notion of death is linked with that of resurrection; exclusion is always followed by a new integration" (*ibid.*, p. 79). In this way beliefs in an afterlife can be seen as meeting the threat that death makes to the social system.

The passage from the visible to the invisible world is similar to other regular changes of state which occur in all societies, to the rites of birth, initiation, and marriage, each of which involves an exclusion—that is, a death—followed by a new integration—that is, a rebirth. This thesis brings Hertz directly to his explanation of the double funeral. Each of these changes of status involves profound modifications of attitude toward the person concerned, modifications that are accomplished only gradually, with the passage of time. This transformation is exactly what the double funeral performs. At the provisional ceremony the body of the deceased is rejected, disposed of, while the soul is separated from the mortal remains. The period of mourning that follows is a period of transition both for the bereaved, who are partially excluded from normal social life, and for the soul of the departed, which occupies an intermediary station between this world and the next; at this stage the soul is sometimes thought to dwell in the vicinity of its former habitat and sometimes considered to have already started on the journey to the other world. At the definitive ceremony the bereaved are finally brought back into the community once again, and the soul joins its forebears in the Land of the Dead.

Like other members of the same school, Hertz displays a tendency to reify society, a tendency that makes for certain misunderstandings. But we may eliminate this difficulty by putting his general point in a slightly different way. Beliefs in an afterlife appear to be related to the basic contradiction that exists between the continuity of the social system—the relative perpetuity of the constituent groups and of their corpus of norms—and the impermanence of its personnel. This conflict between the mortality of the human body and the immortality of the body politic is resolved, in part at least, by the belief in an afterlife. A future existence is postulated as a supplement to man's earthly span, a Land of the Dead as a counterpart to the Land of the Living.

Hertz's discussion throws light on the problem, raised earlier by Tylor, of explaining the universality of the body-soul dichotomy, though Hertz does not himself develop this. Some such dualistic concept of the ghost-in-the-machine would seem to be a "logical" way of putting into words the differences between dream and "real-life" experiences. But this same duality would also appear to be a *sine qua non* of beliefs in an afterlife. For since the body itself is seen to decay after death, it is necessary to posit some other constituent of the human personality that persists. Thus the body-soul dichotomy is to be linked to the same built-in contradiction as beliefs in an afterlife and the custom of the double funeral.

Though Van Gennep generalizes the idea of gradual transition from one status to another to situations outside the life cycle, and develops in greater detail the analysis of other ceremonies, he otherwise adds relatively little to Hertz's thesis. He, too, views death as one of a number of situations that involve major changes of status and that are implicit in the passage of an individual through the social system. "Transitions from group to group and from one social situation to the next are looked on as implicit in the very fact of existence, so that a man's life comes to be made up of a succession of stages with similar ends and beginnings" ([1960] p. 3). Such changes cannot be effected suddenly, by the wave of a wand. They require some formalized public statement and also a period of transition, during which the individuals undergoing the change and those with whom they have social relations can adjust themselves to the new situation. This transition is marked by what Van Gennep calls rites of passage: these begin with the rites of separation, whereby an individual is cut off from his earlier status; there follows the intermediary stage (*periode de marge*), a period of waiting; and the sequence is concluded by rites of aggregation by means of which the person is inducted into the new status.

A large number of these rites center upon the key points in the continual turnover of membership of human groups, namely birth, marriage, and death. Funeral ceremonies are the final and most dramatic rite of passage in the life cycle: the public statements of the separation of the dead from this world, and of the bereaved from the dead, and finally of the aggregation of the ghost of the deceased to the community of the dead and the bereaved to the community of the living.

The approach of these members of the *Année sociologique* school laid out the main lines along which funeral ceremonies have been analyzed by later anthropologists. Radcliffe-Brown was heavily indebted to them for the theoretical framework of his account of mortuary institutions among the Andamanese (1922). So also have been other writers, influenced in turn by him, especially Warner on the Murngin [1937] and on the United States [1959], Gluckman on the Southeast Bantu [1937], and Wilson on the Nyakyusa [1954, 1957]. Malinowski, too, owed a similar debt in the discussion of funeral ceremonies that appears in his well-known essay "Magic, Science and Religion" (1925). Death, he claims, shakes the moral life of the society, and public ceremonials are required to restore the cohesion of the group ([1954] pp. 52–53). In much the same vein, Radcliffe-Brown, following closely on Hertz, had written that "death constitutes a partial destruction to the social cohesion, the normal social life is disorganized, the social equilibrium is disturbed. After the death the society has to organize itself anew and reach a new condition of equilibrium" ([1948] p. 285).

Malinowski attempts to carry his analysis to a further level, into the personality system. Warming to man's predicament in resounding rhythms reminiscent of Sir James Frazer, he is eventually led to perceive funeral ceremonies and beliefs in immortality as the outcome of deep emotional revelations, on the one hand, and as a product of the instinct of self-preservation, on the other. Gluckman ([1937] p. 117), following Durkheim,[8] has objected to analyses of mortuary institutions as a "response of the individual to death," on the grounds that to explain them entirely by the emotional comfort given to the dying person and his survivors is to avoid many of the important problems

---

8 ". . . mourning is not the spontaneous expression of individual emotions. . . . Mourning is not a natural movement of private feelings wounded by a cruel loss; it is a duty imposed by the group. One weeps, not simply because he is sad, but because he is forced to weep. It is a ritual attitude which he is forced to adopt out of respect for custom, but which is, in a large measure, independent of his affective state" (Durkheim [1947], p. 397).

involved, for example the question of why an unloved parent is buried with the same full ceremony given to a loved one. Malinowski at times played down the institutionalized aspect of these phenomena, and also introduced psychological simplifications in the shape of hypostatical instincts. Nevertheless, he did bring out what other writers have sometimes overlooked: that these institutions must be analyzed on both the social and the personality levels, which are indeed interlocking, not discrete systems. Hence sociological and psychological theories must be consistent with one another.

It should be noted in this context that although recent psychological research has failed to confirm the presence of any instinctive fear of the corpse, there has been an increasing emphasis on the incidence of mourning and grief in early childhood following the loss of the loved object. After examining the evidence for such behavior in animal species, Bowlby notes that although there are a number of differences, there are also striking similarities that suggest the presence of instinctual processes [1960]. In his reports of acute grief in adults, Lindemann observed how the preliminary phase of mourning and despair, characterized by "a painful lack of capacity to initiate and maintain organized patterns of activity" ([1944] p. 142), is followed by a phase of recovery during which a reorganization of attitude takes place not only in respect to the image of the lost person, but also in the context of new relationships. Loss of patterns of conduct is one of five main features of acute grief that he distinguishes, the others being somatic distress, preoccupation with the image of the deceased, guilt, and hostile reactions. These observations (and those of Marris [1958]) are consistent with the approach adopted here and indicate how standardized procedures assist the process of reorganization on a personality level.

Gluckman's criticism of Malinowski, and more particularly his own analysis of these practices, emphasizes another point, raised by the school of *Année sociologique* but neglected by many other writers on this subject, namely that mortuary institutions are not to be considered merely as "religious" phenomena, in the sense of ways of acting associated with the "supernatural" world. Indeed, since I shall be concerned with the interdependency of mortuary beliefs and practices with the other aspects of LoDagaa social life, particular attention will be devoted to the other, "secular," elements. Of great importance here are the social control functions of ceremonials. Funerals are inevitably occasions for summing up an individual's social personality, by a restatement not only of the roles he has filled, but also of the general way in which he has conducted himself during his lifetime. The composition of the obituary, whether a written report in a newspaper, a funeral oration in an ecclesiastical building, or a mimetic performance at the graveside, involves, directly or indirectly, a public reformulation of social norms that itself serves as a sanction on behavior. Of equal importance is the way in which mortuary institutions perform this function by providing for the differential treatment of the bereaved in the funeral ceremonies, the corpse at burial, and the dead in the afterlife (Goody [1959*b*]).

Then again, there is the redistributive aspect of funeral ceremonies. Psychoanalytic writers have pointed to the adaptive aspects of mourning behavior. In the first phase, the reaction to loss may lead to a restoration of the lost object in cases of separation, for example, when a child screams for an absent mother. In the second phase, disorganization occurs and a successful outcome involves a withdrawal of emotional concern for the lost object and a preparation for attachment to a new one (Bowlby [1960; 1961]). A similar reorganization centers upon the rights that the dead man held. Just as the death of an officeholder requires the installation of a new incumbent ("The king is dead, long live the king"), so many other rights and duties of the deceased have also to be transferred to surviving members of the community; in particular, property, sexual rights, offices, and certain roles may all require perpetuation in this manner. Without some system of inheritance and succession, of intergenerational transmission of these exclusive rights, social life would be marked by disorganization rather than by relative continuity. The cost at which this continuity is obtained, the conflicts over the methods of transmission, are, as I have already noted, one of the central interests of the present study.

In this chapter, I have tried to present some of the main contributions to the study of the institutions that turn upon the ineluctable fact of death. In general terms, the broad historical development has been from the "rationalistic positivism" of the English intellectualists Tylor and Frazer, who sought the origins of religion in the body-soul dichotomy, to the sociological approach of Emile Durkheim and the French school, who concentrated upon group goals and interests, particularly in their integrative aspects. To this must be added the contribution of Freud, who, among other important insights, focused attention upon the conflict situations inherent in any personality system. In this respect Freud did for the personality system what Marx did for the social system; though both had their prescriptions for eliminating future conflicts, they also perceived the inevitability of such conflicts under pre-existing psychical and social conditions.

Here, then, are the principal sources upon which this study of **mortuary institutions will draw.**

CHAPTER III

The Analysis of Ceremony and Rite

Well here again that don't apply
But I've gotta use words when I talk to you.

ELIOT, *Sweeney Agonistes*

My main purpose in this book is to examine certain differences in the mortuary institutions of two communities, the LoWiili and the LoDagaba. In order to establish the nature of these differences, it is essential first to describe in detail the ceremonies that are performed at a person's death. Any such account of ceremonial or ritual institutions raises problems of methodology that have provided a continuous source of controversy for the various branches of the social sciences involved in their interpretation. Some of these discussions appear to have arisen out of ambiguities in the concepts rather than from the complexities of the material, and it therefore seems appropriate to consider some of the general issues at this point, insofar as they bear upon the subsequent analysis.

CEREMONIAL

Among the LoDagaa, most funerals and ancestral sacrifices are public ceremonials of the kind that Durkheim took to be the epitome of religious behavior. It was such performances as these that also occupied Radcliffe-Brown's attention in his account of the ritual beliefs and practices of the Andamanese; here he defined ceremonial as those collective actions, required by custom, that are performed on occasions of change in the social life. This last phrase touches upon the function of *rites de passage*, those ceremonies among which funerals stand out as the most vivid example. However, not all the performances that we shall consider involve changes of status of this kind, and rather than think in terms of functions and explanations applicable to all ceremonials, it is first necessary to make some discriminations within this general category.

In his book *Les Rites de passage,* Van Gennep not only called attention to the way in which certain ceremonies serve to announce and to enact changes of state, but also spoke of two kinds of change that he referred to as *les passages cosmiques* and *les passages humaines.* The first give rise to regular ceremonies set within the seasonal or calendrical cycles, like harvest festivals and the Adae rituals performed by the Ashanti at the end of each twenty-one-day period; the second pertain to changes within another cycle, that determined by the span of human life.[1] It is convenient further to differentiate the second category into those changes of universal application that all members of a community undergo, birth, marriage, and death, and those of a more restricted kind that involve the transfer of limited roles, for example chiefship, or membership in selective associations such as the title-taking societies of West Africa or the fraternal organizations of Western Europe.

The two cycles are not, of course, totally independent; initiation, a life-cycle ritual, is often a mass ceremony held at a specific point in the calendar. Birth and death do not give the same latitude for adjustment, but nevertheless the ceremonies that attend them are not immovably tied to precise physiological changes. Moreover, ceremonials that occur at the installation of a new officeholder, such as the coronation of a king, may be linked either with the life cycle or with the cosmic cycle. If the reign is normally ended only by natural death, then the investiture is set within the life cycle. But if the period of office ends after a specified length of time, as with the ideal type of "divine kingship" or with the American presidency and other elected offices, then the ceremony is geared to the calendrical system.

Apart from these regular ceremonies governed by the demands of the human and cosmic cycles, other performances of a similar kind are carried out in irregularly determined situations of crisis. Among the LoDagaa, sacrifices are made to the ancestors and to the Earth not only at fixed junctures, at moments of passage, cosmic and human, that constitute points of transition in the social life, but also upon occasions of misfortune, when a child is ill or when drought threatens. Indeed the

---

[1] Chapple and Coon make a similar distinction between "rites of passage" and "rites of intensification," the former term being used for disturbances in the equilibrium of the group that are caused by an individual, as in a funeral, and the latter for changes affecting all the members of the group, as in ceremonies connected with the alternation of the seasons ([1942] p. 397). This classification seems less satisfactory to my mind, since among the LoDagaa, for example, funerals demand the greatest social participation of all such occasions.

majority of sacrificial offerings are of this occasional kind; Turner [1953] refers to them as rituals of affliction and Wilson ([1957] chap. 7) as rituals of misfortune. Such performances mark changes in the social life only in the purely tautological sense that any interpersonal behavior may be said to do. With regard to the rationale of rituals of affliction, the function ascribed to them by the actors themselves (i.e., the ex-pressed or manifest purpose) is primarily that of solving specific prob-lems. Cyclical ceremonies, on the other hand, though they may embody acts directed to the solution of these matters, as a Sunday service its prayers for rain, are not necessarily oriented in this direction and may be simply affirmatory or "expressive," to use a term often used by Rad-cliffe-Brown, Parsons, and others. However, I prefer to avoid this epithet which, though it purports to refer to the actor's frame of reference, is in fact employed in a somewhat loose manner, and rites and ceremonies are deemed to "express," in some undefined way, "social structure," "society," or "ultimate values."[2]

In referring to the functions of cyclical ceremonies as affirmatory, I am of course echoing Radcliffe-Brown, who wrote: "The ceremonial (i.e., collective) expression of any sentiment serves both to maintain it at the requisite degree of intensity in the mind of the individual and to transmit it from one generation to another. Without such expression the sentiments involved could not exist" ([1948] p. 234).

This approach derives from Durkheim, and is influenced by Shand, a psychologist whose work on sentiments had considerable influence at the time. Durkheim himself spoke of religious forces as correspond-ing to "objectified social sentiments" ([1947] p. 324, n.1). Indeed it was this feature that he selected to differentiate religion from what he con-sidered to be the more individualistic sphere of magic; in speaking of religious action, Durkheim means in effect ceremonial.

There is a danger in this approach, however rewardingly pursued by these two writers, in that it appears to say more than it does. Inter-preted in the widest sense, the statement that all ceremonial has an affirmatory or integrative function is tautologous; for clearly any repe-tition of normative behavior in some sense reinforces the norm. How-ever, there does seem to me to be a way in which this claim may be made more meaningful. Looking at ceremonials in terms of the changes in the social relationships of the actors involved, we can see how these performances differ according to whether the human or cosmic cycle

---

[2] This matter is discussed at greater length in my article "Religion and Ritual" [1961*b*].

is involved. Ceremonies in the human cycle announce and enact changes in a person's status, that is, his position in the social system. Similar changes of position are involved in those ceremonies that increase the social distance between groups, as when a previously exogamous clan divides into two intermarrying units.

Ceremonies of the cosmic cycle, on the other hand, are usually simply affirmatory in that they restate established positions and relationships, often in the highly charged manner that led Chapple and Coon to speak of them as rites of intensification. For instance, the Odwera or New Yam Festival of the Ashanti, while strengthening national identity and reinforcing a particular set of cosmological beliefs, at the same time reaffirms certain features of the political organization; for at this annual event divisional chiefs must repair to the capital to pay homage to the paramount ruler. Indeed, a demonstration of the affirmatory or integrative aspects of such a ceremony consists basically in an analysis of the personnel involved and the extent to which their acts in this context intermesh with their behavior in other institutional complexes. In other words, the study of such performances is essentially the same as that of any other kind of social action; it involves an exploration of relations of interconnectedness.

The chief function of the third type of ceremony, rituals of affliction, is not in promoting changes in the system of social positions, nor yet in reaffirming existing relationships, but in re-establishing those that have been disturbed. These relationships include not only ones involving supernatural agencies but also those between human beings themselves, as when a period of warfare is ended by a formal peacemaking.

The affirmatory role of ceremonial procedures of which Radcliffe-Brown speaks is, then, essentially an aspect of social control. But the same writer also describes ceremonial as having a somewhat different control function, as providing a "free expression" of anger and other suppressed, or partially suppressed, feelings. This idea has had widespread currency. Aristotle spoke of the cathartic effect of ceremonials, with particular reference to religious dramas. In more recent times, Freud has emphasized the therapeutic, remedial results of "acting out." Certain types of group therapy are based on the dramatic performance of incidents in the individual's life, a procedure resembling the verbal exploration of the mind that constitutes the psychiatric interview. But whatever the position in therapy, in ceremonial it is controlled rather than free expression of feeling that is important. Funerals control grief by providing standardized forms of expression. And they control not only the sense of loss of the loved one, the personal deprivation, but also the guilt and self-accusation that so often accompany the departure of a close kinsman.

Because of this interlocking of the social and personality systems, it is clear that the attitudes "expressed" in ceremonial, as in other forms of standardized action, are defined primarily by the social system. When a LoDagaa widow is ritually washed to test her for or purge her of the adultery that might have caused her husband's death, this procedure bears witness, among other things, to the tension that centers upon the allocation of relatively exclusive rights over women in a polygynous society. In other words, not only does ceremonial map out the pattern of social relations, whether by enacting a change of position, or by reaffirming the existing schema, or by re-establishing the *status quo* after a disturbance; it also gives controlled expression to personal emotions that demand some formal outlet as well as to the conflicts to which any particular set of social relations give rise. Although there is no exact correspondence, the ties and cleavages in the social system are often experienced as friendship and hostility, love and hate, in the personality system. If we interpret cleavage in the rather special sense—not of the absence of a social relationship, but of a social relationship characterized by a hostile component, that is by negative as distinct from positive acts—then ceremonials may be said to demonstrate the ties and cleavages of the social system, as well as to act out the positive and negative feelings of an individual actor.

This aspect of ritual is somewhat different from the reaffirmation of social "sentiments" or institutions that was previously discussed. For the reference is not to the reinforcing of social norms as such, but to the controlled expression of forces that might tend to upset the social system from within. In order to clarify this statement, we may turn to Gluckman's analysis of what he calls rituals of rebellion, especially his treatment of the role of women in Zulu and Swazi ceremonial [1954]. By the regular re-enactment of an unsuccessful rebellion, the women make what is from one standpoint an outright affirmation of male supremacy. From another point of view, these acts demonstrate tensions in the social structure that appear to derive from the contradiction between the dominant economic role of women in agriculture and their subordinate role in the rest of the social system. But the chief function of the ceremony in this context is that by making such a conflict overt, it relieves and controls the situation of tension. This is what, following Schurtz, we may refer to as the *Ventilsitten* or safety-valve function of ceremony.

The safety-valve function of ceremonial in the social system is the counterpart of its cathartic function in the personality system. However, the acting out of contradictions in ceremonial may anticipate and help to control the development of conflicts on the personality level, that is, if the action of the ritual is successful. Thus rituals of female initiation may go some way toward relieving the difficulties inherent in the onset of puberty as well as publicly announcing that the girls have reached a marriageable age, and funeral ceremonies may serve to counter the grief generated by loss and separation at the same time as reallocating the rights and duties of the deceased with regard to roles, property, and women.

RITUAL

The term ritual is one that has been used in diverse ways, receiving almost as much abuse as the word myth. In anthropology it came into prominence as a way of referring to the whole field of magico-religious practice and belief and so avoiding the need to differentiate between magic and religion, a distinction that, as Marett had pointed out, involved certain difficulties. Thus when in his essay on taboo (1939) Radcliffe-Brown speaks of ritual acts or values, he contrasts these with technological acts in much the same way as Tylor and Frazer had distinguished magic and religion from science ([1952c] p. 143). There is this difference, however, that Radcliffe-Brown, and most subsequent writers, have identified ritual with the sacred, a concept that was developed by Durkheim to replace the earlier trichotomy, which he regarded as unsatisfactory, and that served as a basis for his alternative to the minimum definition of religion put forward by Tylor.

Durkheim's dichotomy between the sacred and the profane seems to me no solution to the difficulty. One of the main grounds upon which he bases his proposal to adopt the sacred as the criterion of the magico-religious is that this division is one recognized in all societies. This I believe to be no more true than in the case of the natural-supernatural distinction, which he rightly notes is a categorization imposed by the European observer upon the practices and beliefs of other societies.

If these ideas are not universally, or even widely, present as folk concepts, that is, concepts employed by the actors themselves, do they have any advantage over the magic-science-religion trichotomy of the earlier English "intellectualists"? In a searching discussion of this question, Parsons singles out the "symbolic" nature of Durkheim's concept of the sacred as its basic positive criterion, in contrast to the intrinsic means-end relationship that characterizes profane action ([1937] pp.

430–31). Radcliffe-Brown also differentiates ritual from technical acts by their expressive or symbolic element ([1952c] p. 143). But it is not easy to discern what Parsons, Radcliffe-Brown, and others intend to imply when they speak of the sacred or ritual as symbolizing "ultimate values," "social function," or "social structure." Is it not that, failing to find the "intrinsic" or "rational" means-end relationship that is assumed to underlie technical acts like the hoeing of a garden plot before planting, these writers "explain" the residual category of acts as "symbolic"? An act that has no "rational" meaning is assumed to have a hidden rationale.

Thus it would appear that insofar as the dichotomy between the sacred and the profane, the ritual and the technical, is valid, it harks back to the distinction between rational and irrational action that lay at the heart of the trichotomy used by Tylor and Frazer. Indeed, if we interpret "science" in the broad way that was intended, the two types of classification are virtually identical. The world is indeed divided in two domains, as Durkheim and Malinowski contended, but it is a division imposed by the European observer.

Despite the attempts at refutation, then, the nineteenth-century distinction between the rational or empirical (the scientific or the technical) and the non-empirical (the magical and religious, or the ritual) has formed the basis for all later theoretical discussions. In one respect there has been some development: namely, in the further division of acts that have no intrinsic means-end relationship into the non-rational and the irrational. To this distinction, I will shortly return. First, however, I want to follow through the main implication of the argument. It is that we must base our analysis of ritual on a recognition of the wide discrepancy, built into the most central concepts of the sociology of religion, between the actor's and the observer's point of view. For better or for worse, we must accept the limitations imposed upon us by the rationalist dichotomy between "technical" and "ritual" acts. I am concerned to emphasize this point, because many theoretical treatments of "ritual" or "ceremonial" base their argument upon the differences between rite (*ritus*) and other customary ways of acting (*mos*), whereas in fact this distinction is of very limited analytic significance. The preliminary focus of attention must be shifted to the similarity of all custom, whether rites or mores, as data for sociological analysis; for the problem of establishing the "meaning" of a social act is not radically different in the two cases.

What is involved in determining this meaning? Without wishing to enter into the many epistemological problems that this raises, I nevertheless regard it as impossible for the sociologist to ignore this question altogether. By so doing he only adds to the existing confusion.

As a starting point, we may distinguish two broad levels of analysis, which, following Merton's discussion of "function," we may call the manifest and the latent. The manifest or expressed meaning (Richards [1956], p. 112) of a word, a gesture, or an object, or of an act consisting of a sequence of such units, is established by asking the persons concerned—a procedure which, though deceptively simple in appearance, is less so in practice. Even if the question "What do you mean?" is translatable at all, it may not lead to the series of verbal equivalences the Western observer desires. A possible alternative is to ask, "Why do you do that?" but this may lead no further than the reply "Because our grandfathers did so," which serves merely to assure the outsider that he is dealing with institutionalized behavior of some duration.

The other extreme is for the observer himself to allocate meaning to an action he perceives, which he does by bringing to the situation his own scheme of interpretation. And, as in the case of the linguistic assumptions of Max Müller and the psychological interpretations of Freud, Jung, and others, the frame of reference is often one hidden from the actor, or at any rate not the one in terms of which he sees himself as acting. Following Flügel ([1932] p. 365), I would speak of these forms of interpretation as cryptophoric.

Between these two extremes fall the interpretations of the sociologist, which depend upon an elucidation of what may be spoken of as the idiomatic meaning of social acts. Such interpretations must necessarily be based upon the meanings given by the actor himself. But they go beyond the actor's interpretation in two ways: first, in viewing individual acts as part of a total system of social relationships, a standpoint that even the best informed and most sensitive participant finds difficult to take; second, in seeing customs in a wider setting than the experience of one culture alone provides.

To do this we must start with the manifest meanings themselves, as derived from the study of particular contexts. Then these specific usages can be compared one with another to produce a definition of the range of meanings of such and such an act or object. This approach was explicitly developed by Radcliffe-Brown in his analysis of Andamanese ceremonial and is excellently demonstrated in Srinivas's account of the Coorgs of South India; it is summarized in the following three principles:

(1) When the same or similar custom is practiced on different occasions, it has the same or similar meaning in all of them.

(2) When different customs are practiced on one and the same occasion, there is a common element in the customs.

(3) If two customs are found associated with one another on different occasions, then there is something in common between the different occasions (Srinivas [1952], p. 72; Radcliffe-Brown [1948], p. 235, [1952c], p. 147).

In practice, the application of this method of internal comparison means that although mortuary institutions may lie at the center of our interest, they cannot be understood without reference to other situations in the social life of the LoDagaa. Consequently, the continuity of the account of their funerals must at times be broken by allusions to other ceremonial sequences, such as the initiatory proceedings of the secret Bagre society.

This method of contextual comparison, the method of dictionary construction, is of course applicable to particular concepts as well as to the more complicated acts of which Radcliffe-Brown was writing. For example, in order to understand the meaning of the "sweeping" of a person who has come in contact with the dead body, we must examine the other contexts in which the verb *pir,* which I translate as "sweep," is used. This procedure at once raises a point of theoretical importance that has already received some discussion in connection with the term "ritual." For we find that the contexts include acts that would normally be considered as "ritual," for example the "sweeping" of the Earth shrine with a special sacrifice when a person in the parish has killed himself. And the term also refers to a woman sweeping up the dust and other refuse from her rooms, an act that we would consider to be "technical" or "rational," in the sense that the means employed and the end obtained are recognized by us as intrinsically related in ways that are in principle subject to testing by logico-empirical methods.

In the previous paragraph, I have, by the use of quotation marks, not only distinguished one type of sweeping from another, but also suggested that the "sweeping" of the Earth shrine is a metaphoric extension of the "non-ritual" usage. From the actor's point of view this may or may not be the case. For instance, a Christian in contemporary Western society, when asked to explain what he means in saying that baptism "washes away" his sins, may reply that by undergoing such a lustration he is making a declaration of faith and announcing his membership in a particular religious body whose promise it is that the sins of the members will be forgiven them. Here the sense of the term "wash" in a religious context is seen by the actors as a metaphorical extension of the technical usage.

On the other hand, when a LoDagaa declares that the bathing of the widow during the funeral ceremony cleanses her from her husband's "dirt" (*deo*), the actors themselves give no primacy to any such pragmatic or "rational" implications. It is the same with the concept "sweep." The actors make no general distinction between the removal of what we would call the mystical pollution that is thought to be present as a result of the widow's contact with her late husband and the removal of the dust that has accumulated on the compound floor, except in terms of the severity of the consequences of not carrying out the operation in question. In this latter case, the observer cannot say that a metaphorical usage is involved, since, from the actor's point of view, there is no primary point of reference.

Nonetheless, actions such as the bathing of the widow are frequently spoken of by anthropologists as symbolic. From one standpoint all social action that involves the use of words and gestures is symbolic. However, social scientists use the term in a more restricted way to refer to "modes of action so constructed that they 'stand for' or 'signify' other modes of action or events" (Nadel [1951], p. 261). How is this applicable to the instances mentioned above? In the first case, we can point to the explanations of the people themselves and say that baptism is a symbolic act that "stands for" something the actors designate. In the second case, we can speak of symbolic behavior only by imposing a distinction from the outside. We perceive that from our standpoint certain forms of lustration achieve pragmatic ends by "rational" means, whereas other actions, described by the same term, do not. Thus our distinction once again rests upon the dichotomy between rational and ritual action.

The purification theme is of frequent occurrence in funeral ceremonies; so, too, are acts of reversal. But most frequent, perhaps, are the acts of separation and aggregation. We spoke earlier of the different phases of funeral ceremonies and of the other performances that involve changes of social position—the phases of separation, transition, and aggregation. Here we are concerned more specifically with the acts that mark changes in social distance. A typical act of aggregation is tying, a ritual metaphor that often occurs in marriage ceremonies. In the LoDagaa funerals, the same act is performed to restrain the bereaved and to keep the errant soul within the confines of its human dwelling. Similarly, a typical rite of separation is cleaving or cutting, a metaphor that often occurs when an exogamous unit splits, or during funerals when the hair of the head is shaved.

Although I have spoken of these themes as being embodied in a cultural tradition, they have often a wide cross-cultural distribution. Purification, for example, is frequently associated with the removal of dirt, the cleansing of the exuviae of the body; and the theme may be elaborated in non-physical spheres by the concept of pollution. Sweeping and bathing are typical acts of purification. In many cases we are dealing not with an indefinite range of possible "symbols," nor with the more or less arbitrary association of sign and referent we find in language, but rather with certain nuclear clusters of acts, certain general themes, certain widespread applications of the "association of ideas." Acts that maintain the input-output system of the human body are given a generalized significance as acts of aggregation (eating, sexual intercourse) and acts of separation (the removal of dirt and exuviae), respectively. From the observer's standpoint, the meaning of an act can be seen as built up through associations, certain of which are common to many societies. Purification by lustration is one such constant.

In these two sections, I have discussed some of the general problems to which an analysis of ceremonial and ritual gives rise. The central theme running through these diverse comments relates to the difficulties created by the attempt of Durkheim and others to reject the definitions of earlier writers in the field of comparative religion. In order to avoid certain problems he saw in using the concepts of Taylor and Frazer, Durkheim defined his center of interest as the realm of the "sacred," which he declared was universally distinguished from the world of the "profane" by the actors themselves. This last assumption is hardly justified by the facts, and it is necessary to recognize that the use by the sociologist of the sacred-profane dichotomy, or the distinction between "ritual" and other acts, is usually based upon our own "rationalistic" frame of reference. By "ritual" I refer, therefore, to a category of standardized behavior (custom) in which the relationship between the means and the end is not "intrinsic," that is to say, is neither irrational nor yet non-rational, and by "ceremonial" to a sequence of ritual acts performed in public.

Paradoxically, the importance of recognizing the basis upon which we make these distinctions lies in realizing their relative unimportance for analytical purposes. If we accept the proposition that the basis of the dichotomy is a matter of "rationality" as defined by the observer, we can appreciate that for most sociological purposes all customs, whether rites or mores, can be treated from one and the same standpoint and that the problem of determining the meaning of social acts is not radically different in the two cases.

FUNERAL CEREMONIES OF THE LODAGAA

In dealing with the LoDagaa ceremonies I shall in the main adopt a chronological form of presentation, since this is simplest for the reader to follow. This approach has the disadvantage that it precludes the grouping together of similar rites and therefore involves a certain degree of repetition. It will also prevent the full development of an examination of the ceremonies role by role, as suggested by Gluckman ([1937] p. 119); although this type of analysis forms one of the central interests of the present study, it would be impossible to collect in one place the data on how the son, wife, or brother acts during the course of the various ceremonies without repeating much of what has already been presented in the chronological analysis.

One advantage of following the sequence of events is that it permits the tracing of the actual transformation of a human being into an ancestor. There is a further advantage, of some importance when we are trying to ascertain the differences between these communities, in that a chronological account reduces the likelihood of one's selecting from the material on the basis of a predetermined thesis. I have attempted to reduce the effects of unconscious choice by presenting as full a description as possible. This description is based in the first place upon the funerals of adult males among the LoWiili, persons of different age, sex, or community being mentioned only where differences of custom are known to exist.

There are differences of custom not only between the major groupings of "peoples," but also within each community. Special forms of funeral ritual serve to distinguish patriclans, and their constituent segments, from units of similar structural order. For example, among a certain agnatic group in Birifu, the Daboo patrilineage of the Naayiili clan sector, the smock in which the corpse is arrayed is removed shortly before the actual interment. This action is of significance to the observer only when it is seen within the context of a general custom of shrouding the corpse for burial. It is one of those standardized forms of action that the members of national, kinship, and other groups seize upon to assert their own identities, either against the world as a whole or else against members of similar collectivities. There is therefore little to be gained from inquiry into the correlatives of such emblematic devices beyond a certain limited point; they are simply ways of announcing and enacting the existence of such and such a collectivity.

These diacritical features of social relationships, to use Nadel's phrase, are tied both to categories of social role and to groups; the Doctor of Philosophy is distinguished by a red hood, the French Republic by its tricolor. However, the reasons for choosing one color as against another are likely to be of peripheral interest in the general analysis of the system of social relationships. Of course, the choice of one particular emblem rather than another will doubtless be related to the whole complex of culturally determined themes. The fact that the Chinese use white and the Europeans black to indicate mourning is not in this sense accidental. Moreover, it may sometimes be possible to trace the specific historical factors behind the choice. But often, as the changes in the color of Christian mourning garments suggest (Goody [1960], p. 44), the most important consideration in the choice of such emblems is that they should be different from those adopted by similar groups, an everyday example of which is the use of school colors and college crests.

The distinguishing features of clans, which I do not discuss in this analysis, differ in this respect from the variations of custom that are to be found among the peoples I speak of as the LoWiili and the LoDagaba. For, as we have seen, there are no units of a political order beyond the settlement for which diacritical differences could have significance. Culturally, one community melts into the next, and no groups emerge that could be called tribal. There appears no call for diacritical features on this level, since until recently there were no collectivities of greater dimensions than the settlement or clan that had any continuing importance for the actors themselves. In view of this and other considerations discussed in the opening chapter, it seems reasonable to place a different analytic significance upon the differences between these communities than upon the differences between clans. But the real test of the correctness of this assumption must lie in our attempt to explain the nature of the differences in the funeral ceremonies of the two communities in terms of other aspects of their social systems, in particular the type of property relations.

The full complement of funeral performances occupies some twelve to fifteen days and is spread over a period of at least six months and sometimes as long as several years. In view of the complexity of these performances, it seems desirable to give the reader some idea of the over-all sequence of events before we start on the detailed analysis.

The series of funeral ceremonies consists of four main sequences, distinct in time one from another. The first, the burial service, begins at the moment of death and lasts for some six or seven days, depending upon the sex of the dead person. The observation that the ceremony commences at the moment of death is not as unnecessary as might first appear; for in European societies the burial service is often deliberately delayed, whereas in others, and especially those in which the custom of live burial is found, it begins when an individual is considered to have completed his role in life (Rivers [1926], pp. 40–43). Effectively, such a man has served his human span and is outside the society of the living.[3] The LoWiili do not bury these moribund individuals alive, nor leave them to die like the Eskimo and other nomadic peoples, but I did hear of a sick man who took an "unconscionable time a-dying"—he had lost the critical faculty of speech—and, it was said, had finally to be helped on his way to the other world.

Thus the importance in ceremonial of the physiological processes of "birth and copulation and death" depends to a considerable extent upon social factors; as far as the social system as a whole is concerned, they constitute points of entry into, and departure from, the system of social roles and groups. Rites of passage, such as baptism or naming, weddings, and funerals, may as a consequence have a greater social significance than the birth, the commencement of a sexual union, and the death they commemorate.[4]

The burial ceremony (*kuur*) is divided into two phases, separated by the disposal of the corpse itself. The first is the public, exoteric part, held in the open area near the house of the dead and continuing for three days until the body is interred. However, burial occurs somewhat earlier when it is a child who has died, or when the corpse is rapidly decomposing, or when farming has still to be done. Most LoDagaa rituals take place when the productive season is over, for then there is not only time, but also enough grain to make the porridge and beer without which no major ceremony is complete.

The pre-burial phase of the ceremony is the most elaborate of all, consisting of a large number of different ritual "scenes." By this I mean short sequences of acts, like the fooling of the joking partners. There are too many such scenes to list here, but it is helpful to think of this complex burial phase as falling under the following main heads: (1) the preparation and disposal of the corpse; (2) the mourning of the bereaved and of the other members of the community; (3) the sepa-

---

[3] "This is so because, due to the weakening of their faculties, they have ceased to participate in social life; their death merely consecrates an exclusion from society which has in fact already been completed, and which every one has had time to get used to" (Hertz [1960], p. 85).

[4] "It is impossible to interpret the body of facts that we have presented if we see in death a merely physical event" (*ibid.*, p. 76).

ration of the living from the dead by mimetic and other rites that involve the reaffirmation of the solidarity of the descent group; and (4) the redistribution of certain marginal roles of the deceased.

After the burial takes place, the private, esoteric phase of the ceremony begins. It consists of four ritual scenes, each distinctly separated one from another, that set the pattern for the performance of the last two of the three subsequent ceremonies. These scenes may be described as: (1) the distribution of the flesh of the animals killed to the name of the deceased; (2) the bathing and whitewashing of the widow preparatory to the redistribution of the dead man's rights over women; (3) the meal consumed communally by the orphans preparatory to the formal redistribution of the dead man's role as father; and (4) the rites in the dead man's room preparatory to the redistribution of his property.

The second funeral ceremony, or Diviners' Beer, held three "weeks" after the burial, is concerned with discovering the cause of death. The LoDagaa week consists of six days, and, like subsequent ceremonies, these rites begin on the actual day of the week on which burial took place.

The third ceremony, or Bitter Funeral Beer, should take place at the beginning of the rains and should last three days, exclusive of the brewing of the beer. The first and third phases of this ceremony are similar to the whitewashing and property-distribution phases (2 and 4) of the post-burial performances. In the second phase the provisional ancestor shrine is placed in the dead man's byre, marking a transitional stage in his passage from the role of living father to that of ancestral father.

The earliest occasion on which the final ceremony, or Cool Funeral Beer, can take place is shortly after the first guinea-corn harvest following the death, provided three months or so have elapsed. Whether or not it is performed as soon as that depends primarily upon the state of the stocks of guinea-corn, considerable quantities of which are required for contributions in kind and for the food and beer needed to feed those who come from a distance. The three phases of the previous ceremony occur once again, but in a different order as well as in a rather different form: (1) the making of the final ancestor shrine and its entry into the dead man's byre; (2) the bathing of the women, their final release from mourning, and the redistribution of the rights in them that were held by the dead man; and (3) the final rites preparatory to the redistribution of the property. (4) In addition, there is a further rite that consummates the process begun by the orphans' meal in the post-burial rites; this is the public assumption of the role of "father" by the classificatory "brothers" of the dead man.

On one level, the whole sequence of ceremonies can be considered in terms of Van Gennep's schema as:

A. The performance of rites that *separate* (1) the deceased from the living, that is, from the bereaved, from the various groups and quasi-groups to which he belonged, from the community, and from his roles, offices, property, and rights over women; and (2) the bereaved from the other members of the community.

B. The performance of rites that *aggregate* (1) the deceased to his ancestors and to the Land of the Dead; and (2) the bereaved to the community from which they have been temporarily separated, a process that includes the redistribution of the relatively exclusive rights.

This, then, is the outline of the funeral ceremonies of the LoDagaa and will serve as a guide to the detailed study of these performances that is presented in the following chapters.

PART TWO

Death

CHAPTER IV

The Day of Death

Permettemi un momentu
Ch'eo mi avincinghi a la tota;
Perche a pienghie sempre solu
Lu core nun si cunsola.

Allow me to come, for a moment,
To the funeral table;
For the sorrowing heart cannot find consolation
In perpetual solitude.

Corsican vocero or keen

THE APPROACH OF DEATH

When a man is thought to be on the brink of death, the senior male in the compound personally informs those of the dying man's close agnates living nearby and sends boys or young men to tell others living away from the settlement. The closest patrikinsman of a man, the father, brother, or son, or the husband of a married woman, is known as the senior mourner *(kutuosob,* "the owner of grief") and is ultimately responsible for seeing that the ceremony is properly performed.

The sick man's sisters, and, among the LoDagaba, their sons, are also told. They are the ones who, together with his wives, should attend the dying man during his last hours; for the moment of death he should be sitting up, preferably in the arms of a close kinswoman. Indeed it is sinful for a man to die lying down, as if he were a slave with no one to take care of him, and a payment should be made to the Earth priest who provides two poles of ebony *(gaa: Diospyros mespiliformis)* with which to move the corpse. For when a child is born, the midwives catch its head to prevent its touching the ground, and the Earth is thought to be angry if humanity, having grasped hold of a man, should then let him go before he has breathed his last.

Whereas in both communities a man's close kinswomen attend him in his sickness, among the LoDagaba this assistance is set within the context of matriclanship. As a man once remarked to me, "If I suddenly got ill, which God forbid, my mother's 'sister' would come to see me. If one of my matriclan (*ma nir*) doesn't come when I'm ill, to turn me over when I need it, who is there to help me? I'll die with my head on my mat." The word *nir* has the general significance of a person, while *ma nir* means "one of my own people" and was here used quite explicitly to mean a matriclanswoman.

It is important to note that among the LoDagaba it is the male offspring of these same women who will inherit the movable property of the dead man in the absence of a full brother. In such a case, the sister's son may also be called to the deathbed; for if he is the heir, he has certain duties to perform as soon as the funeral begins. In one instance when a man in middle age had died, the killing of the funeral animals had to await the arrival of his full brother from a distant town, even though his father was still living; the reason given was that father and son do not "eat" together, that is, inherit movable property, and it has to be a member of the same property-holding corporation who points out the beast to be slaughtered.

The heir also has duties regarding the money left by the dead man: in both societies it is he who distributes a proportion of it to the bereaved, to the deceased's widows and to the children, so that they may scatter it to the grave-diggers and musicians at the funeral, in gratitude for the services they render and as a demonstration both of the wealth of the departed and of the respect in which they hold him. Since a man's money is usually buried in large pots somewhere on his land, he has to inform the heir not only how much should be expended in this way, but also where his wealth has been hidden. However, in practice, this information is usually conveyed to the heir indirectly; for a man often prefers to tell the hiding place to a favorite son rather than to the legal heir. When the late chief of Birifu died, he told the secret to the son on whom he most relied, although his full brother was heir to the property. In a case I knew of among the LoDagaba, an old man told his youngest son, the one who continued to work with him when the other offspring were farming on their own. In both communities, however, the confidants were jurally and ritually supposed to reveal the hiding place to the true heir; but whether or not the possessor of such a secret tells of all the concealed wealth is a matter which, though often talked about, is difficult for an outsider to ascertain.

The money buried in this way consists of both cowries and metal currency. As often with customary usages and especially with language, traditional forms persist longer in ceremonial than in mundane contexts. In funeral contributions, as in marriage payments, the shell money is the preferred medium.

While these persons are being informed of the death, the women of the house make preliminary preparations for the brewing of beer, a task that takes a full two days even after the grain has been malted.

THE ANNOUNCEMENT OF DEATH

Death is a matter of public concern both within the settlement and beyond its boundaries. It is announced in three ways. The moment of death itself is marked by the loud wailing of women; it is these lamentations that inform the immediate neighborhood, which consists mainly of members of the local sector of the deceased's patriclan. Later, the playing of xylophones spreads the news to the whole settlement as well as to nearby parishes, and the particular tune indicates whether it is a man or a woman who has died. More distant kinsmen receive the news by messenger (*koyiri*). The first of these methods establishes the fact of death itself, the second the sex of the deceased, and the third the individual concerned. The mother or widow of the dead man, accompanied by a female companion, may be seen half running, half walking, along the path leading to her natal home, crying bitterly as she goes. Sometimes the actual task of informing her kin is taken over by another woman, but whether a man's mother is alive or dead, her agnatic kin must be informed of the death of their sister's child.

The xylophones, which vary in size between three and five feet in length, should be played continuously throughout the ceremony, usually two at a time. But it is the first player to arrive on the scene who receives of the Fowl of the Xylophone (sometimes a guinea-fowl), which the senior mourner kills by beating against the slats of the instrument. Subsequent players are rewarded by the cowrie shells that those attending the funeral throw on the xylophone. These contributions can amount to quite a considerable sum; I saw one rather accomplished player collect 1,800 cowries in the space of about half an hour, and this he divided in equal portions with the two drummers who accompanied him on wooden drums (*ganggaa*).[1] The amount of cowries received certainly bears some relation to the skill of the player; not all are so amply rewarded for their pains.

The range of attendance at a funeral depends on the status of the

---

[1] The LoDagaba of Tom play this drum only at the funeral of a man who has killed another man; there is no such restriction among the LoWiili.

dead man, the spread of his kinship ties, and the means of communication that are available. Broadly speaking, participation in funerals, even of one's clansmen, is defined by the distance that the sound of the xylophone carries; the same is true of help in war. However, if close agnates have migrated farther afield, messengers may be sent to inform them of the death. The arrival of a messenger imposes an obligation to attend, or, in the case of an old man no longer able to make distant journeys, to send a son as representative. The coming of motor vehicles has made it possible to maintain such relationships over much greater distances than before. Newly established LoDagaba communities some hundred miles away on the road to the south continue to keep in touch in this way with their parent settlements. For this reason, the existence of transport is an important factor in determining the direction of contemporary migrations.

Not all deaths are mourned in public. In the case of those who have died an evil death (*kũ faa*, "bad death"), the body has to be quickly disposed of by various means. This category includes those who are killed by lightning, or by other actions of the Rain shrine, and those who have sinned against the Earth (that is, witches, suicides, and persons who have been sold into slavery). It also includes those whose death is the result of a mass epidemic, who are consequently buried in a communal grave. In all these instances, and in the case of unweaned infants, only the immediate relatives are informed.

Nor is a funeral invariably held at the place of death. A woman who dies on a visit to her father's homestead is carried back to her husband's home after the preliminary bathing has been completed. If this is not possible, either because of distance or because of some other factor, then the burial service is celebrated first at the place of death and later at the husband's home. Among the LoDagaba, unless the second installment (*doẽ*) of bridewealth has been paid, the husband's agnates do not have the unequivocal right to bury the body of the dead woman. It is said of them, "they don't own the dead body" (*be be so a kũ*). If the wife's lineage wished to enforce their claim, they could arrange for a third party to scatter some ebony leaves outside the husband's compound; after this act no one will dare to continue with the funeral, since the Earth has now been invoked.

Although I have often heard of the possibility of such action, I have never come across an actual instance of it. This, I believe, is because the dead woman's kin never make such a threat unless there is some other cause for dispute, in addition to the debt itself. And the husband's patrilineage either settle the matter there and then or else call upon joking partners to intervene. The latter dissuade the woman's kinsfolk from taking so drastic a course by saying "What do you want with that rotten thing? Let's all mourn together and bury the body here." Indeed the husband's group are moved to act in this situation not so much from the fear that the corpse will be carried back to the dead woman's home, but rather from a sense of shame (*vīī*) at having the dispute publicly raised in this way. Moreover, there is always in the background the generalized threat that if the wife's group are not given satisfaction, they might attempt to dissuade their daughters from making similar marriages in the future.

A further consideration with regard to the bridewealth debts is that the removal of the corpse is not the most effective of the retaliatory pro-'cedures available. For the creditor lineage can simply cancel an existing or future marriage payment to the husband's group. It is for this reason, I believe, that when I questioned a group of LoWiili on the matter, some denied that the second bridewealth payment remains a debt after the woman's death; what in fact happens between members of nearby lineages is that the outstanding amount gets set off against other transactions. It is therefore to be expected, and my data confirm this suggestion, that the threat to remove the corpse of the dead wife would be made only between distant patrilineal groups with relatively few relationships to be disturbed.

In my interim report on the LoWiili, I remarked that formerly a woman's lineage were entitled to remove the corpse in the absence of the cattle payment ([1956*a*] p. 51). Further inquiries make it appear that this was never more than a formula for getting a hearing for another wrong. I gave too much weight to this threat among the LoWiili, which is less common than among the LoDagaba. However, in both societies there is a recognized connection of jural status with place of burial, which even if it operates mainly in anticipation, has nonetheless a considerable influence over people's actions. A LoWiili case will make the point. When Gandaa, the late Chief of Birifu, died, two of his widows went to live with a pair of full brothers, who were his classificatory "sister's sons." At first, these men asserted that they had a full claim on the women, although they recognized that any children they might beget would be considered offspring of the dead man. Some two years later, a child of one of the widows, who had accompanied his mother into concubinage, died, and the chief's patrilineage carried the dead body back to be buried in their own cemetery. This was galling to the "husband," who then told me that he now wanted his mother's brother's people to accept the requisite bridewealth payments; for as things stood at present, if his "wife" should die, the chief's lineage might bring yet greater shame upon him by carrying her corpse away to be interred.

"If you haven't sent the cattle payment," the LoDagaa claim, "you own neither the body of your wife nor the flesh of any animal she may kill." Just as it is highly unlikely that a woman's kin will actually lay claim to her corpse, it is also most improbable that a woman will kill a wild animal, since she owns neither bow nor gun. But it does occasionally happen. In one much quoted instance, the wife of a Birifu man discovered that an antelope had run into the byre, so she seized a bow and shot it. At this point the husband came along and stepped in to finish off the dying animal, for fear, it was said, that she would always be upbraiding him with the taunt "Who is it that's killed a wild animal around here?"

Why should acts of such infrequent occurrence be continually used as indices of the status of a married woman in respect of her husband's and her natal kin? The second installment of the bridewealth, the cattle payment, is demanded by a woman's natal kin when she has provided her husband with some two or three children; in other words, she has given assurance of her fertility and has helped to "build the house" into which she has married. The payment represents an acknowledgment of a contribution made over a considerable stretch of time, and one that is implied in the original transaction: the balance of rights between spouses and between affines is not altered in any major respect. But from the standpoint of the husband and his group, this second transfer of property demanded by the bride's kin is conceptualized as an acquisition of further rights. That these rights are of little practical importance is beside the point; objectively, they simply mark the fact that such a transaction has occurred, but to the husband's lineage they appear as a material extension of interest, a viewpoint that serves to rationalize the transfer of further wealth to the wife's kin in respect of the children she has already borne.

Just as a woman's funeral could be used by her kinsfolk to call attention to a wrong believed to have been done, so the kinsmen of a dead man might attempt to collect outstanding debts during the mortuary service on the grounds that cows are required for killing to the dead man's name. When the representative of those patrilineages who have received wives from the deceased (the wife-taking in-laws) arrive on the scene, they may be called over and given a piece of fibre and told, "Perhaps you've got no rope. Take this home, tie it round the cow's leg, and bring the animal here." The fact that this is an occasion for settling debts may be one aspect of the requirement that all the wife-taking in-laws should attend the funeral before the actual burial takes place. In any case, the demand for unpaid bridewealth could be easily reinforced at this moment by the retention of the wife concerned, who would of course be present attending her kinsman's funeral.

The wife-taking in-laws of the deceased are obliged not only to be present but also to contribute an "in-law fowl." At one funeral I attended, the actual burial was held up until the arrival of the dead man's sister's husband, even though the corpse was rapidly putrifying. This fowl is a compulsory gift to the dead man's patrikin in recognition of the rights that they still exercise over their sister and of the obligations that the husband owes as a son-in-law. For these rights are not extinguished by the death of any one member of the groups involved, excepting only the wife herself.

Equally, a man should not put himself in the wrong by failing to attend the funeral of his wife, and it is said that formerly he would have lost all claim to the children of the marriage had he done so. To refuse (LD *zagri*) a wife's funeral had therefore the same consequences as rejecting the wife herself, although this situation had been modified by certain decisions in the local magistrate's court by the time of my stay.

Attendance is also compulsory for wife-giving in-laws. If a woman dies, her kin are directly concerned to see she is given a proper burial; in the case of a man's death, the widow's kin publicly reaffirm their right and duties toward her. This process is one that involves the taking rather than the giving of property; but the widow's kin do contribute grain for the final ceremony, when the widow is released from her ties to the dead man. In addition, they can make a voluntary gift of a fowl and a bunch of guinea-corn heads, if the relationship has been especially satisfactory, and this is usually presented in the course of the funeral orations.

In all parts of this region, a man who is buried away from the village in which he resided also has a funeral ceremony performed for him at his own compound, when concrete evidence of his death is brought there. On the report of a man's death reaching his village, a close agnatic kinsman goes to try to discover the truth of the story. The funeral does not begin until he returns with an article of clothing or some other possession, which is then placed upon the funeral stand. The death is thereby established, and the ceremony takes place as usual, with the article of clothing being interred in the place of the dead man.

THE WASHING OF THE BODY

When they hear the distinctive sounds of grief issuing from the dead man's compound, those women from the neighborhood who are acquainted with the funeral procedures gather there to arrange for the bathing of the corpse. There are two points to note about the women who carry out these tasks. First, they are the classificatory "wives" and "sisters" of the deceased, a fact of general significance that will be discussed later in this section. Second, these arrangers of the corpse are always women of an advanced age. It is not merely that time brings with it the responsibility and knowledge necessary to perform the complex series of rites. It is prescribed that these women should have passed the menopause, that they should, to use the LoDagaa phrase, have "turned to men" (*lieba daba*). They can no longer perform the main task of women, the bearing of children, and are, as it were, asexual. This attribute permits them to carry out intimate physical acts on members of both sexes, an attribute that in Western European society is ideally associated with the doctor. But there is a yet more general aspect of this role of the older women, and one with parallels in many other societies.[2] In a social system in which authority is largely vested in males, there is a strong tendency to equate the authority figure with maleness, or at least with asexuality. This strain toward consistency in the social system is the counterpart of generalization on the personality level. Among the LoDagaa, it works out in the following way. Authority, ritual and otherwise, is normally vested in men; within the general category of women, it is those past the menopause who most nearly approach the male.

The old women proceed to bathe the dead man in hot water—formerly they rubbed the corpse either with *kãbur,* the black, greasy byproduct of shea butter, or else with chewed groundnuts—in order to remove all the body dirt (*deo, deghr*). The widows are not allowed to do this themselves, lest they should attempt to commit suicide by biting the body of their dead husband. For it is thought that a widow might try in this way to follow her husband to the Land of the Dead. Were her mouth to touch the corpse, she would consume some of the dirt of his body, any contact with which is so dangerous that it requires a purification to be performed by the grave-diggers, who have been rendered immune from the consequences of pollution by their special "medicine." I witnessed one such incident in which, directly after the burial, the widow was led to the grave, where a new-laid egg (*jel paala*) was broken over her forehead in such a way that the yolk fell onto the grave itself.

This ritual act, involving the use of a new-laid egg as a purifying agent, also occurs during the course of the LoWiili ceremony known as

---

[2] Van Gennep ([1960] p. 145) remarks that old women are often either identified with men or else become leaders in ceremonies restricted to females.

Vukãle. This performance takes place toward the end of February, not only among the LoWiili, but also among the neighboring Dagaba and DagaaWiili, and has the expressed purpose of banishing various diseases from the parish. Groups of unmarried girls and young boys who have not yet reached puberty walk around the homesteads within their minor ritual area and sweep all the dirt (*deo*) from the floors of the rooms, singing as they do so. One of the older girls sings the first phrase, and the whole group joins in the alternate lines.

Here there are sores,	*Natir ben be,*
May they go away;	*O yi ye'e;*
Across the river,	*O yi Man gon,*
May they go away.	*O yi ye'e.*

In subsequent verses of the song, the names of other diseases are substituted for "sores." When the rooms have been swept, the house is then covered in whitewash splodges. In return for their services, the children are given food, which they take to the west, or Lo, boundary of the ritual area, that is, the boundary nearest to the River Volta. Here they take a housebat, feed it with porridge and relish, and bathe it in a stream. Then, one of the children, holding the bat and a new-laid egg in his hand, throws them both toward the river. The inhabitants of the neighboring area afterwards perform the same ritual, and in this way disease is cast out successively from one community to the next.

This ceremony brings out four metaphors of purification that also recur constantly in the course of the funeral services. The first is purification by water. Lustration takes place when the bodies of the dead person and the bat are bathed.

The second is purification by the breaking of a new-laid egg. This act transfers the impurity from the widow to the corpse in the one case, and from the community to the bat in the other. The association of the egg with birth and hence with newness make it a satisfactory vehicle for such a purpose. But there is a further element involved. The white of the egg has a metaphoric connection with the sticky substance found inside the stem of the okra, and both of these were associated by informants with semen. The link here is not only the similar tactile properties of the three substances, but also their color; for white objects are employed in a variety of such contexts, as can be seen from the ritual procedure of whitewashing.

Whitewashing is the third mode of purification and the one that most clearly displays the complex nature of such procedures. Writing of a similar color identification among the Andamanese, Radcliffe-

Brown remarks: "The association of light and dark with euphoric and disphoric conditions respectively has a psycho-physical basis, for it seems to be universal in human nature" ([1948] p. 316). But while the LoDagaa associate white with cleansing, they also link it with death, just as white is the color of mourning in China. This latter connection appears to be largely a matter of differentiation, a method of setting the bereaved apart from the remainder of the community, and the cleansed house from those that have not yet been visited. The importance of the purely diacritical aspects of so many of these standardized procedures was noted by Van Gennep with regard to mutilations of the human body ([1960] p. 74). Its relevance to the present context, though differentiating sects rather than roles, is emphasized in the injunction issued to the early Christians to wear white at funerals, "not black as the heathen do" (Duncan-Jones [1932], p. 618).

Yet a further element lies behind this act of whitewashing. The whitewash is dug from the earth and has strong associations with the mystical aspects of the land; in other contexts its application appears to have the effect of calling upon the Earth shrine to bear witness to certain deeds, so that if things go wrong, supernatural sanctions will come into play. In the Vukãle ceremony the association with the Earth is certainly relevant, since it is the ritual area that is being cleansed; but there is none of the character of an ordeal that marks the whitewashing both of the surviving spouse (especially the widow) and of initiates to the secret Bagre society. In the latter case, the Earth provides a sanction against the neophyte breaking his vows, in the former against a failure of the surviving spouse to confess any complicity in his or her partner's death. However, in all three cases the whitewashing has the simultaneous effect of purifying the parties and of differentiating them from the rest of the community.

The fourth method of purification common to both these ceremonies is sweeping. To sweep the dust is also to cleanse the house of disease, for dirt has the generalized significance of "mystical defilement." Sweeping is therefore an act of purification. It may also be one of separation, as is the case with all the foregoing rites. When a man's soul (*sie*) is thought to have left his body, his father or another close agnate performs a private rite to purify the body and so allow the soul to re-enter its proper dwelling. The man is literally swept with the fowl and the guinea-fowl that are sacrificed to the shrine indicated by the diviner. In the words of one informant: "The exit of the soul leaves all the skin dirty (*ka fu sie yiina fu yanggan zaa dioro*) so that you have to sweep away the dirt (*fu na piira a dioro*) and put it on a shrine so that your soul can return again (*bin a tiib yang ka fu sie natwona kpe*)."

A similar rite is carried out by a craftsman when he sells a xylophone he has made, for it is feared that the soul of the maker may have entered into the instrument he has created. The immaterial substance has therefore to be separated from the material object with which it has associated itself and made to return to the human body in which it normally dwells. The Earth shrine also has to be "swept" when one of its congregation commits a heinous sin, such as suicide; this is done by the piacular sacrifice of a dog, which is brushed against it, slaughtered, and then thrown aside. Only the joking partners of the parish can eat the flesh of such animals.

All these methods of purification are concerned with the removal of various kinds of "dirt," of which the most important are the exuviae of the human body. These adhere to the clothes a man wears, to the objects he uses, and to the persons with whom he has been in closest physical contact, especially his wife. Hence all these things and people are the subject of particular attention during the funeral ceremonies. Dirt is conveyed from person to person by physical contact, particularly during sexual intercourse, partly through sweat, partly through the seminal fluids. The strong association of dirt and coitus is perhaps also connected with the dual functions of the sexual organs; for in W. B. Yeats's words, love has "raised its mansion in the place of excrement."

The exchange of body dirt creates an intimate bond that may be dangerous for both parties. The surviving partner of a marriage has therefore to be cleansed by bathing. The transfer of body dirt, particularly in sexual intercourse, leaves a person defenseless against certain sorts of malevolent attack, especially witchcraft. Among the LoDagaba, witchcraft is believed to be practiced mainly by one matriclansman against another; this does not mean that the hostility necessarily stems from a matriclansman, but that any aggressor would have to employ such a person as an agent. Most LoWiili do not formulate any such restriction, although mothers are quite often accused of killing their children. But in both societies another flank lies open to attack by witchcraft. As far as mystical aggression is concerned, intercourse places the sexual partners firmly in each other's power, even though they are members of different descent groups. This is one of the reasons why a spouse's jealousy is so dangerous, a fact that in general tends to make a husband treat a wife, and especially so in a plural marriage, with considerable respect for the prevailing norms. It places a sanction on the behavior of the man rather than the woman, because if a husband loses his wife, except by divorce, he can only acquire another by making further bridewealth payments. A woman, on the other hand, has no such obstacle placed in the way of her remarriage; indeed by the leviratic rule she is automatically allocated to another man when her present husband dies.

Nadel ([1954] p. 172) deals with a similar problem when he attributes the Nupe male's fear of a woman's witchcraft to basic sex antagonisms, that is, to his resentment of female dominance in sexual relationships, a universal situation of conflict that various societies work out in different ways. In the LoWiili context, I would relate the emphasis on female witches to a more general phenomenon, role inferiority. Because of their subordinate position, both in social and in physical terms, women are seen as having more frequent recourse to mystical modes of attack than men, to whom other forms of action are available. This fear of what she may secretly do constitutes a limited guarantee that a wife will be reasonably treated, despite her relative lack of jural status and physical strength.

As among the Tallensi, then, dirt and soul are closely associated (Fortes [1949], p. 58). Indeed the one seems to be the material agency of the other. The nature of these beliefs will be further elucidated during the analysis of the ceremonies, but their permeation throughout the whole series of rites has necessitated a preliminary look at some of these interconnections. We can now return to the account of the preparation of the corpse.

When the women have bathed the body, they put some melted shea butter on their palms, stretch out and withdraw their arms twice in quick succession, and on the third occasion anoint the corpse with oil. Anointing the body is part of the normal routine of bathing, but what I call the ritual of pretended gesture (*tun*) is specific to funerals and to similar performances, such as those connected with the Bagre society. These pretense rituals serve to point up an occasion that is marked off from the ordinary, and they can therefore be considered as an example of those rituals of reversal, so often found in funeral ceremonies, in which actions are performed in a manner different from, and often opposed to, the ways appropriate in normal circumstances.

This formalization of the usual ways of acting is also a technique of dealing with mystically dangerous persons and is always adopted by the LoDagaa when dealing with the dead themselves as well as with those who approximate, albeit temporarily, to such a condition. Thus offerings of food to ancestor shrines, to widows in mourning, and to those undergoing initiation into the Bagre society are all made with gestures of pretense. In the second of these examples, it is the widow's former association with the dead man that places her temporarily in this special category. In the third case, all Bagre neophytes are "killed" during the course of the long series of initiatory rituals they have to undergo on becoming members. In part, this pretended killing is a homeopathic protection against sickness, but as Van Gennep has emphasized, it also marks a change in the status of the participants, whose former position is, as it were, killed off. Funerals are the supreme example of the ceremonials of passage and as such often form the model of other such ceremonies. Initiatory rituals frequently include the "killing" of the novice, whether in the secret associations of West Africa or among the Masonic lodges of Western Europe.

These rituals of pretense are carried out three times for a man and four for a woman. The common use of three and four in Africa is an example of a widespread association of male and female with odd and even respectively, a fact that should possibly be related to the uniqueness and duality of the most prominent anatomical features distinguishing the two sexes, namely the penis and the breasts. According to Dieterlen ([1951] p. 5), the Bambara who live to the northwest recognize three as representing the penis and testicles, and four the four lips of a woman. I myself heard no such explanation from the LoDagaa; the explicit association of three and four with the sexes generally is certainly much wider than any reference to specific sexual characteristics.[3]

At a LoWiili funeral I attended in Biro, the southern part of Birifu, the head of the corpse was shaved directly after the body had been bathed. The shaving of the head also occurs as part of the procedure of cleansing the surviving partner of a marriage, as well as the parents after the death of a child. This act of cutting falls into the general class of acts of separation; shaving the head not only differentiates the individual concerned, it also cleanses by removing some of the bodily excrescences upon which dirt accumulates. The same act occurs again in the initiatory rituals of the Bagre association as well as in the soul-sweeping ceremonies. Indeed it is of such widespread occurrence in this and in other cultures that it can, as I have earlier noted, be considered the typical act of separation, just as tying is the most typical act of aggregation. Some writers have interpreted hair-cutting as a substitute castration; in the present instance, a cryptophoric interpretation of this kind appears uncalled for.

Even at this early stage in the obsequies, the particular form of ritual employed depends upon the roles the dead man has filled, the social groups to which he has belonged, his personal achievements in life, and finally the cause of his death. For not only is a person's formal status,

[3] When rituals are performed a different number of times according to sex, this is indicated in the text by putting the number for a woman in parentheses.

his inventory of roles, made quite explicit at his funeral, but the ceremony in fact defines his general position, his standing, in the community in which he has lived. Attention has already been drawn to the over-all differences in treatment accorded to the corpse of an unweaned child and to those who have died "evil deaths." There are also many more specific variations in custom. As far as the bathing of the corpse is concerned, this is differently performed for two categories of person, those who have died a "death by arrow" (*pĩĩ kũ*) and those who have killed another human being (*ziēsob*).

"Deaths by arrow" include suicide, for which expiatory performances have to be undertaken at the Earth shrine, and other deaths associated with poison (*lo'*). Persons who die from certain festering sores are similarly treated; so, too, those who are killed by snakes. In the latter case, the quiver, a man's most important object of property, cannot be hung over the shoulder of the corpse until the snake that killed him has itself been killed and its skin draped on the funeral stand. If this is not done, there can be no cure for any other person who is bitten by the same reptile. Moreover, the body cannot be left all night on the funeral stand which is erected outside the compound, lest other snakes should be attracted by the smell and bite those who sleep there. Hence the corpse is carried inside each evening until the day of burial.

The body of such a person is bathed in a whitish mixture of malted guinea-corn flour (*kai*) and water. The use of flour paste is a special sort of purification, rendered necessary by the presence of poison. When the corpse has been washed in this manner, it is not arrayed in the usual smock, but is placed upon the funeral stand in nothing but a pair of shorts.

The other variation in the way of burying the corpse reflects not the manner of death, but an aspect of the status of the dead man, namely whether or not he is a homicide. Indeed, a detailed examination of a funeral ceremony will reveal all the roles of importance that he has filled in his lifetime and that are expunged or inherited at his death.

The corpse of a homicide is too dangerous either to be supported or to be bathed by women, at least until after a sacrifice has been performed. On his deathbed, such a man is left to die lying down. After he has died, four other homicides take ebony poles and roll the body over three times. The men carrying out these acts are inhabitants of the same ritual area, and they are allowed to be clansmen of the deceased, but not members of the same patrilineage, since these are felt to be too closely related. When the body of the homicide has been turned over in this way, a certain root (*soro: Cochlospermum tinctorium*) is procured, the one used in the purificatory rites that the killer undergoes immediately after a slaying. One of the homicides chews a portion of the root, and the reddish fragments are spat on the dead man's left arm, the one that held the bow.[4] The throat of a cock is then cut so that the blood drips onto the same arm, and, as always in the sacrificial procedure, some tail feathers are plucked out and stuck in the tacky blood. Following the sacrifice, the hunting horns (*wera*) used to announce the slaughter of an animal in the hunt or of an enemy in war are blown loudly, while the homicides perform a mimed dance, enacting the dead man's feats in battle.

One other feature concerning the preparation of the corpse should be mentioned here. If a woman dies in childbirth, she cannot be buried without the child first having been removed from her belly. This is a taboo of the Earth. For no infant is given a normal funeral, and mourning is confined to the parents alone. I shall discuss the reasons for this later, when analyzing the different modes of burial. Here it is sufficient to say that an infant cannot be buried below the surface of the earth. Consequently, if the mother was interred with the infant in her belly, the anger of the Earth shrine would be aroused against the survivors. A post-mortem operation has therefore to be performed, and this can be done only by a homicide whose medicine protects him against the mystical consequences of dissecting corpses.

I was also told that the same operation would be carried out on a man who died of a swollen belly (*pur paala*), although I never came across an actual instance of this. A swollen belly has various possible causes, but the most probable is that the sufferer has practiced witchcraft and in consequence of this has died an evil death (*kũ faa*). Witchcraft is associated with the stomach in various ways. A person only practices witchcraft if his belly is black: that is, if he is angry either with a particular individual or with humanity at large. It is believed by some that a witch's belly contains a number of hard objects, though the LoDagaa perform no autopsy to discover these. The diagnosis of a swollen belly as having been caused by the practice of witchcraft is not only connected with the idea of the stomach as the seat of the emotions. It also springs

4 The root employed in this particular rite may vary from clan to clan, for the homicide medicine certainly does. However, I believe *soro* plays a prominent part in all the major purificatory rites for homicides; this is presumably connected with the fact that the root turns red when cut or broken, thus recalling the shedding of blood. The words for blood (*zĩĩ*) and for red (*zio, zie*) may be etymologically connected. The name for the homicide medicine (*ziẽ*) also appears to form part of the same associated series of concepts, the general importance of which is discussed at the end of the following chapter.

from the belief that witchcraft is a sort of greed, a hunger for meat; its practice is likely to make a person physically fat. Formerly, the customary way of dealing with a suspected witch living within the same ritual area was to take him to the Earth shrine, where he was made to drink a mixture of soil and water. The belly of a witch was thought to swell until he died; the innocent suffered no harm.

In discussing the old women who lay out the corpse and the homicides who prepare the body of one of their fellows, I remarked that the persons called upon to perform these tasks are never close relatives of the deceased. Extreme distress, particularly in severe cases of separation, often leads to incapacitating anxiety and grief in the bereaved. But this system of allocating tasks to more distant kith or kin is not simply a direct outcome of universal psycho-physical reactions of mourning. For the categories of both the bereaved and the helpers are subject to social definition. Indeed, among the LoDagaa the principle of "not burying one's own dead" is elaborated into a major mechanism of social interaction. The exchange of services of affliction between social groups and persons is an important method of building up a network of interrelationships, especially insofar as neighbors are concerned.

This exchange of services of affliction has functionally much in common with the exchange of gifts, as discussed by Thurnwald, Malinowski, Mauss, and others. Malinowski's account of the *kula* trading expeditions showed how relatively complex social relationships were established upon bases other than the exchange of economic goods and services that accompanies technological change and the consequent development of an elaborate division of labor. Although differentiation of function arising directly from the productive system is to some degree more intrinsic to a social system (in that there are fewer alternatives for social action), the exchange of ritual services is equally capable of bringing otherwise discrete groups and persons into lasting social relations. To this extent Durkheim's assumption that an increase of moral density depended, in the last resort, upon occupational differentiation in the economic sphere, and this in turn upon population density, requires some modification ([1933] p. 268).[5] Indeed, his suggested schema of development from mechanical to organic solidarity can be seen as

[5] The need for modification does not depend upon an acceptance of Parsons's argument that Durkheim was "biologizing" social theory ([1937] p. 323), an interpretation that has recently been rejected by Schnore [1958]. On the other hand, Durkheim's initial failure to grant a *conscience collective* to societies with mechanical solidarity, another point that Parsons makes in his perceptive commentary, is closely related to my own criticism of his causal association of increasing "moral density" with technological progress.

yet another attempt, similar in kind to the one of Spencer's he was engaged in dismissing, to clothe technological innovation in the garb of moral progress. On the one hand, increasing complexity in social relationships does not appear to lead to a change in the kind of bond visualized in Durkheim's dichotomy. On the other, complexity may arise from a ritual division of labor as well as from an economic one, from an exchange of ritual goods and services as much as from an exchange of economic ones.

Several writers have noted the importance of the exchange of rights over women in building and maintaining social relationships, and Lévi-Strauss [1949], following Tylor's well-known statement [1889], has argued that the rejection of the sexuality of the sister was man's first step from nature to culture. By denying oneself access to the sister, one is forced into a wider network of relationships. But however it was "in the beginning," the incest taboo certainly has no monopoly in this respect; for taboos on the disposal of the dead, to take but one example, work in a very similar way.[6] By denying a person access to the dead bodies of his near kin, the field of social interaction is again extended. "Funeral friendships" are in this respect functionally similar to marriage. Indeed, for the very reason that services of affliction do not have the same biological basis as rights in women, they possess a yet greater potential for elaboration, so that a whole hierarchy of exchanging groups may be erected. As with marriage exchange groups, the collectivities involved in services of affliction may be paired (direct exchange, as in groups practicing prescriptive bilateral cross-cousin marriage), or linked in a linear series (circular or indirect exchange, as with groups practicing a certain type of prescriptive mother's brother's daughter's marriage), or else they may be diffusely organized.

Ritual services among the LoDagaa mostly operate by paired exchange, as when two groups consisting of one or more patrilineages act as grave-diggers for each other. On the other hand, three or more groups sometimes engage in a diffuse exchange of services of affliction, so that when one is in need of assistance, the members of all the other groups participate.

Before examining this system of transactions in greater detail, there are two points of general relevance arising from Figure 4 (p. 66). First, the diagram, as presented, relates to acts for which the group is homo-

---

6 Hocart speaks of these arrangements as "mutual ministrations" and emphasizes that intermarriage is only one form of such "reciprocal duties"; unfortunately his discussion and analysis of the subject are confused by a concern to construct "dual organizations" ([1936] p. 263).

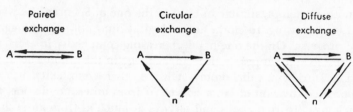

FIG. 4.—Some types of exchange.

geneously organized. That is to say, each of the relevant members of Group A acts toward Group B in approximately the same manner. But such, of course, is not always the case. Some discussions of the exchanges involved in cross-cousin marriage fail to give adequate recognition to the fact that even if each member of Group A acts in the same manner (for example, by marrying his mother's brother's daughter), the transactions, though identical from one standpoint, may relate some members to Group B and others to Group C, D, etc. In other words, the pattern of exchange, looked at from a particular level of group structure, may be heterogeneous rather than homogeneous. Therefore, in any discussion of exchange, the group reference needs to be clearly specified. Otherwise there is the danger of inferring a system of circular exchange at the level of the inclusive group merely from data indicating that each of the members carried out a similar type of marriage. Prescriptive cross-cousin marriage may operate heterogeneously rather than homogeneously and thus give rise to a diffuse arrangement (the third type in Figure 4), such as results from the straightforward application of a rule of exogamy.

Second, the diagram refers not only to the exchange of identical goods and services, as between the LoDagaa groups that carry out reciprocal ritual services for one another, but also to the exchange of equivalent goods and services, as when a body of specialists performs certain rites on behalf of the rest of the society, or of a particular social group, and is rewarded for these services by money or by other means. Leach's criticism of Lévi-Strauss's analysis of Kachin marriage turns on the point that the latter's interpretation does not allow for equivalent as distinct from identical reciprocation (Leach [1951]). In the context of funeral services equivalent but not identical return occurs when a specialist group acts as grave-diggers for the whole community in return for a cash payment. The fact that these specialists may form a pariah group warns us against trying to view all or most social behavior as exchange, a concept that carries the implication of reciprocal interaction. For such a view overlooks the position of groups who are obliged to perform services that the society recognizes to be inadequately rewarded, obliged either by the threat of force, as in certain conquest situations, or by the existence of other sanctions. In other words, it may neglect the power or authority differential between the parties involved in the transfer of goods and services.

The exchange of ritual services may take numerous forms, and in funeral ceremonies we are primarily concerned with those that I have called services of affliction. Since the widows and sisters of the dead man are considered to be too close to bathe his corpse, the task is allocated to classificatory "wives" and "sisters." However, although it is a "sister" who goes into the dead man's room, props up the corpse in a sitting position, and finds the grease for rubbing on the body, the "wives" and "sisters" do not themselves take the leading roles in these ceremonies. Instead, they get some woman from outside to organize the proceedings, while they act as her helpers. The attitude behind this dependence upon distant help is succinctly expressed in the proverb "A person with a long face cannot suck his own wound" (*No wo'o sob be muore o tuore*). In any situation of distress there are certain members of the community who stand in relationships that oblige them to assist the sufferer. Thus this proverb does not merely imply a negative prohibition against helping oneself; it is a positive injunction upon others to come to one's aid. The range of persons from whom this assistance can be expected is of course a matter for social regulation. Indeed such regulations are a most important part of the framework of the organization of social groups, and an understanding of the operation of these services must be sought within the context of the system as a whole.

Among the LoWiili, the actual disposal of the body is carried out not by members of the same lineage as the deceased but by more distant agnates, or even by members of another patriclan. They must be near but not too near, removed but not too removed. Indeed, descent is not necessarily involved at all; it is rather a question of proximity. One needs to be able to call on people who can come immediately a death occurs and who are acquainted with the nature of the ground in which the grave has to be dug. The groups that perform these services for one another I call "burial groups." In some LoDagaba parishes, on the other hand, a system of diffuse rather than paired exchange operates in this context; any grave-digger from a neighboring patrilineal group other than that to which the deceased belongs may come along and help.

There are a number of other services—for example, the rites surrounding the carving of the ancestor shrine—that have to be performed by a person of the same agnatic descent, however distant. A totally unrelated person cannot carry out such ministrations on behalf of the bereaved. Among the LoWiili, these "funeral groups," which are responsible for many of the reciprocal services the obsequies demand, consist of one or more patrilineages that exchange services with other patrilineages of the same clan sector. As we noted earlier, by comparison with the LoWiili, the LoDagaba clan sectors are relatively undifferentiated from the internal standpoint; the funeral groups are formed by the local sector of a patriclan that operates reciprocally with the sector of a linked clan resident in the neighborhood, and the necessary services are carried out by members of another named descent group that claims a common origin with that of the dead man in the distant past. Thus among the LoDagaba the same funeral services are performed by groups that are of a higher order of segmentation, though there is little difference in numerical strength. For the LoDagaba show a tendency to greater fragmentation of patriclans and less emphasis on genealogical reckoning in group contexts. The local sector of a LoDagaba patriclan is not divided into a recognized number of lineages that participate as collectivities. The greater stress on membership of uterine descent groups coincides with less emphasis on specific genealogical reckoning in the patrilineal ones. The LoDagaba sacrifice depth of genealogy and thus limit the possible extent of lineage organization. Instead, the same range of differentiation, or order of segmentation, is achieved by having numerically smaller patriclans and placing greater importance on the linkages between them inside the parish.

In one part of Birifu (LoWiili), an intermediary situation is found, essentially similar to that in Tom (LoDagaba). Biro, in the south, is occupied by two patriclan sectors, Gomble and Biro proper, who intermarry and perform funeral services for each other. They recognize one another as agnates (*yidem,* "housepeople") and maintain that in times past they formed a single exogamous group, but later divided because they were unable to find enough brides from outside their ranks. This situatioń, however, is exceptional; for normally the LoWiili funeral groups consist of lineage of the same clan sector, who also refer to each other as *yidem,* and sometimes, in this context, as *sããbir,* "children of one father." The Naayiili clan sector, for example, has five constituent lineages, which form two reciprocating groups of the kind mentioned above.

Still other services are carried out by the joking partners of the deceased. (By joking partnerships I refer to relations between members of social groups as such; I speak of the similar institution between specific kinship or affinal roles as joking relationships.) In the early stages of the funeral, the joking partners often act as companions to the bereaved, whom they restrain from doing harm to themselves in their grief. Later in the ceremony, the partners will jointly engage in performing a series of grotesque acts that help to distract the mourners and so adjust them to the loss.

Joking partnerships work on a more inclusive basis than either the burial or the funeral groups, operating between clans or in some cases between groups of linked clans. In a system of double clanship, reciprocal services may of course be based upon both sets of descent group; in these two communities, both matriclans and patriclans are paired in joking partnerships, and funeral ceremonies provide the main occasion on which they come into play. In each case the joking partner is able to "make hot things cold"; this he does, actually and metaphorically, by "throwing ashes," the cool residue of the hot fire.

The operation of these "cathartic" services, which groups perform reciprocally for one another, will become clearer in the course of the analysis of the ceremonies. But it is worth emphasizing here that they serve not only to relieve affliction but also to create bonds of a political kind. By the externalization of these duties toward one's dead, as with the externalization of rights over the sexuality of one's female kin, a system of exchange is built up that in itself makes for the rule of law and order. For by such methods, positive relationships are established between groups, and these provide a strong sanction against acts that lead to a breakdown in the system of reciprocal services. In this way, the system of reciprocating groups tends to perpetuate not only the specific services in the context of which the groups have emerged—burial or funeral services, for example—but also positive social relationships in general. Both the exchange of services and the threat of the withdrawal of reciprocity are mechanisms of special importance to segmentary or stateless systems, those in which central institutions for the maintenance of social control are absent.

THE ARRAYING OF THE DEAD

When the old women have anointed the body, they take a length of white cloth and wind it around the waist of the dead man. They then proceed to attire him in the finest clothes, a white smock, long baggy trousers, and a hat, usually a red fez. The white cloth, the most important item of the corpse's apparel, is usually purchased by his patrilineage with money collected at previous funerals. In the case of poor households, the corpse is sometimes stripped of all else before the actual burial occurs, but the piece of white cloth is never removed from the man's waist. It is said that formerly only an old man was buried in a smock which was otherwise taken off and washed in ashes ready for the next funeral.[7]

For those belonging to the Bagre society, especially if they are poor, the piece of cloth and the clothes (LD *bag foba*) may be bought out of the money (LD *bag libie*) collected by senior members during the initiation ceremonies. Clothes can also be supplied to needy members during their lifetime, one of the several ways in which the Bagre functions as a "friendly society."

The LoDagaa are ignorant of the art of weaving. In the market, they purchase strips of material, three inches wide, made either in the north, as the generic name "Mossi cloth" indicates, or else woven in the strangers' quarter (*zongo*) of one of the small towns situated along the main trade route running between the Ashanti, Gonja, and Wa to the south, and the countries of the Niger bend to the north. This material is subsequently sewn into clothes either by a local man or by one of the foreign traders. Thus all woven cloth is associated with foreigners, and particularly with Moslem strangers.

Funeral attire has even stronger associations with foreigners. The funeral smock is an example. It differs from the ordinary smock—the normal wear for a man when he is not working in the fields—in that it is either entirely white or at least not striped with red.[8] (The prohibition on red thread in the cloth may be related to the similarity in color between this and blood.) The emphasis on white is, as I have remarked, an aspect of purificatory ritual among the LoDagaa; but the connection of the white smock with Islamic dress must also be taken into account, as the other garments more clearly demonstrate. The long baggy trousers have obvious Moslem associations. Formerly, only a skin penis sheath was worn by the men, while a youth tucked his penis under a string tied around the waist. But nowadays the everyday wear in the fields, in the house, or in the market is a pair of shorts, either of factory-made cotton or else of hand-woven Mossi cloth. Trousers are rarely worn by the LoDagaa, except by those who have acquired chiefship since the establishment of a central administration by European powers. The

[7] I was told that the Tiedeme and some other clans in Tom formerly used to bury their dead in a sheepskin, and that when they changed to Mossi cloth they put a small piece in all the old graves lest the ancestors should become angry.

[8] There are only four color names in Dagari: *soola*, *sebla*, translated as black, but covering most dark colors; *zio*, *zie*, translated as red, but ranging from yellow to the deepest red; *pla*, white; and *ulu*, grey.

use of trousers in funeral ceremonies reflects Islamic influence, as both their shape and their use by persons of high status indicates. But the clearest indication of all is the wearing of the red fez, which elsewhere in the region is linked both with Islam and with positions of authority.

Thus the corpse is not merely dressed; it is dressed up. The name of the clothes given to indigent Bagre members (*bag foba*) indicates this, for *foba* means "showy." The clothes used are high-status objects, associated with chiefs claiming positions of political authority or with Moslems claiming a special relationship with the supernatural. Furthermore, both classes of person possess not only high status, albeit in neighboring social systems, but also riches, the chiefs from tribute, the Moslems from trade. The material achievements of the dead man form a constant theme throughout the celebration of his obsequies; indeed the whole distribution of meat, and therefore to some extent the attendance at the funeral, depends upon the savings he has made during his lifetime by investment in livestock. Dressing him in fine clothes is thus a means of honoring him and his earthly attainments; it also testifies to the prosperity and well-being of the social groups to which he belonged.

There is another reason why the corpse should be arrayed in this way. When the neophytes of the Bagre society complete their initiation, they dress up in a very similar manner and then repair to the market place, which they walk around in formal procession. Both the procession and the elaborate attire constitute public announcements to the community that a change of status has been effected. Thus, in funerals as in other *rites de passage*, both human and cosmic, the adoption of formal clothing emphasizes not only the distinctiveness of the occasion but also the occurrence of a change of public import and, in addition to this, the status—particularly the achieved status—of the dead man.

This interpretation is supported by the fact that both in the Bagre initiation and in funerals the women, too, are dressed in smocks. Although I was once told that the only women to be clothed in a smock were those who had passed the menopause and were said to have changed to men, I saw no evidence of this in contemporary funerals. All corpses except those that had been killed by poison (*pīī kū*) are dressed up in smock, trousers, and fez before being placed upon the funeral stand. In everyday life these garments are worn exclusively by males. Women normally wear nothing but perineal bands on which are hung some fresh leaves. On market days and other special occasions, they usually wrap a short piece of "Manchester cloth," a towel, or a length of wide-loomed "Yoruba cloth" over the leather bands. In recent years the better-off women have taken to dressing in longer cloths that cover the body from the breasts down to the knees.

At death a young girl has a small strip of cloth tied around her waist, but an older woman is always dressed in perineal bands made of goatskin, which are the matron's wear par excellence. On these bands hangs a bunch of fibres teased into many strands, which is described as her "leaves," the usual decoration a woman wears behind and sometimes in front. An old woman will collect and prepare the vines (*byuur*) needed to make this "horse's tail" for her own funeral; hanging on the wall of her sleeping room, it is the harbinger of mortality, a recognition of the inevitability of death.

In addition to these special items of female apparel, a woman's corpse is dressed in male costume, an act that is not in this case an instance of the reversal of roles. It is not transvestism, but rather a function of the paucity of women's clothing and the lowliness of their general status; until recently, when they acquired the ability to purchase imported cloth, women's main method of dressing up was to put on men's apparel. And this, from society's standpoint, is to adopt the insignia of higher status.

There is, however, one feature of the arraying of the corpse that does demonstrate the use of reversal procedures and how they may serve to direct attention to the distinctiveness of the occasion, especially at the funeral itself, which celebrates the antithesis of life. For the smock is not placed on the dead man in the ordinary manner; instead it is turned inside out, an act analogous to the reversing of firearms at military funerals in Europe. Moreover, all the pockets of the gown are cut away, making it impossible, the LoDagaa say, for the dead man to take anything with him. For they believe that the soul of a living person might accompany the dead man, a possibility against which elaborate ritual precautions are taken at various stages during the performance of the obsequies. The persons whom the deceased was most fond of are especially vulnerable. Young children are in the greatest danger of all and are often disguised by ashes, whitewash, or beads, so that they will not be recognized by the ghost of the dead man. For it is feared that the dead may try to perpetuate their network of social relations in the next world by dragging their close associates with them. In the case of the widow, precautions are taken not only against the possibility of her voluntarily following her husband, but also against his forcing her to accompany him to the Land of the Dead.

This fear of the dead man's intervention is related to the conflicts inherent in close relationships of all kinds. But there is also a cosmological aspect deriving from a contradiction involved in the very idea of an afterlife. The minimum definition of survival implies that an entity or essence associated with a human body persists after death. The inevitable link between the personality of the individual in its living and dead states means that the ghost or spirit tends to be treated as if it still possessed the desires and wishes of the living. And hence, as in the present case, the dead body is often provided with food, drink, and other material objects for the journey it is about to undertake.

Among the Ashanti, slaves were formerly killed to accompany dead chiefs to the other world. The custom of suttee, which existed among some Indian castes in the last century, was similar in certain respects, although there the widow followed the dead man of her own volition. The Hindu practice brings out very clearly one crucial aspect of the problem; for whether or not the widow was burnt on the pyre, her dead husband was visualized as retaining his right of exclusive sexual access in perpetuity. The prohibition on her remarriage emphasizes the central contradiction involved in the idea of survival after death, namely, the endowment of the dead with the attributes of the living. By a variety of procedures the living attempt to separate themselves from the dead, and one way in which they do so is by creating an image that is, partially at least, a human image. For in the long run the spirit can only be conceived in terms of human wishes and desires, and religious relationships must be regulated upon this basis. So the dead man is given food he cannot eat, objects he cannot use, and rights he cannot exercise. Yet at the same time a major purpose of the funeral ceremony is to divest him of rights that were vested in him as a living person. He can no longer be granted the full quantum of rights he held in life; for unless an irreducible minimum of these are separated from him and transferred to the survivors, the social system cannot perpetuate itself.

A partial solution is to grant the dead man a token of the rights he earlier held; one wife or one slave may be sacrificed upon the grave, the kinsfolk taking the rest. The LoDagaa adopt a similar procedure with regard to grave goods. In most cases only nominal quantities are supplied for a man's last journey. When larger amounts are offered, they are consumed—as are the majority of sacrifices everywhere—by those who remain behind. The "communal meal" is on one level a function of the limits inherent in the operation of a supernatural economy.

The major contradiction here lies in dismissing the dead with honor and yet retaining their property without loss. A subsidiary problem arises from the fact that even when temporal objects are offered to the spirits, their enjoyment has to be differently conceived. The offering of token amounts is one partial solution; the concept of a joint corporation such as a lineage, consisting of both the living and the dead, is another. But neither of these ideas altogether solves the central difficulty that is reflected in the fear which the living have that the dead will attempt to perpetuate their network of social ties in ways dangerous to the survivors.

THE DISPLAYING OF THE CORPSE

When the body has been dressed up, the grave-diggers from the reciprocal burial group, or, in the case of the LoDagaba, from neighboring patriclan sectors, take over the corpse from the old women. Grave-digging is a specialized task; its practitioners are required to undergo an apprenticeship that is not only a training for the work itself, but also a protection against the mystical dangers surrounding the bodies of the dead. It is for this latter reason that if a boy should show signs of fear while at a funeral, his father may compel him to help the team of grave-diggers, usually four in number, who are preparing the chamber grave. This may require the use of physical force. My assistant recounted how once at a funeral he had expressed disgust at the sexton's task. Taking this as an indication of fear, his father tried to make him climb down into the grave. The boy refused; his father threatened to expel him from the house, but the boy refused again. Finally the father used his superior strength to force him down.

This incident demonstrates not only the strength of the feelings centered on the corpse, but also a recurrent feature of LoDagaa therapy. The performance of repulsive acts in controlled circumstances has both curative and prophylactic results. In taking medicine, the patient is often obliged to act in a manner that is totally at variance with his everyday behavior. For example, he may have to eat medicine placed upon the rung of the main ladder leading to the flat roof, the place where all strangers, dogs, and children tread on their way into the compound. A LoDagaa considers that to eat in this way is disgusting beyond belief; yet in this particular context the act has a protective function. The cathartic aspect of this procedure is even more strongly brought out in the case of grave-digging, in which the fear of the corpse is purged by contact with the very object of disgust. The performance of such acts that run contrary to everyday modes of behaving serves to inoculate the grave-diggers against the dangers associated with their unpleasant task; and this effect is further reinforced by certain restrictions imposed upon them during the actual burial. For should any of the fluids drip down from the corpse into their mouths, they have to swallow rather than spit them out.

In the preceding section, I pointed out the way in which reversal procedures mark off a special occasion from the ordinary activities of daily life. This differentiating function makes them particularly useful in the public announcement of changes of status. There are three further aspects of reversal rituals that require some comment.

First, reversal procedures may be employed in ceremonies of induction as a test of the neophyte; by performing the tasks set, he establishes his fitness to belong to the group or, alternatively, to change to a higher status. This aspect relates more directly to entry into selective associations, such as secret societies, college fraternities, and the like, but is not altogether absent from initiatory performances in general, as, for example, the induction into the "fraternity" of grave-diggers, which, because it is a specialist association, is necessarily selective. When the reversal concerns a strongly sanctioned prohibition, by the very act of breaking the social norm the initiate forges a bond with the other members of the group as against the rest of the world. This feature of reversal procedures cannot be overlooked in a treatment of the initiatory procedures of organizations such as Mau-Mau. But to discuss this in greater detail would lead into the whole problem of deviant groups, which involves more than the single, controlled reversals of accepted procedures that we are concerned with here.

Second, rites of reversal may be utilized to reinforce a norm, a use that is associated with general changes in status rather than in the membership of selective groups. By sleeping with the wife of a distant kinsman on a ceremonial occasion such as an Australian corroboree, the ideal norm of individualized rights in women may be reinforced. I do not only mean that the controlled breach of the norm may reduce the likelihood of transgression at other times; that by permitting the occasional expression of sexual desires for forbidden objects, there may be less danger of coveting a neighbor's or a kinsman's wife during the remainder of the year. I mean in addition that controlled breach, by drawing attention to the existence of a norm, may call for its observance, just as myths of the primeval incest of the twin siblings may reinforce contemporary prohibitions on the sexuality of the sister.

Third, reversal procedures may have attributed to them the therapeutic and prophylactic effect noted in connection with the LoDagaa fear of the corpse. It is possible that, as in the case of permitted breaches of the sexual taboos, some of these procedures may in fact have em-

pirical effects of this very kind. For example, the performance of a
wholly unpleasant task was included in the ritual administered to new
supplicants at all the medicine shrines that I observed in detail. These
shrines are approached mainly in times of distress, and the inclusion
of deliberately revolting acts in the rites necessary to obtain medicine
(as in the purification of an individual who has killed another human
being) inoculates the participant against anxiety. The formalized transgression of certain strongly held norms—and none is more strongly held
than those intimately connected with the input-output system of the
human body, the oral, anal, and genital activities—may release anxiety
that has been generated in quite other contexts. Thus the efficacy of
the medicines derives not only from the client's belief in their powers,
but also from the specific nature of the acts he performs and their network of associational meanings. Reversal is an essential constituent
of this process.

Induction into the grave-diggers' fraternity involves the consumption of a special powder known as *bo tĩĩ* or *tĩĩ tuo*, which, following the
general usage of writers on Africa, may be called "grave-medicine."
Tĩĩ, however, denotes any material that confers special powers upon
its possessor. It covers the substances employed in magic both good and
bad, both black and white. It refers also to materials European scientists would regard as having an empirical effect—DDT, aspirin, and the
like—as well as to the ingredients of the potion brewed by the witches
in *Macbeth*. The phrase "he has medicine," *o tera tĩĩ*, can be used of
someone who has extraordinary powers, whether he employs these to
become a successful hunter or to destroy an enemy by mystical means.
It would be used of the medicines offered by Government clinics as well
as those provided by LoDagaa grave-diggers. In other words, the concept of *tĩĩ* crosscuts any rational-irrational, natural-supernatural, sacred-
profane dichotomy. True, it implies a recognition of some sort of a
duality between normal and non-normal (as distinct from abnormal),
but this is implicit in any conceptualization of the norm. To assert that
all societies have such a dichotomy is hardly a statement likely to pro-
voke dispute. On the other hand, to identify this dichotomy with the
division of the world into the sacred and the profane seems to me misleading, particularly when it is suggested that the area defined by the
sacred represents the field of religious behavior.

Grave-medicine is purchased from one of the senior members of the
fraternity living in the particular settlement and is consumed at the
mouth of the grave after a burial has taken place. There the medicine
is mixed with some porridge made from the guinea-corn thrown at the

feet of the corpse. The first act of anyone coming to a funeral is to halt before the dead body, cast some cowries at the foot of the corpse, and then stand in front of the xylophones and toss more shell money on the instruments that are being played. The former contributions are collected by the grave-diggers, the latter by the musicians. It is said that in earlier times heads of guinea-corn were thrown in this way. And today the close mourners, who have to make contributions of this kind throughout the entire ceremony, will often give grain rather than cash.

Thus grave-digging is a lucrative if not an honored task. The income of its practitioners is further increased by the sale of medicine. Although in theory this gives the purchaser the right to share in the work and therefore in its rewards, this right is exercised by a comparative few, the remainder consuming the medicine only as protection against the mystical dangers that surround the corpse.

When the grave-diggers take charge of the body, they first loosen the limbs and then carry it outside the compound. This cannot be done by the ordinary exit. The traditional LoWiili compound has no door, except one leading into the byre, from which there is no access to the rest of the building. To enter the house you have to climb a wooden ladder that leans against the outside wall, which leads onto the flat roof. From there you descend by means of another ladder into one of the open courtyards. For the dead body, however, a special hole had formerly to be made in the wall of the courtyard belonging to the set of rooms in which he died. On the other hand, the bodies of young infants were passed over the top of the courtyard wall, as was also done if babies had to be taken from their natal compound before the "outdooring" ceremony at three (or four) months of age. In each case the normal exit by the rooftop was forbidden. The LoDagaba enter their compounds through the byre, but nowadays both they and the LoWiili often leave a gap in the yard wall for easier access, maintaining that there is no longer the same need for protection against sudden attack. It is through this gap that the body is usually passed.

Here again the reversal theme is apparent. And once again there are additional explanations for this practice that interlock with the system of cosmological ideas. The removal of the corpse by a special exit is of widespread occurrence, and Tylor has associated this procedure with the attempt to prevent the ghost from finding his way back to his house and harming those he has left behind. In its most extreme form this belief involves the abandonment or destruction of the house itself (Tylor [1920], II, 25). Similar ideas are certainly to be found among the LoDagaa. But there is also an element in the procedure

that is specific to their own cosmological system. For either at the foot
of the ladder leading to the roof, or in the doorway of the byre, or sometimes in a position halfway between, are buried three stones taken from
the grove that surrounds the local Earth shrine. This household shrine
to the Earth is believed to bring increase to the inhabitants, human and
non-human, and to ward off death and disease from the compound.
Indeed, if a death occurs within three years of building the house, it is
felt that the Earth (or sometimes the ancestors) has not approved the
site, which is consequently abandoned. It is this opposition between
death and the shrine that is partially avoided by taking the corpse
through another exit.[9]

When the corpse has been carried outside, it is leaned against the
wall of the byre and seated on the wooden board that serves as its door
(kpaan); a man is placed in a cross-legged position, and in the case of a
woman the legs are laid straight out in front. Occasionally, an animal
known as the Going Out Cow, Gõ Yi Naab, used to be tied up outside
the exit to the house and the body lifted over it. I myself never witnessed this event, for recent cases are few. At the funeral of the late
chief of Birifu, a great number of cows were killed, among which was a
Going Out Cow. On this occasion, I was told, the meat went to the
women living in the compound, although Rattray states that it belongs
to the patriclan ([1932] p. 441). It is my impression that such a cow
was never killed except for someone who possessed a large number of
livestock, in other words, very rarely.

Across the folded legs of the dead man his bow is laid, and over his
shoulder is slung his quiver. The xylophones brought from nearby
houses then start to celebrate his achievements as a warrior and as a
farmer; the public aspect of the funeral has now begun. Beside the
corpse sits the wife of one of his sons or some other woman from his
compound, trying to flick the flies away with a cow-tail whisk. On the
rooftop above, the senior mourner takes some bunches of guinea-corn
heads (kajin) from the granary and lets them fall around the dead body.
He also drops other produce of the fields, Na'angmin bum bure zaa,
all God's planted things. A similar rite is performed at the last two
funeral ceremonies, when the deceased is formally brought back into
the compound again in the form of an ancestral shrine. Other members

---

[9] Van Gennep offers a generalized version of this explanation when he maintains
that the corpse is taken through an alternative exit because the main doorway is
sacred ([1960] p. 25); I would prefer to phrase this more concretely and say that the
doorway itself is often connected with the well-being of the house and its inhabitants,
either by association with specific supernatural agencies or in terms of the more
diffuse beliefs, such as the idea of "luck," which we might call preternatural.

of the lineage, those who have granaries, may make a similar offering of guinea-corn, but more usually their contributions take a monetary form, that of cowrie shells. All shells (*paala per libie*) and produce (*zangbume*) thrown around the corpse are the property of the grave-diggers; they cannot be touched by anyone from the dead man's own lineage, and more particularly those who are likely to inherit his property or marry his widows, since this is his dirt.

Meanwhile the grave-diggers begin to prepare the funeral stand at a convenient spot near the compound, the exact location depending upon the state of the crops and the position of the shade trees. The stand—known as *pandaa* before, and *paala* after, the body has been placed there—consists of four newly cut ebony posts, which are driven into the ground about three feet apart to form the corners of a square. The association of ebony with death has already been noted in describing the preparation of a homicide's corpse. Should the custodian of the Earth shrine wish to expel an inhabitant of the parish, he may drive an ebony stick into the ground outside the offender's compound. In any other circumstance, except in the erection of the funeral stand, there is a strong prohibition on this act. It is thought that death will come to the man in question, or else to one of his close kin, unless he leaves the ritual area within a short period of time.

Halfway up the posts that form the framework of the construction, transverse poles are fastened with fibres to make a rough platform for the body. Guinea-corn stalks are fixed on top to form a roof, and around the sides are hung sleeping-cloths of Mossi or European origin that have been borrowed for the occasion from the neighboring houses.

Among the LoWiili, a grandfather is never placed upon such a stand. For the three days of the pre-burial rites he remains with his back resting against the house he has created, squatting upon the same byre door or wooden bench where as an old man he had spent so large a part of his day. Although the LoDagaba do not differentiate a grandparent in this same manner, in both communities he is accorded a special form of burial. He is not buried in the cemetery serving a group of houses—in the grass (*mwo puo*), as the LoDagaa say, that is, in the uncultivated land—but in a grave dug in the courtyard of his own home. For it is he who has successfully established that home by producing two generations of descendants, an achievement that is recognized by this distinctive treatment.

A grandmother is also honored in this same way. When a woman has stayed a long time in her husband's house and has a married son with children of his own, she is said to have become a house-owner (*yirsob*). Indeed, already when she has borne three or four children, she is allowed to look inside the main granary of the house, an act otherwise forbidden to wives. Such a woman is therefore given a burial that is similar in many respects to that given to a man of the same status.

Here again the values of the society, to use a much-abused phrase, are enshrined in funeral customs; the system of status evaluation emerges in its concrete reality, the procedures themselves offering positive sanctions on the desired goals.

THE CELEBRATING OF THE DECEASED

By the time the body is propped up against the wall of the byre, a number of people will have collected outside the compound, and they now cluster around the xylophone. It is the *Lo jil kpēē*, the large Lo xylophone, that is used initially. On this are played the standardized tunes mentioned before, by which those living at a distance can tell whether it is a man or woman who has died. There are words for these tunes, but, as usual with LoDagaa xylophone music, they are rarely sung. For a man, the words of the first song are:

> *A nyāāgala gan,*
> A great man lies down,

> *Ka zaa baara.*
> And all is finished.

The second goes:

> *Tamyuur be ko,*
> They've killed a great warrior,

> *Tam loora biu,*
> So tomorrow we'll fight.

At this the senior mourner runs hither and thither, grasping his bow, as if he wished to go and revenge his kinsman. It is said that formerly, if this song was sung, the death had to be revenged, the human debt collected, before the funeral could be continued. Having paid tribute to the dead man's prowess as a warrior, the xylophone player praises him as a farmer.

> *Kuora gandaa kpi,*
> A great farmer has died,

> *Be na ngma gandaa ne.*
> They'll mark out a strong man's strip.

In an alternative version, the last line runs:

> *Be kon boona saab.*
> They [the household] will no longer eat.

Ability as a farmer is measured by the crops one harvests and by the strength of one's arm. In communal hoeing parties—the normal method of farming for the younger men—each person is allotted a strip of land, and there is great competition to see who will finish first. *Gandaa ne* means a strip that only a strong man can tackle.

Hearing this song, the senior mourner takes out a bunch of guinea-corn heads and other farm produce—millet, groundnuts, maize, and yams—and throws them on top of the xylophone. This the musicians will keep, together with a fowl that the chief mourner kills by beating against the instrument. The bunches of guinea-corn heads, the commonest kind of funeral contribution, are tied together at the previous harvest, when the senior member of the farming group selects the best-looking heads for seed purposes and has their stalks woven together for easier handling.

Farming and hunting are the central activities of a man's life and until recently the two main methods of increasing wealth. Someone who had become rich through farming was known as a *kukuur na,* master of the hoe handle, while a good shot with the bow or the gun was known as a *tamyuur na,* master of the bowstring. These are the only two contexts in which the word *na,* cognate with the term for "chief" in centralized societies in the Voltaic area, appears to have been used. Whereas formerly it meant a rich man or a man of influence, the LoDagaa now use the word to refer to a Government-appointed chief.

The words of the similar songs sung at a woman's death are:

(1) *Fu yũon tintin na tshe,*
You're left quite alone,

A kũ na ko-a.
Now death has taken her.

(2) *Poole be sora nen;*
This girl never asked for meat;

O ma do' võvõ ti kpi.
She who cooked well is now dead.

A sire paa lona.
Her husband has suffered a heavy loss.

It will be seen that in the case of a woman it is the loss to her husband that is stressed; this emphasis is partly a function of the sex of the musicians and partly a reflection of the position of women as jural minors. A woman is buried in the cemetery near her husband's home, and, provided the bridewealth payments are complete, the responsibility for the actual performance of the funeral falls to his patrilineal group; a daughter is "another person's corpse," as a man once told me. Nevertheless, her patrikin keep a watchful eye on the whole proceedings, and at the Final Funeral Ceremony her temporary ancestor shrine —for as a jural minor she will not have a permanent one carved for her— is carried back to her natal home and placed in the byre beside the shrines of her male forebears. The conflict between her role as wife in one lineage and daughter in another is evident throughout the course of the ceremonies. But on this particular occasion it is the woman's role as wife that receives the emphasis.

These set songs that are played on the xylophone are not specific to any individual but celebrate a man's roles as warrior and as farmer, his task of defending the community and of providing for his household; and, in the case of a woman, her roles as mother and as wife. These are universal roles that all men and women fill in their day and are therefore celebrated quite impersonally for any member of the community who dies.

The women then celebrate the achievements of one of their sex as the men do for one of theirs, and after these songs have been played, the "co-wives" and "husband's sisters" of the dead woman, those who have collaborated with her in her capacity as wife, bring out some of her cooking pots and calabashes, which they break at her feet. Like the farm produce dropped around a man, this act pays tribute to her domestic achievements. In addition, the woman's husband also contributes farm produce for her funeral, partly as a reward to the xylophone players and partly as a public acknowledgment of the help she has given him on the farm, which is further recognized after the burial by the presentation to her patriclan of a "beast of farm-clearing" (*vaar daar dun*).

When the grave-diggers have erected the funeral stand, they carry the corpse from the doorway of the byre and place it in a sitting position upon the platform they have made for this purpose. Once again the achievements of the deceased are celebrated, not only in music but also visually; for here he sits surrounded by the attributes of wealth. There are the clothes in which he is dressed, the brightly colored cloths decorating the stand, and, nearby, the wooden boxes in which people keep their most valued possessions. These boxes are not of local manufacture, but are usually brought back from the South by young men to hold the goods they have purchased out of the proceeds of their dry-season labor. As with the cloth, these boxes do not necessarily belong to the deceased. He may have had but one box; the remainder are lent by kinsmen or neighbors.

The dead man's bow is again laid across his folded legs, and the quiver hangs from his shoulder. He may have other weapons—a gun (*malfa*), a straight sword (*tokoli*), or a spear (*panna* or *kamfin*)—but the bow is the real sign of an adult man. The bows of the members of his clan sector are suspended upside down on one of the supports of the funeral stand, or stacked together on the ground nearby. To hold a bow upside down at any other time is felt to be dangerous; arms are reversed to indicate the reversal of normality. By piling their bows together, the clansmen salute the dead man in his capacity as a warrior and as a hunter, and at the same time assert their solidarity in the face of the loss of one of their number.

The dead man's achievements as a farmer are recognized by the farm produce hung on the framework of the funeral stand. Like the money strewn around the corpse, this belongs to the grave-diggers. So does the fowl (*bo nuo*) that is tethered to one of the poles and presented by the senior mourner to be sacrificed at the spot where the new grave is dug. Other fowls, and even a goat, may be tied in the same way, and these too belong to the sextons, as well as the money that is continually being thrown at the corpse by newcomers and by the bereaved.

More grain may be stacked in the baskets at the foot of the stand. Contributions to the funeral expenses include a bunch of guinea-corn heads from each member of the clan sector who is head of a compound. This grain is used to make obligatory gifts to in-laws, to the gunmen who fire their weapons, and to the attendant musicians. But it also plays something of the same part in relation to farming that the stacking of the bows does to hunting; it celebrates the achievements of the dead and emphasizes the solidarity of the survivors in regard to yet another joint activity.

Among the LoWiili, a further acknowledgment of the prowess of the dead man may be placed near the stand. If he has accumulated a large amount of money, either by farming or by other means, a sealed pot of his cowries may be dug up from its hiding place and laid at his side.

The signs that celebrate the achievements of dead persons naturally indicate their sex roles, because of the sharp division of labor between the two sexes. As a man is given his bow and quiver, so on a woman's lap will be placed her personal basket (*tiib pele,* or "shrine basket"), and in her hands an unscraped calabash bowl.[10] As the men of the clan

---

10 Sometimes a calabash is also placed at a man's side, so that he may drink on the way to the Land of the Dead.

sector piled their bows nearby, so their wives each bring some of the leather bands in which an adult woman is dressed and hang them on the funeral stand. This is done in recognition of the common roles they jointly filled, or, as the LoDagaa say, "to prevent themselves dreaming of the deceased," and idea that is explained later in the discussion of mimetic rituals. If the woman is known for the beer she brews for sale, a ladle is placed at her side. Meanwhile her feet rest on a pot used to cook the soup or relish that accompanies the basic dish of porridge.

The calabash, basket, and soup pot are, like her clothes, the material extensions of a woman's personality, carried with her wherever she goes, just as in the days before the coming of the Colonial Government a man was never without his bow and quiver. These objects remain part of her personality even after death. The basket, with its rim decorated with cowrie shells, is the one in which a woman keeps her most personal possessions, her shell money, her cosmetics, and her individual shrines, such as the one to her destiny (*ngmin*) or to the "beings of the wild" (*kontome*). When she goes any distance from her room, she will carry it on her head, balanced on a ring of twisted grass (*tasir*).

Apart from her clothing and her shrine basket, the calabash is a woman's most characteristic possession. At her death, it is placed upon her lap, in the same position as a man's bow. During her lifetime, she carries one in her basket wherever she goes, in case she wants to drink water on the way. She will swear one of her gravest oaths "to her mother and her calabash," that is to her dead mother. For among the objects a woman possesses there is always hidden a special calabash to be used at her own funeral; should she fail to put one aside, her co-wives would mock at her poverty and lack of foresight. For how else will she scoop up water to quench her thirst on the journey to the Land of the Dead? And with the pot she can prepare food wherever she is. Yet at the moment of burial, the pot and calabash are broken, an act that again brings out the contradiction that lies behind material dealings with a spiritual world.

There are a number of other visual indices of the status of the corpse. In the case of an unmarried male, his penis is tied under a band round his waist as if he were a young boy; this gesture of shame is to be interpreted as a penalty for not having undertaken the role of husband, essential to the group's continuity. In addition, a bachelor's bow is broken after his death; it is not needed as an ancestral shrine, for without descendants he can have none.

At the funeral of a woman, there are other visual signs that reflect her ability and achievements in the realm of procreation. A woman who has not succeeded in giving birth to children is seated upon a large earth-filled pot, the bottom of which has been broken. This act appears to express the complete failure of her procreative powers. An indirect acknowledgment of a woman's positive achievement as a mother is later made by placing a small calabash in the mouth of the last of her offspring to die, signifying that the progeny of one woman (*ma per,* a mother's stem) has come to an end. An alternative is to close her mouth by tying together the two ornaments that project from her upper and lower lips. These acts of closure show the importance given to the offspring of one womb as against the offspring of one penis, even in patrilineal contexts. The last child of a woman is singled out in several ways, for it is he who marks the end of her procreative powers. When she can no longer give birth, then she has "become a man." In these various ways, then, customary behavior places greater emphasis on the fertility of females than of men; for it is the former that is of greater importance in securing social continuity. Institutionalized arrangements exist among the Lo-Dagaa for overcoming masculine infertility; after suitable sacrifices to the ancestors, another member of the patriclan can deputize for an unsuccessful male. But for the procreative powers of a woman there can be no similar substitution.

CHAPTER V

The Day of Death: Mourning the Dead

> In sorrow of soul they laid on the pyre
> Their mighty leader, their well-loved lord.
> The warriors kindled the bale on the barrow,
> Wakened the greatest of funeral fires.
> Dark o'er the blaze the wood-smoke mounted;
> The winds were still, and the sound of weeping
> Rose with the roar of the surging flame
> Till the heat of the fire had broken the body.
> With hearts that were heavy they chanted their sorrow,
> Singing a dirge for the death of their lord;
> And an aged woman with upbound locks
> Lamented for Beowulf, wailing in woe.
> Over and over she uttered her dread
> Of sorrow to come, of bloodshed and slaughter,
> Terror of battle, and bondage, and shame.
> The smoke of the bale-fire rose to the sky!
>
> *Beowulf*

The stage is now set; kinsfolk and ritual specialists have completed their preparations, and the body of the dead man now rests upon the funeral stand, ready to receive a mourning tribute from all those dwelling in the neighborhood, as well as from other kinsfolk who live at greater distances. For the messengers have now set off to other villages, and the music of the xylophones has spread news of the death throughout the parish, and to nearby settlements as well. All those who hear the funereal notes, however faintly, have some obligation to attend. Indeed, such occasions are the most important times when members of the ritual area congregate together in any sizable number. And apart from the premium placed upon attendance, to stay away can be taken as a sign of possible complicity in the death.

The acts of mourning I want to discuss in this chapter are of three kinds: first, the mourning of the bereaved, the close kin of the dead man; second, the mourning of the general body of spectators; and last, the rituals of mourning connected with the agnatic clans.

METHODS OF RESTRAINING THE BEREAVED

While the xylophones are playing, the lineage "wives" and "sisters" of the dead man walk and run about the area in front of the house, crying lamentations and holding their hands behind the nape of the neck in the accepted attitude of grief. The close male kinsfolk act in a similar manner, though they are somewhat more subdued than the women. From time to time, one of the immediate mourners breaks into a trot, even a run, and a bystander either intercepts or chases after the bereaved and quietens him by seizing his wrist. Those continuing to display such violent grief are secured round the wrist by a length of fibre or hide, the other end of which is held by a companion or follower of the bereaved.

This role can only be filled by a person standing in a certain relationship, the complex definition of which derives from the system of double clanship; for it should be someone who is a joking partner in the matriclan framework and at the same time a member of another lineage within the same patriclan. When his father died, Ziem, from the Tshaa quarter of Birifu, was followed for three days and nights by Tuőzie, a classificatory "brother" of the same patriclan, but belonging to a different patrilineage. Round his right ankle, Ziem wore a piece of string (*myuur*), made by rolling the outer cover of the dawa-dawa pod (*Parkia oliveri*) on the thigh. The deceased's sisters and daughters, however, had fibre (*byuur: Hibiscus cannabinus*) tied round the wrist or the waist, one end of which was held by the funeral companion. The fibre is not strong enough to prevent the mourner from breaking away, but it nevertheless implies the exercise of restraint. For the closest mourner the material form of restraint is more effective, and a strip of hide, usually cowhide (*ganaa*), is tied firmly to the wrist, around which a piece of cloth has first been wrapped.

These different methods of tying and restraining the bereaved are indices of the socially expected reactions to grief on the part of various categories of person and are therefore of particular value in elucidating certain general aspects of these roles. The modes of restraint employed for the different kinship positions are as follows:

Man's funeral

Father	Tied by hide
Mother	Tied by hide
Wife	Tied by hide
Brother	Tied by fibre
Sister	Tied by fibre
Son	String tied around the ankle
Daughter	String tied around the ankle

Woman's funeral

Husband	Tied by hide and cloth; string around waist and ankle
Father	Tied by hide (in the case of an unmarried daughter)
Mother	Tied by hide (in the case of an unmarried daughter)
Brother	Tied by fibre
Sister	Tied by fibre
Son	String tied around the ankle
Daughter	String tied around the ankle

The use of hide is limited to the persons who are presumed to lose most by the death, and of these a husband suffers hardest of all. It is only within this first category of bereaved that ritual precautions are taken against suicide. The second category of close mourners includes those who are considered less likely to do themselves harm; not only the kinsfolk listed above, but any other close affinal, agnatic, or matri-lateral relative who runs about in front of the stand may be caught and tied round the wrist with fibre. In the third category come the children of the deceased who, though they are usually followed by a companion, wear only a piece of string tied round the ankle and often another tied round the neck. Sometimes a daughter may be seen with fibre round her wrist, but this is not common.

In general terms, the first of these categories includes the conjugal and parental roles, the second those of siblings and other kinsmen of equal status, and the third the filial role. The differences in the stand-ardized physical restraints appear to indicate a diminution of the grief expected to be shown by each of these three classes of kinsfolk in this same order.

Before analyzing these categories of bereaved in greater detail, note should be taken of some other ways in which mourners are visually dif-ferentiated. The young children in the deceased's compound, and sometimes the children of a dead man's full sisters or those from a dead woman's natal home, have ashes painted on their faces, usually on the first and third days of the funeral, and are made to wear, bandolier fashion, strings of cowries known as *libie siore*. A string of this kind is normally worn only by adult women on festive occasions. At a funeral two such strings are tied together by a joking partner of the father's matriclan and hung over the child's shoulder. A grown man may also be made to wear such cowries, if the dead person was a friend (*ba*), a lover (*sen*), or a grandparent. I have also heard of an instance in which these were put on a younger full brother of the deceased. Indeed, al-though the procedure is obligatory only for young children, a joking partner may require anybody who shows excessive grief to wear the strings, and in return for this service he will be given a few cowries. The persons distinguished in this manner turn out to be those who have been on terms of exceptional friendship with the dead man. In other words, the wearing of the string of cowries indicates a personal relationship with the deceased closer than that implied by the norms themselves.

The use of ashes for "cooling" in situations of crisis has already been remarked upon. Because of this property, ashes are of value in warding off the ghost of the dead man, which at this phase in the ceremony is thought of as especially "hot," that is, dangerous to mankind. In addition, a further thematic element is present. The ashes smeared on the children's faces serve to disguise them from the deceased. Sometimes, too, the daughters of the deceased who have attained puberty and, less frequently, his wives and full sisters are dressed in men's smocks for similar reasons. Because of the smock and the ashes, the dead man may be led to place the person concerned in the wrong role category. One LoDagaba man explained to me that you put on ashes for a father's father but never for a father. But the joking partners do put ashes on young children when the father dies, so that he will not recognize them and will think of them instead as grandchildren.

Transvestism also seems to play its part in the use of the strings of cowries previously mentioned. Young children of both sexes are disguised by wearing the apparel of adult women, but otherwise the wearing of these strings at funerals is largely confined to men. I have also on occasion seen women with them over their shoulders. These may be women who have reached the menopause and are "disguising" themselves as fertile wives. However, I omitted to ask the questions that would enable me to confirm this suggestion. In the other cases, the transvestism, the reversal of sex-linked clothing, is not, as it was in the earlier example of the wearing of smocks by women, a matter of using high-status apparel that happens to be associated with the opposite sex. Nor does it represent an actual reversal of some aspects of the sexual role. It is a mask deliberately adopted to suggest to the ghost that the wearer is other than what he is.[1]

Why is it that near kin require to be protected from the ghost in this way? The dead are visualized as actively endeavoring to maintain the network of social relationships that had surrounded them during their mortal existence. One way in which they may attempt to do this is by forcibly abducting the souls of those who were closest to them.

---

[1] The phenomenon of mourning disguises is discussed by Frazer ([1918] III, 236, 298) and by Crawley ([1932] pp. 224 *et seq.*).

The various disguises that his possible victims adopt prevent the ghost from recognizing his favorites and therefore from removing them to the Land of the Dead. The danger in which the living think of themselves in regard to the dead can be seen as an aspect of the ambivalence present in all close social relationships. But as far as the young children are concerned, another factor is perhaps at work. Their particular vulnerability can be partly explained as an institutionalized manifestation, a social projection, of the anxiety that centers upon infants, particularly in a society in which the mortality rate is very high. The more general aspects of this question will be considered in connection with the way in which infants are buried; but it may be remarked here that both the absence of any public ceremony and the standardized hostility with which such a corpse is treated are consistent with this suggestion.

A further means of protecting the living against the dead is revealed in the methods of restraining kin. It will be recalled that persons tied with hide and fibre are distinguished from the offspring of the deceased, who have only a string tied around the ankle. The string is not in fact an attempt to restrain them; this their companions do by seizing the mourners' wrists. It is rather a protective device comparable to the disguises adopted to deceive the ghost. Here the tying of string round the ankle is thought to prevent the bereaved's soul from leaving his body. At the end of the therapeutic ritual known as "sweeping the soul," during the course of which an errant soul is made to re-enter the body it has abandoned, a string is also tied round the patient's ankle. In both cases the string binds the soul within the human frame. For outside the body it is an easy prey for witches and other malevolent agencies, such as the ghost of the dead man, from whom at his funeral the danger is seen to come. Another reason given by the LoDagaa for performing this rite is to soothe the patient's anxiety; it is done, they say, *ka fu pla yaghra* (LD), a phrase best translated as "lest your heart jump." If your heart is troubled, then your soul is likely to be in danger, for it may have left the body that houses it.

This same act occurs at other points in the course of a LoDagaa funeral. Immediately after the burial, a female joking partner ties a string round the neck of the dead man's children. The surviving spouse is similarly treated during the course of the whitewashing; at this time ashes are also placed upon the head of the widow or widower, and in the latter case another piece of string is tied round the waist. Here again these acts are protective devices taken to prevent the ghost from doing harm to the members of his elementary family.

Having reviewed these various methods of distinguishing the classes of mourners, I shall now return to a consideration of the three main categories of bereavement: parent-child, conjugal, and sibling bereavement.

Parent-child Bereavement

I have already noted how the methods of restraining the close bereaved, who fall mainly within the dead man's families of orientation and procreation, reflect the socially recognized attitudes toward him. In this respect the parental is sharply differentiated from the filial role. A man will be expected to display great grief at the death of a young son, one, that is, who is past infancy and has acquired a social personality. The older the son, the less pronounced will be the parental grief displayed. Nevertheless, the father is always more affected by the son's death than the son by the father's, and although the son has a funeral companion, he is not restrained in any other of the formal ways. Indeed, the son has to be protected from his father's ghost and is even suspected of being responsible for his father's death. The reverse never occurs; a father needs no protection against his dead son, nor to the best of my knowledge is he ever directly implicated in his son's death.

Another indication of the same imbalance in the parent-child relationship is to be seen in the occurrence of suicide attempts, which are a standardized method of demonstrating grief at the loss of a relative. The following two examples will show the differences involved. When Duure, the wife of Wura (Tshaa, Birifu), returned home one day from fetching firewood, she was too tired to carry her large bundle up to the roof and then down again into her own courtyard. So she threw the wood over the high wall of the yard; unfortunately her young son was playing there and was killed on the spot. The distracted Duure stuck a poisoned arrow in the wall and ran toward it; but at the last moment her resolution failed and she turned aside.

Whereas it is recognized that a parent may threaten or attempt to kill himself at the death of a child, the opposite would be unthinkable. When Ziem's father died, no precautions against suicide were taken on his behalf. However, when his young son died some time afterward, he tried to kill himself with a poisoned arrow, and his "father" from another lineage had to bring a pair of the tongs (*tshaaba*) used by smiths, and Ziem was made to grasp these in his hands. The tools of the smith (*saa kpiera*), and indeed the smithy itself, are closely associated with the Earth shrine. "The smithy is (the same in certain respects as) the Earth shrine" (*saa in tenggaan*), say the LoDagaa.

One aspect of this association, possibly the major one, lies in the com-

mon link with iron. Iron ore is dug from out of the earth, and throughout the Voltaic region all unclaimed objects made from that metal
belong to the Earth shrine. In smelting ore and in forging iron, the
smith is working with the earth itself, and his role is in some respects
assimilated to that of the custodian of the Earth shrine. For the smith
who makes the weapons of war can also act as a peacemaker; like the
Earth priest, he can throw ashes and make hot things cold. Hence the
tools of his trade are thought of as having the power to quieten a man
inclined to self-violence, a theory that is supported by the belief that
after holding the tongs any attempt at suicide would prove fruitless;
the wound would only remain open for three (or four) years, causing
great pain to the person who had tried to kill himself. Thus giving the
bereaved the tongs to grasp is like giving a suspected witch some earth
to swallow. Both acts are carried out under the threat of force and both
invoke the Earth shrine. Strictly speaking, however, in the first case
the bereaved is made to take a conditional, though silent, oath; whereas
in the second he is submitted to an ordeal, a mystical test of guilt.

It appears, then, that the parent-child relationship is not evenly
balanced, for the partners neither possess reciprocal rights and duties
nor display reciprocal sentiments one to another. In an equally balanced system, one would expect a similar intensity of grief to be ex-
hibited by both parties. This clearly does not hold in the present case,
the standardized grief displayed by parents being greater than that of
children, despite the acknowledgment of filial piety.

There is a generalized structural reason why the loss of a child
should be felt more intensely than that of a parent. The death of a
member of the junior generation stands in contradiction to the normal
progression of human life. Consequently, a young person's funeral, except that of an infant, is a more bitter experience than the obsequies of
either a parent or a grandparent. Indeed, as far as the grandfather is
concerned, such a man has achieved his allotted span, has a relatively
secure line of descendants, and will be buried in the courtyard of his
own home. Very soon after the beginning of his funeral, his joking
partners begin to clown and the young women to dance, and the whole
funeral is suffused with a spirit of enjoyment rather than of mourning.

Apart from this general factor of the life cycle, there are more specific reasons for the differences in anticipated grief. These reasons relate
to the hidden tensions and overt conflicts between generations, a matter
that will be discussed at greater length in a subsequent chapter. To the
children, the parents stand as possessors of the common cultural heritage as well as of particular rights over property, offices, roles, and
women. But in addition to the generalized tensions between the haves

and the have-nots, there are other problems arising from the process of transmission. For the coming generation has eventually to acquire from their seniors both the cultural tradition and these relatively exclusive rights, the one by the process of socialization, the other by that of inheritance and succession. Conflicts and tensions always develop in the actual process of handing on the social heritage; and when such transmission occurs within a domestic context, as it usually does in non-literate societies, it inevitably involves close kin. In both the LoDagaa communities, residence is based on the elementary family, and consequently it is upon the parents that major responsibility for the child's upbringing falls. Hence the major tensions involved in socialization fall upon the parent-child axis, and upon the subordinate partner, the child, rather than upon the dominant partner, the parent.

With regard to relatively exclusive rights, the situation is rather different. Unlike the common cultural heritage, which from one standpoint can be infinitely divided, these rights cannot be handed over without loss to the original holder. Indeed, in most non-literate societies the senior generation retain their rights to the end, and transmission is often literally a matter of waiting to step into dead men's shoes. Moreover, when the junior generation's main avenue to exclusive rights is by a system of next-of-kin transmission, the shoes in question are those of a near and in some ways dear kinsman. Thus the situation of the haves and the have-nots is exacerbated by the heir's anticipation of the benefits to be reaped after the moment of transfer, which usually coincides with death.

The mother is less likely to be the object of these conflicts than the father. Nonetheless, she does have responsibilities in the socialization of the child that inevitably give rise to an element of hostility in the relationship, especially on the side of the junior partner. This hostility has to be largely suppressed during her lifetime, but is given overt recognition in the differences in treatment accorded to the mother and the child at the other's funeral, differences that reflect the expected reaction to the loss of the other person.

Mother-child conflicts relating to the differential possession of rights affect the sons less than the daughters; but as far as material objects are concerned, both may benefit at her death. However, the tensions over relatively exclusive rights clearly have greater prominence in the father-son relationship, because it is between males that most property is inherited. Moreover, it is the sexuality of women, not that of men, in which exclusive rights are acquired. At this point the differences in the inheritance systems of the two communities become significant; but among all the LoDagaa the father-son relationship is not only a major axis of the socialization relationships, it is also a channel for certain categories of exclusive right.

In the light of the foregoing discussion, we can understand why in the standardized procedures of the LoDagaa, members of the junior generation express less grief at the death of a member of the senior generation than the reverse. But there is a further aspect of parent-child relationships that an examination of the modes of restraining the bereaved brings out. The list of methods of restraint shows that in the case of the death of a married woman, the father and mother are not bound round the wrist with hide, as they are for an unmarried daughter or a son. The major loss involved is now regarded as falling upon the husband rather than upon the parents; for it is he who by the marriage has both acquired rights and accepted duties toward their daughter. Included in these is the right, and duty, of burying her in the cemetery of the settlement in which he lives.

There is yet another feature of parent-child, or more specifically father-child, relationships that mourning behavior reveals and that it seems appropriate to discuss at this juncture. In the majority of cases, a child's *pater* or social father and his *genitor* or biological father are one and the same man. When this is not so, some recognition may be given to the relationship created by biological as distinct from social paternity. This is illustrated by certain events at the funeral of Daazie, who belonged to the Marba lineage of the Naayiili clan in Birifu. This man had long been the lover of Pookũ, a woman whom Batero, a member of the same clan but of the Natsho patrilineage, had inherited from his elder brother. When Daazie died, Boninse, one of the offspring of the union, danced with great vigor and generally displayed more grief than the old man's legitimate offspring. When I discussed Boninse's action afterward, I was told of these adulterine children, *be bong be sãã,* "they know their father." Although their *genitor* was a clan brother of their *pater,* that is their mother's husband, and therefore a classificatory "father," the term *sãã* here carries the implication of biological rather than social paternity. And it was this relationship, of an adulterine child to his *genitor,* that was openly expressed in the mourning behavior. On the other hand, the fact that the other offspring of the union did not participate to the same degree stresses the non-jural nature of this relationship.

Conjugal Bereavement

The close mourners, those tied with hide, include not only parents but husbands and wives. The loss of a spouse is equated with that of a child. The survivor is restrained from self-violence not only by the strip of hide tied around the wrist, but also by being made to grasp the smith's tongs and, after the burial, to drink water sacralized by association with the Earth shrine. Let us consider an actual example.

Namoo was living at a new settlement, some fifty miles to the south of Birifu, where he had taken his family a few years before. His wife was back visiting her natal house when she died very suddenly. A false message was sent to Namoo to say that his father's surviving brother, Batero, had fallen from the rooftop of his house in Naayiili, and had died; it was assumed that a man would react less violently to the news of his paternal uncle's death than to that of his wife. Namoo boarded a passing lorry and came at once. On reaching the outskirts of Birifu, he was met by a joking partner from another patrilineage of the same clan (that is, from the funeral group), who first of all seized his arms and then told him that it was his wife for whom the xylophones were playing. Namoo broke loose from the grasp of the joking partner and ran at full speed to his "father's" compound, to which the body of his wife had been carried. There he was at once caught and restrained by other persons present at the funeral. For the LoDagaa declare that it is better for a man in such a state to be with the crowd rather than on his own lest he try to do himself some harm. Moreover, attendance at the ceremony has another, less explicit, effect on the bereaved. As the funeral continues, their grief is lessened by the performance—both by themselves and by others—of the various formalized procedures. Quite apart from the specific content of the rituals, their actual performance has a purging effect. The LoDagaa, however, take additional precautions against the bereaved, and when Namoo arrived at the scene of the funeral, he was seized for the second time, and into his hands were pressed the smith's tongs.

Although both husbands and wives are tied with hide when a spouse dies, it is expected that greater intensity of grief will be displayed by the man than the woman, and it is he who will be most carefully supervised. Wives are the actual or potential means by which the continuity of the lineage is maintained. The death, particularly of a young wife, entails a total loss of the reproductive powers that the lineage has acquired; for there is no return of the bridewealth in the case of her death, nor is a substitute provided as in the institution of the sororate. If a man has proved himself to be a good son-in-law, his affines may formally point out another girl as his "wife," but he will still have to hand over the full bridewealth if he wants to marry her. On the other hand, the death of a husband entails no comparable loss to the widow nor to her descent group. By the operation of the levirate she automatically has another husband to provide for her, another man's house in which to live, another sexual partner. If she is not satisfied with any of the possible inheritors, she can always try to find a husband elsewhere.

The tying of a piece of white cloth around the wrist of the widower but not of the widow, apparently to mitigate the chafing of the hide, indicates that the LoDagaa expect a greater display of violent grief from the man than the woman. To explain this only in terms of the difference in physical strength is hardly satisfactory, since a man is not ordinarily expected to give vent to his grief to the same extent as a woman. Our alternative interpretation of the relationship between the modes of restraint and the differences in conjugal roles is supported by an examination of the rites of widowhood, the whitewashing and testing of the surviving spouse. These rites also emphasize an aspect of conjugal bereavement that we have already encountered in discussing the concept of "dirt," namely the element of hostility that is visualized as an intrinsic feature of marital relationships. But here we need only make the point that these differences reflect an explicit social situation; for whereas by the death of a spouse a man loses the sexual services of his wife, the widow merely exchanges the services of one man for those of another.

Fraternal Bereavement

The relationship most characteristic of the secondary category of bereaved, as defined by the methods of restraint, is that between siblings. As with most close relationships, the sibling bond contains a hostile component of greater or lesser degree. In patrilineal societies this is likely to be strongest between brothers, less between siblings of opposite sex, and least of all between sisters. In both the second and the third category, the relationships are subject to spatial separation after the sister's marriage, so that even those tensions between brother and sister that relate to the control of sexuality and the exchange of rights over women are lessened by an increase in physical distance. However, it is upon the relationship between brothers that the very existence of the agnatic joint household depends. The normal cycle of development in domestic groups is based upon the fact that the solidarity of the group of brothers, which is strongest while the father is alive, becomes less so on his death. The reason for this greater solidarity in the early years is partly that the father acts as a leader of the agnatic unit in both external and internal affairs, but also that the opposition of the brothers toward that leader serves to consolidate their own relationships. When the major point of reference for their solidarity disappears with the father's death, fraternal tensions come to the fore. In neither of the LoDagaa communities does the joint agnatic household continue intact long after the father dies. Indeed, as I have shown elsewhere (Goody [1958]), there is a tendency among the LoDagaba for fission to occur even before the loss of the father, for reasons related to the system of inheriting wealth. But among the LoWiili the centrifugal force of fraternal tensions is held in check during the father's lifetime.

When fission of the economic or residential unit does take place, the point of reference is maternal origin, the children of a man by each wife constituting a different group. The way in which this subdivision occurs reflects the joint interests that full brothers have in each other's property; for whether wealth is vested in the patriclan or the matriclan, it passes to the full sibling before dropping a generation, to the son in one case, to the sister's son in the other. The problem of inheritance will be more fully considered later. Here it is only necessary to make the point that the sorrow at the loss of a full brother is in each case mitigated by the prospective enjoyment of his wealth, and the procedures of restraint show that no sibling is expected to grieve as deeply as a parent or a spouse.

GENERAL MOURNING

Newcomers to the funeral pause on the path not far from the deceased's compound, break into a half-run, and enter the open space that surrounds the stand. But a man has to take care lest he trip and fall, for to do so means that his soul has left its body, a state of affairs that can only be remedied by performing the ceremony of "sweeping the soul."

Around the sides of this space, unevenly dispersed under the available shade trees, are the spectators, the members of one village (or, within a village, of one minor ritual area or patrilineage) generally sitting in a tight cluster. Such groups will probably have arrived on the scene together, for people do not relish going to a funeral alone. Any occasion on which a man is singled out from the crowd makes him liable to the attention of others and hence a target for the attacks of sorcerers and witches.

The newcomers run across the front of the stand three (or four) times, crying whichever of the funeral greetings is appropriate to their relationship with the dead man. The following are the main cries used on these occasions:

n sãã wei, alas, my father—for any member of the senior generation of one's own patriclan and sometimes for a member of one's father's matriclan.

m ma wei, alas, my mother—for any wife of a "father," or for an older member of one's own matriclan or of one's mother's patriclan. The alternative *ma bie,* "mother's child," may be used for these two categories of kin when the individual addressed is of the same or junior generation to oneself. The cry applies to males as well as females, although the more usual kinship term *madeb,* "male mother," is sometimes heard. *Ma bie* is also used at the funeral of a fellow "sister's son," i.e., of a person whose mother comes from the same patriclan as one's own.

o wei, alas—a cry of general applicability.

n sen wei, alas, my lover—for any woman of whom one is particularly fond.

gandaa wei, alas, strong man—for an old man who has lived a full span.

After they have run into the cleared space uttering their cries, the newcomers pause in front of the stand, regard the face of the dead man for a few moments, then feel in their skinbags or the pockets of their smocks for cowries to throw at the stand. The necessity for recognizing the face of the deceased is one of the objections the LoDagaa have made when in the past the Government and the Christian Churches have suggested that the body should be buried more promptly and the funeral ritual should follow rather than precede the inhumation. The LoDagaa strongly oppose what they regard as indecent haste. One reason given is that such a change would introduce the possibility of burying alive a person who had simply lost consciousness. They also argue that a person may know many people by sight, particularly children and adolescents, whom he does not know by name. A man has an obligation to attend, for at least part of the time, the funeral of another member of the parish, and of members of clan sectors adjoining his own, whether or not they inhabit the same ritual area. He has a further obligation to attend the funeral of an acquaintance who lives within a day's walk, there and back. There are a number of people in neighboring settlements whom one is not sure whether or not one knows, or only knows of, and this doubt can be resolved only by seeing the face of the dead man. Since some kinsmen have to come from distant parts, the displaying of the corpse for three days is considered necessary in order to insure that all may see the dead man before he is buried.

However, it is not only the faces of the half-remembered dead that one pauses to recognize at the funeral stand. A man has to be convinced by visual evidence that the particular person he knew is no longer alive. Once this has been established, the survivor can take steps to readjust to the loss. Thus the gesture partakes of the nature of a farewell in that it puts a formal end to a sequence of communicative acts, just as the beginning of such a series is usually marked by a set greeting, often accompanied in European society by physical contact in the form of a kiss or the shaking of hands.

Those newcomers who have brought guns shoot them in the air, an act that they may repeat at any important stage of the ceremonies. For this they are rewarded with gifts of guinea-corn from the chief mourner, with cowries from the bereaved, and with a fixed amount from the general collection for expenses. Although in other societies shooting is often said to ward off the ghosts of the dead, no such reason was given to me here. The LoDagaa, following a custom widespread among the peoples of this region, shoot guns to welcome important strangers. At funerals they are similarly honoring the dead.

The Orchestra

After recognizing the deceased, the newcomers go over to the xylophones and throw more money to the players. By this stage of the ceremony, the musicians will have changed over to the *Dagaa* type of xylophone, which has eighteen slats as against the fourteen notes of the *Lo* instrument. Funeral chants, as distinct from the songs mentioned earlier, are sung only to the music of the *Dagaa* xylophone.

Xylophones are usually played in pairs, by a leading player and his accompanist. In addition the funeral orchestra consists of a drum (*ganggaa*) made from a hollowed-out tree trunk, covered at both ends with cowhide, and beaten at one end with a pair of stubby sticks. This drum is used solely at the funerals of adults, or in ceremonial contexts in which its association with death is relevant; and only a man who has lost his wife may possess one. The cowhide with which the drum is covered is taken from a beast known as the Cow of the Rooftop, which is killed at each funeral. Another type of drum, the *kuor,* is also occasionally played with the *Dagaa* xylophone; it is made from a large gourd, and the membrane consists of the skin of a monitor lizard.

Funeral Chants

The newcomers gather round the xylophones and begin their lamentations. Persons from the same patrilineage or settlement who have arrived earlier at once arise and join them; for if only a few are singing, they are thought to be more exposed to mystical dangers. Others among the spectators then cluster round. Should one of the newcomers be accomplished at funeral chanting, he will begin to sing; otherwise the task is undertaken by anyone who is practiced in the art. The singer is subsequently rewarded by a share in the money thrown to the musicians and by gifts from the clansmen and from the wife-taking in-laws of the dead man.[2]

The funeral chant (*long*), though it always includes standardized phrases of a proverbial kind, is largely impromptu. Its variability, its length, its condensed and idiomatic language, and the conditions under which it is sung make it difficult to take down on the spot. I give below an example from the funeral of a five-year-old boy, whose father was still alive, to illustrate the tone of such chants and the attitude adopted in the face of the loss of one of the members of the society. The sentiments expressed are often bitterly hostile to the deceased, who is accused of abandoning those whom he leaves behind in the world of the living. This bitterness is most intense when the death is least expected, especially, that is, at the funeral of a young child.

> *O sãã tũ anga ko wa de a yerme.*
> The father has sent the boy to fetch his loads.

> *Ba vuõna a kalinyãã ti tshe a sambala.*
> They pull up the good grass and leave the bad.

> *O sããmine nibe 'yer bo'or ko kyen soro.*
> Some of his "fathers" spoke about a sacrifice and he has
>   gone to ask about it.

> *Ba na baara ti nyi ngmẽ nuru ka baar.*
> They'll all finish and you'll grieve till the last.

> *Ti wa yiri ba nye doo yee.*
> We came to the house and couldn't find him anywhere.

> *Baa mi gan gbim o sãã tampur zu.*
> A dog always lies quietly on his master's midden.

> *Ti wa na ir de ti ka ti kul, ye ye.*
> We've come, so jump up and welcome us and then we can all
>   go home.

[2] I distinguish between wife-taking and wife-giving in-laws in order to avoid the ambiguity involved in the use of "in-law" and "affine." By wife-taking in-laws I mean those to whom a man has given rights over women, in contradistinction to the wife-giving in-laws, those from whom he has acquired them. In using this terminology, I wish to make it clear that these transactions are rarely, if ever, viewed by the participants as occurring between whole descent groups, but rather between small subdivisions of them. Moreover, the distinction is not present in their own kinship terminology, although the persons to whom a man is related through "sisters" and through "wives" are in fact differentiated in a number of contexts.

1. Children from the
dead man's compound,
with their foreheads
whitewashed and
strings of cowries
over their shoulders

2. The orchestra: *Dagaa* xylophone
and tree-trunk drum

3. A general view
of the funeral dancing

4. A classificatory "wife"
offering a pot of beer
to her dead husband
in the course of
a funeral speech

5. A classificatory "wife" of the dead man whisking the flies away from the corpse

6. A friend bringing a fowl to the dead man's kinsmen

7. A new grave,
nearly finished

8. Dividing the C‹
of the Rooftop

9. The women
continue to dance,
even after the body
as been taken from
the funeral stand

10. The grave
of an unweaned child

11. Agnates of the dead man
collecting the
funeral contributions

12. Water being pou
on the hands
of the widows
before they are fed
and whitewashed

13. Ancestor shrines in the byre of an abandoned house

14. A classificatory "sister" of the deceased being restrained by another woman

15. The sacrificer tapping his knife on the shrine while the officiant addresses the ancestors. These shrines (belonging to the Tiedeme patriclan) are slats of stone that are kept outside the compound; they act as substitutes for the usual wooden figures

16. A recent widow, still covered in whitewash, attending another funeral in the neighborhood

In most of these chants the pretense is made that the child is not really dead at all, but either absent or sleeping. This refusal to recognize death is particularly apparent in the last of the sentences of the chant.

Whereas the members of other descent groups generally chant songs of abuse, the deceased's own lineage sing the praise chants (*dano* or *kuonbie*, literally "crying words") belonging to their own clan. The passer-by sometimes hears these chants of praise being sung by the women as they stand grinding the corn. When one of the Tiedeme of Tom dies, the singers will cry out:

> *Ngmaam ble zu mele liɛ̃ o minga.*
> A small monkey strangled itself with its tail.

And:

> *Bandaa lo yagli.*
> A lizard fell and hung itself.

Both these animals have totemic connections with the descent group in question, and no clansman may either kill or eat them. The reason given for the prohibition is that the animals have at one time in the distant past come to the aid of an ancestor in a critical situation. Consequently all the present members of the clan owe their existence to the monkey and the lizard. It was said, for instance, that when the slave raiders once came to the village, they destroyed the compounds of other patriclans all around, putting the inhabitants to the sword. But the ancestor of the Tiedeme, dozing under a tree, was awakened by a lizard jumping down upon him and so managed to escape.

Not only has the lizard an intimate connection with the clan, but in the funeral chants the clansman is actually spoken of as a member of the totemic species. These totemic beliefs appear to be very similar to those reported from many other parts of Western Sudan (e.g., Fortes [1945], chap. 8). In some clans a food prohibition, such as the taboo on eating food out of a basket, operates in precisely the same way as the avoidance of an animal species. In only one instance I know of is the prohibition not oral in character: the Haiyuri, who trace their origin to the Mossi (the northern people noted for their weaving), prohibit the throwing of cloth from one person to another.

Although these prohibitions vary considerably, they nearly all refer to eating and mostly to animal species. The species, however, are by no means all of utilitarian value. Indeed, except that the animals are never domestic, the species tabooed by the LoDagaa seem to have no common characteristic, and the prohibitions upon them appear to be replaceable by ones referring to non-totemic objects. All these taboos function mainly as emblems, as distinguishing features of clans. Moreover, in situations in which the basic norms of clanship—those governing sexuality (exogamy) and aggression (abstention from internal attack and mutual assistance in war)—are latent, such taboos provide a more effective source of clan solidarity than the name of the group itself. In other words, they supply continuing reference points for group cohesion.

But does this diacritical function provide a sufficient explanation of these totemic phenomena? Radcliffe-Brown [1929] accounted for the choice of particular species in Australia by referring to their economic and ritual value in social life; among the LoDagaa, on the other hand, the animals are of trivial importance. Nor is there a general association of the objects of the natural world with particular local or descent groups in the manner discussed by Durkheim and Mauss in their paper on primitive systems of classification [1901–2]. Nevertheless there is, I suggest, a cosmological aspect even to African totemism of this more limited kind, and the predominance of natural species can be interpreted as acknowledging the continuity of man with other living things. Other features of this generalized respect for nature are more appropriately considered in the context of hunting, which is treated later in this chapter.

The chants of other clans refer to avoidances, shrines, and legendary incidents peculiar to that descent group. When sung for a woman, such chants include a generic name, applicable to any female member of the clan, which always ends with the suffix *ma,* meaning "mother." Among the LoDagaba the chants sung at a man's funeral include those of his mother's patriclan, but at the end of the chant is added the word *nyiena,* which signifies the root of a tree that burrows underground and then sprouts up elsewhere, a concept that epitomizes the diluted agnation, the residual rights, transmitted through women. This lateral relationship contrasts with the strictly unilineal tie referred to by the word *per,* as in *ma per* (matrilineage) or *sãã per* (patrilineage), one literal meaning of which is the bole or lower trunk of a tree. The botanical images neatly convey the sociological distinctions.

Funeral chants are sung only to the *Dagaa,* never to the *Lo,* xylophone. The LoSaala, the inhabitants of the Lawra area, who have no xylophones of the former type, do not chant at funerals and distinguish themselves from all the neighboring peoples whom they call *Dagaa* by reference to this fact. The funeral songs played just after the death has occurred should be accompanied by the *Lo* xylophone; among the LoPiel of Tom, however, this instrument is rapidly disappearing, and the songs often have to be played on the *Dagaa* xylophone instead. This disappearance seems to be related to the more general movement away from *Lo* customs and toward *Dagaa* ones that I have discussed in my earlier monograph [1956a]. The type of xylophone played is seen by the peoples of the area as one of the most important indices of cultural affiliation.

Dancing

These two types of xylophone each have their own particular dances, the leaping movements of the one (*Dagaa wobo*) requiring a quite different technique from the shuffling steps of the *Lo* dance. The xylophone has to be played continuously day and night throughout the mortuary ceremony, and when no chants are being sung, the musicians play the accompaniment for funeral dances, either *kuur bine* on the *Lo* xylopohone, or *sebr* on the *Dagaa*. Especially during the earlier phases of the funeral, the senior mourner and the close bereaved are constantly running hither and thither and are restrained by the persons in charge of them, particularly when they display inordinate grief or run away from the area immediately surrounding the house, since it is feared they might do themselves or others harm. While running to and fro one of the bereaved may suddenly break into a violent dance to the rhythm of the music. Spectators who are of the same sex jump up and join in, and, if they are men, will hold up a bow or a throwing-stick in their right hands. The closer the kinship tie with the bereaved, the greater is the obligation to participate in the dance he has initiated. The dancers start from the perimeter of the circle formed around the funeral stand, dance toward the corpse, then break off and retire to the places where they were sitting.

Most of the dancing is done by the women, a custom that I have sometimes heard strongly criticized by the men, who say that women come to funerals only to dance. Although the men also take pleasure in dancing for its own sake, they dance for other reasons as well, as a mark of respect for the dead man and as a means of dissociating themselves from the activities they have performed with him during his lifetime, an aspect of mimetic acts that will be explained in the section on clan rituals. In fact, these same considerations enter into the women's dancing, but there is yet another aspect to the dances performed exclusively by males, which lends force to their contention. Such dances are in part a formalization of the ways in which grief is expressed. As we observed in connection with the funeral songs, these earlier gestures include threats against those who, by mystical or other means, have been the cause of death, and the seizing of clubs or bows is also a formalized gesture of defiance. Gradually, however, the men's dance of war gives way to the women's dance of peace.

Mystical Retribution

Attendance at all the funerals in the neighborhood is by no means automatic. To go to the funeral of someone who had done you a wrong that has not been expiated is to invite mystical retribution.[3] This complex belief covers a wide range of acts and resembles the Tallensi ideas of *tyuk* and *dulem* (Fortes [1949], pp. 35, 219). Two specific examples will serve to outline its meaning.

When Der of the Kusiele patriclan from Lawra (LoSaala) died, his death was diagnosed as an evil one, *kū faa*. He was said to have hired a witch to attack another resident of the house in which he dwelt, an agnatic kinsman of his, and for this the compound shrines had killed him. After his death, a full brother inherited his widow, a woman whose own brother was shortly afterwards killed by the same compound shrines for a similar offense. To understand this marital situation, the reader must know that the main compounds in the oldest ward of Lawra, known as Yikpēē, "the big house," are very large, containing as many as a hundred persons under one roof. Among these are a number of "sisters' children" born out of wedlock, and these attached members of the patriclan usually marry within their natal compound.

Der's widow wanted to give her brother a proper burial instead of having his body, together with his personal possessions, interred in the bank of a stream outside the parish, as is the fate of witches in that part. She therefore seized the wooden boxes in which her brother kept his possessions and took them to her own room. By this attempt to thwart the shrines, she placed herself in an impure state; she was a "spoiled woman," *pogh sangna,* a phrase otherwise used only of a wife who has committed adultery that has not yet been expiated. When the brother of her late husband, knowing what she had done, took her as his wife, he invited mystical retribution upon himself. He had, in effect, condoned a wrong to the descent group without the proper sacrifices having been made.

---

[3] The ways of inviting mystical retribution of this kind fall into two categories. If, owing either to bravado or to failure to ascertain the facts by divinatory procedures, you attend the funeral of a man in whose death you have been implicated, then you are said to *kpen tule,* to "enter" *tule.* If, on the other hand, a man has stolen some goods of yours and you curse the thief, then should you knowingly or unknowingly drink beer bought with the proceeds, you are said to *di tule,* to "eat" *tule.*

The second case concerns the wife of Menuõ of Tom, who left him to go to the town of Lawra, where she became pregnant by a lover. Since no bridewealth payment had been made by the man with whom she was living, Menuõ was still her jural husband and therefore the *pater* of her offspring. When she was about to give birth, she left Lawra; but instead of going to her husband's or her father's house, which were both in the same settlement, she went to the neighboring village of Yipiele, whose inhabitants stand in joking partnership to the people of Tom. In due course the woman's father was informed of the birth of a child and sent a messenger to tell Menuõ. To publicly establish the paternity of a newborn child, the husband presents his wife with a gift of guinea-corn (*pogh tshi*). When the messenger arrived, therefore, Menuõ turned to his sister's son, Domulko, who happened to be present at the time, and told him to open the granary and take out three basketfuls of grain. When I asked him why he could not do this himself, Menuõ replied that since his wife's lover had not yet sent the adultery payment (*paa bume*, "things of the vagina"), he would have invited mystical retribution had he done so. A sister's son, on the other hand, can perform such dangerous tasks without fear of supernatural punishment, for his compound and granary are protected by different shrines and by different ancestors, and hence he stands in a proper position to assist in difficult situations of this kind. Had Menuõ himself dispatched the heads of corn, he would have appeared to condone an offense against the descent group, an offense that it is the specific duty of the compound shrines to punish, unless appropriate measures have been taken to expiate the wrong.

There are other occasions when a person is said to invite mystical retribution. If two men who have slept with the same woman accidentally touch each other's hands when eating from the same bowl, they render themselves liable to the same sort of supernatural sanction. If a man tries to drop "medicine" into his brother's granary and is killed by a shrine for this offense, the surviving brother will invite retribution if he attends the funeral. It should be added that the granary shrines, known as *bur kokor ngmin,* are different for brothers who farm separately, although their ancestor shrines are, of course, the same. The concept of *ngmin* resembles that of the Tallensi *yin* (to which it is etymologically linked) in its association with specific individuals and their personal destinies.

The danger of attending any funeral is that if a man has any responsibility in the death, and of this he may be unaware, he may lay himself open to attack from the very shrines that would normally protect him. In each of the instances given above, a person invites retribution by acting toward someone who has wronged him as if nothing had happened. By so doing, a man is, as it were, spurning the shrines who assist and protect him. Having implicitly or explicitly called for their help, he is now acting in a manner that might seem to reject or deny their intervention. The most extreme example of such behavior is attendance at the funeral of a man in whose death one has had a hand. In other words, this belief serves to reinforce the system of supernatural sanctions by making it dangerous for a person to interfere with the working out of mystical vengeance, whether or not this has been deliberately invoked. The norms must be observed. The leviratic spouse should have expiated her sin; payment must be forthcoming for the wife's adultery. These matters pertain to the society's basic norms, whose transgression no man has the power to condone.

There is a medicine (*tule tĩĩ*) that may be taken to offset these dangers, either when one has already invited retribution or when one has to carry out an act that might lead to such a consequence. However, a person does not always know whether or not the danger exists, and ignorance of the law is no defense against supernatural vengeance.

Not only may a person be held responsible when he is unaware of doing wrong, but he may also suffer for the sins of others, particularly those of members of the same descent group. At the funeral of Namoo's wife, referred to earlier, no member of the closest patrilineage of the same clan attended, since Namoo had recently abducted the wife of one of their sister's sons who had lived among them since he was a small boy. To attend would have been to invite mystical retribution upon some member of the group.

The dangers of retribution are such that most elders take precautions before attending a funeral at which there is even the slightest possibility of running into trouble. Before setting out, an elder will kill a fowl to one of the medicine shrines in the house. If the fowl is accepted—that is, dies on its back with wings outstretched—then no mystical danger need be feared, and it is safe for the compound head and all the other residents who fall under his ritual jurisdiction to go to the funeral. Often a fowl will be killed by the deceased's own housepeople if they suspect that there is something wrong. I was told in Tom that before the funeral of an Earth priest could begin the representatives of the other local clan sectors, known in this capacity as *kuomber*, would first go to kill a black fowl at the Earth shrine, taking with them five hundred cowries. I presume that if the fowl is refused, the elders then know that some reparation has to be made to the shrine and would consult a diviner to discover the proper way to expiate the sin.

CLAN RITUALS

Acts of a mimetic kind are of frequent occurrence in funerals as in other ceremonial sequences. In the LoDagaa mortuary rites there are two main types of mimetic action, the first relating specifically to membership of the patriclan, and the second to the life cycle of the individual. Rites of this latter kind are among the events taking place on the second day of the burial ceremony, but the principle behind them will be elucidated here, because in the present context it is more explicitly stated by the actors themselves.

Clearly, one of the functions of these mimetic performances is to serve as an obituary, a celebration of the achievements of the dead man. But the double-edged nature of funeral ceremonies that has struck so many observers is as apparent here as elsewhere. For such performances not only reaffirm the solidarity of the living members of the group in the face of death; they also deliberately eliminate the dead man from their midst.

When I speak of the process of disassociation that eliminates the dead man from the network of social relations into which he had formerly fitted, I do not mean that his social personality ceases to exist for the other members of the group, but only that the part it plays in their activities is radically changed. The first task is to increase the social distance between the living and the dead. The LoDagaa state this by claiming that the purpose of these mimetic acts is to prevent themselves from dreaming about the deceased. Dreaming is associated with divination. Through the medium of dreams, supernatural agencies can communicate with the living, and the ghost may reveal the true cause of his death to a sleeping friend. Any dream can indicate the origin of the mystical trouble (*bo'or, bagr*) that has befallen a man, and a diviner should be consulted to find out the appropriate measures to be taken. The dreams of the diviner himself may also reveal the cause of the misfortune, and a miniature sleeping mat—one of the many objects (*kpaara*) that he shakes from his bag when about to divine—is often held up in his hand at the beginning of a session, while he studies how it sways, now this way, now that.

People prevent themselves from dreaming of the dead man by the homeopathic expedient of engaging in any task that they were wont to perform jointly with him when he was alive. Thus the major group activities in which the individual participated during his lifetime are re-enacted during the course of the funeral ceremonies. Not only the mimes connected with the life cycle, but also the funeral divination and the clan rituals—that is, the procedures that center upon the solidarity of the patriclan—are said to prevent dreams. It is these clan rituals, carried out by members of the reciprocal funeral group, that constitute the next phase of the ceremony.

Clan rituals celebrate the achievements of the dead man as a warrior and as a hunter, and aggregate the relics of the men and animals he has slain to the totality of such relics belonging to the ancestors of the clan sector. In these activities it is not only his individual attainments with the bow that are celebrated. The whole ritual stresses how his victories both in war and in hunting were essentially dependent upon membership of a social group. The material manifestations, the "objective correlatives," of this dependence are the arrow poison and the two protective medicines (one for hunting and the other for homicide), which are all three closely connected with the shrine of the patriclan itself.

Among the LoWiili, the brewing of arrow poison (*lo', logh*) is usually a matter for the patrilineage. However, any person learning that a particular section of his clan is about to prepare a fresh mixture, a task that is undertaken about once a year, can send his arrows along to be daubed with the thick, black fluid.

Although the ingredients of the mixture are sometimes thought of as identical for the whole clan, this is not always the case. A lad who is brought up among his mother's natal kin will inevitably come to depend upon their arrow poison. And so not all the members of the clan, nor even of the local subdivisions, may in fact possess the same recipe for the brew. Moreover, a person may deliberately seek new ingredients if his original brew is not proving a success. (Arrow poison differs in this respect from protective hunting medicines, which are always associated with a particular clan shrine.) These additions to the poison are either revealed by the beings of the wild or else acquired by purchase from a more successful marksman. Thus, although the intrinsically effective ingredient in these poisons is strophanthus, the effectiveness of a poison is attributed by the actors not so much to the common element as to other ingredients such as snakes' heads that are not in themselves fatal; and these are the ones that differ from clan to clan and sometimes from person to person.[4]

In addition, each poison has its own specific injunctions and prohibitions, and it also has its particular cry (*suono* or *dooro lo' yuor*). However, the cry that a man actually uses always includes the one associated with the hunting medicine, which is the same for all lineage members because it is linked to the clan shrine. The shouting of this cry at the

[4] Apart from strophanthus, the LoDagaa also use as poisons *Calotropis procera, Elaeophorbia drupifera,* and *Sapium* sp.

moment when the arrow leaves the bow is believed to increase the efficacy of the poison; for if an animal is struck, it cannot then run so far as to get lost in the bush. The proper working of the poison depends, therefore, upon the observance of certain injunctions and prohibitions that are specific to the poison, some of which are linked with the patrilineal descent group, and others, such as abstention from sexual intercourse beforehand, which are general to all participants in warfare and the hunt. Thus success in war and hunting is attributed to the social elements in the situation, and especially to the knowledge and power one obtains from membership of a particular patriclan, rather than to the natural component, the intrinsically effective strophanthus.

The clan not only helps in the killing of men and animals; it also provides protection against the dangers inherent in success. For although these acts are usually considered honorable achievements, they are nevertheless fraught with mystical dangers that have to be warded off by taking certain medicines. The hunter must be especially wary of the animals known as bad or dangerous (*dun soola,* literally, black animals). This category includes both domestic (*yir dun*) and wild (*we dun*) species and has no direct connection with the objective dangers that a European might see in these animals. The domestic animals spoken of as "black" are the cow (*naab*), the sheep (*pir*), and the dog (*baa*); the wild ones include the elephant (*wob*), the lion (*gbiung*), the buffalo (*we naab*), the leopard (*luora*), the hyena (*kpintin*), the hippopotamus ('*yen*), the boar (*duo*), the kob (*wal piel*), the crocodile (*iiba*), and a species of small antelope (*wal soola*), as well as the crown bird (*brungmaan*) and an unidentified species of bird known as *dulu.*

Although the category of dangerous animals crosscuts the distinction between wild and domestic animals, there is an important difference. In the first place, a domestic animal is normally killed only in sacrifice, an act that counters the mystical dangers involved. In the second, these domestic animals appear to be called black because they can be used in grave ritual situations, such as the sweeping of the soul. But with wild animals, the danger lies in the actual slaughter of one of the black species, sometimes said to possess medicine and to know witchcraft, and a person who does this is treated in a similar way to a homicide. The name *kpirme* is used for the special meal made both for a man who slays a black animal, and for a man who kills a fellow human being. While the rites performed when the hunter returns from the chase vary with the species he has killed, in general he cannot drink water until he returns to the settlement, where he is fed with a soup made from the liver of the slain animal mixed with the hunting medicine (*we tīī*) of his patriclan. This medicine is prepared by the lineage elders, who are known in this context as the "tree root diggers," since roots form the basis of most medicine. Except in the case of the birds, the flesh of the animal is cooked some days later at the house of a member of the hunter's own patrilineage, where the "clan shrine" (*dooro tiib*) is kept. Here, too, is the pole to which the skulls of the smaller animals are tied (*yaaro,* or *dooro, lo' daa*) and the pot of water (*piora*) in which the hunter dips his fingers before setting off for the communal hunt. Indeed, whether the bush animal is of a dangerous or a safe species, some of its flesh is cooked and eaten communally, together with a specially prepared porridge into which a little of the medicine has been mixed.

The hunting shrine is frequently the same as the clan shrine. When this is not the case, the two are closely associated, and so, too, is the arrow poison used by members of the clan sector. Physically there is no one altar for the whole dispersed descent group, only the separate altars attached to each patrilineage. Nevertheless, this whole complex of shrines, medicines, and associated rituals and beliefs serves as a focus of unity; for they are visualized as identical throughout the clan, all of whose members are dependent upon them for success with the bow as well as for protection from the consequences of killing.

This dependence is re-enacted in the course of the funeral cere-monies. The skull and horns of all the ritually dangerous animals a man has killed are added to the clan relics. The horns of the smaller animals are hung on the hunting pole, known as "the pole of the clan's arrow poison," while those of the larger ones are aggregated to the pile that is then placed in the dead man's byre.

When the funeral is well under way, some six men under the leader-ship of the elders of the clan sector go to the house where the last death of a member of that group took place.[5] There in the byre are kept the horns (*kpiin iile*) of the larger of the dangerous animals killed by the dead ancestors. These horns are gathered up and borne in slow pro-cession, to the accompaniment of a hunting whistle blown by the leader, the most senior member of the sector to be present at the time. When the procession arrives at the funeral, the points of the horns are thrust into the earth in front of the stand. Other hunters present at once jump up and begin to dance, simulating the stalking of a wild animal, the drawing of the bow, the release of the arrow, and occasionally breaking out in victory halloos. Anyone who wishes to show that he has killed more dangerous animals than the deceased can seize the horns and dance with them, holding them above his head.

[5] In Tom (LoDagaba) the relics of the men and animals killed are kept in the senior house of the clan sector and are taken back there after a funeral.

The horns are in fact brought out at the funeral of every adult male; for all have eaten the hunting medicine of the clan at the communal meal that is prepared when a wild animal has been killed by a clan member. With the relics of war, the procedure is somewhat different. These trophies consist of a number of slats of wood (*ziē tender*), each one representing a man slain by a member of the clan sector. They are brought out for any person who either is a homicide (*ziēsob*) or has eaten of the medicine (*ziē tīī*) which, like hunting medicine, is taken for protection against the dangerous consequences of killing.

A person who has killed a man is immediately taken by other homicides in his own clan sector to the house where the medicine is kept. There he is forced to eat food mixed with this powder, one ingredient of which is the liver of a dead person, and he has to drink water in which the bones of a victim have been boiled. This brew is drunk from a skull euphemistically called a "head calabash" (*zu ngmaan*). When a man had killed an enemy in war, he tried to sever the head from the body and take it back to his homestead. The jaws were then tied together with hide, and the skull itself was placed in the byre with the ancestor shrines, to be brought out with the wooden slats at the victor's funeral. In homicide rituals the top of the skull may be used as a drinking vessel, as if it were an ordinary calabash.

The name "head calabash" is also given to the half-gourd which, painted with whitewash and decorated with feathers, is sometimes worn by a man who has killed a wild animal. If the animal was a "dangerous" one, a small piece of the skin is fastened to the top of the headdress. This calabash is the one taken by hunters on their expeditions so they can scoop up water from pools during the course of the hunt, which may last over several days. Nowadays it is little used among the LoWiili, but is more frequently found among the Lo peoples of the Ivory Coast and the Upper Volta. It represents one of a number of ways in which the treatment of a man who has killed a wild animal resembles that accorded to a homicide. For example, in both cases the food with which the protective medicine is mixed is eaten with the left hand, the hand normally reserved for sanitary purposes. As in so many societies, left-handedness is "sinister," and in this instance its use represents a reversal of everyday ways of acting.[6]

[6] My observations on this question run somewhat counter to Hertz's assertion that the right hand is always sacred, the left always profane ([1960] p. 110). I feel the difficulties inherent in the attempt to reduce social phenomena to terms of the sacred-profane dichotomy put such an assertion in doubt. One might describe the use of the left hand in these rituals as a "profanity," but one can hardly deny that the context is "sacred." It is a profanity because it reverses the normal course of action,

The food is not eaten from a bowl, but is put in dirty places—the mat on which a menstruating woman has slept, or a step of the ladder by which people climb up to the roof. The consumption of food that had been contaminated in this way would otherwise be utterly revolting, and indeed it requires an effort on the part of the individual to avoid vomiting. Although the content of the ritual varies in different descent groups, there are two constant elements, the eating of food and medicine from dirty places and the consumption of a portion of the body of the slain. Both these acts are deliberately disgusting, reversals of ordinary procedures. The consumption of part of the liver of the dead man is, in fact, the polar opposite to cannibalism. Although this rite is often spoken of as "ritual cannibalism," it is more accurate to regard it as a nauseating act performed for therapeutic purposes, as those who had participated in it made clear to me. The general aspects of such reversal procedures have already been noted; those features concerned specifically with homicide will be discussed at the end of the present section.

When a homicide dies, he is first dealt with by other killers; for it is dangerous for women to come in contact with the corpse until the proper rituals have been performed. Later in the ceremony, after the ancestral horns have been displayed, the eldest homicides in the clan sector collect the wooden slats at the house where the last funeral of a member of their "fraternity" took place.

One of these slats, each of which represents a dead man, is made out of the stave of the killer's bow, either when he dies or else when he is given the homicide medicine. Both the slats and the bow-stave are referred to as *tender,* which is also the general term for bamboo. Rattray states that *za tandere,* another dialect form of *ziē tender,* refers to the killer's own bow, which is set aside until his death, when, after being cleansed by a fellow homicide, it is inherited by his son ([1932] p. 442, n.1). Among the LoDagaa, I have only heard the phrase *ziē tender* used to refer to the slats themselves. However, the killer's weapon is treated much as Rattray describes, except that it is not inherited. The bow with

---

which requires that the right hand be used for eating, the left for sanitary purposes. Reversal is the important feature of these acts.

Needham [1960] has recently analyzed Bernardi's material [1959] on the Mugwe, the Failing Prophet of the Meru of Kenya, and offers an explanation for the importance attached to the acts this ritual leader performs with the left hand. During the course of his discussion, Needham refers to the privilege of Ibo homicides of using their left hands for drinking, which, like many Ibo rites, parallels LoDagaa usage. My own data suggest that fuller consideration should be given to the reversal aspect of these customs, which Needham discusses only in a footnote.

which a man has been killed is hung up on the wall away from young children and never used for hunting again. But at the killer's death it is broken in two and becomes a *ziē tender*. Until then it has been known as a bitter bow, *tam tuo*. The phrase *a in tuo* means "that's difficult." Although I have translated it as "bitter," *tuo* does not necessarily carry any connotation of unpleasant taste; it rather indicates an act or object that is set aside from the normal run. Similarly an arrow (*pīī tuo*) that has been in contact with blood is particularly dangerous and must be kept in a special quiver (*lo' tuo*). Among neither the LoWiili nor the LoDagaba are these objects inherited by the heir to the major portion of the property; unlike ordinary hunting equipment, they are assigned to more distant kin.

The bamboo slats are carried to the dead man's compound and then to the funeral stand by the senior homicide in the clan sector, who is followed by an attendant holding an unscraped calabash (*ngman tun*). This contains the thick, sticky mixture of homicide medicine, which, with the aid of a piece of broken okra stalk, the attendant scatters on both sides of him. When the stalk of the okra is broken, it exudes a gluey substance, sometimes compared both with the white of an egg and with semen. The separated fibres of the okra stalk make it a useful instrument for dispersing fluids, and it is employed in a number of purificatory rites for this purpose.

When the slats are carried to the funeral stand, they are placed in a shallow hole and covered with earth. The small mound is then spread over with branches of thorn to prevent man or animal from coming into even indirect contact with these mystically dangerous objects. Behind the leader and his assistant follow several younger men armed with bows and arrows. All gather around the buried slats, and each man in turn takes the calabash containing the medicine and anoints himself on the toes, chest, head, and back. A dog is then seized and pushed against the thorns a number of times before having its head cut off. The blood flows onto the thorns and into the calabash, and the body is thrown aside to finish its death throes. Taking up the calabash once again, the participants anoint themselves a second time. When this is done, they engage in a war dance (*be derena*) not unlike the hunting dance performed earlier.

The sacrifice of a dog is reserved for the most difficult rites.[7] If a

---

[7] Labouret suggests that formerly a dog was killed over the animal horns as well as over the wooden slats ([1931] p. 323). In Tom, I was told that the broken bow-stave is tied to the dog.

member of a parish has been killed by another inhabitant, the clan sector involved has to provide a dog to be slaughtered at the major Earth shrine before any further expiatory action can be undertaken. This rite is known as "sweeping the Earth shrine." In another yet more interesting metaphor the sacrifice is said to "shave the head of the Earth shrine" (*puon a tenggaan zuru*). When an unweaned child dies, the parents' heads are shaved at a ceremony that corresponds to the third of the full funeral performances; until this has been done, they cannot engage in sexual intercourse. The inhabitants of a parish speak of themselves as children of the Earth shrine, and it would appear that in sacrificing a dog after the death of one of their number, the congregation are treating "mother earth" in analogous fashion.

Formerly the flesh of a dog was forbidden to women, but this prohibition is no longer strictly observed. However, the animal sacrificed on this occasion is tabooed by men as well as by women. The carcass of the animal killed during a homicide's funeral can be claimed only by an individual who has surpassed the dead man in the number of his victims, although he will share the flesh among the other homicides present. The gradual disappearance of warriors who took part in the fights of the pre-Colonial period has led to difficulties in the performance of these rites, and nowadays men may claim a share of the flesh if they have merely eaten the protective medicine. Even so, I have never seen any junior men eat this meat, and the head, which, with the liver, constitutes the most significant part of any sacrifice, is always reserved for real killers.

On one occasion when I was present, a fowl was killed instead of a dog because, it was said, the dead man had killed his "brother"; intraclan homicide requires the protective rites, but carries none of the prestige of slaying a victim in a fight in which the group can participate as a whole. On another occasion, the slats were brought out without a dog being killed, and it was explained that although the deceased had shot a man with an arrow, someone else had already shot the man beforehand.

Like the vulture, the dog has close physical contact with human flesh; it is sacrificed only when an actual killing has occurred. Formerly no woman ate of its flesh at any time; the same prohibition applies to the vulture, except that men, too, are forbidden to touch it unless they are homicides.

Although homicide medicine, like hunting medicine and arrow poison, is basically the property of the patrilineal descent group, a man can also acquire such medicine from the mother's patriclan. Should this in turn be inherited by his agnatic offspring, the result will be to create differentiation within the patriclan. There is another way in which such differences arise. If a killer is mystically troubled by the blood he has shed, a diviner may direct him to procure some more effective medicine from another source. Indeed, the diviner may require someone to eat homicide medicine even though the person has not actually killed a man. The following case illustrates certain of these points. The wives who bathed the late chief of Birifu during his last sickness were treated with medicine in order to mitigate the harmful effects of close contact with a dying killer. Being unable to move from his sickbed, the chief had sent one of his sons to fetch some renowned homicide medicine from a distant Wiili settlement to which certain of his kinsmen had migrated. This son had also to become a "homicide" (*ziẽsob*), a rite that involved the shooting of a dog as a substitute for a human being. Formerly, I was told, a dead body preserved in clay was used as a target. A person who has performed these rites is said only to have "eaten the medicine" (*o dina tĩ*); he has not become a homicide proper (*ziẽ soola,* a black killer). In earlier times, after an enemy had been killed, the younger members of the killer's lineage were given a similar opportunity of becoming homicides by proxy. The dead body was set up encased in clay so that all might shoot at it.

As the funeral ceremonies demonstrate, not only is a distinction made between the real killers and those who have only eaten the medicine, but there are also differences within the category of true homicides, differences that are significant indices of the LoDagaa moral system.

All killers, honorable or despised, have to be treated with homicide medicine, and even if the victim was a fellow clansman, the killer is still given the protective medicine and qualifies for the status of *ziẽsob*. However, at the funeral of such a man, who is, of course, subject to other more severe sanctions against intraclan homicide, the full ritual is not performed; the deceased is denied the sacrifice of a dog, since this is reserved for achievements in extraclan fighting.

The most honored achievement in the "fraternity" of killers is to have slain a man in warfare, that is, when fighting on behalf of the group, whether this be the descent or the local group. Socially approved homicide, though like all killings mystically dangerous, ranks high in the LoDagaa scale of values. It is the mark of a real man. "What a man!" (*O in daba*) the spectators at the funeral exclaim, as they watch the dog's blood dripping onto the assembled trophies of the clan.

Why is it that the slaughter of animals and men, whether under honorable or dishonorable circumstances, is viewed as dangerous? Why is it that the descent group not only assists its members in the killing, but also protects them from the consequences of their acts? Even the slaying of an enemy in battle, which in one way meets with full social approval, is considered mystically dangerous, and the returning hero is made to undergo a series of revolting procedures.

The LoDagaa would attribute the necessity for such precautions to a fear of revenge by the soul of the dead man or animal. But though it is possible to view these rituals as one of the implications of beliefs in the persistence of the soul after death, the widespread nature of this phenomenon and its association with other ritual themes invites a different explanation.

All societies must maintain a double attitude toward the taking of life, both of human beings and of animals. Under certain circumstances the killing of members of another group is an honorable act; under others it is not. These circumstances vary according to the state of social relationships between the groups concerned, whether they are at war, feud, or peace, and to the social distance between the parties involved. Among the LoDagaa it is never permissible to kill a member of the same patriclan, and no state of war or of feud can exist between the segments. Between more distant groups, on the other hand, it is doubtful whether formerly there could be anything called a state of peace; to kill a member of a group with whom the clan sector was at feud was nearly always permissible, for it served to redress the balance of wrongs invariably seen as weighted in the opponent's favor.

Thus in killing as in other spheres of human action the applicability of a particular norm depends upon the social distance between ego and alter and the balance of positive and negative acts existing between them. Homicide must at some point be forbidden within the system of local and kinship groups in order that people may carry out their productive and reproductive tasks. Consequently, even though norms may be stated in such universalistic terms as "Thou shalt not kill," the implied conclusion to the injunction runs "a member of the same group." Alternatively, the restriction may not apply permanently to certain groups, but only under certain conditions, as, for example, "except in times of battle," when appropriate behavior switches from pacific to warlike at the operation of a trigger mechanism such as a declaration of war. Or, again, the application of a moral norm that has been phrased in general terms may be limited even with respect to members of the same group if they have committed a crime defined as heinous. Thus, in certain cases, the norms relating to a particular type of act, such as killing or sexual intercourse, have to be completely reversed not only at specific periods but also at significant points in the social structure.

Every society maintains some such double standard toward the taking of human life, and this in turn gives rise to certain problems of a general kind. Basically these spring from the contradiction, explicit or implicit, between the principle of reciprocity and that of self-protection, between violent retaliation for wrongs done, or believed to have been done, and the "sanctity of human life." When a universalistic injunction is accompanied by a particularistic application, as in the Christian ethic, the contradiction is explicit, it exists within the actor's frame of reference and may lead to the formation of ideological subgroups who reject the use of weapons and the imposition of capital punishment. Among other peoples such as the LoDagaa, the contradiction is implicit, and may be eased by treating all taking of human life as mystically dangerous and by subjecting the killer, whether hero or murderer, to certain humiliating but therapeutic procedures.

The killing of animals gives rise to similarly contradictory attitudes toward the shedding of blood. Of the smaller animals of no economic importance some are savagely destroyed by the LoDagaa, whereas to kill others is considered wanton destruction of life. My cook would attack violently a certain type of lizard whose coloring appeared to lend support to the belief that it was the cause of leprosy, and yet he reproved me when I swatted flies and grasshoppers whose presence annoyed me, not because of a specific totemic belief but because I was killing a harmless creature. *Na'angmin be bobra ka fu ko-ona,* I was told by another man. "God doesn't want man to kill such creatures. They don't bite nor are they food. If you do that, God will kill you in like fashion."

These special attitudes toward certain animals are held by the whole community; indeed, the division into black and white species is reported from many parts of Africa. But other beliefs are linked to particular subgroups of the society, and it is these that are often spoken of as totemic. I have already suggested that although the emblematic role of such beliefs is clearly of great importance, there is also a cosmological aspect to them, and this bears upon the problem I have just discussed. For the individual, the "sacredness" of the clan emblem institutionalizes conflicting attitudes toward the killing of animals; on the community level, the species killed by society as a whole is spared by one of its constituent segments.

The LoDagaa, unlike some communities in Australia, do not of course perform any ceremonies deliberately designed to increase the number of the totemic species. Nevertheless, I do not think that considerations of economy, in the broad sense of the management of expenditure, are irrelevant here.

Let us first take domestic animals. In agricultural societies, livestock is valued both on the hoof and on the table. First, it is often a means of acquiring social status. Second, indiscriminate slaughter only leads to future deprivation. In order to maintain the economic system, domestic animals must be given due value both alive and dead.

Less directly, the same considerations apply to hunting societies. The over-hunting of wildlife brings diminishing returns, so that a double standard may also have "survival value" as far as the provision of meat is concerned. By this I do not intend to imply that all totemic species are important economically; they are no more so among the LoDagaa than elsewhere (Worsley [1955]). Nevertheless, if we consider natural resources as a whole, such prohibitions may be related to contradictions inherent in maintaining "the balance of nature" and at the same time defending oneself from attack and supplying oneself with meat. Like the double attitude toward the killing of men, this built-in contradiction of the human situation is expressed in magico-religious acts and beliefs of the kind we have examined. Indeed, any explanation of the animal dichotomy should take into consideration the possibility that the double attitudes toward the killing of natural species may represent an overspill, a generalization, from those that center upon the killing of men. For among the LoDagaa, as in most societies, a certain continuity is perceived between all living things, which appears not in any formal doctrine of evolution, but rather in the many stories about animals and their interaction with human beings as well as with other animal species. This recognition of the affinity between animals and men may contribute to the dichotomizing of attitudes and behavior toward the killing of natural species, since the destruction of both involves the shedding of blood, the stoppage of breath, the halting of motion.

Not only are the concepts of blood (*zíí*) and breath (*nyovuor*) of central importance in linking the animal with the human world, but they also ramify throughout the whole range of beliefs connected with life and death, homicide and hunting, sex and childbirth. Blood is clearly associated with childbirth and menstruation; infertility may be caused by the failure of the blood of the man and woman to mingle; it is an essential part of humankind, and its outflow spells death. Indeed the LoDagaa often identify homicide, of the non-mystical kind, with "the shedding of blood" (*zíí tshiir*), and it is precisely this act that is man's gravest sin against the Earth on which he dwells. Blood in the veins means life, but on the ground, death. When a domestic animal is killed in sacrifice, the throat is cut and the blood usually caught in a pot. Some may be allowed to fall on the altar, but never, I think, to spill indiscriminately upon the earth. It should be added that among the LoDagaa the deliberate killing of livestock is nearly always carried out as a mystical act, an offering directed to some supernatural agency. In one way, the shedding of the blood of the sacrifice upon the shrine subtly resolves the human dilemma of which I have spoken; for not only is the responsibility for the deed thrown onto superhuman powers, but these agencies are even conceived of as being gratified by the act.

Frazer accounted for the widespread taboos on blood, especially the reluctance to shed blood upon the ground, by the belief that it was the dwelling place of the soul ([1911] pp. 247–48). In many cases a more satisfactory explanation would link the mystical significance so often attached to blood to a recognition of its dual aspect, as creator and sustainer of life within the body and as the mark of death outside. But yet a further duality is involved, one that relates to my main contention; for the blood of the slain is again dichotomized into that legitimately spilt in the course of law and in war on the one hand, and that shed by the murderer on the other. The elaboration of acts and beliefs centering upon blood appears to derive not only from its obvious importance to human life, its "social value," but also from the conflicting norms that surround its shedding.[8]

I suggest, then, that the fact that we kill some men and not others, some animals and not others, and that we have to husband animals at the same time as destroy them gives rise to problems similar in kind to those involved in rejecting some women as sexual objects and accepting others. Looked at either as a means of establishing interrelationships between persons of different social groups or else as an indispensable step to achieving a measure of stability within the upbringing group, either way the incest taboo is of fundamental importance to human societies. But its adoption inevitably creates a segmentation of the moral and conceptual perspective by dividing women into the touchables and the untouchables. And what may be regarded on one level as a structural duality in the sexuality of male and female members of the com-

---

[8] There is a similar duality in the killing of domestic animals, some of which are eaten by the worshipers and others which are rejected. Robertson Smith's fascinating account of sacrifice, piacular and ordinary, discusses many of the points I have touched upon here, the kinship of men and animals, the sanctity of cattle, the significance of blood ([1927] esp. chaps. 8–10). The explanation I offer dispenses with the need for the dubious developmental hypotheses to which he resorted in order to account for apparent contradictions in his data.

munity appears on another as ambivalence with respect to intercourse itself. The sexual act as such is dangerous as well as pleasurable, a duality that is in turn manifested in institutionalized behavior, ranging from the extreme case of rejection by specialist groups such as monks and nuns, to restrictions that operate only at certain places and at certain times, to the idea of copulation as a transfer of "dirt."[9]

The same range of reaction turns up in connection with killing. In less differentiated societies, the restrictions apply universally but intermittently. In those with more elaborate systems of stratification, an entire caste like the Brahmans may entirely abjure aggressive action between men, as well as the killing of animals and even the destruction of certain plants that bear a resemblance to animals. Indeed, in India, it is precisely the group that attempts to inhibit all aggression that also leans heavily toward the rejection of sexuality. Elsewhere, too, groups that make a profession of purity act in a similar manner toward sex and aggression. However, in contemporary European societies, with their looser systems of stratification, these same contradictions are brought out most clearly in the behavior of minority sects that adopt vegetarianism, practice non-violence, or restrict sexuality. It is relevant to remark in this general connection that children in Western society sometimes appear to have conceptual difficulties in assimilating the reversal of attitudes that the slaughter of both men and animals entails, and that

---

[9] Crawley made a similar point in *The Mystic Rose* (1902), when he insisted that "sexual intercourse, even when lawful morally and legally, is dangerous first, and later sinful" ([1932] p. 182). He attributes this attitude, and the associated sexual taboos, to the danger of confusing male and female roles by the close contact that intercourse involves, for it might lead to the interchange not only of generative fluids but also of sex-linked qualities.

Crawley goes on to derive incest and marriage from the same cause. There are, I believe, more satisfactory "explanations" of incest than this, and it would be more consistent with the general trend of my argument to reverse his nexus of dependence between incest and marriage on the one hand and double attitudes toward sexual intercourse on the other. For incest and marriage in themselves split the sexual universe into two parts; and aside from the division of the opposite sex into the permitted and the prohibited, there are equally universal restrictions that apply to the number and circumstances of permitted liaisons, even with possible sexual partners. However, the very universality of these institutions makes it well-nigh impossible to offer anything substantial in the way of proof and disproof. If one turns to animal societies for a negative case, it could perhaps be argued that the close relationship between sex and aggression in groups without restrictions of the incest type suggest that the double attitudes are not dependent upon the presence of a taboo of this kind in any simple way (e.g., Zuckerman [1932], pp. 232 *et seq.*). But the evidence here is not sufficiently clear to be of any great help; for example, recent field studies of baboons by Washburn and others are beginning to modify the picture of their sexual behavior presented by Zuckerman, largely on the basis of research on captive animals.

these difficulties may be eased by protecting some animals as pets and accepting others as food.

In conclusion, then, although hunting is from one viewpoint a highly honored pursuit, success in the chase also brings formidable dangers of a mystical kind. These dangers are mitigated partly by the many prohibitions placed upon hunting, especially those taboos of a totemic nature that prevent each clan from killing certain species, and partly, too, by the rituals that have to be undergone by a man who has slaughtered a wild animal.

The same is true of homicide, of killing a member of the human species; even when it is honorable, it is also dangerous in some way to the person doing the killing. Even when it is not an offense in legal or jural terms, the act is one that requires a social readjustment. The form of the adjustment varies, of course, from society to society, although some "solutions" have a wider distribution than others. But the many indications of a double attitude to particular killings should, I suggest, be related to the contradictions that exist with regard to killing in general; it is because of this segmentation of the moral norms that even the appointed executioner has to wash the blood from off his hands.

CHAPTER VI

Adjustment to Loss: The Second Day

Musha, said I to myself, I don't know in the world why they make it so fine, for in three days' time it will be deep in the clay. How strange are the ways of the world.

O'SULLIVAN, *Twenty Years A-Growing*

Most of those who attend the first day of a funeral leave long before the sun begins to set. But the xylophones continue to play, though more sporadically, and persons close to the dead man settle down to spend the night in front of the house of mourning. In small groups the women curl up in their sleeping cloths round the fires of dry millet stalks, while the men cluster around the xylophone to talk amongst themselves and eventually to stretch out in its vicinity and drop off into a fitful repose. To spend the night in this way is a mark of respect to the dead and to the close bereaved; and the men and women who do so form the nucleus of the crowd that gathers for the second day of the performances.

During the course of the three days that precede the burial of the dead man, the tone of the funeral changes from grief to resignation and finally to acceptance. In the earlier stages the near mourners display considerable distress and are restrained by funeral companions, persons who are not so closely tied to the deceased. Gradually, the physical presence of many people, the comfort offered by friends and joking partners, and the very performance of a series of established ceremonies all take their effect. There is a routinization of grief, a systematization of mourning, which represents adjustment to the loss of the dead man.

One striking aspect of this process of the return to normality is the increase in the activities revolving round the supply of food and beer. It is one of the duties of the companion of the bereaved to see that he eats and drinks. From time to time he will lead him to a neighboring house where beer has been brewed, and the two will sit and drink for a while, usually at the expense of the other men who happen to be present. Indeed, a favorite gesture of friendship at a funeral, made usually to the senior mourner, is a gift of cowries known as "funeral water" (*kuur kwõ*). This he may use to purchase beer for himself and for people attending the obsequies who have had some distance to travel.

Those coming from out of town have to be supplied with victuals if they stay overnight. However, most people who live at a distance do not arrive until the second day and will often set out on the return journey the same evening. They will probably be offered beer by the kin of the dead man, but for food and additional beer they depend upon what they bring with them and what they can buy locally. So every funeral becomes a small market. Some women bring beer and others cooked foods such as boiled groundnuts and sweet potatoes.

The emphasis of the funeral now shifts from restraining the grief of the bereaved to promoting the opposite reaction, laughter. This process was once explained to me in the following way. On the first day, the dead man's wives and sisters are caught and tied; then they cry, because they don't believe that he is dead, but think that he just sits motionless (*be be tiera ko kpina; o zina*). On the second day, they know for certain that he is dead, for his soul has left his body (*o sie yiina*). Now the women of the dead man's patriclan, his "sisters," playfully seize any of the wives of the male members, his "brothers," tie fibre round their wrists, and call them "close mourners" (*kutuodem*), in this way activating the joking relationship that exists between a woman and the wives of her male clansfolk, whom she calls by the same term as they do, namely, "my wife" (*n poo*).

It is not only between in-laws of the same generation that such behavior occurs. I have already spoken of the role of joking partners in the early stages of the funeral, how such men are often called upon to help modify the grief of the bereaved. On the second and third days of the funeral, the joking aspect of the partnership comes to the fore; instead of applying direct restraints on the bereaved, they now guy their behavior in front of the assembled company.

There are two main sets of joking partnerships among the LoDagaa, between the patriclans and between the matriclans, but the emphasis given to these varies in the different communities. Among the LoWiili, patriclan partnerships are not of great importance. The situation that usually seems to bring them into play is when a man has broken one of the prohibitions associated with his descent group; a joking partner may then be called upon to help set matters right. The matriclan partnerships, on the other hand, are more often spoken of in conversation, and they play a prominent part at funerals. On the second day of the obsequies, the joking partners of the deceased demand contributions of cowries (*lonluore libie*) from members of the deceased's own matriclan. There are only four main matriclans, Some and Da, and Hienbe and Kambire, two of which usually tend to be numerically dominant in any one settlement. The settlement is therefore roughly divided between those playfully asking for money and those reluctantly giving it. Refusal to contribute brings forth a wealth of abuse, directed partly against the dead man, but also against his whole clan, especially in the form of allusive references to traditional stories told about the origin of each matriclan. At one funeral, I saw an old and respected woman wearing a man's smock and performing a grotesque dance in front of the funeral stand. Here she mimicked the "disguise" adopted by close female relatives in the hope that the matriclansfolk of the bereaved would give her something to make her stop. The money-raising aspect aside, such comedy clearly has the effect of distracting the grieved and amusing the crowd.

This function is even more apparent among one of the LoDagaba communities, the LoSaala, than it is among the LoWiili. On the second day of a LoSaala funeral I attended at Gbiiri, a woman suddenly began to plaster ashes upon the face and chest of the close agnatic kin, wives and sister's children of the dead man. She turned out to be a joking partner of the deceased, and her action was the signal for others to do the same to the spectators. One woman, for example, had an old basket tied round her neck by the joking partner of the matriclan to which both her father and the dead man belonged, an ironic comment upon the measures taken to relieve the grief of the bereaved themselves.

The dead man belonged to the Kambire matriclan, and his children were therefore "children of Kambire" (*Kambire biir*). The joking partners of the Kambire are Hienbe. When the bereaved had been plastered in this manner, women whose fathers were Hienbe (that is, *Hienbe biir*, "children of Hienbe") ran round the spectators, seizing all the female offspring of Kambire men they could recognize and covering the upper part of their bodies in mud. Initially it is the task of joking partners to restrain the children of the deceased in their grief. At a later stage they display their relative lack of involvement in another way, by guying the behavior of the bereaved, by vigorous dancing, and by other exaggerated ways of acting.

When the women had finished with the females, one of the men of the matriclan pointed out to them some of the male children of Kambire fathers. These people were also threatened with a plastering unless they contributed money, and this led to more horseplay in which the men joined. One hefty ex-soldier put up great resistance and had to be thrown to the ground several times by a group of men before he could be given the treatment meted out to those who refused. Even after he had been covered in slush he still showed fight, and the struggle only stopped when a "mother's brother," in this case, a senior male of his own matriclan, came over and quietened him. The soldier then borrowed a string of cowries and danced vigorously in front of the funeral stand, "restrained" by the man who had been mainly responsible for having him plastered. He came over to where I was sitting and, pretending to be dumb, begged for shell money. I explained that since my father did not belong to the Kambire clan I need make no contribution. But his companion, who spoke for him, retorted that he now considered himself one of the bereaved (*kuurdem*) and as such was requesting cowries to buy beer and quench his thirst (*kuur kwõ*).

I have described the activities of joking partners at this LoSaala funeral because they were more in evidence there than at any other funeral I attended. In comparison, the part played by joking partnerships among the LoWiili is more limited. Indeed, the LoWiili only demand joking partners' money at the death of an aged person, someone who merits burial in the courtyard.

We have already seen that among the LoSaala joking behavior comes to the fore after the most bitter stages of the funeral have passed. It can therefore be understood that in all these communities the older the deceased, the more joking at his funeral; for the loss is less acutely felt than in the case of a younger man. A fundamental difference exists between the attitude to the death of a person who has lived his full span and produced male heirs, and to that of a younger man dead before his time. The first allows of a gradual elimination from the network of jural and individual ties; the community anticipates the readjustment required. On the other hand, an unexpected death causes a sudden rent in the fabric of relationships and makes greater demands upon the system. Rattray quotes a man from the neighboring Dagaba peoples as saying, "The funeral of a young person is a very sad thing; the funeral of an old person is a subject of laughter" ([1932] p. 423). This is just as true of the LoDagaa; the change from grief to resignation takes longer to accomplish in the case of a young man. And although joking behavior is instrumental in effecting this adjustment, it can be brought into play only when the tension begins to relax.

Although the age of the deceased accounts for certain differences in the conduct of joking partners within each community, it does not explain the differences between communities. The lesser emphasis on such behavior among the LoWiili appears to be associated with the smaller part played by the matriclans in general, since it represents a restriction of their functions. Moreover, if, as I assume, there has been a movement away from matrilineal institutions among the LoWiili in the recent past, one would expect to find evidence of this in the contrast between the funerals of the younger and older members of the community.

So far, I have compared only the LoWiili and one of the LoDagaba communities, the LoSaala, and from this it appears that the role of the matriclan joking partners in funerals is consistent with the degree of emphasis placed on matriclanship in other contexts. When we look at the other LoDagaba community, the LoPiel, a further complexity arises; for we find that patriclan partnerships are even more important than among the LoWiili, despite the presence of property-holding matriclans. For example, when I attended a LoWiili funeral for an old man, it was the women belonging to his matriclan's joking partners who at one point in the ceremony tried to collect the money thrown at the stand for the grave-diggers. Among the LoPiel, exactly the same acts were thought of as the main feature of patriclan joking partnerships. However, the matriclans certainly also had a role there in the network of joking partnerships. It is they who daub with whitewash persons begotten by the deceased's matriclan and who, in a more private capacity, kill a fowl at a dead elder's house to see whether a funeral should be held at all.

It is difficult to examine the operation of this partnership in detail, for there was little joking of any kind at the LoPiel funerals I attended in Tom, possibly owing to the influence of Christianity, which is negligible in the other areas in which I worked. My evidence therefore derives from statements about what formerly happened as distinct from the observational data presented for the other two groups. It is possible that formerly the matrilineal joking partners were more active at LoPiel funerals than I have suggested. But if the LoPiel have in fact always placed greater emphasis on the part played at funerals by patriclan joking partners than either of the other two communities, what is the explanation of this?

If we compare only the LoPiel and the LoWiili, it might be suggested that there was an adjustment of the relative weights placed on the alternative lines of descent, an increase in the role of the matriclan in the transmission of property being balanced by compensating emphasis upon the patriclan in the exchange of these funeral services. This type of explanation provides a neat solution that can rarely be rebutted.

Reference to the LoSaala, however, brings out the difficulties involved. For here the matrilineal inheritance of movable property is accompanied by an increased emphasis on the matriclan in this and in other contexts. A more probable interpretation seems to be that in systems of double descent certain tasks are transferred fairly easily from one system of descent groups to the other; activities that in one community are carried out by patriclan joking partners may in another be performed by their matrilineal counterparts. There is nothing that intrinsically ties such relationships to one line rather than another. What is important is that joking partners should be available to act as a counterbalance, and sometimes as a counterirritant, to those who have suffered loss: that there should be an explicit category of persons who can fill this useful role, which, though limited to a specific situation, bears some resemblance to that of the licensed fool at the medieval court.

There is one final aspect of this institution upon which I wish to comment here. The association of joking with the performance of services of affliction is a common feature of "funeral friendships" and one to which Griaule [1948] drew attention in his phrase *l'alliance cathartique*. In his stimulating treatment of the subject of "friendship" relations, Radcliffe-Brown criticized Griaule's use of this phrase and at the same time restated his earlier thesis that joking was a form of controlled antagonism, an expression both of detachment and attachment. We have seen that relative lack of involvement is an important aspect of these partnerships; indeed, it is because of their intermediary position that the joking partners can perform services for each other in times of crisis. There are other situations in which joking partners hurl insults at one another, when they may be thought of as engaging in a kind of moral equivalent of war, to use William James's phrase. Between relatively distant groups, this form of relating is in effect a substitute for more overt forms of aggression. And following a suggestion in psychological literature, Griaule claimed that such behavior in itself constitutes a cathartic purification of a part friendly, part hostile relationship.

But the action of the joking partners at funerals is somewhat different from this, for one of the two sides plays a distinctly passive role. The joking is directed by one side against the other, and it appears as an expression, and as an instrument, of the general change in the funeral ceremony. Insofar as these acts are instrumental in effecting this change, the joking partners may be regarded as performing a service of affliction on behalf of the bereaved, and it is certainly in such a light that the LoDagaa themselves view this behavior. There seems therefore to be some justification for the use of the phrase *alliance cathartique,* although only in a somewhat different sense from that implied by Griaule.

It should be noted that the LoDagaa regard joking, and to a lesser extent the ability to perform more specific services of affliction, as standing opposed to the unity in adversity that is demanded on the one hand by close ties and on the other by respect relationships. For instance, I had noticed how a frequent companion of mine used to joke and play with friends of his own age at funerals in his wife's home, although he was at the same time very punctilious in his attendances. However, when he encountered in-laws of a senior generation (*diem*) his attitude quite changed; for, he explained to me, "when your senior in-laws cry, you cry; you cannot play." The same is said of members of the patrilineage of one's mother; with them one does not snatch, one shares, one does not joke, one cries.

CHAPTER VII

The Burial of the Dead

"Don't you know," said he, "that it is not right to take a short
road with the coffin to the house of the dead nor yet with the
corpse to the grave?"

o'sullivan, *Twenty Years A-Growing*

MIMETIC PERFORMANCES OF ECONOMIC ACTIVITIES

The third day of the mortuary ceremony, the day of burial, opens with
the funeral hunt (*kuur mwo*). This token hunt is carried out by the
reciprocal funeral group of the agnates of the dead man and his mother,
sometimes in consort, sometimes separately. The role of the mother's
patrilineage here, as at other stages in the funeral ceremonies, is an instance of the important part played by matrilateral relationships in
societies with exogamous patrilineal descent groups.

When the sun is well up, the lineage males foregather with their
bows and arrows, their muzzle-loading guns, their throwing sticks, and
their dogs. They set off to some uncultivated land or to a field of
stubble and there try to flush a hare or a wild guinea-fowl. Whether
or not they have any success, they return shortly to the place of the
funeral. Anything caught during the course of the hunt would be
placed at the foot of the funeral stand, but I have never seen any booty
brought back from such expeditions.

This token hunt is a mimetic activity, similar in its explicit purpose and its implicit function to the mimetic rituals of the first and
second days. The survivors not only enact the achievements of the
deceased, but "act away" their associations with his ghost. In the words
of the LoDagaa, they repeat their joint activities for this last time in
order to "take out the dream"; that is, to prevent themselves from being
troubled by the dead man.

Hunting is not the only joint activity treated in this way. Usually some token farming is carried out on the same day. Members of the same farming group as the dead man, the group that jointly fulfills its obligations to in-laws, gather together with their hoes and start to weed the ground around the compound. A householder (*yirsob*), even if he still had such a commitment to his in-laws, would normally send the younger male members of the compound in his stead, and consequently no ritual hoeing takes place at the funeral of an older man.

The southward, dry-season migration of young men in search of temporary work is also regarded as a communal activity from which surviving participants must expunge their memory of the dead man. The distinguishing possession of a returning migrant is the wooden box in which he stores the things he has purchased with his earnings. As I have mentioned, these boxes (the dead man's and others brought from neighboring houses) are usually piled up at the foot of the stand to demonstrate the achievements of the deceased. When a man dies, those who have worked with him in the South may gather together and, putting the wooden boxes on their heads, carry them in procession as if they were returning to their homes after a season's hard but profitable labor in the richer areas of the country. I once saw the following episode. Some fifteen men were walking in procession, carrying loads, when several others approached, stepped up to a couple of the returning migrants, and pretended to question them as if they were police. A fight ensued, and the other actors joined in what proved to be a very realistic performance.

Shooting cowries is yet another such communal activity. Among the LoDagaba, this form of gambling was very popular in pre-Colonial days; inveterate gamblers journeyed round the various weekly markets, staking not only their money, but sometimes their cattle, their crops, and even their wives. I knew one man who claimed that his mother had changed hands in this way. Heavy gambling may take place during the funeral of an old man who has engaged in this pursuit during his lifetime.

At a woman's funeral there are parallel mimetic rites connected with her various domestic activities. Her small children may gather round the foot of the stand and be given a meal such as she used to prepare for them. Her patriclan "sisters" and the wives of her clan "brothers" and her female friends all bring earthenware pots or calabashes to the funeral, in the same way that men bring bunches of guinea-corn heads when a fellow clansman dies. The pots are placed around the stand; but just before the burial, the women who used to go to the pool to fetch water with the deceased collect them up, walk with them on their heads four times around the dead body, and then cast them to the ground so that they break into a multitude of small fragments. A few of the pots, however, will be salvaged from the pile by a joking partner and given to the full sister of the deceased.

These same women, who have worked with the dead woman either as a sibling, co-wife, or sister-in-law, go off into the bush to cut some firewood, which they bring back on their heads and again carry round the stand. On one occasion, the women also collected leaves of the kind they hang upon their waistbands.

These various mimetic performances re-enact the typical communal activities of men and women. Not only do they serve to restate publicly the behavior appropriate to male and female roles; they also help to redefine the social networks of the survivors which have been temporarily disorganized by the death of one of the persons significant to them.

FUNERAL SPEECHES: FRIENDS AND LOVERS

The actual burial is preceded by a series of funeral speeches addressed to the deceased. At a woman's funeral, these may be given by a female friend (*tshene*), by a lover (*sen*), by her children, or by her husband; at a man's death, it may be a male friend (*ba*), a lover (*sen*), a wife, the father, or the bride-giving in-laws. There is no overriding obligation upon any one of these people to make a speech (*mwolo*). Should a particular person choose to do so, it would be taken as an indication of the good personal relations, beyond strictly jural demands, that had existed between the two of them.

Both in form and in content these speeches closely resemble one another. A person approaches the stand accompanied by someone from his own clan sector to act as his crier and repeat the staccato phrases of the oration at the top of his voice for all to hear. At the side of the speaker and his crier stands a woman bearing on her head a pot of beer. When these three stand before the corpse, other members of the same clan sector get up from where they are sitting and gather round to form a semicircle facing the corpse. If the speaker is a friend of the deceased, which is the role most frequently celebrated in this way, he will tell in his speech how their friendship arose and the ways in which the dead man had helped him. Then he makes an offering of twenty cowries, which, he declares, is to pay the ferryman to transport the dead man across the river dividing the Land of the Living (*tenggaan tiung*) from the Land of the Dead (*kpime tiung*). Often the gift of twenty cowries is made with the further suggestion that these will allow the dead man to return at night and tell the speaker the cause of death, and, if necessary, to consult an other-worldly diviner about the matter. Having offered the cowries, the speaker produces the head of an arrow attached to a broken shaft (*pĩĩ ngmaa*). The barbed iron point is stuck in the hat that the dead man wears, so that on his way to the Land of the Dead he may have some means of shooting the witch who killed him. These arrows are subsequently given to the reciprocal funeral group, as are other "hot" or dangerous items of the dead man's possessions.

At this point the pot of beer and a cock are produced; they, too, are to help the dead man on his last journey and to enable him to be revenged upon the witches or sorcerers who killed him. These gifts are offered first to the dead man, and then the speaker asks that they be taken by anyone willing to replace the dead man as his friend. If no one is willing to accept the beer and the fowl, the speaker declares that now he knows his friend is indeed dead, for no one will ever take his place. If a man wished to end the relationship without speech-making, he would simply tie the cock to a post of the funeral stand, where it becomes the property of the grave-diggers.

As an example of such an oration, I give the text of a speech made by a LoSaala youth from Lawra at his friend's funeral (pp. 134–35). To a greater extent than any other instance I recorded, it elaborates upon the journey to the Land of the Dead and raises the question of the cause of the death. One point in particular may give the reader some difficulty. The speaker tells the dead man that even if his death was caused by another mortal, he should still carry on with his journey. But this advice contradicts the speaker's real intentions, for he knows that these remarks will only anger the ghost, so that he will at once return to take his revenge upon his killer. This question of vengeance will receive more attention when we consider the ancestor cult and beliefs about the afterlife.

The fact that the fowl and the beer, the main elements in the gifts offered to the dead man, are also offered to the person who is prepared to fill his place in the dyadic relationship emphasizes two of the main features of funeral ceremonies. There is, on the one hand, the physical separation of the deceased from the world of the living and his social separation from the network of relationships that surrounded him; on the other, there are the integrative aspects, the redistribution of the rights and duties of the dead man and his incorporation into the community of the ancestors.

The question of the redistribution of rights and duties calls for some discussion at this juncture. For the presentation of the gifts is not merely a celebration of the way in which the deceased acted in a particular role; it is also a public request for another person to fill the gap left by the dead man in the social network of the bereaved. The problem of replacement is a matter of finding somebody else not only to fill a prescribed role, but to fill it as satisfactorily as the deceased had done. The institution of funeral speeches demonstrates how even aspects of social relations that have little or no jural significance are readjusted during the course of the ceremonies by the mechanism of direct substitution. The LoDagaa are loath to extinguish any of the dead man's relationships; hence the funeral ceremonies provide institutionalized methods for the taking over of these roles by other persons. During the course of the burial service certain relationships that have been marked by satisfactory personal feelings are provisionally reorganized, and among these are the relationships centering upon the dead man's activities as friend and lover. Then, at the final ceremony, his roles as husband and father are also formally handed over to others.

It is true, of course, that in any system in which the kinship terms denote classes of persons rather than individuals, the place of any particular person is in a sense automatically filled by another member of the same category. But what occurs in the LoDagaa funeral ceremonies is a formal transfer of position. Not all the dead man's roles are treated in this way, and no specific substitute is provided for the dead man as sibling and as son. The formal perpetuation of some roles rather than others appears to depend upon the part they play in the total social system. The continuance of the role of husband, by means of the levirate, is related to the fact that when the deceased acquired rights over women by the transfer of bridewealth, he did so as a member of a property-holding corporation. The perpetuation of the role of father is associated partly with the need to provide guardians for jural minors, but also, on a more general level, with the maintenance of the authority structure of the society; for it is not only the fathers of young persons who are replaced.

In a general and very important sense, all roles exist independently of the individuals who occupy them. But here we are dealing with a different phenomenon. By this mechanism of substitution, specific networks of social relationships are maintained intact despite the death of one of the individual members, when this is important to the social system. Thus the roles of husband and father are reallocated; whereas, in the absence of similar structural reasons, those of sibling and son are not.

O be in bummo.
I've come for no bad reason.

Etshe ma ni a fu tũ ta
Just that you and I were inseparable

a yoo vla vla zaa.
and went everywhere without any trouble.

E ka i Na'angmin tome
But it was God's will

ka diã biu
that this morning

ka be buole fu kũ.
people should say you were dead.

Etshe ma ni a fũ
But you and I

mi dong nebe
used to walk together

a nibe zaa bongnia.
and all men knew it.

Etshe Na'angmin wa de fu.
Then God came to take you.

Alena n yil
So I said to myself

n na wana
I would bring

a dãã yuor nya.
that pot of beer.

Alena ti dong ir
Thus we used to do

a nibe zaa nyere.
for everyone to see.

Alzu n wana
So I brought along

dãã yuor nya wa kob
this beer to give you

e fu nyuu.
to drink.

Etshe lo sor vla, vla, vla
Have a good journey

o ko yi yil fu zie.
and may nothing trouble you.

Etshe a nuura,
And this cock,

fu na dena
take it

tshereni.
along with you.

Fu na mani gani zie kõ,
If you want to go anywhere,

a nuura o na ma tshong a zi lighe,
the cock will always get up at dawn,

koli,
and crow,

e fu le ir
and you'll get up too

le tsheri.
and set off again.

Fu na tera a nuura vla vla vla
Look after the fowl well

tshereni.
as you go on your way.

O na wan kolena e fu ir.
If it crows, get up.

Deb zaa ma tshereni
Every man who sets off

e tera nuura.
takes a cock with him.

Fu na tan a fu yir,
And when you reach your house,

fu puri fu nibe vla vla zaa.
greet all your people warmly.

E yil be kabe
May there be nothing wrong there

e be kana a ting vla.
and may they look after the place well.

Etshe alena in nire naa
Whether it was that somebody

wa bong a fu zie
killed you

ma ni fu na tshole-a
because you and I went together

a nibe puo be pele;
and people were angry (lit. "their bellies
    were not white");

al wa i nire-no na bong a fu zie,
whether it was because of this you were
    killed,

bi fūno wa bobr nira
or because you yourself wanted (to eat)
    somebody

a Na'angmin wa ir fu,
and God took you away,

fu na doniu tsheri
go ahead

n wa tur fu pur.
and I will follow you.

Etshe a lizer na n kofu
And these twenty cowries I give you

fu na tsheghi
so you may pay

na a Man
at the River

etshe gon.
and get across.

Nye sor vla
Have a good journey

e tshen fu nibe zie.
and go to see your people.

Ni a pīī nya,
And this arrow,

fu na de tshen
take it along

teb a suoba.
and shoot the witch.

A dāā nya,
As for the beer,

na'a nuura,
and the fowl,

ka nir wa be be
if there is anyone

ka tin le ter ta
who will be to me

a le na ma ni n ba,
as my friend was,

o de a dāā a yong nuura.
let him take the beer and fowl.

Ti nir be kabe,
But if there's no one,

yi bar me n dire kuoneni,
let me drink and weep,

ti bong ka a baara diā.
and know that the friendship dies today.

Among the LoDagaa, friendship between males is the most important of these self-perpetuating relationships outside the sphere of kinship and affinity. As in the case of the institutionalized friendships that make possible certain widespread systems of trading such as the *kula* of the Trobriands, one of its main functions is to supplement the ties of extraclan kinship, either by binding together individual members of potentially hostile groupings, or by creating additional bonds with persons belonging to the groups into which one marries (which are in a sense opposed to one's own agnatic group by the very fact of being composed of non-clansmen).

The institution of friendship has received comparatively little attention from anthropologists; for example, there is no entry under this heading in the index to the latest edition of *Notes and Queries*. This neglect is particularly strange in view of the fact that in our own society friendship networks often have some of the functions that are elsewhere allocated to local or descent groups. Herskovits has discussed the importance of the role of best friend in Dahomey ([1938] I, 239). Fortes mentions the existence of friendships among the Tallensi, where he sees them as arising out of kinship ties. He writes that although friends are not necessarily kinsmen, they very often have common kin ([1949] p. 337). Among the LoDagaa, as among the Australian aborigines, any two individuals can find a kinship term by which to address one another, so that all relationships may be said to occur between kin. But for the LoDagaa, friendship is nevertheless something different from kinship. It crosscuts kinship ties and is a voluntary relationship differing in this respect from the joking partnerships existing between descent and other groups, which are often spoken of in accounts of other African societies as "funeral friendships."

To emphasize the independent status of these ties, some account of the development of friendship between males (*balo*) is necessary. Spontaneous friendships arise in a person's first work group, that is, in the small groups of young boys who are sent out to keep the livestock away from cultivated land during the season when cattle might trample upon the growing crops. These boys leave early in the morning and do not return until nightfall. Whereas the child's peer group has previously consisted largely of children from his own and adjacent compounds, usually members of the same clan sector, he now meets lads from other clans inhabiting the same or neighboring settlements, those same groups from which his wives will probably come. It is from his fellow herd-boys that a man will usually choose his particular friend. Friendship in this sense is essentially an extraclan relationship. Moreover, it would be unlikely for a boy to find friends among his mother's patriclan; for with members of these groups standardized relationships already exist. Friendship voluntarily extends "close" ties outside the usual range of such relationships. "People are like the shoots of a creeper," one man said to me on the subject of friendship, meaning that connections spread everywhere.

I use the word "friend" here to translate the more restricted usage of the word *ba*, which in its most general sense can be used for any other male with whom one is on good terms, even an agnate or a matrilateral kinsman. This wider usage, however, does not imply the specific obligations that are involved in extraclan friendship. A best friend, as distinct from a friend in the more diffuse sense, may be called upon to help on any occasion, when a debt presses, when negotiations with prospective in-laws are required, and in many other circumstances. No formality marks the beginning of such friendship, though I once heard it said that formerly great friends might cut their wrists and drink each other's blood. Nor is there in principle any limitation on the number of best friends a person can have.

At the death of such a friend a man takes to the funeral a white fowl and a bunch of guinea-corn heads or twenty cowries. These gifts are either offered formally during the course of a funeral speech, in which case a pot of beer and a broken arrow are also given, or else presented to the patrilineage of the dead man to be given to one of his children, or possibly to a "brother" if the children are too young. The person who accepts these objects then becomes the friend of his dead kinsman's former friend. He has the same obligation toward him as the latter had toward his father or brother, and will make the same presentation of the "friend's fowl" (*ba nuura*) at the funeral of the man whose gifts he has taken. In this way the friendship may be handed down from generation to generation.

The institution of friendship between males differs from the other types of personal relationship that are celebrated in funeral speeches. In the other cases, too, an individual may seek a substitute for the original partner. At the death of his lover a man may offer a guinea-fowl, the bird that replaces the fowl in most ritual acts concerning women. This gift may be taken by a woman married into the same lineage as his late mistress. Nevertheless, friendships between persons of different sexes, between women, and between in-laws are more transitory than those between males, and in this sense are less relevant to the wider social system.

One example may serve to illustrate the persistence of these relationships over time. My field work among the LoDagaba was mainly carried out at Tom, the birthplace of Timbume, a member of my staff, who had not visited the village for many years. When we arrived there, his own patrilineage paid little attention to us, although perhaps the lack of a senior man had something to do with this. His mother's patrilineage, with whom he had lived after his own father had died, were certainly more solicitous. But the person who took him under his wing was the friend of his late father. This man was introduced to me as "my father's friend," and this was the reason constantly given for his allegedly disinterested attentions. The institution of friendship is more widespread among the LoDagaba than the LoWiili, a fact possibly connected with the smaller agnatic clans; but among both communities it is an important form of interpersonal relationship, and one which, by the particular method of its perpetuation at the death of one of the partners, is set within a lineage context.

By the same mechanism, the lover relationship perpetuates itself after the death of one of the partners. Both men and women address and refer to a number of people of the opposite sex as lover, just as they do friend. But a man's true love is a woman who declares so openly by bringing him a dish of shea butter, or by always putting aside a pot of beer for him whenever she brews. "A lover is sweeter than a wife," a man once told me, and all those present agreed. She has no jurally enforceable rights and obligations; what she does is done on a voluntary, personal basis. The LoDagaa maintain that such a relationship can only exist between men and women who are not married to one another. They also say that marriage, essential for the establishment of conjugal families and for the legitimization and socialization of children, changes the very basis of this "love" relationship. You can beat a wife, they say, but never a lover, for she would only go elsewhere.[1] And though most men will only rarely be seen sitting and talking to their wives, and never drinking beer cheek by cheek out of the same calabash, a lover will often be called over to chat and to drink in this way.

Sometimes the relationship is given an even more formal recognition than this. If a husband sees his wife continually putting beer aside for another man or displaying affection in other ways, he may approach his wife's "lover" with a request to bring a fowl and 360 cowries. The fowl will then be killed at the ancestor shrines of the compound, and the woman and her lover can then sleep together without any fear of an accusation of adultery being leveled against them. Of course this sacrifice would be undertaken only if good relations existed between

---

[1] Labouret states that a man can beat his lover if she is unfaithful. He describes a more institutionalized form than I encountered ([1920] p. 281).

the men concerned and if the husband had more than one wife. In any case, this custom is, I judge, but rarely practiced.

An alternative method of formalizing the relationship is for the lover himself to approach the husband through an intermediary, possibly one of the husband's brothers. This custom is known as "the lover enters the room" (*sen kpe diu*) and has a further variant. If a husband cannot have children by his wife, he may approach an elder of his patrilineage and ask him to arrange for another member, a classificatory "brother," chosen by the woman, to sleep with her. Tauxier and Labouret raise the question as to whether this custom, also reported by Rattray for the neighboring Sisala and Dagaba, should be considered a form of polyandry. Writing about the "Dagari" (i.e., the LoDagaba), Labouret ([1920] p. 280) treats the lover as co-husband on the grounds that by entering into such a union he is obliged to farm for the senior husband, just as the latter has to farm for the girl's in-laws. This kind of farming service is also found among the LoDagaa, but it hardly warrants the name of polyandry. Although the relationship is of a more permanent kind than the sexual access that hospitality requires among the Eskimo, I would nevertheless consider this a form of cicisbeism, a legitimization of equal access to married women, rather than an instance of polyandry. The existence of farming services makes no real difference. Indeed, the reverse situation occurs among the LoDagaba where, unlike the LoWiili, women do light work on the farm, and the mistress may bring her female friends to weed a groundnut field for her lover. In neither case does farming imply a marital relationship. And even when the lover produces a fowl to be sacrificed to the ancestor shrine, this act serves only to legitimize access; the woman's husband remains the *pater* of her offspring, whoever the biological father may be. An institution somewhat closer to polyandry of the adelphic kind exists in the LoDagaa custom whereby the wife of the elder of twin siblings is accessible to the younger until the latter marries a wife of his own. But I would again consider this to be tolerated access, rather than polyandry, since the children are all regarded as born of the elder brother.

There is one final point to note about the funeral speeches, another indication of the standardized differences in the grief displayed at the funerals of young and old. I have never heard a formal speech at the funeral of an old man; for such a person has usually become so infirm that he has ceased to maintain the affective relationships that call forth these orations. His surviving contemporaries are few, and even the authority of his lineage position may in practice be exercised by another. At his funeral the chants are more tempered, and there is in general greater emphasis on the reallocation of the major roles of the deceased than on the readjustment of these relationships of a personal, non-jural character. But although in these circumstances there is no set speech, friendship, as distinct from extramarital love, does receive institutionalized recognition; for it has more than an individual significance, being set within the framework of lineage ties. Whatever the age of the dead man, his best friend will bring a "friend's fowl," which is accepted by one of the deceased's close agnates. Friendship is the only one of these relationships likely to persist into old age. Moreover, it is the only one to be given recognition in this way by the descent group.

CARRYING THE CORPSE TO THE GRAVE

The speeches over, the funeral moves rapidly toward the actual burial. This is immediately preceded by the disposal of the medicine associated with the dead man's shrine to the beings of the wild, often known in the literature of West Africa as fairies, and which I have elsewhere referred to as hill and water sprites (*kontome*). Among the Lo-Wiili the majority of adults have shrines to these beings, whereas among the LoDagaba shrines to "gods" (*ngmini*) are correspondingly more frequent; both are used for divinatory purposes. The medicine associated with these beings of the wild has to be neutralized before burial, since unlike most other shrines this is personal to the dead man. The rite is carried out by four men and four women belonging to the reciprocal funeral group to that of the deceased, or to that of her husband if she is a married woman. Two of the women are "wives," and two "daughters," of the deceased; and apart from the leader, the men are his "sons." These eight persons enter the dead man's byre in slow procession to fetch the medicine. They emerge, male and female alternately, and walk three (or four) times round the stand, halt in front of the body, then raising the palms of their hands together, blow the powdered medicine over the corpse. Rattray was told that "The power of the dead man's 'medicine' is thus spoiled, and he is prevented taking it away with him" ([1932] p. 444, n. 1).[2]

With the throwing away of this medicine, the climax of the funeral

---

[2] The reference is to the disposal of the medicine of the *Batibe* shrine, a kind of specialized sprite shrine associated with carved wooden figures, which are often connected with divination. I have seen this rite performed at only one funeral, whereas the disposal of the sprite medicine was a constant feature of LoWiili funerals.

is reached. The four men who have participated go over to the xylophone, where they are joined by others. The women, on the other hand, gather round the corpse, lamenting. At the xylophone the senior member of the reciprocal funeral group, or someone delegated by him, chants three (or four) times the solemn phrase,

A baara ye-e.
All is finished.

The cry is taken up in a heart-rending fashion by all those standing around. Then the xylophone plays a particular phrase three (or four) times,[3] and at this signal the grave-diggers approach the stand, throw off the cloths, wrap the body in a new mat, and bear it away to the grave. The women wail at the top of their voices while the men chant loudly around the xylophone. At this critical moment the surviving spouse is held firmly by funeral companions. I have seen a husband dragged bodily from the scene to prevent him trying to follow his dead wife. At the same time the xylophone plays more vigorously than ever, and some of the younger women dance with all their energy as the body is carried off. In the old days this moment was a still more anxious one, since (as in many parts of Ghana) the carrying of the corpse to the grave was sometimes used as a method of discovering who had killed the dead man.

The grave-diggers who are not actually carrying the body hastily tear down the stand, collect the crops, money, and fowl that belong to them, and carry off the wooden posts, to throw them in some stream bed where they can cause no harm. The grave-diggers come back later and brush with ebony leaves the cloths that have been lent to decorate the funeral stand, and these can now be collected by their owners.

If the dead man was a real homicide, a further ceremony has to be performed, after casting away the medicine but before the final notes are played on the xylophone. The senior homicide approaches the corpse carrying a small chicken, while other members of the lineage blow war and hunting horns and bear their bows and arrows in a menacing manner. Their leader takes a piece of the *soro* root (left near the dead body from the earlier ritual), peels a portion of it, and cuts a V-shaped slit in it. Having done this, he slits the throat of the chicken, letting the blood drip over the *soro* root and upon the left shoulder of the corpse. At this the men surrounding him break into a war dance, in which the other homicides are particularly conspicuous, displaying

---

[3] This phrase consists of chords of the second and seventh, followed by the third and eighth, notes; these pair are both "brothers" (*yoor*), that is, intervals of an octave.

their bravery by kicking at the xylophone and threatening each other with their bows. This is the final public rite of those that serve to purify, celebrate, and dismiss the dead body of a man who has killed another human being.

THE BURIAL OF THE BODY

The grave-diggers begin preparing the grave on the first day of the burial ceremony, directly they have finished erecting the stand. What they have to do depends upon the social condition of the individual to be buried in it. For in the whole sequence of funeral ceremonies differences in the form of burial are perhaps the most precise summation of the social personality of the deceased. In this more than in any other aspect of the ceremony, the controlling factor is a social one, particularly since the mode of burial varies not only with status distinctions of a relatively permanent kind, but also with the manner in which an individual has conducted himself within a given role. For example, in many societies royalty is accorded a different form of burial from commoners, and these special procedures may be linked, as among the Ashanti, to the sacredness of kings and to their "divinity" after death. But in addition to this, we often find that wrongdoers of one kind or another, parricides, suicides, witches, are given forms of burial that radically distinguish them from those who have observed the social norms.

These general principles hold true for the LoDagaa, among whom there are three main modes of disposing of the dead. The normal form is inhumation in a bell-shaped chamber, either in the local cemetery or else in the courtyard of the compound itself; the second is the building of a mound above the corpse; and the third consists in burial in a trench grave.

Cemetery Graves

In ordinary burials it is customary to dig a new grave (*bo zio,* a "red" grave) in the local cemetery for each group of full brothers, a long and arduous procedure. There is approximately one cemetery for each patrilineage, the members of which usually live close together. Burial is a matter of locality rather than descent; husbands and wives and members of other lineages living in the same house are all buried in the neighborhood cemetery, the location of which is determined partly by dislike of transporting a rotten corpse for any great distance and partly by the need for sufficient depth of soil in which to dig. Interment in a cemetery is known as burial in the bush, *mwo puo.*

Like house-building and farming, the digging of a grave makes direct use of the soil, and throughout the Voltaic area these activities are frequently associated with the Earth shrine. Among the LoDagaba, as in many neighboring communities, it is the custodian of this shrine who selects a suitable place for a cemetery and marks out the opening to each grave with the aid of a large, unscraped calabash. This he places on the ground where the grave is to be dug and then sprinkles some ashes around the perimeter of the gourd. After this he sacrifices the fowl provided by the senior mourner and formally begins the task of digging the grave by breaking the ground three times with his hoe, as he does when a new house is built and sometimes when new land is brought under cultivation (Labouret [1931], p. 324; Rattray [1932], p. 445).[4] The LoWiili, however, delegate this task to the grave-diggers themselves, for what appear to be purely numerical reasons. The parish of Birifu is so heavily populated that it would be virtually impossible for the custodian to carry out the duties of marking out each grave and digging the first sod for the foundations of every house, as is done in neighboring communities. These tasks are decentralized to the level of the minor ritual area, where such matters are integrated with the organization of the clan sector.

The opening of this grave is only big enough to permit a body to slide into it. It widens out into an oblong or a bell-shaped chamber, in which two "benches" of earth are left for the corpses, with smaller heaps for headrests. When the grave is finished, it is inspected by the senior mourner or his lineage elder. If a woman is being buried, then her own patrilineage have to say the word before the actual interment can take place, unless the cattle payment, the second installment of the bridewealth, has been paid. A guinea-corn stalk is placed across the mouth of the grave in order to stop the souls of those attending from entering, voluntarily or by force, and hence from getting buried together with the corpse. The same protection is often given to the pots of beer brought to the funeral; for it is feared that ghosts, the transformed souls that have not yet settled in the Land of the Dead, may contaminate the liquor by trying to drink it.

The grave is now ready. The LoDagaba bury their dead only in the morning or evening; for they believe that when the sun is shining directly into the tomb, someone's soul may be basking there. The LoWiili are aware of this belief, but the question is not one that con-

---

4 In Birifu the digging of the grave is sometimes begun with an axe-blade fitted to a long, straight stick.

cerns them greatly. When the time of burial arrives, the grave-diggers wrap the body in a mat and carry it to the grave, which has been temporarily covered with a pot. The senior sexton takes a piece of thorn tree, a knife, and a spiky grass called *kalinyãã*, which looks like wild barley and is used in a number of other purificatory procedures, in cleansing the Earth shrine during the expiatory rites for a suicide and in washing an ancestor shrine in the course of the subsequent funeral ceremonies. These sharp objects will expel any soul that, deliberately or accidentally, may have entered the grave.

One man stands inside the chamber, the top of his head just showing through the narrow entrance; a cloth is held up to screen the operations from the spectators, and the body is passed down inside the grave for burial. There the corpse is laid on its side in a sleeping position, with one hand under the cheek and the other folded across the chest (Rattray [1932] p. 446). A man is laid on his right side, facing east; this is done, they say, so that the rising sun will tell him to prepare for the hunt or for the farm. A woman rests on her left side, facing west, so that the setting sun will warn her when to prepare the meal for her husband's homecoming.

Earlier we saw how male and female were associated with the numbers three and four respectively, while here they are linked with east and west, with the rising and setting of the sun, perhaps even with day and night. The asymmetric duality of the sexes, of odd and even, and of the right and left hands are often connected with one another in man's picture of the world, and at the same time the terms in each pair are allotted different moral values.

Hertz sees the distinctions that relate to man's body, together with those applied to spatial orientation, as having their origin not in facts of a physical order, but in the opposition of the sacred and the profane; they form part of "the dualism which is inherent in primitive thought" ([1960] p. 110). Recourse to the sacred and profane dichotomy as an explanatory device seems to me no more useful here than in other contexts. Part of Hertz's difficulty lay in the fact that he was avowedly looking for "origins" of universal (or near universal) human phenomena; satisfactory evidence for making an assessment of this kind is hard, if not impossible, to produce, and Hertz adopts the usual Durkheimian approach of playing down the significance of the physical data. In view of the sway of instinctual psychology at that time, such an orientation had, and still has, much to be said in its favor. But it was also part, as it still is, of the ideology of the attempt to gain independent recognition for the social sciences, just as attempts to devalue the physical, as against the social, differences between male and female have served the feminist cause. I am only concerned to point out that if the problem of social or non-social determinants, of nature or nurture, is capable of any solution at all, it should be approached from a more empirical angle than marks the work of many investigators.

In the present case, one does not need to look much further than "the nature of things" to find an adequate basis for many "dualistic" conceptions of the human body and its sexual roles, and even of certain aspects of the asymmetrical value accorded to the opposed terms. "Social" elements are, of course, also relevant, particularly in accounting for the differences between societies. But it hardly needs the apparatus of comparative sociology to demonstrate that man prefers to classify in terms of a small, rather than a large, number of categories. One aspect of this so-called "primitive dualism" is simply the fact that in conceptualizing A, one implies non-A, or, in other words, B. That the LoDagaa link such opposites together in networks of association is only to be expected. What one has to guard against is giving them too great an importance by too readily extending their scope.

There are three general points to bear in mind about the elucidation of such networks. First, it should be clearly stated whether such a categorization is an explicit part of the actor's frame of reference, or whether it is a construct of the observer's—not an easy injunction for the anthropologist to follow. Second, in deriving generalized tables of equivalence and schemata of a very abstract kind, it must be remembered that the more general we make our categories, the greater the probability that an impressive quantity of material can be classified under them.[5] Third, it should be kept in mind that most associations of this kind are contextual, as Evans-Pritchard has insisted in his analysis of Nuer symbolism, whereas tables of equivalence tend to suggest that the associations that they record apply in every situation.

One could extend the LoDagaa dichotomy between male and female categories somewhat further than I have done here. For example, the Earth is held to be feminine, the Sky (or Rain) masculine. On the other hand, there is no indication that the LoDagaa make any general association between the Earth and either the number four or the direction

---

[5] For ingenious examples of highly generalized tables of equivalence, see Hocart [1936], p. 227, and for a cogent discussion of the dangers involved, see Brough's criticism of Dumézil's *L'Idéologie tripartie des Indo-Européens*. Here Brough tries to show that the tripartite structure with its three functions, which Dumézil regards as typically and exclusively Indo-European, can also be discerned with equal ease in the ideology of the Ancient Hebrews, given a sufficiently sympathetic observer (Brough [1959]).

west. The Earth is female in its procreative aspect; however, it is linked not only to the planting carried out by women, but also to the preparation of the fields, the tending of the growing plants, the harvesting of the ripened grain, all of which are in the hands of men. In other situations, the Earth as the inhabited area stands opposed to the uninhabited Bush, in others to the Ancestors; but it would be misleading to associate the last two terms of the "equations" on these grounds alone. We are faced here with networks more complex than radical dualisms or tripartite divisions.

When all is finished, the tomb is closed. It may be covered with either a pot or a stone. A grave covered with a pot is known as *yaaro* and is never reopened; only when the last child of one mother has died, when the full sibling group has ceased to exist, will the grave be covered in this way. As I have remarked, a small round calabash is put in the mouth of the last member of a group of brothers to die. This metaphor of closure implies finality and is indicative of the weight placed upon the group of full brothers, those defined by reference to one mother. The other type of normal grave, known as *yoo kpul,* is covered with a stone, which can be removed if another sibling or a sibling's wife is to be buried in the same tomb. But the grave is never reopened in the case of certain "bad deaths" (*kũ faa*)—that is, when the immediate cause of death has been snake bite, leprosy, severe headaches (probably cerebrospinal meningitis), continuous coughs (possibly tuberculosis), anthrax, pox, or elephantiasis—because of the supposed danger of infection.

When the tomb has been covered, the four grave-diggers grasp the same hoe and dig into the piled-up earth that has been taken from the grave. Whereupon the senior grave-digger takes a calabash of water and splashes it on the earth that they have gathered together. Each then takes a turn at mixing the earth and water into mud, passing the hoe swiftly from one to the other as they finish. The senior man fills the gaps around the side of the pot or stone; each of them then grabs a handful of the swish and, passing it around the grave three times, lets it fall onto the surface of the pot. Each, again, takes more mud until the pot or stone is covered completely. Finally, they dig up some dry earth to spread over the whole. Sometimes, at the end, the handle of the hoe they have used is stuck on top of the mound.

The grave is now properly closed. A woman belonging to the burial group fetches a calabash of water in which the following have been soaked: strophanthus leaves, the main constituent of arrow poisons; heads of the sharp-pointed *kalinyãã* grass; and *kõkõ* leaves (*Ficus gnaphalocarpus*), another tree with many ritual usages and one especially associated with the beings of the wild. The senior grave-digger takes the calabash and makes three attempts to pour the liquid upon the outstretched hands of the grave-diggers. On each occasion they withdraw their hands and allow the water to fall upon the grave itself. The fourth time they let the water run over their hands, and all wash together, thus cleansing themselves from contact with the corpse. This ritual of pretended gesture is the same as that adopted in earlier dealings with the dead. All that remains is for the grave-diggers to divide out the money that has been thrown at the foot of the funeral stand, to cut up any chickens or larger animals that have been tied there, and to collect any crops or other objects to which they are entitled.

Courtyard Graves

I have already mentioned the various ways in which the funeral of a grandparent differs from that of a younger person. Perhaps the most dramatic manner of celebrating their different status is the mode of burial itself. For whereas other members of the community are carried "into the bush" for inhumation, grandparents are buried inside the courtyard of the house they have helped to "build," in an old grave (*bo soola*, a "black" grave), constructed in the same manner as those located in the cemetery. Since I have already considered the social implications of grandparenthood, I shall confine my attention to one particular rite that occurs at such burials.

Before the grave is finally closed, a crowd of women and small children collect around the opening of the tomb; the senior grave-digger takes the children one by one and bends their heads over the hole (*be mwoli a boo*), supposedly three times for a boy and four for a girl, in return for which the mother hands him a few cowries. In Tom, the child is actually taken into the grave and made to hack away at the earth three times as if he were a grave-digger, collect the soil in a calabash, and then empty it out again. Children below the age of puberty are not usually permitted at funerals, but those who are still being breast-fed are often carried there on their mothers' backs. Moreover, children belonging to the compound of the dead man are bound to be present for at least part of the time. These children who attend are especially susceptible to maleficent influences present at the place of burial, and the homeopathic measure described above is taken to prevent them from dreaming of the deceased (Labouret [1931], p. 324). It is also supposed to prevent any harm coming to the child from treading on the courtyard grave. Sometimes at ordinary funerals one post of the stand is left in position after the body has been carried off for burial,

and mothers bring their children to a grave-digger, who puts their heads
or hands against it (*be longnina daa*), and often sprinkles some ashes
on their hair, so that no harm will come to them if they accidentally
touch such a post in the future.

The rule that young children should not attend these performances
is one of a number of rules excluding children from adult activities,
such as full-scale hunting; so that when they have to accompany the
mother, special protective procedures are required. But, as I have remarked in another context, there is a further element in the situation.
Children are the most vulnerable members of the community; the high
rate of infant mortality is a constant source of anxiety and is connected with a large number of practices centering upon various medicine
shrines. Consequently, when young children come near the scene of
any death, they are subjected to special precautions against possible
dangers.

The grave is closed by the grave-diggers in the normal way. A day
or two after the interment, the women of the neighborhood come and
plaster the top with one of their waterproofing mixtures, usually of
cow dung and swish. For this they are rewarded by the housepeople,
as well as by any passer-by, whom they may call upon to contribute a
handful or two of cowries.

Mound Graves

The digging of a new chamber grave is a long and arduous process,
and the privilege of being buried in one is not extended to those members of the community who are considered dangerous and who therefore have to be disposed of either as quickly as possible or else outside
the boundaries of the parish altogether. When a serious epidemic causes
many deaths in a short space of time, a common trench grave is dug for
all the corpses. But in other cases, the principle underlying the special
mode of disposing of the dead appears to be the avoidance of burial
within the earth itself. For the Earth is not only the custodian of
corpses; she is also the guardian of the living. In this second capacity
she is associated with the main activities of human life—farming, childbearing, housebuilding, smithying, trading, the making of pots, and
the playing of xylophones. This dual aspect of the Earth is a prevalent
feature of West African religions and indeed of the beliefs of many
other agricultural societies. In Ashanti, the dichotomy is recognized
in the distinction between *Asaase Afua,* the fertile Earth, and *Asaase
Yaa,* the barren Earth (Meyerowitz [1951], pp. 76–77). Among the
LoDagaa, the interment of an evil-doer below the surface of the earth

might adversely affect any of these important activities, especially the fertility of crops and of women.

One way of minimizing contact with the earth is to build the grave above ground. The corpses of young children, those who have not yet been weaned and can neither walk nor talk properly, are buried under a pile of earth at the side of a crossroads on the path leading to the mother's home. The pile is covered with thorns to keep the dogs from scratching up the corpse, and also it is said to keep the "spirit" of the child from escaping. On top is placed the wicker cradle in which the child slept, and through it a stake is driven.

An unweaned child is only a potential human being; he has not yet achieved a social personality. For the emergence of a new personality is not necessarily tied to the moment of birth. In European societies, some religious groups fix upon an earlier point in time, whereas the LoDagaa, like many African peoples, settle upon a later one. For them, a child is not entitled to a human burial until it has been weaned, a process that does not normally take place until the third year of its existence. Up to this time the child is orally dependent upon the mother, and its social personality is in most contexts merged in hers. An infant of this age is considered to be without two of the basic attributes of humanity—the capacity to walk and to talk. Yet another criterion for the presence of a social personality, a criterion with a number of implications, is whether or not a following sibling has been born (*o tera tuuri*). When a new infant arrives, then it is thought that the first child is no passing visitor.

Thus the LoDagaa display no public grief at the death of an unweaned child, for it is not yet accorded human status. Indeed, if the child dies before being ritually taken out of the house three (or four) months after birth, not even the parents always mourn. For an older but still unweaned child, the parents may weep, but the xylophones are silent; the funeral is almost entirely a domestic affair. The mother, accompanied by another woman, goes off to tell her natal kinsfolk, and the father is taken to a neighboring house and given drink. Meanwhile the sextons break the child's eating gourds as well as the pot that has been used for heating the "medicine" in which the child is bathed. As a reward they collect the few guinea-corn heads and cowries that have been thrown on the corpse. The assembled company wait for the mother to return with some of her kinswomen; when she arrives, a little milk is squeezed from her breasts to be fed to the dead child, and the burial takes place without further ceremony.

It is not simply that children of this age are no loss to the wider community beyond the elementary family. Children who die young are seen as doing so deliberately; they are a positive danger and are often spoken of as beings of the wild (*kontome*) who have come to plague the mother. It is not just a question of getting rid of them, but doing so for good; for they may play this trick of being born and dying a number of times in order to harass the parents. The driving of the stake through the cradle is an attempt to prevent such a child from returning again to the belly of his mother and so spoiling her parturition (*dobo*). A child whose elder sibling has died is believed to be that elder sibling himself, though no longer possessed by a sprite. He is known as a *tshaakuor* or *lewa*, "one who comes back," is called by the special personal name of Der, or Yuora in the case of a girl, and is usually marked on the cheek with a cut so that he can be identified if he dies and returns again yet a third time. Sometimes the grave-diggers will make a series of cuts on the corpse of such a child. These cuts resemble the facial marks normally worn by the "Farafara," which is a generic name given to Mossi-speaking peoples of the Bolgatanga area, such as the Tallensi, with whom there is a joking relationship of the most inclusive range. Then when the same mother bears again, the women who first bathe the newborn child look for evidence of such marks, and if they discern any, exclaim: "He's come back! He's come back!" (*o le ba wa*). The intended effect of such cries is to shame (*yongna vii*) the errant child into staying on this earth; for it is thought that if he knows that others are aware of what he is about, he will no longer plague the mother.[6] If these measures are not effective and a third death occurs, the body is buried not on the side of the path leading to the mother's home, but in one of the tall anthills scattered throughout the bush, so that the child's remains will be utterly destroyed. A burial of the same type is given to a child who has been grossly deformed from birth.

The burial at the crossroads with a stake driven through the grave bears a striking similarity to the treatment of murderers, and particularly witches, in medieval Europe. Indeed, such a practice continued in England well into the last century. This similarity derives, I believe, from the fact that in the burial both of infants among the LoDagaa and of the blood guilty in Europe, the community is concerned to separate completely certain categories of unwanted persons from the living and

---

[6] I have also known such cuts to be made as a kind of disguise on older children who are suffering from some sickness; a sickly child may also have his or her name changed for a similar reason, and the tribal name "Mossi" is sometimes used for such a purpose.

from the ordinary dead. They are separated, of course, by the mere fact of being distinguished. But more precise images are involved. The stake is driven through the corpse not only to destroy it but to fasten it to one place. At the same time, burial at the crossroads involves an image of dispersal, both because the paths go their different ways and because it is a place where strangers foregather. In addition, the LoDagaa say that even if the sprite did break loose, the crossroads would confuse its attempts to return to the mother's womb. Thus the same ritual themes appear to be common to this type of burial in both these societies.

Trench Graves

When a number of people die as the result of an epidemic, they may be buried all together in a trench grave. Individual graves of this kind, dug in the bank of a river or in the dry bed of a stream, constitute one way of dealing with sinners against the Earth shrine. For it is said that when the rains come and the river rises or the stream bed fills with water, the corpse, or at least its impurities, will be washed outside the confines of the parish. The underlying theme is indeed very similar to that behind the treatment of the bat in the Vukãle ceremony.

This is but one of the ways of distinguishing those who have died an evil death (*kũ faa*) and have been killed by the Earth shrine (*tenggaan kũ*). No public mourning takes place, for it is forbidden to play the xylophone, an instrument closely associated with this shrine. If the funeral service cannot be performed, the bereaved do not go into mourning, nor is an ancestor shrine carved for the deceased, since these are intrinsic parts of the subsequent ceremonies.

Sins against the Earth shrine include a number of wrongs: witchcraft, suicide, being sold into slavery, the shedding of blood of any member of the parish, sexual intercourse outside a habitation, hoeing (that is, using iron) on the weekly day of rest, and the theft of Earth shrine property, such as cowries paid as fines, stray livestock, and lost metal objects. Each of these offenses is in principle subject to the sanction either of a curtailed service or of a special form of burial—and sometimes both. That is to say, an offense is subject to this sanction unless it has been expiated by payments to the Earth shrine, or unless the lineage elders are ignorant of the sin or choose to ignore it. But ignorance, deliberate or accidental, may lead to further complications, in that future disasters may be attributed by a diviner to this additional failure to conform to the requirements of the Earth.

When Gbaa, a LoWiili elder, died during the dry season, he was buried in the courtyard of his house as befitted a man whose sons were married and had several children of their own. In addition, he was the senior of the three lineage heads of the Tshaa clan sector of Birifu. Later, during the wet season, there was a short break in the rain sometime in June, which, though not an unusual occurrence, always causes great anxiety, since it comes at an awkward moment for the growing crops. The Earth shrine was approached, diviners were consulted, and various proposals were put into effect. One of these was the removal of Gbaa's corpse from his courtyard grave for reburial in an oblong trench dug in the side of a stream near his house. The rains, it was believed, would wash the body out of the ritual area and carry away the impurity so that the earth would no longer be contaminated.

The reason given for what was to me a surprising transfer of the body of an old and respected man to a sinner's grave was as follows. In his youth, Gbaa had been sold as a slave (*gbanggbaa*) by his own family. In time of famine it was not unusual for a man to protect his children by selling them to someone living in an area less severely affected. Usually this presented no great difficulty, since famines were local in character; moreover, there was an extensive demand for slaves in the South. Later Gbaa returned home to Birifu, but no sacrifice was performed to the Earth shrine. This is considered essential, since, so far as the parish is concerned, to be sold into slavery is to lose one's birthright. Re-entry to the ritual congregation can be effected only by making the proper payments to the shrine, by killing a dog "to shave the Earth shrine's head." Unless this is done, a member of the parish who returns from slavery is buried in the same way as an outsider purchased by one of its inhabitants. He is interred in a trench grave at the side of a watercourse—not carried there, but dragged by the ropes used for tying the posts of the funeral stand. None of the later ceremonies is performed on his behalf, and hence no ancestor shrine is carved in his name.

Among the LoDagaba, but not among the LoWiili, a witch is buried in a similar manner. In Lawra, for example, such a person is carried to a marsh on the edge of the parish and buried there, together with his personal possessions. For witchcraft is an offense against the Earth, and formerly the shrine was used in order to test the validity of accusations of witchcraft.

Among the LoWiili there is no special piece of ground put aside for the burial of witches, and I have only known this one case, not one involving witchcraft, when the body was interred in the bed of a stream. But there is no mourning and no playing of xylophones at the death of a witch. The body is simply disposed of as quickly as possible in an old grave, which is never again reopened.

The method of ascertaining whether or not a person is a witch is related to the discovery by divination of the cause of death, a subject treated more fully in the account of the next ceremony, known as the Diviners' Beer. But there are other ways of discerning witchcraft. The LoWiili, for instance, reckon that anyone who dies on a day known as Nakwol Market, a day especially associated with the Earth shrine, is thereby shown to have practiced witchcraft. This means that the burial service cannot be performed unless an expiatory payment is first made to the custodian of the Earth. But when the debt has been paid, the mourning is carried out in the normal way at the next funeral that the lineage performs. For example, the death of Ngminvuor of Birifu was just such a double occasion. A year previously, Guon, the widow of his father's brother, had died on the wrong day and had not been mourned. But the debt had now been paid to the Earth, and a cow that had been received as part of Guon's daughter's bridewealth was killed for her to give to her husband, who had been dead long since.

Apart from this automatic attribution of witchcraft, there are a number of other reasons for holding up burials. As I have earlier remarked, if the patrilineage owes a debt to the Earth shrine, the priest may stop the funeral until it has been settled. Should he overturn a xylophone and throw a few ebony leaves on the slats, no one will play the instrument again until after a settlement has been arranged. However, although this procedure was much talked about, I have never attended a funeral at which it was carried out. As a sanction it stays in the background, more as a threat than an actuality; for in fact the master of the Earth is reluctant to take the initiative in action of any kind. Among the LoWiili, the payment of the expiatory sacrifices is usually left entirely to supernatural jurisdiction; if a member of the lineage is subsequently afflicted by a disease, or some similar trouble arises which is traced by the diviner to the earlier failure to pay, the lineage then has to decide whether or not to carry out the obligation. Among the LoDagaba, however, the Earth priest may be forced to take a decision when he is called upon to mark out a new grave; to do this for a person in debt to the shrine would only bring retribution upon his own head.

In the majority of cases, however, the decision whether or not to accord a person a full burial is made by the lineage itself. In his account of the neighboring peoples of the Upper Volta, Labouret states that a fowl is always killed to the compound shrines before mourning begins in order to discover whether the deceased was a witch ([1931] p. 319). Among the LoDagaa, an elder will often make such a sacrifice before he attends a funeral, outside as well as within his own clan sector; but I am not sure if this is done in every case or only when some suspicion has been aroused.

It is evident that the lineage has a good deal of latitude in deciding whether the funeral of a particular individual will or will not be carried out; they may or may not pay the debt to the Earth, they may or may not sacrifice to the compound shrines. At the funeral of Gbaa, a respected elder, no attention at all was paid at the time to his ancient sin against the Earth; his transgression was only remembered later when a drought ensued. On the other hand, when a person is considered less worthy, for whatever reason, this fact will be in the minds of those responsible for carrying out the funeral. For example, in the compound of Bõyiri of Birifu, there was living a distant clansman, Baabaa, who had fled from the authorities in the Ivory Coast. When his wife died, no mourning took place and upon inquiry Bõyiri let it be known that he had killed a fowl to the household shrines and that it had been revealed that something was wrong. The woman herself was not popular, and Baabaa was in a marginal position, since he had no close ties with the group. Both for these reasons and because Baabaa farmed on his own, Bõyiri felt under no strong obligation to bury the dead woman with full ceremony; indeed, discussing the incident over a pot of beer, someone remarked to me that Bõyiri had not performed the complete funeral because he wanted to save money.

In this case the deceased was a woman, and her husband had no close agnates either in Birifu or in the neighboring settlements. But a compound would never take upon itself the sole responsibility of canceling the funeral of an adult man of the lineage, indirect though the procedures of divination are. This would be done only with the general agreement of the other close agnates. The LoSaala funeral of Der, whose death has already been mentioned in connection with the concept of mystical retribution, was stopped on the first day, when it was shown he was a witch, and his body was carried off to be dumped in the marsh. But here the other lineage members were present, and it was not left to one man to decide.

The point I wish to stress in connection with the burial of witches is that although certain of the diagnostic procedures appear to be semiautomatic in their operation, in fact a number of alternatives are open to those responsible for the funeral. First, the preliminary killing of a fowl may simply be omitted. Second, when a fowl is killed there is often some room for doubt as to whether it is accepted or refused. To be accepted the animal must die on its back; but sometimes when the bird lies on its back before it is dead, the sacrificer will snatch it up lest in its final throes it turn the wrong way. Third, even if the sacrifice does indicate that the dead person is a witch, a further fowl may be killed at another shrine to make sure the first result was not a mistake. And, last, the agnates may decide, whatever the sacrifice or the day of death may indicate, that they will expiate the dead man's offense and have him buried in a proper manner.

In these various ways, the opinions of a man's agnates are brought to bear upon the question of how he will be disposed of after his death. These opinions will clearly reflect both his position in the group, as with Baabaa's wife, and the way he had conducted himself during his lifetime, as in the case of Der. The non-performance of the funeral constitutes part of the system of moral and ritual sanctions against witchcraft, accusations of which are linked with a failure to adhere to social norms, owing either to social marginality or to excessive hostility in personal relations.

Finally, it should be noted that it is not only ex-slaves and witches who may be buried in trench graves, but others who have sinned against the Earth shrine and not expiated their offenses, a category that includes suicides and all those who have shed the blood of another member of the congregation. For to bury in the ground those who have broken her taboos is thought to anger the Earth and to impair the fertility of the land. In a community with limited techniques of producing and storing food, the possibility of a bad harvest provides a very potent sanction on human behavior; for it threatens the community's very existence.

CHAPTER VIII

Income and Outlay

They laid him brawdawn alangast bed. With a bockalips of finisky
fore his feet. And a barrowload of guenesis hoer his head.

JAMES JOYCE, *Finnegans Wake*

When the body has been buried, the onlookers soon disperse. Some of
the women present may be moved to perform a final dance in front of
the stand, and the grave-diggers may be asked to "inoculate" some
children by touching their hands or foreheads against one of the posts.
But this is soon done and only a small number of men are left, waiting
to carry out the final rites of the burial itself.

During the course of the ceremony, various monies have been collected from those attending, and this, as well as part of the dead man's
wealth, is used to make gifts to those who have helped. After the body
has been buried, further payments of money and of guinea-corn are
made to persons who have assisted in the performances; and, most
important of all the funeral expenditures, certain animals are killed to
the dead man, and the meat distributed among his kinsmen. Entitlement to portions of the meat is closely linked with the obligation to contribute to the funeral expenses, and hence a direct balance is maintained
between income and outlay. So that the reader may see these payments
within the wider context, I begin by recapitulating the gifts and contributions made and received during the course of the burial service
and attempt to present a balance sheet of funeral prestations. However, since the slaughter of the animals and the distribution of their
flesh is such a major feature of the ceremonies, this matter will be given
separate treatment in the following section.

FUNERAL PRESTATIONS

Funeral prestations, especially the division of the slaughtered animals, are of particular importance in that they reveal perhaps more

clearly than any other set of acts the kinship and descent organization of the two communities. The situation is extremely complex in view of the system of unilineal descent groups based upon both the uterine and the agnatic lines. But it is in this context that one of the reasons for the stress laid by the LoDagaa upon funeral ceremonies becomes apparent: in an area where the political system is so diffuse, funerals provide descent and local groupings with a means of cohesion.

Income

In considering the income of funeral ceremonies, we may make a rough distinction between voluntary and compulsory contributions.

Voluntary contributions are divisible into the following three categories:

(1) "Funeral water" (*kuur kwõ*), money that is offered to the senior mourner by his friends so that he can buy beer for himself and his guests.

(2) Individual contributions to the grave-diggers, which are thrown at the stand, and to the musicians, which are cast upon the xylophones. Such a gift is normally made by an individual upon arrival, but close kinsmen approach the stand or orchestra at any time during the course of the ceremony and throw further sums. Some of the money thrown by the bereaved belonged to the deceased; for many of the expenses of the funeral are a charge upon his estate. Hence a pot of cowries is often set aside for this purpose before a man dies; the person responsible for its distribution is the heir to the wealth, among the LoWiili the patrilineal heir and among the LoDagaba the matrilineal heir.

(3) Gifts offered to the deceased by friends, lovers, and others in the course of their funeral speeches. Only in the case of male friends is there a definite reciprocal character about these gifts, and this is associated with the institution of "perpetual friendships."

Compulsory contributions are also of three types, two of which have already been mentioned during the account of the burial ceremony:

(1) "Joking partners' money" (*lonluore libie*), a contribution demanded by the joking partners from the clansfolk of the deceased in order, they maintain, "to bury the dead man," that is, to buy a fowl to tie to the stand for the grave-diggers. In fact the money is retained by the individual who begs it. If none is forthcoming from any particular person, the joking partner abuses the clan of the deceased and behaves in a ridiculous and unseemly manner. Among the LoPiel these funeral joking partnerships operate mainly in the context of patriclanship, and among the LoSaala and the LoWiili of matriclanship.

This contribution, often made under the threat of verbal or physical sanctions, is compulsory in a somewhat different sense from the other prestations in this category, the sanctions for which are less direct but graver in their consequences. I include it here because it is in a sense a counterpart of the main funeral contributions described below.

(2) The "father-in-law's fowl" (*diem nuura*) and the "brother-in-law's fowl" (*dakye nuura*), a contribution consisting of a cock and a bunch of guinea-corn heads, brought along by those who have received wives from the deceased, that is, those who are married to his sisters or his daughters. If a woman dies, the sons-in-law bring a guinea-fowl in place of a cock. I have known some wife-taking in-laws to make a contribution of this kind at the death of any member of the wife's compound.

Occasionally the dead man's wife-giving in-laws also present a "fowl" to the bereaved (in this case a fowl, a poisoned arrow, and a bunch of guinea-corn heads), and this contribution is often placed on the funeral stand of their son-in-law. Although this gift, too, may be called the "in-law fowl," it in fact differs from that mentioned above, being one of the voluntary gifts accompanying a funeral speech and hence given only if personal relations between the affines have been particularly good.

(3) The major contributions to funeral expenses consist of the twenty cowries collected from persons standing in certain specific relationships to the deceased. The contributions are of three kinds—"byre money," "matriclan money," and "treebole money"—and are usually made on the third day, shortly before the actual burial. Elders from the patriclan of the deceased sit in front of the funeral stand collecting the "byre money" (*zo libie*), while members of his matriclan accept the "matriclan money" (*beltaaba libie*). There are significant differences between the two communities with regard to the collection of these contributions; I shall therefore report the LoDagaba situation first, since this is more straightforward, and note the LoWiili variations afterwards.

The byre money consists of twenty cowries contributed by all agnates who are heads of compounds. From this and the other funeral monies the main expenses are met. Unless an agnate has made such a contribution, he is not entitled to share (*puon*) in the Cow of the Hoehandle (the animal killed to celebrate the dead man's prowess as a farmer); nor do I think a non-clansman would have any of the flesh cut for him unless he had made his contribution. It should be added that there is a further restriction on the consumption of this meat, since no one can eat of the funeral animals unless he has himself lost a parent of the same sex as the deceased.

Among the LoWiili, the range of contributors is wider and includes the head of every compound present at the funeral, or rather the head of every farming group, each of whom has a separate granary (*mwo puo libie*). Those persons who are also patriclansfolk of the deceased give twenty cowries, not only for themselves, but also for every married man in their farming group (*kuur libie*).[1]

The twenty cowries from matriclansmen of the deceased is collected separately. In this system of double clanship, the body of the deceased is vested in both patriclan and matriclan; it is the responsibility of each to provide a proper burial for its members, and these funeral contributions—the one made by matriclansmen, the other largely by patrikin—ensure that the necessary expenses can be met. The payment of the first of these contributions, the matriclan money, entitles a person to a portion of the Matriclan's Cow (*bel naab*), also called the Cow of the Rooftop (*gaar naab*), because the carcass is dragged up to the flat roof of the compound to be shared out. One of the rear legs of this cow is allotted to the matriclansmen who have given twenty cowries to help bury their "brother."

The third contribution of shell money is known as "treebole money" (*tieper libie*), and is due from all members of the matriclan of the deceased's father; it was this gift that the joking partners at the Gbiiri funeral were guying when they threatened the bystanders with a mudbath. Out of this, two hundred cowries are taken to purchase a fowl for the grave-diggers. It can then be said that *"Kambire"*—or whatever matriclan it may be—"have buried their child." Such a gift entitles the contributors to the "father's leg" (*sãã gber*) of the Matriclan's Cow, "father" here being interpreted in a matrilineal context and referring to members of the deceased's father's matriclan, all of whom can say of the dead man or woman, "I bore him" (*ma-no doo*). When a woman dies this contribution is made by the husband's matriclan.

Among the LoWiili, the situation varies. At a woman's funeral I attended in Biro, a settlement to the south of Birifu proper that I have classified as LoWiili, all members of the deceased's father's matriclan were called upon to contribute to their "daughter's" funeral expenses; of this money two hundred cowries were used to buy the fowl, and the rest added to the other monies collected at the same time. However, I have attended other funerals at which an elder of the father's matriclan, one who is also a near agnatic kinsman, has provided the cowries for the grave-diggers' fowl, and no further contributions were made. But even when one man makes the contribution it is thought of as coming

[1] I have heard it maintained that only compound heads who are clansmen should give byre money, as among the LoDagaba, but this is not the normal practice.

from the whole clan; in Birifu itself, I once saw a man voluntarily present twenty cowries on the grounds that the dead man, a member of his father's matriclan, was his classificatory "father." Looked at against the background of other differences between the two communities, the twist that the LoWiili give to this institution is of considerable significance, since it indicates a shift in the responsibilities of matriclan membership, or rather a tendency to confine these responsibilities to persons who are doubly clansmen of the dead man.

If we compare the way in which these funeral contributions are made in the two communities, we find that whereas the ideal patterns, the statements about what should happen, are almost identical, the practices differ. Among the LoWiili there is, as we have seen, a restriction on the contributions demanded from the matriclan of the dead man's father. Corresponding to this there is a widening of the range of byre money, which is given by any compound head present—that is, by any compound head from within the parish—and by patriclansmen and members of the mother's clan sector from without. Even the range of the contributions made by the deceased's own matriclan shrinks; for normally only persons who are also members of the same patriclan sector as the dead man will hand over twenty cowries. The next section will show how these contributions are directly linked with the mode of distributing the meat of the funeral animals and how this in turn is linked with the system of inheritance.

Outlay

The various monies collected by the elders of the lineage are subsequently gathered together in one pile, and when the burial has taken place, the following payments are made to those who have rendered services. The figures given are representative rather than standard, since the payments are not necessarily the same in all cases.

To the owner of the *Dagaa* xylophones	700 cowries
To the owner of the *Lo* xylophones	500 cowries
To the owner of the wooden drum (*ganggaa*) .	300 cowries
To the owner of the gourd drum (*kwor*)	60 cowries
To those who brought guns	200 cowries

In addition, two hundred cowries may be given to the grave-diggers in place of the fowl, and a further twenty to the person who later whitewashes the surviving spouse. The remainder of the money is kept for a future funeral in the lineage, to buy the strips of white cloth that are tied around the waist of the dead.

Gifts of guinea-corn, which may also be added to any of the monetary prestations, have to be made as follows: (1) one basket to the widow's patrikin and (2) one basket to the mother's patrikin. These gifts of grain, together with the fowls contributed by the wife-taking and wife-giving in-laws, define the most important relationships into which a man enters through marriage: those with the kin groups to which he is tied through the women his own kin have taken as wives—that is, his mother and his spouse—and those with the groups to which his kin have given wives, in particular his sister and his daughter.

At the death of a wife, the husband makes a further prestation to his affines, known as the Beast of Farm Tidying. A consideration of this outgoing gift is best deferred until the discussion of the other funeral animals in the next section. However, the reference to the Beast of Farm Tidying serves as a reminder that not only do funeral prestations have to be examined as a whole; they also have to be thought of in terms of the total exchange of rights and duties between persons and groups. An attempt to place funeral prestations in the more inclusive context of transactions between affinal and matrilateral kin is made later in this chapter (Figure 7). But the pattern of these funeral prestations between affines is shown in Figure 5. Two aspects require some comment. First, except for the voluntary gifts accompanying funeral speeches, all these prestations are between males, that is, between jural majors. Second, again disregarding the voluntary gift of a fowl by the widow's father, there is a certain imbalance in the pattern of gift-giving, because, while contributions are received from the wife-taking affines of the same and the junior generation, they are given to the wife-giving affines of the same and the senior generation. In other words, no gift is made to the kin of the son's wife nor received from the husband of the father's sister, since these relationships are of lesser consequence in the total social network.

These baskets of guinea-corn are gifts from the dead man's granary, not to one individual, but to the whole lineage into which his mother and his wife were born. Thus the gift to the widow's kin, for example, is spoken of not as a gift to the dead man's in-laws, but as a gift to the "house" of his wife's father (*põõ sãã yidem tshi*), and it is shared by the members of the clan sector. These gifts emphasize the fact that the patriclan never entirely gives up the claim on its female members, even in respect of their fertility. On one occasion, when the basket did not appear to him to be sufficiently full, I heard a man threaten publicly to take away his sister's children if the proper measure was not at once produced. The "children" he spoke of were married and had offspring

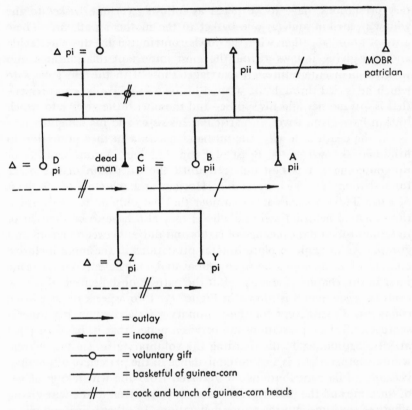

FIG. 5.—The transfer of funeral prestations between affines. The persons involved are distinguished by letters and allocated to patriclans (pi, pii) in order to show the way in which this figure links with Figure 7 (p. 170).

of their own. It is this residual claim on the children of the sibling excluded from inheritance that lies behind certain of the complexities of sister's son–mother's brother relationships in many patrilineal societies (Goody [1959a]).

THE PROVISION OF THE COW OF THE ROOFTOP

When these prestations have been made, the remaining task before the company disperses is the slaughter of the funeral animals and the distribution of their flesh. These animals are killed to the name of the dead man. I use this phrase to distinguish the slaughter of funeral animals from sacrifices proper, which are said to be given (*ko*) either to the ancestors or to a particular shrine. The funeral killings differ from such sacrifices in two respects. First, the animals are not killed at any altar, but beside the entrance to the dead man's compound. Second, no prayers are uttered nor does any specific request accompany the slaughter. Indeed, the animals are killed in honor of the dead man rather than being given to him, although failure to kill an animal at the time of the funeral gives rise to a future debt to the ancestor concerned. I therefore use the phrase "kill to the name of the deceased" in order to indicate that although I regard this as a preliminary to later sacrifices to his ancestral spirit, the slaughter of these animals also celebrates his achievements upon earth.

The animals killed in this manner fall into several categories: the Going Out Cow, the Cow of the Rooftop, and the Cow of the Hoe-handle, to mention but a few. A full list of the livestock killed at the ceremonies at which I was present is given in Tables 1 and 2. I would stress that these were instances that I actually observed; for informants habitually exaggerate the number of beasts killed at a kinsman's funeral and are unlikely to be any more precise about the funerals of non-kinsmen at which their participation is necessarily more limited.

The inaccuracy of informants in this matter arises not only from this general factor, but also from a situation specific to LoDagaa obsequies. Our examination of the funeral contributions has shown that although the ideal norms of LoWiili behavior are in most cases very similar to those of the LoDagaba, the actual patterns may display significant differences. As might be anticipated, the same is true of the distribution of the meat of the animals killed; for the payments of cowries are thought of as an entitlement to portions of the flesh. This disparity constitutes one of the most significant differences between the two communities and hence a major focus of our treatment of these ceremonies. But there is a further point upon which this discrepancy throws light, a point concerned not with the differences between the two communities, but with the process of change itself. It would appear, for reasons I cannot present here, that the LoWiili have been subject to a complex process of change that is reflected in the observed differences between the ideal norms and the actual patterns. Of course, such discrepancies characterize all societies; indeed, moral injunctions are not infrequently couched in terms that render them virtually impossible to put into practice. But in the present case we are dealing not with ideal formulations of this highly generalized kind, but with precise statements for the conduct of certain ritual procedures. On this level the disparity between the ideal and the actual is to be interpreted not as a permanent aspect of the social system, but as a stage in the readjustment of ritual and belief to meet changes in other parts of the system.

In order to establish the existence of the differences between the two communities and of the discrepancies between stated and actual behavior, and in order to indicate the apparent cause as well as the actual correlates of these differences, it is necessary to examine in considerable detail the livestock slaughtered at the funerals and the manner in which their flesh is distributed. While the reader may not find the minutiae of great interest, such an examination is one of the few ways open to the social anthropologist to demonstrate, rather than simply assert, the correctness or otherwise of his conclusions. First, therefore, I shall deal with the provision of funeral animals. The bare details of these transactions are recorded in Tables 1 and 2.

TABLE 1.—ANIMALS KILLED AT BURIALS OF ADULT LoWiili MALES

Name and age of deceased	Animals Killed	Comments
Gbaa (Tshaa) over 65	Cow of the Rooftop (daughter's bridewealth) Sheep of the Hoehandle	Killed to the name of his younger brother
Daazie (Naayiili) over 65	Cow of the Rooftop (daughter's bridewealth) Cow of the Rooftop (daughter's bridewealth) Sheep of the Hoehandle	Killed to the name of his younger half brother Killed to Daazie
Tontol (Baaperi) over 65	Cow of the Rooftop, given on the hoof to mother's patriclan (Cow of the Byre) Goat of Divining Sheep of the Bowstring Sheep of Chicken-rearing	A long discussion took place to the effect that the first should have been killed by the patriclan as at the previous funerals, and that an animal should have been killed to the hoehandle
Yitu (Ngmanbiili) 30	Goat of the Hoehandle	
Ngminvuor (Tshaa) 35	Cow of the Rooftop, his living brother's Cow of the Byre Sheep of the Hoehandle	Killed to his father to give to his father's father
Zuon (Naayiili) 30	Cow of the Rooftop, to mother's patriclan (Cow of the Byre) Cow of the Rooftop, to own patriclan (Cow of the Byre) Sheep of the Hoehandle Goat of Butchering Sheep of Trading	

TABLE 2.—ANIMALS KILLED AT BURIALS OF ADULT LoDAGABA MALES

Name and age of deceased	Animals killed
LoSaala	
Der (at Gbiiri) 60?	Cow of the Rooftop Cow of the Hoehandle Sheep of the Hoehandle Goat of the Bowstring (given by his younger full brother) Goat of Trading
LoPiel	
Der (Dakuone) 50?	Sheep of the Rooftop Sheep of the Hoehandle
Katu (Nambegle) over 65	Cow of the Rooftop Cow of the Hoehandle Cow of Groundnut Farming (*singbie naab*) Cow of Gambling

From this list of the animals I saw slaughtered at the funerals of adult males, it appears that the most frequent victims are the Beast of the Rooftop and the Beast of the Hoehandle. Animals bearing these names were provided on eight out of the nine occasions. In some instances it was a cow and in others a sheep or a goat. Cows and sheep are, in a sense, treated as equivalent in the magico-religious context, and the LoDagaa often speak of sheep as "cows" when they are to be offered to some shrine. As Evans-Pritchard points out for the Nuer, this usage derives not from any characteristic of the "primitive mentality" as such, but from the fact that in these situations the lesser animals are held to represent the greater ([1956] pp. 128, 131). Although they are equivalent in respect of their potentiality as sacrificial victims, the animals are not held to be identical. Consequently, it is still possible to take the type of livestock killed as an index of the significance of the offering made.

Measured by the size of the animals slaughtered and by the occurrence of delayed offerings to persons who have died sometime earlier, the Beast of the Rooftop is clearly the most important of all. This animal is variously known as the Cow of the Rooftop (*gaar naab*), the Matriclan's Cow (*bel naab*), and the Cow of the Dispersal of the Funeral (*kowel naab*). Such a cow should be killed to every adult male who has produced male offspring, and the responsibility for doing so lies with the inheritor of the man's wealth. If no such offering is made, either at the burial service or upon some later occasion, no agnatic descendant of the deceased should have a cow killed to his name, lest the dead ancestor, angry at seeing a member of his lineage receive what he has not yet been given, and fearing, too, the comments of his fellow ancestors, should vent his wrath upon a member of the clan who has thus humiliated him. No one's wrath is to be feared like that of an ancestor, for he knows the secrets of the house in which one dwells and of the shrines which protect it; there is no evading his revenge.

The cow will not necessarily be killed to a man's name at the time of his own funeral; of the five instances from Birifu, in three the cow was in fact killed to the name of an agnate who had died some time previously. At Ngminvuor's funeral the elder of the clan sector reminded the chief mourner, the full brother of the dead man, that no cow had been slaughtered to the name of their paternal grandfather. The beast was therefore killed to the dead man's father, Sortshera, to be handed on by him to his father, Gbalgbe (Fig. 6).

This attempt to by-pass the debt to Gbalgbe will probably fail, for it is likely that any future misfortune that descends upon Albaa, or upon a member of his immediate family, will be related by the diviner he consults to the fact that before Gbalgbe had had a cow killed to his name, one was offered to his son. However, although Gbalgbe got no cow, he automatically "received" a leg—the father's leg—of the animal killed to his son, the meat of which was eaten by those members of his matriclan (KorenDa) who also belonged to the same patriclan.

Among the LoDagaba, too, the Cow of the Rooftop may be provided many years after the actual burial of the person to whose name it is killed. But the basic difference between the two communities is sharply

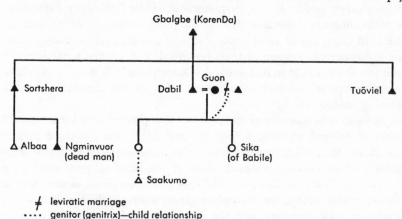

FIG. 6.—The genealogy of Gbalgbe's descendants.

brought out by the fact that the provision of the victim is the responsibility not of an agnate, as among the LoWiili, but of the matriclan in general and of the heir in particular. This direct connection between the provision of the main funeral cow and the inheritance of wealth is made by the people themselves. The LoDagaba recognize the obligation to supply such an animal only when the dead man has left property of value that has been inherited in the uterine line; the funeral cow is in fact taken as an indication that there is more livestock to come. In the words of one man with whom I was discussing this matter, "How can your mother's brother ask for a cow to be killed to his name when he has left you nothing to kill?" Furthermore, the obligation to provide for the former holder of the livestock is not extinguished by the slaughter of this animal alone. The livestock, which comprises the bulk of the matrilineally inherited wealth among the LoDagaba, may increase under the heir's supervision, and the dividend on the original "capital" may be held to warrant the sacrifice of an additional victim at the ancestral shrine of the original owner. That is to say, a subsequent misfortune in the domestic family may later be attributed by a diviner to the failure to sacrifice further animals to the dead man. As we shall see in the discussion of manes worship, sacrifice to the ancestors is closely linked with the mode in which the objects of sacrifice have been passed down from the dead members of the community. The obligation to provide cattle to the original owner is thought of as enduring in perpetuity (*o be baarei*).

Among the LoDagaba, then, the Cow of the Rooftop is provided by the uterine kinsmen of the deceased, whereas the LoWiili view this as a responsibility of the patriclan. Both maintain that no cow should be killed to a man's name until his agnatic forebears have all been satisfied. But although the LoWiili assign responsibility to the patriclan, there are nevertheless non-agnatic elements about the ways in which they set about the provision and distribution of this cow. There is, of course, no question of the sister's son having to supply the animal, since the heirs to the wealth are always agnates. Nevertheless, a matrilateral as distinct from a matrilineal element is present; for in three of the five LoWiili funerals at which a Cow of the Rooftop was killed, the animal had been indirectly acquired from the dead man's maternal uncle. How is this to be reconciled with the absence of uterine inheritance?

I have described elsewhere the practice whereby a man lends his sister's young son a fowl to look after (Goody [1956a], p. 58). If the youth successfully rears the chicks hatched by this hen, his mother's brother allows him to keep some if not all of the brood. This hen is the beginning of the boy's personal wealth. At some later date the uncle may do the same with a sheep, and finally with a cow. The original animal is known as the Cow of Breeding (*naab gwöl*), and its offspring as Cow of the Byre (*zo naab*), because it is given to the sister's son for having looked after the animal in his own compound. When the Cow of the Byre itself multiplies, one of the offspring should be sacrificed at the shrine of the mother's brother and yet another at that of the father, lest the wrath of the dead be visited upon their descendants. This animal is often killed at the funeral of the original recipient and constitutes not only an offering to the ancestor in question (the mother's brother), but also a celebration of the name of the man who has just died (the sister's son). At the funeral of Zuon (LoWiili), when two Cows of the Rooftop were killed, one was divided among the deceased's patriclan in the usual manner, and the other given to members of his mother's patriclan, who proceeded to cut it up on the spot and distribute it among those present. In the course of another LoWiili funeral, that of Tontol, who was certainly the oldest man in the whole neighborhood, it transpired that on his deathbed he had made a request for a live cow to be sent to his mother's patrikin, and this was duly done. When the agnates of the old man were drinking beer after the burial, a heated argument arose among them, the majority maintaining that this cow ought to have been kept and killed at the funeral. Tontol, however, had been aware that his mother's brother had to be satisfied first, and his clansfolk decided to exercise their prerogative of taking the animal back to their own settlement.

We see, then, that both the LoWiili and the LoDagaba tend to kill as Cow of the Rooftop an animal that has been acquired through female ties. But what the LoWiili regard as a transaction between two patrilineages, male property being vested exclusively in these groups, is among the LoDagaba a transaction within the matriclan itself. Although in both cases the Cow of the Rooftop may be acquired through the mother's brother as a result of the customs relating to the Cow of Breeding, the transfer is differently conceived. In the first case, the animal is regarded as property that has changed hands from one patrilineage to another; some compensation has to be made, not because it is considered as an enforceable debt but in order to avoid mystical dangers. In the second case, cattle are exclusively vested in the matriclan, and the slaughter of the Cow of the Rooftop is a preliminary to the redistribution of the deceased's wealth within that group.

Among the LoWiili, the loan of a cow by the mother's brother gives the sister's son the right to retain one of the offspring; the inclusion of this cow as part of his patrimony is conditional upon the return of one of its own offspring to the patrilineal ancestors of the mother's brother in the form of a sacrifice. These are the conditions under which the cow acquired through a matrilateral tie can be incorporated in the wealth vested in the patriclan. The killing of such a cow at a funeral does not therefore diminish the body of the inheritance, since the sacrifice would have to be made even if no death had taken place. The mortuary ceremony simply provides the occasion for discharging a prior obligation. Thus the choice of an animal of this kind to be killed as Cow of the Rooftop fulfills a double purpose.

The same double function is achieved when a cow received as part of a daughter's bridewealth is killed as Cow of the Rooftop, an event that I observed in three of the LoWiili funerals. The second installment of bridewealth, known as *doẽ* becomes due when a woman has borne her husband two or three children. Her fertility has then been proved, and two cows should be sent to her natal kin. One of these, known as the Cow of Childbearing (*bidoo naab*), or alternatively as the Daughter's Cow (*pooyaa naab*), must be sacrificed to her agnatic forebears. Once again the killing of such an animal not only publicly celebrates the dead man, but also appeases the ancestors by giving them what is already their due.

Among the LoDagaba, a Cow of Childbearing cannot be used as the Cow of the Rooftop but only as the Cow of the Hoehandle, an offering described in a subsequent section and associated with agnatic ties. The LoDagaba say that it is right that the Cow of Childbearing should be killed to the father's name as a Cow of the Hoehandle, since it was by the strength of his arms that he provided food for his children and enabled his daughters to grow up into marriageable young women. It was also in this way that he obtained their mother; an important part of the marriage transactions consists in farming for the in-laws, and even the cash payment of cowries provided by the father or the mother's brother is looked at as a return for the farming one has done for them. Looked at from another point of view, a man's main opportunity for gaining wealth is by farming, and his achievements in the fields are celebrated by killing the Cow of the Hoehandle to his name. He is only able to produce more than his household consumes if he has sons to help him. But if most of his children are girls, though he must work hard to be able to feed them and will have little or no surplus to invest in livestock, he does receive their bridewealth when they get married.

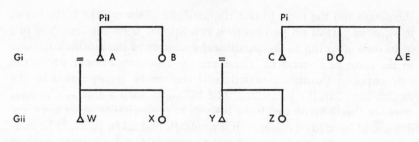

| Genera- | | Patriclan (p) | | | LoDagaba |
tion (G)	Time (T)	ii	i	Transaction	differences
Gi	Ti (marriage)	A+ ⟶	C+	Rights over women (including potential fertility)	
		A+ ⟵	C+	1st bridewealth (cowries and farming)	
	Tii (birth of 2 or 3 children)	A+ ⟶	C+	Rights over women in respect of Y + Z (proved fertility)	
		A+ ⟵	C+	2nd bridewealth (cattle payment, out of which one animal can be used as Cow of Rooftop)	Only used for Cow of Hoehandle
	Tiii (end of childbearing)	A+ ⟵	C	3rd bridewealth (rarely paid)	
	Tiv (death of wife)	A+ ⟵	C	Beast of Farm Tidying, B's ancestor shrine, and a token "bridewealth" of 20 cowries	
	Tv (death of wife's brother)	pii ⟵	C	Cock and bunch of guinea-corn	
	Tvi (death of husband)	pii ⟵	E	Basket of guinea-corn to senior in-laws	
		A ⟵	E	100 cowries, guinea-fowl, and fowl taken by brothers-in-law	
		B ⟶	E	Widow's 20 cowries	
		B ⟵	E	100 cowries from new husband (levir)	
		pii ⟶	pi	Father-in-law's fowl (voluntary)	

FIG. 7.—The transactions between affines and matrilateral kin. Letters refer to the genealogy above; + means other members of the patriclan involved.

Genera-tion (G)	Time (T)	Patriclan (p)		Transaction	LoDagaba differences
		ii	i		
Gi–Gii	Tvii (adoles-cence of Y)	A $\longrightarrow$ Y		Cow of Breeding (including potential fertility)	
	Tviii	A $\longleftarrow$ Y		Cow of Breeding returned	No return in life, since movable property is inherited by Y*
		A $\longrightarrow$ Y		Retention of Cow of Byre	
	Tix	A $\longleftarrow$ Y		Return of offspring of Cow of Byre, its slaughter at the funeral, or its sacrifice to ancestral shrine	Provision of Cow of Roof-top and sub-sequent sacri-fice to ances-tral shrine
Gii		W+ $\longleftrightarrow$ Z+		Limited obligation to send daughter as wife to mother's patrikin, so cycle begins again in opposite direction†	Stronger obli-gation to make such a marriage (i.e., FASIDA for male)
		X+ $\longleftrightarrow$ Y+		MOBRDA marriage also possible, with repetition of cycle	

Fig. 7 (cont'd).—*Among the LoDagaba, an additional transaction occurs here; Y farms for A and receives help with bridewealth in return. † This marriage could also be shown as an exchange between members of Gi, since it is implicit in C = A.

Though he can use this to marry wives only for his sons, not for himself, he can, on the other hand, spend ("eat") it; he thus becomes a rich man (*na*), and it is this fact that is celebrated at his death by the slaughter of a cow. In the same way during a man's lifetime, he has an obligation to kill to his dead father and father's father animals acquired either by farming or by the marriage of his daughters; the two sources are not only identified in sacrifice, but also assigned to the same cycle of inter-change in the over-all network of prestations. And although among the LoDagaba animals derived either from farming or from a daughter's bridewealth are later transmitted by uterine inheritance, at this junc-ture they are treated as self-acquired property and used to celebrate the prowess of the man who acquired them. If the daughter's bridewealth was treated as a Cow of the Rooftop, then it would be distributed by matriclan membership and not by the patrilineal ties with which the hoe and bridewealth are most closely connected.

In concluding this section, I would draw attention to the further parallel between the Cow of Childbearing and the Cow of the Byre. From the standpoint of the male members of a patrilineal descent group, both are acquired by virtue of female links; the bridewealth counterbalances the transfer to non-clansmen of rights over females of the group, while the Cow of the Byre derives from transactions between persons belonging to different descent groups but linked by women. The pattern of these transactions over time is illustrated in Figure 7. Only the major operations involving rights over women and property are shown; in addition, of course, a number of other important rights and duties characterize these relationships, such as the services a sister's son performs for his mother's brother. Analytically each particular transaction needs to be referred to the totality of social actions involved.

THE DIVISION OF THE COW OF THE ROOFTOP

The methods of distributing the flesh of the Cow of the Rooftop in the two communities display differences of the same order of significance as the provision of the animal. But whereas differences in the obligation to supply the victim are directly related to the system of inheritance, differences in the distribution are linked, in the first place, with the main monetary contributions made at the funeral. These monies were discussed in detail in the previous section; but, as a reminder to the reader, a summary of them is presented in Table 3.

The method by which the flesh of the Cow of the Rooftop is distributed is shown in Table 4. The basic difference between the two communities turns on the allocation of the four legs of the butchered animal. These legs belong to the joking partners, the "fathers," the "brothers," and the "sons." In both communities the group to which the kinship term is applied is defined by matriclanship. The "fathers," for example, are the members of the father's matriclan. But among the LoWiili, just as the matrilineal funeral contributions are limited to those matriclansmen who are also members of the deceased's patriclan, the right to the flesh of the victim is restricted in a similar manner. Let me illustrate this by some actual examples, first among the two LoDagaba communities and then among the LoWiili.

I attended the funeral at Gbiiri of a LoSaala man whose mother and father both belonged to the Kambire matriclan. Like most matriclans,

TABLE 3.—THE FUNERAL MONIES

LoDagaba		No. of cowries	LoWiili	No. of cowries
Byre money	*Zo libie,* by all agnates who are compound heads	20	By all compound heads present, outside the clan sector (*mwo puo libie*)	20
			By all married men within clan sector (*kuur libie*)	20
Matriclan money	*Beltaaba libie,* by members of deceased's matriclan	20	By members of deceased's matriclan who are also members of his patriclan	20
Treebole money	*Tieper libie,* by members of matriclan of the deceased's father (or husband's matriclan in the case of a married woman)	20	By a member of same matriclan and patrilineage as the deceased's father (or husband's matriclan and patrilineage in the case of a married woman)	200

this consists of two exogamous sections, one being known as "red Kambire," or "Kambire slaves," and the other as "black Kambire." The "children's" leg, the right front leg, was taken by those in the deceased's patrilineage whose fathers had been Kambire, and that evening these persons gathered together to eat the meat at a communal "orphans' meal." The "brother's" and "father's" legs, on the other hand, were taken to the house of the oldest member of the Kambire matriclan in the parish, who later had the flesh divided out between all the clan members.

The LoPiel apportion the cow in a slightly different fashion, although they use the same terms to describe the limbs. Whereas among both the LoWiili and the LoSaala the four matriclans are divided into two pairs of joking partners, Some and Da, and Hienbe and Kambire, among the LoPiel, the Some matriclan stands in opposition to all the remaining three groups, Kambire and Hienbe being regarded as subgroups within the Da. My example comes from the funeral of an old woman in Gwo; but the difference in sex does not alter the principles according to which the meat is divided. The Cow of the Matriclan was provided by her full brother, who, like her, belonged to the Kpo-Da subsection of Da; their father belonged to the SomDa subsection.

TABLE 4.—THE DIVISION OF THE COW OF THE ROOFTOP

Portion	Recipients	
	LoDagaba	LoWiili
Right front leg with skin (*lonluore bo*)	To the joking partners of the deceased's matriclan	To the joking partners of the deceased's matriclan, usually limited to those belonging to his patriclan as well
Left front leg (*bibiir bo*)	To persons whose fathers belonged to the matriclan of the dead man*	To the children of the dead man and their close agnatic "brothers"
Rear leg (*sãã gber*)	To the matriclan of the deceased's father	To the members of the matriclan of the deceased's father within his patriclan
Rear leg (*beltaaba gber*)	To the deceased's matriclan	To members of the deceased's matriclan within his patriclan
Fillet (*sie*)	To the mother, or to a female member of the same matrilineage	As the LoDagaba
Nape of neck (*nyũũ*)	To the widows	As the LoDagaba
Head (*zu*), entrails (*nyage*), half liver, half kidney, half windpipe, lungs (*fulan fuur*), stomach (*pur*)	Used for preparing the orphans' meal	As the LoDagaba, although the Cow of the Hoehandle may also be used for this purpose
Front three (or four) ribs (*jello*)	To those who cut up the meat (usually the "children" of the dead man's matriclan)	As the LoDagaba
Hide (*gan*)	For the repair of the treetrunk drum	To those who brought guns
Lower jaw (*yeleor*), chest (*nyãã*), half windpipe (*kokor wir*), half liver (*soor*), half kidney (*zooro*), udder (*bori*), heart (*sutshir*), inside belly (*purble*), stub of tail (*zukoor*), ? (*parinyo*), ? (*alinbie*), tip of ear, and small portions cut from back legs†	To the owner of the *Dagaa* xylophones	As the LoDagaba

* I have also heard this called the *paa bie bo,* the leg of the children of the vagina; it is sometimes confined to children of the "house," as among the LoWiili.

† The meat for the xylophone owner and for the widows and children is known as the "bitter meat" (*nen tuo*), and its distribution varies a little from lineage to lineage. The owner of the *Dagaa* xylophone usually cuts some meat for the owner of the *Lo* xylophone.

In this case the animal was slaughtered by the grave-diggers, who kept back certain portions of the meat for themselves. Other parts were put aside, some for the "mothers" and some for the meal to be prepared for the orphans on the following day.

The "children's" leg was sent to the Government-instituted chief, a practice that has been established in many parts of this area since the introduction of these offices by the Colonial administration; but the leg still retains the original name and occasionally even falls into the "children's" hands. Generally, however, the "children" have to be given some other portion, and this happened in the present case. The other front leg was seized by Some, the joking partners to the Da group of matriclans, and the remainder of the cow was then carried on top of the flat roof, where only Da were permitted to gather. While the flesh was being cut up, the matriclansmen sat on the low wall that ran around the roof of the long central room of the house. One of these spectators remarked to me as he sat there, "It is a SomDa child who has come up on the roof (*SomDa, be bie anga na do a garo zu*). Now they really know he's dead. He's no longer a human being (*Be bong ko kpina. O be in nie*), but has changed to meat (*o lieba nen pampanna*)."

The meat divided on the rooftop consisted mainly of the legs allocated to the "fathers" and "brothers." Since both the deceased and her father belonged to the Da matriclans (KpoDa and SomDa), the meat was cut up and piled in one place to be shared among the various Da subdivisions, who are said to eat together (*be zaa long dire*). But since all the remaining matriclans other than Some are held to constitute a single inclusive group, members of these three matriclans had to be given their own portions. So the meat was divided into two equal parts, one of which was left there to be shared between SomDa and KpoDa, the two groups directly involved, while the rest was carried onto the roof of an adjoining room, where it was further subdivided between MeDa and Dabire on the one hand, and Hienbe and Kambire on the other. The men gathered around the meat that had been allotted to their clan, and this was portioned out by the senior member present, who said as he did so, "See your clansman" (*Nye fu nir*).

The implications behind these words will be discussed later in connection with the orphans' meal. Here I want only to point out that the principle behind the distribution of meat in both LoDagaba groups, the LoSaala and the LoPiel, is basically the same. There is no limitation either upon the members of the matriclan who contribute to the funeral expenses or upon those who share in the Cow of the Rooftop. The additional complexities among the LoPiel arise only from the differences in the organization of the matriclans. In the context both of joking partnerships and of the distribution of the funeral meat, the four independent matriclans of the LoSaala act as paired moieties among the LoPiel, with Some on the one hand opposed to the remaining three matriclans on the other.

When we turn to examine the LoWiili situation, we find that the statements made about the distribution of the flesh of the Cow of the Rooftop are virtually identical with those made by the LoDagaba. There is the same division of the legs between the joking partners, the "fathers," the "brothers," and the "children." Actual practice, however, varies in certain significant ways. It will be recalled that although the contributions of matriclan money among the LoWiili are theoretically made by all members of the deceased's matriclan, in practice such monies are largely restricted to those persons who also belong to his patriclan. So, too, the meat of the Cow of the Rooftop is distributed only within the patriclan. Thus, in relation to these acts the boundaries of the matriclan are, in effect, confined within those of the patriclan itself. It is true that matriclansmen belonging to other patriclans could contribute their twenty cowries at the funeral, and if they wished they could no doubt discover when and where the cow was to be killed and successfully stake their claim to a portion of the meat. But to do so would be most unusual. Compared with LoDagaba usage, the sharing of the meat of the Cow of the Rooftop has in fact become the prerogative of the members of the patriclan.

At the LoWiili funeral of Zuon, for example, the limbs were called by the same names as those mentioned above, but the meat was divided into a large number of small pieces, one for every adult male of the dead man's patrilineage and one for every patriclansman present. No consideration was given to claims based on matriclanship alone. Thus the narrowing of the range of contributions is paralleled by a contraction of the range within which the meat of the Cow of the Rooftop is distributed. In Zuon's case, no matriclan money was collected, although a member of his father's matriclan still gave the two hundred cowries for the grave-digger's fowl. The decision to forego these contributions was made by the lineage elders on the grounds that there remained in the house only young men of a different matriclan from that of the deceased, who was SomDa, and that if they collected this money now, none of them would be in a position to make return gifts at SomDa funerals in the future. The reason given appeared to be simply an excuse to cover a move to eliminate matriclanship in this context. For what we are observing here is the readjustment of funeral institutions to a form more consistent with the system of property relationships.

THE PROVISION AND DIVISION OF OTHER ANIMALS

Next to the Cow of the Rooftop the most important funeral offering is the Cow of the Hoehandle (*kukuur naab*). This is one of a number of animals that may be killed at a funeral, depending upon the wealth of the dead man and the means by which he gained it. Of these means the most usual, and the most prized, is farming. By good husbandry, a man may acquire a small surplus of grain at the end of the year. This he sells in the market, and after making various purchases for himself and his family, he often invests the remainder in livestock, a fowl, a goat, or possibly a sheep. By the natural dividend of his investment, or by the addition of the gains of equally fortunate years, the farmer may eventually be able to buy a cow, which is called the Cow of the Hoe-handle. Such capital accumulation is punctuated by sacrifices to the patrilineal ancestors; for in both these communities the hoe, like the techniques of farming and the land itself, is inherited patrilineally. And one of the animals accumulated in this way is killed at the man's funeral and stands as a tribute to his ability as a farmer.

Wealth gained by other means also merits the slaughter of a domestic animal at the funeral. At the burial service of Gandaa, the late Chief of Birifu, in 1950, his younger full brother had the following animals killed to his name:

A Cow of the Bowstring (*tamyuur* or *pĩĩ naab*), bought with wealth gained by robbing men of their livestock.

A Cow of Target-shooting (*tefa naab*), bought with wealth won at this sport, which serves as practice both for war and for hunting.

A Cow of Bangle-making (*bõ zu naab*), bought with wealth gained by casting small objects of brass and bronze by the *cire perdu* process.

A Cow of the Xylophone (*jil naab*), bought with wealth gained by playing or making these instruments.

A Cow of Figure-carving (*baatibe naab*), bought with wealth gained by making the wooden figures that form part of certain shrines, notably those built to the beings of the wild.

The late chief did not, I think, make enough money in each instance to be able to purchase a cow with the proceeds from that pursuit alone. But he was a wealthy man and had accumulated enough cattle over the years to enable his heirs to kill a cow in commemoration of each of the activities in which he had engaged.

The killing of these animals has yet a further purpose, since the destruction of part of the property is thought to make the rest safe for the

heir. These same two aspects, celebration and protection, are also present in sacrifices to the ancestors. The "cooling" of property owned by
the dead man is a major concern of the heir even after the funeral ceremonies are finished. This concern is linked to the situation of tension
that exists between holder and heir while the holder is still alive. His
death transfers the scene of the conflict from the human to the supernatural sphere of relationships. Here the spiritual beings involved
are the ancestors; and the socially expected fears of the inheritor
toward them are apparent both in the prophylactic rituals he under-
takes and in the general anticipation that the dead forefather will display hostility, as well as friendliness, toward his own descendants.

Other animals may occasionally be killed in recognition of other
means of accumulating wealth. These include livestock obtained with
the profits made by trading, butchering meat in the market place, rear-
ing fowls, or divination. In the case of a woman, a Beast of the Beer
Ladle (*dãã sule*) is killed if she has purchased livestock with the money
made by the brewing and selling of beer. But of all these animals, the
Beast of the Hoehandle occupies a special place because of the central
position of agriculture in the economic life of the LoDagaa. Since famine conditions are never far off, the additional effort made by a good
farmer may be the means of saving his dependents from starvation. The
man who works hard at his farm is highly spoken of. In communal
farming the competition to finish one's allotted strip ahead of everybody else instills the same values in the young men. To farm well is to
be honored by all. The special position of the Beast of the Hoehandle is
manifest in the restrictions on the behavior of men who have not yet
been able to put aside sufficient money to acquire an animal. As with
clan taboos, these prohibitions are of a comparatively insignificant kind
and are to be regarded primarily as emblems indicating the importance
of agricultural activities to the community as a whole. Persons who
have been unable to acquire such livestock are not allowed to bathe
either in the water that has collected in the hole made when earth was
excavated to build the compound (*tamboo kwõ*), or in the water in
which the grain is first soaked when being prepared for the brewing of
beer (*kai kwõ*).

Since the wealth of any particular farming group is nominally vested
in its senior member, only the head is strictly entitled to a Cow of the
Hoehandle at his funeral. But if the group has been successful, it is recognized that the labor of junior members has materially contributed,
and a beast known as the *natshiin dakoora,* the Herder's Throwing Stick,
may be slaughtered at the funeral of a dependent member. This animal

takes its name from the fact that the junior members of a farming group look after its herds, especially during the season of growing crops. For at that time a man is justified in taking extreme measures against animals that persistently damage his fields. In the old days the herder had also to be a person who could defend his charges against attack, but nowadays one sees children as young as six or seven doing the job. An alternative name for this animal is the Bachelor's Cow (*dakuor naab*). It is killed for a man who has earned the help of his father in making a bridewealth payment, but has not yet taken a wife; the father pays out at the funeral what he would otherwise have paid out at the marriage.

From a purely visual point of view, the Cow of the Hoehandle is certainly the most prominent of the animals slaughtered to a man's name. For during the earliest stages of the burial service an animal of the dead man's herd is seized by men of the reciprocal funeral group and dragged to the scene of the ceremony. Some of the younger men then struggle to overturn the beast by seizing it by the bottom of the legs. When they finally succeed, the feet are tied together so that it cannot move away, and the cow is left lying like this until the time comes for it to be slaughtered, three days later. Formerly, the end of the tail was snipped off and thrown on the body of the deceased, and the legs of the cow were broken; but this practice has been effectively suppressed by the Administration as inhumane.

The reciprocal relationship between funeral groups is often expressed in terms of tying up this animal; the phrase "we tie for each other" (*ti lona ko*) means that the two groups cooperate in this and other funeral tasks. Moreover, the group that tie the Cow of the Hoehandle also consume its flesh. This animal cannot be killed, cut up, or shared by the deceased's own group, but only by the reciprocal funeral group, who divide the flesh among those of their members who have lost their fathers.[2] As the LoDagaa say, "People cannot eat their own dirt" (*be kantwõ di be deo*); hence a close, but not too close, group of agnates must do so on their behalf. The left front leg of the animal is, as usual, reserved for persons who stand in some sort of joking relationship. In this case the leg is taken not by the matriclan joking partners but by the "sister's sons," who often play a similar role (Goody [1956a, 1959a]). However, it is not the "sister's sons" of the deceased's own group who snatch the leg, but those of the reciprocal funeral group. Thus the catching, butchering, and distributing of the Cow of the Hoehandle form one of those ritual services that are the subject of exchange

2 Not all patriclans in Tom have this prohibition on the meat of animals killed at the funeral, but it is very generally observed in the district.

relationships between patrilineal groups. What is too "dirty" for one's immediate agnates to perform is allocated to more distant kinsmen on a reciprocal basis.

This same principle is at work in the distribution of the meat of the Beast of Farm Tidying (*vaar daar dun*), the corresponding animal killed when a woman dies. This animal is offered by a husband to his dead wife's patriclansfolk in appreciation of the assistance she has given on his farm. The first payment of bridewealth transfers the right to the woman's labor from her lineage to that of her husband, although her father still gets some assistance from her at harvest time. From this point of view, the presentation of a Beast of Farm Tidying is not an inescapable obligation on the husband's lineage, since they have already acquired rights over the woman's agricultural activities. Rather, it is a form of thank offering for the way she has worked. On the other hand, to omit this offering would certainly cause offense between the descent groups concerned.

Although the dead woman's lineage receive this gift, they are not themselves allowed to consume the flesh. The animal is handed to the reciprocal funeral group, who later return part of the meat to the husband's lineage to be used in the preparation of the "orphans' meal" for the dead woman's children.[3] Once again the original recipients "cannot eat their own dirt."

Both the Beast of the Hoehandle and the Beast of Farm Tidying are provided and distributed on a patrilineal basis. Farming is specifically linked to the agnatic line, since it is in a subdivision of the patriclan that land is vested, and consequently it is this group that forms the basis of the local units cooperating in productive activities. This is brought out in comparing the distribution of the Cow of the Rooftop, as carried out by the LoDagaba, with the Cow of the Hoehandle. The latter is given to members of the reciprocal funeral group, a patrilineal unit, rather than to the matriclans; the left front leg is taken by an agnatically defined "sister's son" instead of by the matriclan joking partners. Then again the Cow of the Hoehandle is said not to have a fillet (*sie*[4]), which is the portion of the Cow of the Rooftop assigned to the mother. These facts associate the Cow of the Hoehandle (and the same is

---

[3] When a man dies, the LoWiili sometimes cut parts of the Cow of the Hoehandle for the same purpose. But the LoDagaba expressly forbid this and maintain that the Cow of the Rooftop must be used, thus illustrating the greater emphasis placed on matriclanship in relation to orphanhood.

[4] In humans, *sie* means waist and is associated with childbirth and menstruation. It is differentiated from *sie*, the soul or double, by being spoken with a high instead of a low tone on the *e*.

true of the Cow of Childbearing) with sacrifices to the ancestors, the flesh of these sacrifices being distributed on a patrilineal basis. "Hoe cows and bridewealth cows are the same," I was told: both are sacrificed to the ancestor shrines. And indeed among the LoDagaba the sons of the dead man can take a Cow of the Hoehandle out of their father's byre to be killed at his funeral, even in the absence of the heir; whereas the decision about the Cow of the Rooftop and any other cows must wait upon the heir's arrival.

Let me summarize the central points of this extended treatment of the funeral monies and of the distribution of meat to which they are linked. The main compulsory contributions consist of twenty cowries from the members of both the patriclan and the matriclan of the deceased. The money collected in this way is used to pay some of the funeral expenses. The payment of these twenty cowries entitles the contributor, if he is otherwise qualified, to a portion of the Cow of the Rooftop or the Cow of the Hoehandle. Among the LoDagaba, the former commemorates the death of a member of the matriclan, the latter celebrates his achievement as a farmer, an activity specifically linked with the agnatic line.

The statements about who ought to contribute money and receive meat are to all intents and purposes the same in both communities. Among the LoWiili, the divergence between ideal and actual is particularly noticeable, and in practice the stated norms are reinterpreted in terms of the dominant property relations. In situations in which the LoDagaba would work on a matrilineal basis, the LoWiili, who inherit all property patrilineally, virtually limit both the contributions of money and the distribution of flesh to those members of the matriclans concerned who also belong to the dead man's patriclan. The LoWiili system means in effect that the allocation of the meat is nearly the same whether it is made on the basis of agnatic or of uterine descent. For the four categories receiving the legs of the animal—namely, joking partners, "fathers," "brothers," and "sons"—cover almost the whole of the patriclan, since there are only four main matriclans to which they belong. What happens is that the meat is lumped together, cut into small portions, and given to all members of the relevant patrilineal group. It may also be cut up in this way among the LoDagaba, but the portions are distributed to members of certain matriclans without reference to patriclanship.

We see here that the exclusively patrilineal system of inheritance among the LoWiili is correlated with the fact that the animals to be killed at the funeral come from agnatic (or matrilateral) sources, not matrilineal ones. The monetary contributions also tend to be restricted to agnates, and so, too, the claims upon the flesh of the animals slaughtered.

The Cow of the Rooftop is in fact becoming virtually a patriclan animal, patrilineally derived and patrilineally distributed. I say "becoming," because the process is observable. The LoWiili of Birifu tend to avoid the name Cow of the Rooftop, since it carries the implication of uterine inheritance; instead they employ a more neutral phrase such as *kowel naab*, Cow of the Dispersal of the Funeral, which is also used by the neighboring DagaaWiili for their main funeral animal, and which has no suggestion of matrilineal participation.[5] A man whose father had taken him from a LoWiili village to live in a LoDagaba one and who was trying to ensure that his own sons succeeded to his wealth told me that he always refused any flesh of the Cow of the Rooftop that was offered him by his neighbors, because his acceptance might lead them to think that he also accepted uterine inheritance.

Not only are the people of Birifu tending to avoid institutions that imply the matrilineal inheritance of wealth; they are doing so quite deliberately. When pressed about a particular animal, they will say, "Yes, this should be divided according to matriclanship. We are cutting it in pieces and giving one to everybody that contributed twenty cowries at the funeral." But they know that the matriclan contributions are rarely collected from or offered by anyone outside the patriclan, so they simply divide the animal among agnates. And it is because this animal has become so closely linked with the patriclan that they can use for this purpose one of the daughter's bridewealth cattle.

The killing of funeral animals should take place immediately after the actual burial; but quite often it is postponed until later that day, or even the following day, partly because there will then be fewer claimants on the meat. After the meat is shared, the widows are escorted to their fathers' compounds, and the near male mourners are taken to drink beer by the persons who acted as their companions during the past three days, together with other members of the clan sector. On the following day the post-burial phase of the ceremony begins.

---

[5] The only monetary contribution of the DagaaWiili, their equivalent of byre money, is called *kowel libie*, a phrase I once heard used by a LoWiili in the same way.

CHAPTER IX

After the Burial

We are so accustomed to the phrase "sackcloth and ashes" in connection with the funeral rites of some eastern nations, that we
seldom think of it as a filthy, disgusting mode of expressing sorrow. The Congo custom is almost identical; the natives rub themselves in the soil and wear their dirtiest garments for several days
after the death of a relative, presenting a shockingly dirty figure.
One has to think it strange that they cannot mourn in a more
cleanly fashion, but such is the custom, and no one can change it.

PHILLIPS, *The Lower Congo*

The burial of the body terminates for the time being the phase of public
mourning, but the mortuary ceremony continues for another three days.
Some of the rites already described may be postponed until after the day
of the interment. The killing of the funeral animals, for example, may
be so delayed, either because of difficulties experienced in finding an
animal or so that fewer persons will be present to share the meat. But
although the post-burial phase of the first funeral ceremony may include
such rites, and is in any case a direct continuation of that ceremony, it
is distinguished by the presence of three separate rituals that are repeated with modifications in the third and again in the last of the
funeral performances. These three rituals are: (1) the bathing and
whitewashing of the widow, (2) the orphans' meal, and (3) the property
rites in the dead man's room. Behind each of them runs a common
theme, the preparation for the final redistribution of the dead man's
rights and duties. The first ritual concerns his rights over women, the
second begins the formal reallocation of his role as father, and the third
deals with his material goods.

THE BATHING OF THE WIDOW

For three days after a man's burial, only women may sleep at the
house where the death occurred, the male bereaved and those who come
from afar being led away to sleep in another compound. Every morning
and evening the women burst into loud lamentations. At night they lie

down outside the house, and if it rains, they go inside the long room, although they speak of this as the byre and therefore maintain the fiction of not entering the house to sleep. In Tom, I was told that formerly men would sleep for four days at the house where a woman had died, but so far as I know this is not done nowadays.

In respect of the bathing and whitewashing of the surviving spouse, the treatment of men and women is markedly different. The imbalance of the conjugal relationship, already noted in connection with the modes of restraining the bereaved, is again brought out in the procedures taken to prevent the widow or widower from committing suicide that are an intrinsic part of the bathing rituals. As in the earlier instances, the measures taken against the suicide of the widower are considerably more severe than in the case of the widow.

To demonstrate the differences in the treatment of the sexes, I shall first describe the bathing of the widower, a rite that takes place outside the deceased's compound on the day following the burial. A matriclan joking partner from within the husband's own patriclan brings a knife, an arrow, and three stones, called *tenggaan kube,* since they are seen as belonging to the Earth shrine. As I remarked earlier, three such stones are also buried under the entrance to the byre of a new compound, and should anyone die there during the next three years, it is thought that the site in question is unwilling to accept the new residents and that they would be wise to move elsewhere. The metaphorical association of three stones and three years occurs again in the present instance; for if a widower tries to kill himself after being made to drink water in which the arrow, knife, and stones are placed, it is said that his wound will remain open for three years. When he gives the water to the husband, the joking partner makes a speech, of which the following is an example:

> In the water you drink, can you see the arrow, the knife and the three stones?
> *Ka a kwõ ka fu nyuura, ka fu ba nye a pĩĩ, ti nye suo, ti nye kube ata?*
>
> With the knife, a person can kill himself. With the arrow, he can do the same.
> *A suo, nire mi tuõ kon a tuora. A pĩĩ, fu mi tuõ kon a fu tuora.*
>
> But look at these stones. Today I give you both the knife and the arrow.
> *Ti nye a be gõn kube anyene. A diã n de a suo ni a pĩĩ koba.*
>
> If you are thinking of killing yourself, of cutting your throat
> *Fũ wa ti tiere ka fu na kon fu tuora, a suo fu*

with the knife, you won't be able to do it. If you take an arrow
ngma a kokori, fu kontwõ kpie. Ka pĩĩ na fu de

and say you'll wound yourself, the poison can't kill you.
yil ka fu na tshorena fu miõ, a lo' kontwõ ko fue.

People would say that the Earth shrine wishes it so,
Ti be na yil ka tenggaan boora,

and others would think you knew something about your wife's death.
ti be mine na yil ka fu bong fu poo zie.

So today we give you these things to cool your anger.
Le zu a diã, ti na ko fu anya, a suur baara.

In time you'll follow your wife; but she can never return to you.
Fu na wa biera fu poo; fu poo kon le wa fue.

If you wound yourself, you'll be sick three years without dying;
Ti fũ wa ti tshor fu miõ fu na gan yuum ata ti fu kon kpie;

and when you recover, you'll have to make a payment to the Earth
shrine.[1]
ti wa ir fu na yaan a tenggaan.

Two features of this speech in particular are relevant to the present
discussion. The measures taken against the widower are an aspect of
the sanctions against suicide that exist in most social systems; however
honorable a solution suicide may provide for the individual, from the
society's standpoint the practice must be held in check. Here it is visualized as a heinous sin against the Earth. But the speech bears on the
problem of social control in yet another way. For by drinking the water
in which the stones of the Earth shrine have been placed, the widower
is in effect taking a silent oath that he has had nothing to do with his
wife's death. If he has been involved, the Earth shrine would allow him
to commit suicide or perhaps bring about his death in another way.

After this speech is over, the widower has his head shaved, and is
bathed and painted with whitewash (*guor*). A piece of string is then

---

[1] I translate the verb *yaan* as "to make a payment"; but the idea of paying the
Earth shrine is rather different from that of paying a fine in Western society. A
fine is imposed from outside and represents the decision or judgment of a central
authority backed by the sanction of physical force. The sanctions for paying the
Earth shrine, on the other hand, are diffuse and largely internal; the actor feels it
essential to make this expiatory payment in order to avoid more trouble from supernatural agencies, although the payment is often postponed until further misfortunes
are attributed to the same cause.

tied round his throat, and finally he is given a stick (*daagbal, daadyura,* or *daatuo,* "bitter stick"), cut by the grave-diggers, to support him on his way. The tying of the string is a protective measure to prevent the soul from prematurely quitting the body. The stick, sometimes said to represent the man's wife, is retained until the final ceremony, when it is broken in two; it constitutes a further precaution against suicide and is given only to men. A similar stick is often carried by a man who has lost a son. The whitewash has a number of metaphorical implications, which have already been discussed. No man may sleep with a woman while the whitewash is on his body, nor may he engage in any fight; thus certain prototypical aspects of the male role are neutralized until the final ceremony. On the other hand, it is dangerous for a man to be whitewashed if his wife is known to be a witch or to have committed an unexpiated adultery, anyhow until reparation has been made. To do so would be to incur mystical retribution.

When a man dies, his widows are bathed and whitewashed in a similar manner. I never witnessed the entire post-burial bathing ceremony for a LoWiili widow, though I did so among the LoDagaba, and in any case the rites are repeated at later services. It was sometimes difficult to attend affairs conducted exclusively by women, not so much because they themselves objected, but because my male acquaintances thought such behavior unbecoming for a man, even for a white man. I was therefore unable to watch these particular rituals as often as I would have wished, and those observations I did succeed in making were interrupted by my being called to share in drinking a pot of beer, an occupation more suitable for men and one in which it would have been uncivil not to join.

A further difficulty lay in the fact that in Birifu a fairly recent practice had developed of postponing the whitewashing of the widows, in doubtful cases, until after the cause of death had been ascertained at the second ceremony, known as the Diviners' Beer. In consequence, the whitewashing was usually carried out very quietly, on the initiative of the senior women involved. In the case of Ngminvuor's widow in Birifu, it was three months after her husband's death that she was whitewashed, and this took place in the rainy season when ritual performances get delayed or truncated, and funerals are less elaborate and less well attended.

The following description, therefore, is of a LoDagaba ceremony, but there seem to be no significant differences between the two communities. On the day following the burial of Katu of Tom, I was at his house watching the distribution of the meat of the Cow of the Rooftop, which had been postponed a day. A woman belonging to the joking partners of the deceased's matriclan walked quietly by, putting ashes on the heads of the young children present and tying pieces of string around their necks. In front of the house, Katu's four widows were sitting with their backs to the wall, preparing long strips of vine (*byuur* and *tangbo*), which they would later wear round their hips.

In all the rites that the widow has to undergo, the people primarily involved are her own kin. Although males do have their part to play, the main roles are taken by her "sisters" (*yebe* or *poghyaataaba*) and her "father's sisters" (*sãã ma* or *pure*). Because the boundaries of kinship categories are defined by patrilineal and matrilineal clanship, both these classes of persons are defined in two ways. For example, my "father's sisters" may be female patriclan members of the next senior generation or any female member of my father's matriclan. The most important people within the general category of "father's sisters" are those defined as such both in patrilineal and in matrilineal terms, especially my father's full sister. It is these doubly defined "sisters" and "father's sisters" that play the important roles in the bathing of the widows, although among the LoWiili little attention is now paid to the matrilineal aspect, and even among the LoDagaba the patrilineal relationship is the more important, since a woman is so strongly identified with her patriclan in matters to do with marriage.

At Katu's funeral, the "father's sister" of the senior widow had gone over to a neighboring house to call an old woman who was known to be well acquainted with the proper funeral procedures. On the arrival of the expert, she and an assistant went inside the house to prepare whitewash and food for the ceremony. Before being bathed, the widows are given a ritual meal. As is often the case with purificatory ceremonies and rites of re-entry, the participants are forbidden to eat any food beforehand. Taking a calabash of water, the leader pretends to pour its contents over the other widows' outstretched hands. This she repeats on three separate occasions, and on the fourth she finally pours some water. Next, the widows are given drinking water, followed by a mixture of flour and water, and the same fourfold procedure is used.[2]

This ritual of a pretended gesture has already been discussed. But here I want to point to an additional feature, its use in contexts in

---

[2] On another occasion the widow was made to link her hands, palms downward, in front of her, and on the back of them more dollops of porridge were placed; these she had to raise toward her mouth three times and then throw away. Next she did the same with the food placed in the palms of her hands, and finally with them stretched out in front of her.

which a person is being put to a test. The force of the procedure derives from the fact that the same method is used in approaching the dead at sacrifices to the ancestors. On this particular occasion the women are tested to see whether they have been faithful to their late husband and whether they are implicated in his death. As I have mentioned, rituals of pretended gesture occur at several points during the esoteric rites of the Bagre society; indeed, one of my companions once remarked to me after watching this part of the ceremony, "Bagre and funerals are just the same." As can be seen more clearly at a later stage in the obsequies, the widows are treated as dead because of their close association with the deceased. They are undergoing a metaphorical burial of the relationship with their late husband.

There is yet a further aspect to the ritual of pretended gesture, one that lies behind so many of the formal procedures of the LoDagaa funeral. The acts that separate the living from the dead are also a testing of their past relationship. The feeding of the widow appears to be a kind of ordeal to test her guilt or innocence; acceptance of the food is the equivalent of an oath to the ancestor shrines, an oath denying complicity in her husband's death. On each occasion that the water is offered to the widows to drink, the leader of the ritual asks, "Shall we give it?" (*Ti ko?*) If the widow agrees, she asserts her innocence, and in particular that she has not slept with another man, an act that during his lifetime might have led to his death and after his burial would cause great offense to his ghost.

This ceremony can be seen as the last supper of the husband and wife. For when the widow's hands are cleansed and she is given water to drink, instead of drinking it, she swills it round inside her mouth and spits it out upon the ground. The food offered to her, consisting of guinea-corn flour mixed with water, is treated in the same way, except that each time the food is withdrawn, it is flung upon the ground. But it is not thrown away. The food, like the water, is intended for the ancestors, into whose company the ghost is about to be received.

Rites that are of major importance to a community often possess a great richness of thematic meanings. In this way they display the ambiguity that is often found in poetry, having not one but many implications both for those who participate and for those who watch. Still another aspect of the feeding of the widows is brought out by the fact that after they have eaten, their mouths are wiped clean by the old women conducting the ceremony. In other words, the widows are treated as little children, unable to do anything for themselves. As in so many societies, the change of status is effected in terms of the image of death and rebirth. Wife becomes widow by dying and being born again.

After the widows have been duly fed, the old women walk round them again, sprinkle some ashes on their heads, and tie a piece of string round their necks, thus repeating the same protective rites that were carried out during the earlier part of the burial service on the small children of the dead man's compound. The senior wife is then taken round a corner (*dapuri*) of the house and stood under one of the gutters that throw the rain water from the flat roof clear of the walls. It is here that women are daubed with whitewash, whereas widowers are always treated at the front of the house (*dondori*). Like the drain outside the wall of the open courtyard, where women urinate and throw their slops, this is a place where water flows and can carry away impurities of both a physical and a moral kind. It is therefore a favorite spot for conducting purificatory rituals. The widow is made to stand on a piece of matting torn from her husband's mat, and her fellow clanswomen (*poghyaataaba*) crowd round while her goatskin waistbands (*gammie*) are stripped off and replaced with the long hanging fibres that were prepared earlier in the day by the various women present.

An appreciation of the significance of this act depends upon a knowledge of the various types of dress traditionally worn by women; for a woman's clothing alters with the physiological and social development of the individual. Before puberty, a young girl will wear either nothing at all or a few strings of small beads (*leo*) round the waist. Between puberty and marriage, her waistbands are strings of dark-stained grasses that hang down to the knees in front (*ganzuole*). Whereas young children can go about naked, girls who have begun to menstruate must wear some covering below the waist, and men speak of the vagina as an ugly thing that must be hidden. After marriage, a woman puts on a thick waistband made of some fifty loops carefully sewn from strips of goatskin (*gammie*), or sometimes rolled out of fibres stripped from dawadawa pods (*sapie, sobie*). With this dress, leaves are always worn behind, and usually in front, to conceal the sexual organs. Occasionally, at ceremonies, women wear the strings of cowries (*libie siore*) that have been mentioned as a funeral disguise. Except for clothes made from imported cloth, which are usually worn on top of the traditional costume, other types of dress are used only in funeral ceremonies.

The fibres in which the widows are now dressed are clearly a form of premarital wear. In other words, the widows are first "buried," then recreated as newborn children, and are now adolescent girls who have not yet acquired a husband. They will only wear adult clothes again at the conclusion of the whole series of funeral ceremonies, when they once more take up their normal position in the community.

Around the widow's head is placed a plain grass band, which has a protective significance. Next, the old woman in charge takes the broken calabash with the whitewash and smears the mixture over the widow, who then steps backward off the mat. As I have earlier remarked in connection with the Vukãle ceremony, whitewashing has the effect of setting the women apart in their new status of widowhood and of purifying them from the dirt of their former spouses; and in addition to this they are subjected to a further ordeal, to a test by the Earth shrine of possible complicity in the death of their husband. On the occasion I am describing, the widows all came through successfully, and one of their sons fetched a xylophone from the house and began to play. Thereupon the two old women conducting the ceremony led a procession of all the participants four times around the instrument, the widows each supported by a "father's sister." These "father's sisters" often whitewash the widow, if a specialist is not called in, but her "sisters" bathe and dress her. Thus it is the widow's own kinsfolk who subject her to these tests in order to free her from blame.

This dance I witnessed celebrated the innocence of the widows. When it was finished, each widow was given twenty cowries by her patriclansfolk to pay the woman who had carried out the whitewashing. The leader of the ritual first of all took the cowries that were offered her and immediately threw them on the ground near the xylophone. The money was later collected by her assistant and would be returned to her at the third ceremony, the Bitter Funeral Beer, at which she is again called to help. Both at the third ceremony and at the Final Funeral she repeats this action, but on the last occasion the cowries are gathered up by a representative of the dead man's patriclan as a sign that the widow has been proved innocent and is therefore acceptable to the husband's lineage as a leviratic spouse. But until then the cowries and the woman remain untouched. At this point she ceases to be a *kpiin poo,* an ancestor's wife, and becomes a *poo kuor,* a marriageable woman. The name *poo kuor* is also given to a young girl who is ripe for wedlock. The equivalent for a male is *daa kuor,* which I have translated as bachelor; the brothers of the dead man are known as *sir kuorbe,* available husbands, since the widow can choose, or be given to, any of these men.

The whitewashing is now over. The fragments of calabash in which the whitewash was mixed are broken into yet smaller fragments by being trodden underfoot. These pieces are gathered up by the old woman who had conducted the ceremony, and she now throws them away to prevent their being touched by another person. In return for her services, she keeps the old leather waistbands taken off the widows. They, meanwhile, have retired to sit under the wall of the house. There they begin to improve upon the dresses in which they have been attired by taking the rough fibres one by one and rolling them upon their thighs. Later on they make these strips into proper waistbands, which they wear until after they have been bathed once again at the third ceremony, the Bitter Funeral Beer.

The widows have now been tested (*polfu be pol be*) for the first time. For the rest of that day they continue to sit outside the house and can neither leave to go elsewhere nor enter the house itself; indeed, even at night they sleep outside the compound. Visitors to the house the next day will inquire of them if they have slept well. At all times sleeping badly is an indication of the presence of some mystical trouble about which a diviner should be consulted; in this case, bad dreams carry the implication that the woman is being troubled on account of her husband's death and therefore suggest her possible complicity.

Later that day the widows are taken to the nearest part of their husband's farm. There they are given a small calabash containing some grains of guinea-corn, which they pretend to plant. This act is performed three times. From now on the widow is able to work again on the compound's farms, as she had formerly done when her husband was alive.

On the third day, the assistants take hold of the mats on which the widows have been sleeping, stand at the foot of the compound wall, and pretend to throw them on the roof. Once again this act is done in pretense three times, and on the fourth the mats are thrown onto the rooftop. From now on the widows can sleep inside their late husband's house. After the throwing of the mat, they are led three times along the track that goes to the bush farms, then three times along the path to the market, and finally they are taken into the house itself. From now on they are free to go where they will.

These various acts concerning a woman's economic and domestic tasks are rites of re-entry into those activities that she performed as the wife of the dead man. Now she is reincorporated into the domestic life of her husband's compound, with one major exception: control over her sexual powers still remains vested in her dead husband. It is with this that the bathing of the widow at the two final ceremonies is primarily concerned. And as with the re-entry into domestic and economic activities, the freeing of her sexuality is marked by the imposition of and liberation from certain prohibitions on her behavior. After the Bitter Funeral Beer, the third of the funeral ceremonies, she can again wear the ordinary attire of a woman, anoint her body with oil, and sit

upon the four-legged stools used by women. The prohibition on remarriage, however, lasts until the final ceremony. Until that has been
performed she cannot have sexual intercourse, nor even drink cheek by
cheek out of the same calabash as a man in the way that lovers do. Nor
can she touch any of her dead husband's clothes, lest she should again
come into contact with his "dirt," from which these ceremonies are
intended to cleanse her.

By these ritual acts the widow is separated from her dead husband
and rejoins, step by step, the normal life of society. The process is
gradual, like the elimination of the dead man from the roles he played
in the social system. Indeed, the two processes run parallel to one another. Even now the dead man continues to be fed as a living member
of the household. Every time food is cooked, a portion is placed upon
the rooftop on the forked stick that is normally used for drying meat
in the sun (*daatshera*). About every three days a small pot of beer is put
on his own part of the flat roof, the part above the room of his senior
wife. If any powdered tobacco is sold in or near the house, then it is
customary to set aside a pinch for the dead man.[3]

All this allocation of food and drink for the dead man ceases after
the ceremony of the Diviners' Beer. But in a sense, of course, these early
offerings are continued in the form of sacrifices to the ancestors, both
kinds of offering being extensions after death of the food that had been
prepared for members of the community when they were alive. So, at
any rate, the LoDagaa conceive of the situation.

At earlier points in the analysis of these ceremonies, I have commented upon various themes that run through the bathing ritual, those,
for example, concerning the use of whitewash and the sweeping of dirt.
I want here to consider these themes again in the context of the conjugal
relationship, especially insofar as these acts represent both a controlled
expression of the hostile element in the relationship between husband
and wife and a sanction against the expression of this hostility in more
dangerous ways.

The whitewashing of the surviving partner is particularly significant
in the process of dissociation and reassociation to which the bereaved
are subjected. For by this act, the widow is set apart from other members of society. The new status of the surviving spouse is publicly pro-
claimed, and at any future funerals in the neighborhood he or she will

---

[3] The locally grown tobacco is cured with salt and ocro, then ground up for use.
It is taken orally by both men and women, being placed inside the lower lip, swilled
carefully round the front of the mouth to activate the saliva, and finally spat out.
Pipe-smoking is comparatively rare.

be expected to take a vigorous part in the dances. But as in the house-cleansing ceremony known as Vukāle, the application of the whitewash purifies as well as differentiates, a point that hardly needs elaborating in view of the metaphorical significance of whitewash in Western society. Association with death is a threat to the community, and those closely connected with the deceased have to be purified of the defiling effects of their contact with him. The whiteness of the paint is visualized as counteracting the blackness of dirt.

But the metaphor has further implications. The defilement of the surviving partner arises not only from a general association with the deceased, but from the most intimate form of human intercourse, the sexual act. The close association in life of husband and wife is seen as a sharing of the dirt of each other's bodies. This concept epitomizes the domestic union into which the two individuals have entered. Living together on any terms means the interchange of body dirt. A member of the patrilineage of a dead man will refuse the meat of the Cow of the Hoehandle, saying, "We cannot eat our own dirt." But the defilement of the spouse is particularly associated with the sexual act itself, with the sweat of copulation and with the exuviae that impregnate clothes and other highly personal possessions. The specific connection of dirt and sexual intercourse is brought out in the sacrifices to expiate adultery that are made at the ancestor shrines of the husband's lineage. The cuckold himself is prohibited from eating the animal provided by the adulterer. To do so would be "to eat one's wife's dirt" or "to eat on the cheap" (*mworeno o dire*).

Whitewashing frees the surviving partner from the intimate relationship with the deceased. A man once told me that unless this rite is performed for a widower, "the woman's dirt will kill him" (*a poo dio na ko ona*)—that is, if he were to have sexual intercourse with another woman. The whitewashing cleanses the dirt of the dead partner and thus enables the surviving spouse to resume sexual intercourse with other persons without incurring the wrath of the ghost. Such precautions against the dead are of course widespread. As Frazer noted:

> The ghosts of dead husbands and wives are commonly deemed very dangerous to their surviving spouses, whom they are thought to haunt in a variety of ways. This they are thought to do especially when the surviving partner has taken to himself or herself a second wife or husband, for the ghost is naturally jealous of the second wife or husband, and seeks to wreak her spite against the new bride or bridegroom. Hence special precautions are commonly taken to guard the widower or widow against the dangerous spirit of his or her departed spouse. ([1936] pp. 199–200.)

The jealousy that Frazer noted in the relationship with the dead spouse would seem to derive from the relationship with the living one. For it will be recalled that our initial premise was that supernatural relationships—that is, those assumed to exist between human and supernatural beings (which I refer to as excorporeal or spiritual relationships), as well as those between the denizens of the other world itself (referred to as incorporeal or heavenly relationships)—derive from the corporeal relationships between human beings themselves. So the precautions taken against a dead spouse can be considered as indices of the nature of the relationship with the living one. They are social projections of the tensions inherent in the conjugal relationship, as is seen in the dangers that the partner's dirt can have, especially in sexual intercourse with other persons.

The imbalance in the conjugal relationship has already been noted in connection with the different methods of restraining the bereaved. There is a similar inequality in the bathing rituals. Although the whitewash cleanses the surviving spouse, neither widow nor widower may engage in sexual intercourse while it remains on the body; however, the length of time the whitewash is worn varies according to sex. A widow observes this ban until the final ceremony. So, too, does a man; but I have heard it strongly argued, by women as well as men, that for a man the prohibition is relaxed after the third ceremony, since a husband with several wives cannot be expected to remain continent for so long a period. In any case, a woman's funeral is completed in a much shorter time than a man's, so that a widower never observes his prohibition as long as a widow.

The difference in attitude to male and female sexuality is most apparent in the case of adultery. For the whitewash not only serves as a mark of differentiation and as a purifying agent, but also has supernatural implications. The sanction behind the use both of whitewash (*guor*) and of clay (LD *yagra*), which is often employed in the same way, lies in their association with the Earth shrine. Both are taken out of the earth, and their employment amounts to the oath "If there has been any unconfessed adultery, may the Earth kill me." But it is the infidelity of the woman, not of the man, that matters. It is he and his lineage that acquire exclusive rights over her sexuality, not the reverse; a man cannot commit adultery in respect of his wife. When a widow is whitewashed, she may die or go blind if she has committed adultery during her husband's lifetime and not confessed to it; whereas for a widower, it is the adultery of his dead wife, not his own infidelities, that may cause him harm while he wears the whitewash. Indeed, if the expiatory payments have not yet been made on her behalf, a man can no more mourn or be whitewashed for an adulterous wife than for a wife who was a witch. Formerly, if the proper payment had not been handed over by the adulterer's lineage, her body was disposed of quickly without any mourning; this is a "bad death," like that of a witch. To perform the funeral ceremony would be to incur mystical retribution (*kpen tule*). For adultery not only infringes rights acquired by the bridewealth payments, but endangers the husband's life. The adultery of a wife can lead to a man's death.[4] Indeed, there are severe taboos among the LoDagaa upon close contact between men who have slept with the same woman, whether or not she is the wife of either. For instance, a man who had slept with the same woman that another man has subsequently slept with may not visit that man on his sickbed, or he will bring about his death—even if the two men are brothers.

These considerations show the great importance placed upon the act of whitewashing in the funeral ceremonies. Indeed, in doubtful cases (and this appears to be all) the LoWiili now perform the whitewashing only after the cause of death has been finally established at the Diviners' Beer. Only then do they know whether it is safe to whitewash the surviving spouse.

This discussion of male and female infidelity necessarily revolves around the sharp distinction that exists between the coital and reproductive functions of a woman, a point that I now wish to develop. Marriage transfers, among other things, rights over the reproductive powers of the woman to her husband's clan, in effect to a subdivision of that unit, and at death such rights remain within the descent group, according to rules that differ somewhat in the two communities. However, rights over her coital services, although in one sense also transferred to the descent group, are exclusively vested in a single person.

The coital and reproductive aspects of a woman's sexuality are not of course separable in all contexts; adultery infringes one set of rights and threatens the other. However, the distinction is nonetheless valid, not only for purposes of analysis, but because it represents the ideas of the LoDagaa themselves. This is clear from the ritual in which the first pregnancy of a girl is publicly announced. Before this performance has

---

[4] The LoDagaa also recognize that the man may have some responsibility in the death of the wife, as is shown by the speech made at the time that the precautions against suicide are taken. But her death could not result from his sleeping with another woman. Associated as it is with male dominance, the "double attitude" toward extramarital affairs of men and of women characterizes monogamous as well as polygamous societies. However, in this latter case it is enforced by the acknowledged right of men to more than one sexual partner within marriage.

taken place, it is said that the girl may be so overcome by any mention of her state that she will have a miscarriage. One night, therefore, when the husband and wife are sleeping on the same mat, members of his compound put a pebble in a new earthenware bowl, which they fill with water. The intruders then go to the place where the couple are sleeping and call out the names of both husband and wife. When the pair reply, the cold contents of the pot are thrown over them, with the words: "Take the fruit and give me the pips" (*yi de duor mogh etshe a dozun kum*). The metaphor refers to the fruit of the dawa-dawa tree: its dry flesh makes a sweet-tasting flour, but, metaphorically, the household is not directly concerned with this, claiming an interest in the seeds alone. A LoDagaa explained the ritual phrase to me in the following way: "The man and the woman sleep together and do not think beyond their pleasure; by performing this ceremony, we tell them to enjoy themselves but at the same time to remember that the child belongs to us all."

A similar custom is found among neighboring communities. The Voltaic peoples in general place little emphasis on marriage ceremonies, that is, upon the transfer of the bridewealth and the change of residence of the woman. On the other hand, ceremonies centering on the conception and birth of children are more elaborate. I suggest that this is related to the conceptual separation of the two aspects of a woman's sexuality, the coital and the reproductive. For the lineage, the procreation of children, not the acquisition of sexual services, is the central feature of marriage; hence it is this that draws greater public attention.

No clearer distinction could be drawn between these two aspects of a woman's sexuality than in the ceremony I have described. The sexual act is severed from its consequence, and the one is related to the conjugal, the other to the lineage, level of organization. The intimacy of the act itself creates interpersonal ties that are realized and given a concrete material counterpart in the sharing of the dirt of each other's bodies. Unless this bond is formally broken, intercourse with the surviving partner of the marriage, even by a member of the same descent group, will arouse the anger of the deceased. Whitewashing after the burial is one of the series of separation rites that sever the conjugal union. These acts continue until the final funeral ceremony, after which the widow or widower is at last permitted to have sexual intercourse again.

Rights over women thus pose similar problems to those posed by the settlement of property. Whereas at one level of analysis such rights are vested in the descent group, they are in fact exercised by an individual by virtue of his membership in the corporation. Within the group, tension exists between those who at present exercise the rights and those who will do so at the death of the holder. Death shifts the critical relationship among the living members of the corporate group. For example, the focus may move from the conflict between adjacent generations to the rivalry between following siblings. But the original tension is not resolved by death; it moves its scene of operation to the context of ancestor worship. The ambivalent attitude toward the near kinsman from whose death one expects to benefit comes to no abrupt end when the death actually occurs. The illicit wish has been fulfilled, and the moment of sorrow is the moment of rejoicing. But the guilt feelings achieve outward expression not only in sacrifices to the dead, but in the precautions taken before any of the dead man's rights are acquired by his fellow clansfolk. Of the rights that he exercises, possibly the most likely to arouse the jealous anticipation of near kin are those over the sexual services of his wives; these are also the rights whose infringement during his lifetime most threatens the structure of the family and the lineage. Ascertaining whether these rights have been violated, above all by kin, is a dominant motif of the funeral ceremonies, particularly in the later stages. Conflict between the haves and the have-nots is an essential problem with which all human societies have to cope, but the actual lines of tension are determined by the particular form of social organization. It is the funeral ceremonies that often reveal these tensions most clearly, for they cannot but enact the conflicts that exist within these intimate relationships.

THE ORPHANS' MEAL

The bathing and whitewashing of the surviving spouse occupy three days and are rituals carried out exclusively by women. On the day after the body has been buried a further ceremony is performed for the children of the deceased in which members of both sexes participate. This is the orphans' meal, prepared by a double "sister," in the sense just discussed, but offered by the reciprocal funeral group. "Orphan" (*bikpibe*) here carries the less usual connotation of the English word and refers to a child who has lost either parent; thus orphanhood corresponds to the state of being "without a father" or "without a mother" that Fortes has so perceptively analyzed for the Tallensi.

When the funeral animals are slaughtered, portions of their flesh are set aside to make this special meal for the orphans, which corresponds in several significant ways to the feeding of the surviving spouse described in the last section. Senior members of the reciprocal funeral group take the cooked meat into the long room of the house in which the man died (*kpiin diu,* the spirit's room) and divide it between the bowls of soup that have been set out there, one bowl for each child of whom the deceased was the social father. By the use of this phrase, I intend to exclude not only his adulterine offspring, but also the children of any widow he has inherited leviratically. For although he is fully entitled to the coital services of such a spouse, her reproductive powers remain vested in her late husband, the person on whose behalf the bride-wealth was paid. The levir is in the position of breeding children to the name of the dead man; consequently the offspring of which he is not the *pater* or social father take no part in the orphans' meal. In this respect the status of levir approximates to that of "authorized lover" mentioned earlier. The lover-mistress relationship may be authorized by the sacrifice of a fowl, provided by the cicisbeo, to the husband's ancestor shrines. But although this act permits sexual access, it carries no rights in any of the offspring. Indeed, a husband who has proved to be infertile may deliberately seek such a lover for his wife in order to obtain descendants. Such offspring should in theory attend the orphans' meal only at the death of their mother's husband. However, in practice such discriminations are somewhat blurred. I have already spoken of the behavior at Daazie's funeral of the children of which he was the authorized *genitor,* in the above sense. The boy who had been dancing vigorously in public later turned up at the orphans' meal and took a portion of the meat without being prevented from so doing. But the absence of a jural aspect to his presence at the meal is stressed by the fact that his full brother, Namoo, born of the same union, did not come, and neither was he sent for.

When a woman dies, the food is cooked without salt, "so that the children will know their mother is dead." Stress on deprivation, on the loss suffered, runs through the whole ritual. In the center of the circle formed by the participants a woman puts a single bowl of porridge, and anyone present who has already lost his father or mother, as the case may be, may begin the meal by taking this portion. As the children are eating the food, the senior member of the reciprocal funeral group says, "It's your father's flesh you're eating" (*Fu sãã nen fu or*). The phrase "your father's flesh" is ambiguous in that "flesh" might refer either to the father's body or to the body of an animal he owned, since the word *nen* is applied to both humans and animals. However, it will be recalled that a similar phrase is used at the distribution of the Cow of the Roof-top, when there was no doubt but that the cow and the man were identified within that particular context. Here, too, an alternative phrasing that the ritual leader may use is "You're eating your father" (*Fu oora fu sãã*), thus making the sacramental nature of the act quite clear.

An understanding of the nature of the orphans' meal depends upon a knowledge of LoDagaa concepts of the human personality, certain aspects of which are common to a wide range of societies. In his analysis of the Trobriands, Malinowski showed how closely their beliefs about the make-up of a human being were linked to other aspects of the social system, especially the organization of unilineal descent groups. The beliefs of the LoDagaa do not display so close a correspondence; but, as Tylor realized long ago (though he placed this insight into the framework of a dubious and untestable hypothesis concerning the evolution of religion), an understanding of mortuary institutions depends upon a knowledge of the ways in which the human personality is conceived by that society. Indeed, without such knowledge, the verbal and non-verbal acts that constitute the orphans' meal can make no sense to the observer.

A human being consists of two elements, the body (*yanggan*, skin) and the soul or double (*sie*), to which the body acts as as a home. Each is essential to the other. Without the soul, the body ceases to live; to live is literally "to breathe." Without the body, the soul becomes an ancestral spirit (*kpiin*). But even in life, the soul is not a wholly ethereal entity completely confined to its material cage, the body. It has an independent, even material, existence in the sense that it may quit its shell from time to time, thereby laying itself open to the attacks of witches. This temporary dissociation of the body and the soul often occurs at night, but the separation may be of a more enduring kind. Such a state of affairs is revealed only when a diviner is consulted, which usually happens after a specific misfortune but sometimes following bad dreams. The diviner then prescribes the ritual known as "sweeping the soul," which, by inducing the wandering element to return to its human frame, leads to the reintegration of the human personality. These excursions of the soul reflect situations of anxiety and, insofar as they expose the individual to attack by witchcraft, indicate hostility in interpersonal relations. Strong attachments may also cause such a separation of the two elements of the personality, as when a soul attempts to follow a loved one who has died, and is driven out of the grave by the sharp instruments of the grave-diggers.

The movements of the soul reflect the relations of the individual with other members of his society; they may also represent an embodiment, on the plane of belief, of his interaction with the physical world. For instance, in the long and complex task of constructing a xylophone,

the instrument is believed to become imbued with the maker's soul.
If it has been made for sale, the craftsman has to undergo a ritual to
withdraw his soul from the instrument he has created. An aspect of his
personality has entered into his creation, and this has to be removed,
lest it harm others or is itself harmed. In this context the man and the
object of his creation are seen as part of one more inclusive persona.

The way in which the soul becomes associated with objects outside
but in close touch with the body has certain resemblances to the idea
of "body dirt" discussed earlier. Anything that comes into close physical contact with a man—his clothes, his weapons, his farming implements—becomes part of his extended social personality, not primarily
because his soul has entered into them, for he did not himself make
these things, but because they are permeated with the dirt of his body.
Such dirt adheres to all those objects and persons with whom a man
has been in intimate physical contact. The material goods with which
he is associated are in fact part of the man himself as a social object;
man, clothes, and tools are aspects of the unit of social relations, a social
personality. It follows logically within this idiom that the flesh of a
man's cattle is his own flesh, just as a man's quiver is also in a certain
sense part of himself.

These phenomena are often discussed under the general heading of
symbolism. But I intend to convey something rather different from what
is usually meant by this term. It is not simply that x (the quiver) "stands
for" y (the man), but that, from the actor's point of view, both form part
of some more inclusive unity, $x + y + \ldots n$, any component of which
may on the principle of *pars pro toto* represent the whole.

Although this formulation of the problem has certain resemblances
to Lévy-Bruhl's treatment of "mystical participation," there are important differences. In an interesting chapter on "The Problem of Symbols," Evans-Pritchard [1956] has pointed out that when the Nuer say
at a sacrifice that a cucumber is an ox, they are asserting not an over-all
identity but only an equivalence in certain limited respects. They have
no difficulty in other contexts in distinguishing oxen from the fruit of
the *cucumis prophetarum*. Among the LoDagaa, the association of
a slaughtered bovine and the corpse of its owner is of this same contextual kind.

But there is more to the orphans' meal than the association of a
man with his property. It will be remembered that when the Cow of
the Rooftop was dragged to the roof at the LoDagaba funeral, a bystander remarked that the dead man had "changed to meat." That this
statement may represent no more than a contextual equivalence is sup-

ported by the fact that when the LoDagaa say of a woman who has passed the menopause that she has "changed to a man," they clearly do not imply that physiologically and socially she is in all respects the same as a member of the male sex. However, the use of the phrase "changed to meat" indicates, in addition to the general association, that the animals killed to a man's name are seen as representing the body that has now been interred. Yet something still remains unexplained. For not only is the cow slaughtered and consumed by the kinsfolk of the deceased, but it is also ritually fed to the children rendered fatherless by his death.

Certain general factors that bear upon this problem have already been mentioned. The killing of animals closely associated with the dead man is similar to the burial of grave-goods or to the slaughter of slaves at the obsequies of Ashanti chiefs. For all these objects are part of his estate; his heirs may eventually inherit, but he, too, is seen as retaining his rights in and his need of these mundane possessions.

There is also a prestige component in the killings that establish the dead man among his ancestors and celebrate his name among the living. The recognition given to achieved prestige emerges yet more clearly in the slaughter of those animals acquired as a result of the various semispecialist activities of the dead man.

The funeral animals, then, are associated with the dead man and, as part of his estate, are slaughtered to his name. So his death is, as it were, repeated in the death of the cow. When the meat of his animal is distributed, the kinsmen are said to partake of the flesh of the dead man. In this manner the sacrament dramatizes the loss to the group and the resulting changes in personal status involved. The dismembering and distribution of the body are final confirmation of the death, just as the communal meal prepared by the patriclan sector establishes the fact that one of its members has slain a wild animal.

But why is the flesh actually fed to the fatherless children? The orphans' meal serves, of course, to confirm the children in their new status as "having lost a parent"; it has a complement in the rites of the final ceremony when the children are formally shown their classificatory "fathers." The orphans' meal is a preliminary to the final redistribution of the roles of the deceased. Henceforth they can eat the meat killed at the funeral of any person of the same sex as the one they have lost. Should any child do this without having eaten the sacramental meal, it is thought that he will not have long to live. For he has declared a parent dead who was yet alive. However, the change of status does not itself account for the stress on the cannibalistic aspect of the meal.

Commensalism in itself would meet the requirements of changed status, emphasizing as it does the unity of the sibling group in the face of loss.

A clue to the other levels of metaphoric meaning is to be found in the complementary rite in the final funeral ceremony when the children are shown their classificatory "fathers." For then the eating of the meat that is given to children is explicitly a test to show whether or not they had any hand in their parent's death. As in the whitewashing of the surviving spouse, this rite is at once a method of social control and a standardized externalization of the guilt feelings of those who benefit by the death. I did not specifically inquire whether the orphans' meal was also intended as a test of complicity, but the assumption seems justified, first, because it accords with similar rites I have mentioned, and, second, because it makes more comprehensible the feeding on the "father's flesh."

The eating of the sacrificial animal has been regarded by Robertson Smith, Frazer, and other writers as essentially an act of union, union with the fellow worshipers and union with the godhead. But among the LoDagaa a further element is present. It is true that eating together is incompatible with acts of hostility; the two are polar opposites. But eating the meat of a cow that represents the father's flesh is also a test of past hostility. The oral internalization of the father constitutes at once an act of union with him and an externalization of the children's guilt. The standardized practices show that the community recognizes that the hostile component in relationships between adjacent generations involves a possible threat to the parents. The children are subjected to tests of their complicity which, if successfully negotiated, help to disperse their own feelings of self-reproach at the loss of the parent.

It will be remembered that before the burial the widow is restrained, lest she should touch the body of her dead husband, and in particular lest she should commit oral aggression against it. Such an act is an act of love as well as of hate; for by biting the corpse she will die and therefore accompany her husband on his journey to the Land of the Dead. Here again two elements are present. On the personality level, eating the father represents the children's ambivalent attitudes of love and hate; on the societal plane, it constitutes an explicit recognition of the double nature of the child-father relationship.

THE SETTLEMENT OF THE ESTATE

During the earlier phase of the burial ceremony, when the dead man is exposed upon the funeral stand, he is surrounded by all his personal possessions. His quiver is hung over his shoulder; his bow is placed across his folded legs, or may be hung upon one of the posts of the stand, together with his wrist guard and his hat. After the interment the grave-diggers take all these objects except the quiver—that is, the bow, wrist guard, hat, stool, mat, and pillow—and hang them on the wall outside the byre. According to Labouret ([1931] p. 326), the Lo peoples of the Upper Volta do this to discourage the ghost's return; for should he attempt to claim the objects that he had possessed in life, he will only bruise himself against the wall on which they hang. Another interpretation was given to me by one informant who said that by putting the dead man's immediate possessions outside the house, the ghost was discouraged from entering and from wreaking harm upon those within. For the ghost haunts only the places where his possessions remain. If he cannot find them, he moves away. As will be seen from the discussion of inheritance, other of the personal possessions of the deceased are also dealt with in a special way so as to prevent the return of the ghost to the Land of the Living; such objects are taken not by the main heir, but by a person in another more distant division of the same descent group.

The object that the LoDagaa particularly associate with manhood in these ritual contexts is the quiver, which is given an important part in the rites performed in a dead man's room both at this time and later during the third and fourth ceremonies. After the burial, the quiver is taken away by the reciprocal funeral group and hidden under a granary. At all the subsequent ceremonies it is brought back by them for the rituals in the dead man's room, and around it are performed those acts dealing with the settlement of the estate. The member of the reciprocal funeral group chosen to carry out the ritual with the quiver also belongs to the matriclan that stands in a joking partnership to that of the deceased. In many of the rituals in these dual clan systems, the proper person to perform a particular act has to be doubly defined in this way, not only by membership of the patrilineal descent groups, but also by membership of the matrilineal ones. In the present case, the selected man is known as the *lo' dielo*, a term used for the person who lays the arrows out to dry when they have had poison daubed upon the lower part of their shafts; the implication behind the use of this term in funeral ceremonies is of a task so dangerous that a man cannot carry it out for himself.

After the orphans' meal the quiver is taken into the room, together with some arrows, an old hoe (*ku per*), twenty cowries, and an axe. Labouret maintains that the quiver is brought here because it is thought that the ghost will also come. When I myself asked why these objects were laid on the floor, I was told: "That is Katu (the name of the dead man); if anyone should tell a lie in the dead man's room (*ko diu* or *kpiin diu*), he will certainly die." In this context the quiver and the other objects do not merely attract the ghost; they are the dead man. The one interpretation does not exclude the other, since it is quite conceivable that the LoDagaa maintain at different times and in different contexts both that the ghost and the objects are one and that they are distinct. Before categorizing such thinking as an example of pre-logical mentality, it is well to recall that most beliefs in supernatural beings contain similar ambiguities; some Christian ideas concerning the nature of the Trinity are not intrinsically of a different order.

The presence of the ghost, in whatever form, serves as a sanction upon the correct settlement of the estate, ensuring that, so far as possible, the property is distributed in accordance with the wishes of the ancestors, that is, in conformity with accepted norms. The opening act in the process of settlement is to determine what the deceased owed and what he had owing to him. The persons attending any such gathering will include the elders of the dead man's patriclan sector, representatives of the reciprocal funeral group, some members of his matriclan—especially the heir among the LoDagaba—his widows, his children, and anyone who wishes to speak about a debt. The senior man at the ritual inquires whether anyone present holds such a debt or has heard other persons at the funeral make mention of one. To establish an effective claim, a person must make a declaration in the dead man's room, either on this or on one of the similar occasions at the last two ceremonies. The elder, and indeed anyone present, will then inquire into the circumstances of the claim. A report by the heir or by any other person of a debt owed to the dead man's estate is discussed in the same way. Those present will consider the circumstances of the debt, whether it should be realized, and by what means.

When the questioning has been completed, the ritual leader offers the worn hoe-blade to the senior son, saying, "The blade is still large enough. Take it to work with, and bring it back here when we need it." The axe, too, is taken by another of the sons, and after these objects have been handed over, the children may begin once again to farm their father's land. In the course of one funeral I attended, at the moment in the third ceremony when these objects are again brought out, a knife, a chisel, a needle, a flint, and a fire-iron were produced in addition to the axe and the hoe-blade. These possessions constitute man's basic tools, the ones that a father gives his son when he sends him out to farm on his own. By their ownership, a man is set up as an independent economic unit. In this ritual, therefore, the sons are established in the world so that they may take over the role of provider from their dead father.

These objects, inherited patrilineally in both communities, are the tools of production that are associated with rights in the people's basic productive resource, the land itself. It must also be remembered that in the pre-Colonial period, iron, of which all these tools are made, was a scarce and valuable commodity. Moreover, it had considerable ritual as well as economic value. The ore was dug out of the ground locally, and therefore had particularly strong connections with the Earth shrine, as did the smelting plant and the smithy. And today any pieces of manufactured iron that happen to be found belong to the Earth shrine, in the same way that all hoe-blades that are too worn for use are placed at the foot of a shrine, either a shrine to the ancestors or one to the beings of the wild. It is just such a hoe-blade that is given to the junior segment of any farming group when fission occurs; at the same time, the father or the elder brother announces, "I can no longer clear away the weeds for you; take this and do it yourself."

The twenty cowries have a similar significance. Among the LoWiili money is, of course, inherited agnatically. The LoDagaba practice uterine inheritance of wealth, but it is recognized that a man will hand over some of his wealth to his sons in the form of gifts during his lifetime, and also that the sons will not reveal all the hidden pots to the heir. Gifts *inter vivos* are legitimate, though they remain open to question; the retention of buried treasure is illegitimate, but people accept the fact that it often happens. The twenty cowries are said to represent this "illegitimately" acquired wealth, but my notes do not show whether the present ritual legitimizes this money and renders it mystically safe for the sons, or whether the money has to be repaid. The first of these alternatives certainly seems the more likely.

The rites in the dead man's room not only establish the sons on their own, but also liberate them from the prohibition on farming that has operated since the day of their father's death. The sons now take away the tools necessary to cultivate the land, which they must later return for the subsequent ceremonies. The twenty cowries lying on the ground are placed among the arrows in the dead man's quiver, which is wrapped up in an old skin that the deceased used to lie on. The bundle is then borne away by a member of the reciprocal funeral group, to be brought out again for the later performances.

Before I conclude the analysis of this part of the ceremony, the inquiries about debts require some further comment, since what is claimed and what is admitted are of paramount importance in examining the

differences between the two communities. At the LoWiili funeral of
Daazie, one of the dead man's sons reported that his father had lent a
sum of cowries to three different men to help them out with their bridewealth payments. At the same time the deceased had said that the children should not ask for repayment, since these men all belonged to his
own patrilineage. Among the LoWiili, then, this group is one within
which wealth is seen as subject to joint rights. On the most general level
the whole patriclan is spoken of as owning wealth in common, but only
within the lineage are such claims effective in distributive situations,
in actual transactions. Although during their lifetime, members of the
same patrilineage will certainly reckon what sums they have lent one
another, at the death of one of the partners in the relationship no action
for recovery will be taken.

Among the LoDagaba it is the matriclan, not the patriclan, in which
wealth is vested, and this is clearly reflected in the rituals held in the
dead man's room. At Katu's funeral, a member of the same patrilineage
announced that Katu had approached his father for a loan of 3,000
cowries and that in the end it was he (the speaker) who had actually lent
the money. It was decided that this constituted a valid claim upon the
estate, which would be settled after the final funeral ceremony. Nor
does this insistence upon the collection of debts apply only to distant
members of the patrilineage. At the same funeral, even the deceased's
own children were specifically asked whether they held a debt of their
father's or he of theirs, an act unheard of among the LoWiili. On the
other hand, the LoDagaba will not ask about the sister's sons, whereas
this would be done among the LoWiili. In practice, however, the latter
do not press any claim against a sister's son at a funeral settlement, since
he could always turn around and say, "I was sucking my mother's
breasts." The passage of property in this way is not uterine inheritance
in the strict sense, but derives from a man's residual rights in the property of his mother's patrilineal descent group (Goody [1959a]).

The widows are always questioned about any outstanding debts
with the dead man. At one LoWiili funeral I attended, the officiant
turned to the wife and asked her, "When you first came to this house,
did your husband lend you any money?" This question refers to the
fact that it is customary for the husband to lend his new wife some
money for trading purposes. This remains a debt that should be repaid
out of the profits as soon as possible. "Yes," she replied, "he lent me
3,000 cowries, but I paid them back to him." However, such claims are
not usually pressed at this time, unless there is some other grounds for
dispute between the various parties involved. At this funeral the same

question was also put to the mother and to the "mother's brother," the representative of the mother's patriclan, who both answered in the negative.

These inquiries about debts are a preliminary to the final distribution of the property of the deceased and, like the other post-burial rites, are repeated in the third and fourth ceremonies. The conclusion of these inquiries marks the end of the first ceremony, the burial service. The next stage in the sequence is the Diviners' Beer.

CHAPTER X

The Causes of Death

I pray you all, tell me what they deserve
That do conspire my death with devilish plots
Of damned witchcraft, and that have prevail'd
Upon my body with their hellish charms?

Richard III (III, iv)

For most non-literate peoples, the causes that contemporary Europeans would regard as natural do not by themselves provide a sufficient explanation of the death of a human being. I do not mean to imply that they are not aware that the bite of a snake can "cause" a man to die. But factors of this sort are seen not as final but rather as intermediary agents. What has to be ascertained is the person or shrine that was associated with the snake at the moment it struck. In the end this resolves itself into an inquiry as to who or what had grounds for hostility against the dead man, and so the cause of death is seen as a function of the individual's network of spiritual and human relationships. Death is treated as a social phenomenon and attributed to some conflict in the social system, either with living persons (witches, workers of curses, and sorcerers), or with past members of the society (ancestors), or with non-human agencies (shrines). It is for this reason that an analysis of the causes to which death is attributed, especially those falling within the first two categories, can give important information on the main lines of tension existing within any particular system of social relationships.

Most deaths, then, are viewed as cases of homicide. But there are two main exceptions, which fall at the extremes of the span of human life: a child who dies before being weaned is not regarded as a human at all, but as a being of the wild that has come to trouble the parents with this pretense of mortality; and the death of a man whose sons have themselves begotten sons is also thought of in a different way. Such a person has reached the end of his allotted span. He is too weak to arouse the anger of shrine, ancestor, or mortal. Moreover, he has won an honorable place in the community by having "established his house," and has thereby achieved man's ultimate purpose on this earth. Only in a case of this kind would no "cause" be given for an adult's death, except that it is an act of God, a decision from Heaven (*Na'angmin kū*); the word *Na'angmin*, God, is compounded of *na*, meaning chief, and *ngmin*, which I translate as deity or god.

I came across one such instance when, although I did not myself attend all the long series of divinations that settle these matters, I was afterwards told the man had died as a result of God's work, *Na'angmin tomeno*. God, or the Heavens, cannot be appealed to; one can make no sacrifice to God because God has no altar. One can swear by God with impunity, for nothing one can say or do can alter his disposition of things. He created mankind (*o ir ti*) as a potter does his pots, he is the supreme deity, but he is too remote to intervene directly in human affairs, either in life or in death. In effect he means little to the LoDagaa except as a final cause by which to explain the otherwise inexplicable. The concept is a similar one to that found among the Tallensi and is best translated as Fate, or the Heavens. By ascribing the death to God, the LoDagaa are saying that it is the destiny of old men to die; there is nothing more to be done.

The attribution of a death to God is rare. Except in the case of an old man, the cause lies elsewhere. As a man once remarked in my presence, "About that death, don't blame it on God; it's to do with us mortals" (*Kungna na kpi, be ta ferai Na'angmin; ti nisaal bongfua*).

These causes, as I have mentioned, fall within three general categories: (1) present members of the community, namely witches, sorcerers, and others using deadly techniques both mystical and non-mystical; (2) former members of the descent group, that is, the ancestors; and (3) supernatural beings, as represented by the great variety of shrines.

At first I recorded the causes of death in terms of these three categories, looking upon them as alternative explanations. It was not easy to gather this information, partly because of its private nature, and partly because a number of apparently divergent opinions were put forward, since more than one diviner had been consulted. Only later did I appreciate that when people said that an ancestor or a shrine caused a death, they did not necessarily mean that the supernatural agency actually killed the person, but that it had withdrawn its protection so that he became an easy prey for witches and sorcerers. One elder maintained that all deaths are in fact due to living persons, whatever other reason people may give, and another said that even in deaths by sorcery, witches are also involved because of their hunger for human flesh. On the other hand, it could be claimed that the supernatural agencies were the cause, since it is they who permit this mystical aggression. Fortes reports for the Tallensi that all deaths are in the last analysis attributed to the ancestors; other beings merely act as agents on their behalf ([1949] p. 329).

There are thus three levels of causation, the immediate, the efficient, and the final. The immediate is the technique used to kill the deceased; disease, snake bites, or other "natural" causes as well as forms of mystical aggression. The efficient is to be found among the members of the community itself, the person who was behind the act of killing. The final cause is an ancestor, the Earth shrine, or a medicine shrine.

Even this does not exhaust all the possibilities in the causal chain. It is sometimes said that the ancestors, the Earth, and the medicine shrines do not themselves have the power to kill a human being unless the person's tutelary (*sigra*) allows it. "How can you harm a cow unless you have the herdsman's (*niikyiine*) consent?" I was asked. A tutelary is not a special sort of spirit or shrine; the word refers either to a clan shrine, which is theoretically the same for all members, or to the specific shrine or ancestor indicated by a diviner as being a man's own guardian spirit. Each individual has such a tutelary, but will not be aware of its name unless a diviner has been consulted. Although an approach to the tutelary is a necessary step in the chain of events leading to a death, people do not usually say, "the *sigra* killed him"; however this name does sometimes occur in the possible causes suggested in the course of funeral divination.

Many attempts are made during the funeral ceremonies to determine why a man died. Broadly speaking, diviners are used to ascertain the final cause, whereas methods such as carrying the corpse indicate the human agent.

Divination is very common among the LoDagaa. Most men are qualified to divine; but there is a great difference in reputation among them, and good diviners are of course most frequently consulted. It is not knowledge of the future that the clients require so much as the cause of present troubles. The head of a compound consults a diviner if something has gone wrong, or if he has had bad dreams. There are a variety of possible agencies that might have caused this state of affairs, and the ordinary mortal requires guidance in finding the right shrine at which to make his offering. Indeed, the diviner is called *bobuura* (*bag-buura*), for it is he who locates (*buura*) the cause of the mystical trouble (*boor, bagr*), that is, the altar at which the fowl has to be sacrificed. *Bagr* is etymologically connected with Bagre, the name of the secret society, and also with Tallensi *bagher,* which Fortes translates as shrine. The LoDagaa use *tiib* for medicine shrine, a word probably connected both with *tīī,* medicine, and with *tie,* tree.

There are many situations in which divination is resorted to. When a man's child is sick he consults the diviner, who formulates a course of positive action, which temporarily relieves anxiety. If this and other measures fail and the child dies, a diviner is again consulted to reveal the cause, so that further deaths may be avoided. Apart from regular seasonal offerings, no sacrifice is normally made to a shrine unless a diviner so directs. Even expiation for the breaking of a taboo, when the person knows he has invited supernatural punishment, is not usually made unless a diviner links some later trouble with the original offense.

Divination is important for a number of reasons. First, the very discussion of intimate details of past events with an "expert" has some cathartic effect for the client in cases in which he is seeking advice on his own behalf. Second, the diviner reinforces the social mores by a firm restatement of what ought to be done; characteristically, he speaks in highly standardized forms of speech, in riddles, proverbs, and short pithy sayings, which embody the traditional standards of the society. Third, and most important, the diviner formulates a "rational" course of action in anxiety situations. Divination, writes Nadel of the Nupe, "is needed to reduce the uncertainties which must arise; it is thus that it becomes a 'prerequisite' of religious no less than of practical action" ([1954] p. 65).

The determination of the cause of death begins with the announcement of the funeral itself; for when a person dies, the senior mourner, and indeed any compound head, may kill a fowl to a household shrine to see whether it is in order for him to arrange the funeral or to attend it. We have seen, too, how the funeral speeches reveal another method of discovering the cause of death, the deceased being asked by the bereaved to visit the speaker during sleep and tell him who was responsible. Then, formerly, the dramatic rite of "carrying the corpse" was sometimes performed. In the rituals conducted during the three days following the burial, the close bereaved, particularly the widow and the children, are themselves subjected to procedures designed to test their complicity in the death. In addition there is another rite, which I have mentioned only in passing, that occurs on the first and often on subsequent days, when a man's fellow practitioners divine at the foot of his funeral stand. This divination is basically a mimetic ritual, the pur-

pose of which is "to take out the dream." But it is also to some extent
an inquiry into the cause of death.

To understand this rite, it is necessary to know that there are two
main types of divination among the LoDagaa, one associated with the
sprites or beings of the wild (*kontome*), and one with the "gods" or
"deities" (*ngmini*). Initiation into both these cults occurs in two stages,
but only after the second stage has been completed is the initiate permitted to practice divination. In the first type, the initiate receives an
L-shaped stick (*daa gwöl*), one arm of which is about a foot in length,
and the other some three inches. In divining sessions, the client grasps
the short end, the practitioner the long, and, with the aid of the particular beings of the wild to whom the diviner's shrine is dedicated, the
stick selects from among a number of objects that the diviner has spread
in front of him. These are usually kept in his goatskin bag, and each
indicates some possible cause of mystical trouble. The result obtained
by this method is checked by means of cowries thrown from a bottle-
shaped gourd known as *diu gan* (inside skin), the answer being given by
the way in which the shells fall.

The second type of divination, divining with the help of the "deities," is carried out by the use of cowries alone. This technique is
acquired only by membership of the Bagre society. After a person has
been inducted into the second stage of the mysteries and become a black
initiate (*bo soola, bag sebla*), he is given a small leather-covered gourd
known as *yuon gan* (outside skin) since it is used out of doors. (Whereas shrines to the beings of the wild are inside the house, Bagre shrines
are invariably outside, often on the neck of the granary, the part that
protrudes above the roof.)

In Birifu, I found that most divining was by appeal to the sprites,
and a considerable proportion of the population had such shrines; an
equal number of shrines belonged to the Bagre society, but the "outside
skin" was not used for divination in the ordinary course of events.
Among the LoDagaba, however, there were very few sprite shrines, but
a proliferation of shrines to the various "deities" (*ngmini*) with which
the Bagre shrine, known as *bag ngmin,* is associated. The lack of sprite
divination was therefore offset by the greater emphasis on Bagre divination. Functionally the systems are similar, and this particular difference
between the two communities appears to have little significance for the
rest of the social system.

The divination at the foot of the funeral stand is carried out in the
following way. If the dead man has been a member of the Bagre society,
the senior initiate in the reciprocal funeral group calls the other black

initiates to come together beside the corpse. Taking the dead man's container, he shakes out the cowries two by two until they fall in a favorable manner, one up, one down. The casting of the shells is repeated in turn by the senior member of all the patrilineages living in the parish, including the deceased's own group. While the initiates shake the cowries, they sing in a low voice one of the Bagre society's songs. The container is circulated three times. When this has finished, any cowries that are lying at the foot of the stand and have not yet been collected by the sextons are gathered up and divided among the black initiates from clan sectors other than the deceased's, who then return in silence to their places. These cowries have to be treated in the same way as the Bagre money (*bag libie*) collected from the neophytes at initiation ceremonies; they must not be mixed with other monies and can be spent only in certain ways. On one occasion that I attended the money was used to buy food; the three patrilineages of Naayiili (Birifu), who constitute a single funeral group, amalgamated their individual shares and on the next market day bought some meat which they all ate together. Such money can also be used for the purchase of apparel for a member's funeral or for a special loan, as when a man wishes to pay a visit to distant kin and requires some ready cash for the journey.

If the deceased was not a member of the Bagre society, but was a diviner by virtue of his possession of a shrine to the beings of the wild, other practitioners gather round the stand and perform a similar series of acts, but using the small L-shaped stick instead of cowries. In his brief account of the "Lobi" (here, LoSaala) people, Rattray maintains that at the death of a man who engages in sprite divination his bag is carried three times round the stand and emptied of its contents. Then with the dead man's own stick, the other diviners seek the cause of his death ([1932] p. 442). I have not myself seen the cause of death divined for at this stage, but Rattray's statement calls attention to the fact that the funeral divination as a whole is not performed simply for mimetic purposes. A knowledge of the actual cause of death is of great importance to those who remain behind.

The main occasion for making these inquiries is at the ceremony of the Diviners' Beer. However, some attention was formerly given to the question during the actual burial ceremony in the widespread custom of "carrying the corpse," a practice that is no longer observed among the LoDagaa. This rite was sometimes performed when the corpse was taken to the grave, but it could also happen earlier in the ceremony. If the bereaved thought it necessary, then at the time when most people were present, that is, on the second day of the funeral, the grave-diggers would be told to take the body into the house, and two matriclan joking partners of the deceased (members, I think, of the reciprocal funeral group) would tie his clothes inside his sleeping mat (*be le'na a seng*). The bundle of clothes, recognized to be a substitute for the corpse itself, was carried on the heads of the two men without their touching it with their hands. The men walked round the spectators, and the person in front of whom the bundle fell was held to be responsible for the death. Labouret ([1931] p. 319) states that an interrogation is made by joking partners or by grave-diggers using the corpse itself, instead of the bundle of clothes, as they remove the body from the house to the stand; he also maintains that other causes of death besides witchcraft are indicated by the way in which the corpse moves. This method is employed by other peoples in the region, but I have not heard of its use among the LoDagaa.

Now that the "carrying of the corpse" is no longer performed among the LoDagaa, the main opportunity for determining the cause of death is at the special ceremony known as the Diviners' Beer (*Bobuur Dãã*), which is said to take place three weeks after the burial, that is, three weeks of six days. However, I know of no case in which this date was actually adhered to, and the stated time is but a rough indication of when the ceremony in fact occurs.

In some funerals, the Diviners' Beer is the last ceremony to be performed. In the case of an unweaned child, when the cause of the death has been ascertained, the funeral, already much curtailed, is brought to an end. When an older child has died, the parents are prohibited from sleeping together until this beer has been brewed, usually about two weeks after the death. The father's head is then shaved by his agnatic kinsfolk, while the mother returns to her own home for the same purpose.

In the case of adults who have no children, the surviving spouse is merely bathed once more in the course of a very shortened form of the final rites and released from his or her relationship with the deceased. Even if a man does have children, should the divination show him to have died an evil death (*kũ faa*), the funeral will only be continued after expiatory sacrifices have been carried out. And unless the two final ceremonies are performed, the deceased will have no ancestor shrine, since this is created in the course of these ritual sequences. However, even if a person is discovered to be an evildoer after he has been buried in the proper way, his corpse is not usually disinterred but remains in its original sepulcher.

At the Diviners' Beer, the divination is usually carried out by a member of the reciprocal funeral group, whereas the questioning is done by an elder of the deceased's own lineage, or by some other senior clansman. In the case of a married woman, the diviner consulted comes from another lineage of her own patriclan, and the questions are asked by an elder of her husband's clan sector. The instances recorded were somewhat confusing on these points, and I suspect that the variations may be connected with the type of divination employed, whether help is sought from the deities or from the sprites. In one case when the latter system was used, the questions were asked by a member of the lineage itself. In another instance, I was told that those joking partners who act in the context of the Bagre performances, members of another patriclan within the parish, should supply the diviner. These usages appear to vary according to the lineage involved and the person who died; but the general practice is for the interrogation to be carried out by clansmen who are not as immediately concerned as the members of the deceased's own lineage, while the diviner may come from a yet more distant group. Moreover, even in Birifu where sprite divination predominates, the Bagre method is more commonly used in funeral divination, for uninitiated persons (*dakume*) as well as for initiates. However, I shall first describe an occasion, the death of a young child, when sprite divination was used.

When this ceremony is performed for a male, members of his own patriclan sector, a representative of his mother's patriclan, and the diviner himself gather at the foot of a tree outside the compound in which he lived. The diviner first smooths a patch of earth on which to throw the cowries. Women of the house then put in front of him a small pot of beer and a dish of porridge. Emptying the contents of his bag on the ground, he addresses his familiar, in this case a being of the wild. This is how the usual divining session begins. Having finished his speech (*o kaab a boor bar*), he tells the client to grasp the foot of the divining stick. The interrogator then calls upon the Earth shrine and the *ngmin* god to help in showing him what caused the death. *"Buon ar a dakyiin?"* or *"Buon so a dakyin ara?"* he asks. Although this phrase appears to mean "Why does the wall of the house stand?," I was assured that it stood for "Why does the wall fall?" (i.e., *ar lon*). The L-shaped stick, which the diviner and client both grasp, the one at the top, the other at the base, is supposedly guided by the diviner as agent of his daimon. It selects one or more objects among the divinatory materials that lie scattered between them, and those chosen represent the agencies responsible for the death; for most of the motley contents of the bag—sheep's tooth, fragment of cloth, oyster shell, river pebble—signify a possible cause.

In this case it was an ancestor. Then, still holding the stick, the diviner takes the small gourd containing his divining cowries and confirms his diagnosis by shaking the shells on the ground each time the questioner calls out the name of a possible agency. At the right name the cowries fall correctly, one up, one down.

"What caused the house to fall?" asks the questioner. "Was it the father's lineage (*sãã yiri*)?

"The mother's lineage (or husband's lineage, in the case of a married woman) (*ma* or *sire yiri*)?

"The Earth shrine (*tenggaan*)?

"The Ancestors (*kpime*)?

"The Tutelaries (*siura*)?"

And the interrogator continues to call out the names of all the various shrines in the compound, until the cowries fall right.

The small pot of beer is poured to the soil (*tinsog*), to the Earth shrine in its universal aspect, and a large pot is supplied for those present to drink. When they have finished, they all repair to the dead boy's room, where soup and porridge are eaten. Some of this food has been previously flicked onto the objects from the diviner's bag. The diviner himself is given twenty cowries and a bunch of guinea-corn heads, and the ceremony is at an end. The ritual is much the same whatever the method of divination used.

The LoPiel version of this ceremony is known as *Bag Pola,* Finding the Mystical Trouble. The word *pola* means "to test." The final ceremony, in which the children are shown their classificatory "fathers," is called *bi pol,* the testing of the children, and the same term is used when speaking of the bathing of the widows. In this ceremony the technique adopted by the LoDagaba is always the Bagre or *ngmin* type of divination.

Until this ritual sequence has been performed, no sacrifice can be made to the ancestors, the fabric of the compound in which the dead man lived cannot be repaired. The house is still ill at ease, since the cause of death is not yet known and may lie within the house itself. The expression used to describe this condition is *a yir tshaan uri,* the house is uneasy; *ur* are the winnowed husks of guinea-corn, which irritate the skin. While the house remains in this state, no sacrifice to the ancestors may be performed within its byre, because it may be the ancestors who have been responsible for the death. Should this prove to be the case, the occupants may be called upon to abandon the compound, for the ancestors may have rejected the site, or the site its inhabitants. To begin to repair a building before the cause of death has been ascertained is to run the risk of incurring yet further supernatural displeasure by attempting to perpetuate what has already been damned.

The actual ceremony begins in the way that all the others do, with the women of the compound, and the visitors who passed the night there, crying their lamentations and bearing themselves in attitudes of grief as if the death had been just announced. Then the men gather round, and a senior member of the Bagre society addresses the deceased's patrilineage in the following vein:

> When your grandfather left your original home,
> *Ka yi sããkum yiina tenkuori,*
>
> perhaps he had made a promise
> *o ta wa faa ko nuor*
>
> saying he was going to unknown parts
> *o yil ka o na kpiera mwo*
>
> and asking the Earth shrine to let him go there in safety
> and raise children;
> *a tenggaan vẽ ko kpiera mwo vla, ko gwöli a bikpibe;*
>
> perhaps he promised to sacrifice to the Earth shrine.
> *o ta wa yong nuor ko na maali a tenggaan.*

Two cowries are thrown from the container. If they fall incorrectly, then further possibilities are tried out until the true cause is discovered. The following list, though not definitive as regards either number or order, is a typical example of the agencies considered.

(1) The Earth shrine of the lineage's former home (*tenkuori tenggaan*).

(2) The Earth, in general (*tambaalo, tiungser*).

(3) The River Volta (*na man*).

(4) The Kambaa River (*kambaa*).

(5) The Wilds (*wie kur*, bush stone).

(6) The Hill (*tong*).

(7) The local Earth shrine (*tiung tenggaan*).

(8) An Ancestor (*sããkum*, grandfather).

(9) The Mothers (*mamine*), that is the mother's brothers, presumably only those within the mother's patriclan.

(10) The Grandmother (*makum*), probably referring to the matrilineage (*ma per*) as distinct from the mother's patrilineage (*ma yir*).

(11) An outside shrine to the sprites *(kontõ yiri)*.[1]

(12) The god in the neck of the granary *(bo kokor ngmin)*.

(13) Rain *(ngmin nyigra,* lightning god).

(14) An unfilled promise made to one of the other compound shrines.

When the diviner has determined the cause of death, beer is brought out for those who have taken part. The drinking of this beer is in itself an ordeal designed to discover the guilty party; for if anyone present has been involved in the death, he will suffer grievously if any should touch his lips. After the beer is finished, the heads of all the offspring of the deceased are shaved, and the ceremony is then at an end.

This rite clearly corresponds to the Diviners' Beer among the Lo-Wiili; but the LoPiel have a further ceremony, also called the Diviners' Beer, which is the counterpart of the mimetic divinatory performances carried out by the LoWiili at the foot of the funeral stand. This ceremony is attended by all senior members of the Bagre society in the ritual area, although it is also held for elders who divine by the other method. As I have remarked, these persons, known as *bo soola* ("black initiates") by the LoWiili and as *bag tshuurdem* ("owners of the Bagre goatskin bag") by the LoDagaba, are distinguished from the members of the junior grade by the possession of the container used to hold the divinatory cowries; they are therefore the only persons capable of carrying out divination of this kind. The diviner clears the ground in front of him, saying, "I've cleared the ground" *(N ngmiera a gbal)*. Then one of the assistants calls out to everybody to be quiet *(O ngmarena a ne)*. Thereupon all are silent while the cowries are thrown as a check upon the findings of the previous occasion. At the end, the diviner is given a bunch of guinea-corn heads, twenty cowries, some porridge, and four pots of beer, which are drunk under the shade tree near the compound. When this is finished, the practitioner announces the time of the next phase, the *Ko Dãã Tuo,* or Bitter Funeral Beer, an indication that all is clear for the completion of the funeral.

I began this chapter by remarking that the LoDagaa attribute death to three types of causes. First, there are the techniques employed, including such procedures as witchcraft (by transvection) and wizardry (by the use of hypothetical projectiles), as well as empirically determinable means, such as the bite of a snake or the poison of an arrow. Second, there is the agent of death, the human being employing the technique,

---

[1] Although this shrine is outside the compound, it is housed in its own little hut *(yir).*

who may in fact be acting on behalf of a third party who has hired him. Last, there are the supernatural powers, who have rendered the death possible by lifting their protection from the dead man.

Although this triple separation of causes is not so explicitly made by the LoDagaa themselves, I do not think this way of putting it distorts their view of things. When a man dies as the result of a snake bite, they will first hunt for the snake. Later they attempt to find who sent the snake and what agencies contributed to his success. Formerly, the carrying of the corpse was used to specify the person publicly. The Diviners' Beer indicates the supernatural agency. It will be noted that in the questions asked of the diviner, no reference is made to death by witchcraft or sorcery. This omission was expressly pointed out to me by one informant, who added that the possibility of death by witchcraft would be determined by the carrying of the corpse and other means. The Diviners' Beer does not disclose which person attacked the dead man, but only what supernatural agencies were involved. It may indicate that witchcraft was used and which patrilineal group was involved, but does not name a specific person. The absence of questions relating to witches and sorcerers supports the suggestion that deaths among the LoDagaa are accounted for at three levels of causation. It is only after these levels have all been satisfactorily settled that the funeral ceremony can be continued.

CHAPTER XI

The Bitter Funeral Beer

O God! a beast that wants discourse of reason
Would have mourn'd longer—married with my uncle,
My father's brother; but no more like my father
Than I to Hercules. Within a month,
Ere yet the salt of most unrighteous tears
Had left the flushing of her galled eyes,
She married. O, most wicked speed, to post
With such dexterity to incestuous sheets!
It is not, nor it cannot come to good.

Hamlet (I, ii)

The third of the funeral ceremonies, known as *Ko Dãã Tuo,* the Bitter Funeral Beer, takes place at the beginning of the rainy season. It consists of three phases. The first of these carries the whitewashing of the surviving spouse a stage further toward completion; the third does the same for the redistribution of the property of the deceased; and the second phase is concerned with the creation of a provisional ancestor shrine for the dead man.

THE BATHING OF THE WIDOW

In order to brew the beer needed for the ceremony, the women have to start two days before the actual time set, and during this period the xylophones are played continuously, as throughout the opening ceremony. Indeed, this sequence is in some respects a repetition of the earlier service. It takes place on the same day of the week on which the death occurred, and the day begins with the wailing of the women of the house of mourning. Toward evening of that day, as the sun begins to set across the Black Volta, women from the surrounding compounds join in the lamentations for the dead man. Meanwhile the young children of the house are once again hung with strings of cowries and smeared with ashes; for this is the time when the ghost of the dead man is supposed to return to visit his former dwelling.

The shaving, bathing, and whitewashing are performed in the same way as at the earlier ceremony. The widows are taken behind the house, and there they step forward, one at a time, beneath a gutter. Standing upon a piece of the same mat on which she and her husband used to sleep together, each widow is stripped and bathed by the women members of her natal lineage (*poghyaataaba*, "fellow daughters"); for she is still considered to be imbued with the dirt of her husband's body. When the widow has been cleansed, she steps backward off the mat and is allowed to anoint her body with oil for the first time since her husband's death. Then she is whitewashed again, but instead of being entirely covered as before, a small quantity of the purifying paste is smeared upon her ears, arms, thighs, and chest. Now she is permitted to wear *mie*, that is, waist bands of grass instead of fibre; these she may blacken and is no longer required to leave them in their natural color, as if she were a young girl who has made herself a dress of bands while out working in the fields. She is on the way to reassuming the dress of an adult woman.

When the widow has been bathed and whitewashed, she is given food in the same manner as before; three times the old woman pretends to give her food, each time throwing it away for the ghost, and on the fourth occasion she finally permits the widow to eat.

A widower is bathed in a similar way, although less whitewash is daubed upon his body. Only after this has been done can he wear shorts (*pietõn*). If he puts on a smock before the final ceremony, then this becomes the property of those who are in charge of the bathing rites, although he is usually allowed to buy it back.

THE CREATION OF THE PROVISIONAL ANCESTOR SHRINE

The second phase of the Bitter Funeral Beer deals with the creation of the ancestor shrine. Such a shrine is made only for a man or woman who has living children. Indeed, the children themselves have to perform the ceremony, and if the eldest of them is thought to be too young, this part of the ritual sequence will be postponed until he reaches adolescence. Only then is the dead man's line of descent considered sufficiently secure, and only then can the children take over the domestic aspects of their father's role. We must differentiate here between those aspects of his role that relate to the domestic group, such as the acts he performs as provider for the household, and those aspects that pertain to his membership of a certain generation level in a specific descent group. The children can take over the task of provider as soon as they are capable of farming on their own; but the position of their dead father in clan and lineage affairs can only be filled at a much later stage in their social development.

The offspring who are eligible to cut a man's shrine include all those of whom he is or will be the *pater,* regardless who the *genitor* may be. If the widow of a childless man marries leviratically, the child of this sexual union can create a shrine for his social father, her dead husband, even though he has never known him in the flesh. Among the LoWiili, there is a corollary of this in that a man's son born of a wife whose bride-wealth was contributed by the mother's brother cannot cut his genitor's shrine, nor make a sacrifice directly to it, since socially he is the child of another lineage. Should he be called upon to kill an animal to his genitor, he could do so where two paths cross (*sortshera*). The son will of course receive the bridewealth cattle for any sister of the same union, but should he sacrifice the Bull of Childbearing to the ancestor shrine of his dead genitor instead of approaching his mother's patrilineal kin, he would certainly die. An alternative for him, especially if he is living at a distance from these kin, is to kill the animal at the crossroads, a place that not only has particularly close associations with the Earth shrine, but also is intimately connected with the ancestors, since at the Final Funeral Ceremony a shrine always rests here before being carried into the byre.

Among the LoDagaba, on the other hand, the fact that the bride-wealth cattle are contributed by his mother's brother makes no differ-ence to the patriclan membership of a man's children; as far as inherit-ance is concerned, rights in women are vested in both the patriclan and the matriclan of the husband, not solely in the patriclan as amongst the LoWiili. This difference is of major importance to the working of the social system. The provision of bridewealth is closely tied up for the LoDagaa with farming obligations, and these in turn with inherit-ance. If a man cannot get help from his mother's brother in obtaining a bride who will breed children to his name, then he is unlikely to farm for him; as they see it, the absence of farming help would be incom-patible with inheritance.

When questioned, some LoDagaa maintained that an ancestor shrine was made for a man only if he was survived by male children. But there are cases when a daughter gets her paternal uncle, the dead man's full brother, to act on her behalf and so perform the rites necessary to create an ancestor shrine for her dead father, even when she is an only child. Although she would have to produce some of the grain and wealth required to perform this ceremony, the remainder she can borrow from her uncle, who would in any case be heir to her late father's property. One speaker said that a debt would be incurred, but it seems highly doubtful if repayment would ever be asked for, or, if asked for, received. That the LoDagaa consider substitution of this kind possible, rare as it must be in practice, is perhaps connected with the fact that under some circumstances a woman can continue her father's agnatic line. I have elsewhere considered the residual agnation that is transmitted through a married woman to her children. But the children of an unmarried girl who remains in her father's house actually belong to her own patrilineage (Goody [1956a], p. 62). "Illegitimate" children of this kind are most likely to be produced by a girl who is lame or blind. But it was said of one attractive LoWiili girl who had reached marriageable age that her father, who had no sons, was keeping her at home until she had produced a male "housechild" for him. Whether the intention of any father or brother is ever as explicit as this suggests is difficult to say, for the comment is of the kind that rejected suitors might be expected to put into circulation.

There was formerly another method by which children became attached members of their mother's patriclan as housechildren. When a husband rejected his wife, the marriage was annulled, and so were his paternal rights over the children. In both these ways, a daughter, who in any case never ceases to be a member of her natal patriclan, can actually continue the direct agnatic line. Any explanation of why the LoDagaa sometimes maintain that even a female child may initiate the preparation of her father's shrine, and of why she has a submerged claim on the property that she requires for the performance, should be related to the foregoing facts. I tentatively suggest that all these institutions are explicable in terms of the residual rights of membership to agnatic groups transmitted through women.

Parenthood is the first prerequisite for having an ancestor shrine carved to one's name; the second is a proper death as distinct from an evil one (*kũ faa*). For example, a person diagnosed at death as a witch would have no shrine; indeed he or she would not even have a complete funeral. As late in the obsequies as the Diviners' Beer, divination may show that no further ceremony should be performed except a much shortened form of the final rites, the cleansing of the surviving partner, known as *Poo Suora Dãã,* when a woman is bathed. However, sins so diagnosed are usually capable of expiation by appropriate sacrifices, should the bereaved wish to carry these out, so that a bad divination is not an insuperable bar to the completion of the full series of rites. To take a LoWiili example, Guon, then an old woman, was unfortunate enough to die on the inauspicious day of the week. As a consequence she was automatically treated as a witch and buried hurriedly with no public mourning. After her body had been disposed of in this way, an expiatory sacrifice was performed at the local Earth shrine. Some time later when her "son" Ngminvuor died, the funeral was said to be a double one, and cattle were killed to both their names.

Another such double funeral was held in Birifu when Piizie's wife died. A few weeks previously Poful's young son had expired. The father had already consulted a diviner during the boy's illness and had been given a rather involved explanation of his sickness. He was told that the boy had been hired by another person to attack his mother by mystical means, that is, by witchcraft. The boy was therefore not given an ordinary funeral at the time, but the matter was subsequently repaired, and the next funeral in the lineage was celebrated jointly for Piizie's wife and Poful's son.

If no expiation is, or can be, carried out, then an evildoer is denied incorporation in the company of his lineage ancestors. One sin that warrants such extreme action (since it is impossible to expiate) is the killing of a fellow patriclansman. In life, such a man is excluded from the congregation of the ancestor cult and ritually prohibited from consuming any of the sacrificial offerings; in death, he is totally and finally rejected from the clan.

The ancestor shrine created at the Bitter Funeral Beer consists of a bamboo rod some three feet long. For a man, the rod used is the one taken from the bow that rested on his lap at the burial service and that has been hanging on the compound wall ever since. From this the ends are cut off at the two points where the bow is notched to receive the cowhide loops to which the bowstrings are attached. For an old man, the shrine may be made from a piece of bamboo cut to the same length as the walking stick on which he leans. In both cases, however, the bamboo rod is only the intermediate form of the shrine. At the final funeral ceremony an anthropomorphic stick is carved and placed in the byre among the shrines of all the earlier ancestors of the compound. In fact, although I speak of a bow-stave as a provisional ancestor shrine, the name "ancestor's stick" (*kpiin daa*) is given only to the full shrine, the other being simply known as a bamboo rod (*tender*).

A woman has a similar straight rod made for her by her children, which is known as her chair (*ko*). At the very end of the funeral it is carried aloft by the grave-diggers' wives and taken back to the byre of her father's house. However, if a woman has borne a son, another shrine of the same kind is made at the ceremony and placed among the ancestors of the husband's lineage, so that her children will have a place where they can sacrifice to her.[1] The fact that a woman's final shrine resembles a man's provisional one is in accord with her status as a jural minor. The LoDagaa are themselves quite explicit on this score, "A woman is not a full person," I was told, "only a half" (*poo be in ni 'bil, o in ni tshier*).

The ceremony begins when members of the reciprocal burial group arrive carrying the bamboo stick and lean it against the outside wall of the compound, slightly to the right of the entrance to the byre. Beside this opening stands the ladder that provides access to the roof and thereby to the house itself. In front of the byre there is an open area where the stones from the grove dedicated to the Earth shrine are buried; these stones, together with the ancestors, are the main guardians of the house. Here, too, are performed the rites of greatest concern to those who dwell within its walls.

The women, who have just finished the second bathing of the widow or widower, assemble on one side of the bamboo stick, while the men sit on the other. These latter include representatives of the mother's patrilineage, of the reciprocal funeral group, and of the grave-diggers, since the stick has to be treated in the same way as the corpse itself. The senior grave-digger approaches the stick with deliberate steps. On one occasion when I was present, the officiant first swept the stick three times with a handful of grass (*mwo pla*) and some *kõkõ*-tree leaves (the tree that is associated with the beings of the wild). Throwing the leaves aside, he then took some beer and flour from a small pot and a calabash that were placed nearby, mixed beer and flour together, and fed the shrine with some of the paste.

After the offering of the bread and the wine comes the blood sacrifice. Taking a fowl in his hand (a guinea-fowl for a woman), the officiant slits its throat and lets the blood drip over the stick. But instead of casting the bird aside to see whether it will fall auspiciously or inauspiciously, he continues to grasp it so that it cannot flutter (*o vuoni a*

---

[1] I have come across two instances when a woman seems to have had only one shrine cut to her name; the special circumstance involved appears to be the ownership of certain shrines.

I should also mention here that once when I was speaking with a man about the shrines in his byre, he said, "That is X, he has only a bamboo rod, he has no children." I have no other information to show that the rites for a married man without children include the cutting of an intermediary shrine (a bachelor's bow is broken), but this may be the case in some lineages.

nuor a daa yong). Finally he takes some tail feathers and ties them round the shrine. This unusual method of sacrifice is one that excludes the possibility of the shrine giving a response to a human question. Indeed, no answer is required, since these sacrifices are simply part of the process of establishing the stick as a shrine. After this sacrifice of the fowl, the daughters of the dead man come forward, each bearing a calabash of porridge and some soup, which they place at the foot of the shrine. Of these contributions the most important is that presented by the senior daughter (*saab maala*).

These gifts of food mark a significant stage in the transition of the dead man from human being to ancestor. While the husband is alive, it is the duty of his wife to prepare food from the raw produce with which he supplies her. After his death, the responsibility for providing food is taken over by the children and their agnatic descendants. The conjugal family does not endure beyond the death of its members, but the clan is seen as existing in perpetuity. In the context of the ancestor cult the unit of consumption is the lineage rather than the family. The offerings of food made by the widow are quite distinct and of a different character. At the Final Ceremony, when she has been cleansed for the last time, she cooks porridge and flicks some on her husband's shrine, an act that serves as one more test to show whether or not she has committed adultery since his death. This done, the widow is free to have sexual intercourse with other men, while her domestic responsibilities toward the deceased are assumed by the unilineal descent group itself. For the custodianship of the ancestors is essentially a matter for the patrilineal group, as can be seen from the fact that at the last ceremony in a woman's funeral her major shrine is taken to her natal compound and there aggregated to those of her own agnatic forebears.

The daughters of the dead man are followed by the wives of neighbors (*semaandem*), mainly the wives of members of the clan sector and of the burial group, who come forward in a mass with similar contributions of soup and porridge. At the same time, the chief mourner, who is standing on the rooftop, lets fall a bunch of guinea-corn heads and small quantities of other crops, which drop upon the stick below. Here he repeats the actions he performed when the corpse was first carried outside the compound, and as on that occasion the grave-diggers collect up the produce for themselves.

As the farm produce falls around the stick, the women break out into a series of loud laments, which gradually subside into a keening much like the funeral chants sung by men at the burial service. The following example is taken from the obsequies of a man. In content such keens are similar to the chants (*long*) sung on the earlier occasion, except that less hostility is displayed against the dead. Here lamentations are sung for the "house" (*yir*) of the deceased, a word that carries the several meanings of the building itself, the persons who occupy it, and the lineage to which they belong. Since these are women's songs, the mother's plight is usually given fuller expression than the father's. In the fifth of the keens given below, a woman asks one of the assembled company to fetch her son from the distant fields and bring him back to the house. This might reasonably be interpreted as a mother refusing to recognize that her son was dead, a theme not uncommon in these songs. However, in this case there is an alternative meaning, for the allusion may be to the possibility of an attack by witchcraft. A good farmer, one who spends much time in his fields, may arouse jealousy among his fellows, which in turn may lead to mystical aggression. The woman therefore asks someone present to fetch her son back from the farm, lest he should suffer the same fate as the dead man. The last chant refers to death in battle. Here there would be no mourning, only revenge. In most cases, however, death is due to an attack by mystical means, and one purpose of the long funeral ceremony is to determine the specific nature of this, lest others be in danger from the same cause.

> *A yir baara.*
> The house is finished.

> *Fu yil ka sãã yiri fu wa.*
> You said you'd come to stay in your father's house.

> *O waara ka a yir lieb tu.*
> He came, but the house gave way to the wilderness.

> *O do'ona bi vla, do'o mani kũ.*
> She bore a fine son, bore him to die.

> *Yi nyo ma bie, o bin a we kuora puo.*
> Go get my son, he's in the far field.

> *Ka pĩĩ na kon bie, be na soona kuon.*
> If an arrow had killed him, they wouldn't be crying.

The keening for a woman is of the same general character. In the examples below, the two central features are again the refusal to accept the fact that a death has occurred and the belief that the dead woman was killed by mystical means because her excellence as a wife and mother provoked the jealousy of others.

O yira diã zor a kola.
She got up today, but wouldn't go to the stream.

Ka bun i nye a gbil-be-don poo?
What's happened to this woman who could never stop chattering?

Ba ma u a poo kuor lengni o poo sire.
They always look after a widow—until she gets another husband.

O so a nuru maal dir ka ba ko ole yong.
It was because she cooked so well they killed her.

N ma yil a yil vla, ka o kore kon.
I always spoke good sense, that's why they killed me.

These chants are not specific to any particular person, but are taken from the fund of proverbial sayings that most LoDagaa have at their command and that represents the pool of collective experience from which they draw to meet recurrent social situations. Any kinswoman of the deceased who can chant, therefore, cries out what she feels to be appropriate, and her words are taken up by the women around her. For many this keening is the saddest part of the proceedings, and I have seen grown men turn away to hide or avoid their grief. Some of the bereaved may burst into tears, others come forward to throw cowries at the foot of the bamboo pole, just as if it were the corpse in the burial service. Indeed, throughout this series of rites, the same actions are performed in the presence of the wooden stick as were previously performed about the corpse itself, so that the dead man actually becomes his own shrine and thereby an ancestor. For the shrine is the material representation of the deceased, an altar by means of which the living may communicate with him. In this way he continues to participate in the system of social relationships, as a supernatural instead of a human being, especially in relationships with members of the patrilineage to which he still belongs. The set of ties of which he was the focus during his life now centers upon his ancestor shrine. We may therefore speak of the ancestor cult as a projection of social relationships in a perfectly concrete and meaningful sense.

When the produce of the fields has been dropped upon the shrine and the keening of the women has died down, the ceremony is brought to an end for that day, and pots of beer are supplied for the participants to drink. A small pot is first offered to the shrine. A little of the liquid is poured on the stick, and the remainder is drunk by any non-lineage members present who have lost their fathers. Larger pots are then brought forward for the spectators (*zingurbe* or *semaandem,* neighbors), one pot for the women and one for the men. The food earlier offered to the shrine can be eaten by anyone who is hungry, with the exception of members of the lineage itself.

The following morning the women of the house prepare more food for the ritual of bathing the shrine. The grave-diggers first have to repeat their acts of the previous evening, pouring flour and beer on the stick, killing a fowl, and tying some tail feathers around it. The chief mourner again drops crops from the rooftop, the women burst into their lamentations, and money is thrown by the bereaved. The four grave-diggers then take up the stick and hand it to a group of three (or four) old women who are wives and sometimes daughters of their lineage. Indeed, help may be given by women of any lineage other than the deceased's, provided they have passed the menopause. The shrine is equivalent to the newly dead corpse and therefore has to be dealt with by the burial group and its wives.

The women performing this rite may act under the direction of the old women who carried out the whitewashing of the widows, but the group mainly involved in that performance is the widow's own lineage. Here it is the reciprocal burial group of her husband. The old woman in charge takes some water and sprinkles it on the outstretched hands of the other women, who then mix together the ingredients with which they will cleanse the shrine. These are the three materials used by the grave-diggers to clean their hands after a burial: the sharp *kalinyãã* grasses, strophanthus leaves, and *kõkõ* leaves, to which are added the sodden malted grains (*bir*) left over from the brewing of the funeral beer (*ko dãã*).

When these materials have been stirred together by the four women jointly, the leader takes more water and pours it over their palms. Now they are fully prepared to receive the shrine itself from the hands of their "husbands," the sextons. The end of the bamboo is placed upon a ring of plaited grass (*tasir*) so that it will not come in contact with the ground, and the old woman holds it by the top with great care. The other women proceed to cleanse the stick with the mixture they have prepared, pretending to perform each action thrice before actually doing it, using the same ritual of pretended gesture that occurred in the bathing of the widows earlier in the ceremony. Again the female spectators burst into lamentations, while the chief mourner once more throws crops upon the shrine, which are gathered up by the women taking part, the earlier contributions having been collected by the men. If it is a woman's shrine, pots are broken by the eldest daughter as at the burial service. The stick is then bathed in water, anointed with oil, doused in beer, and finally carried by the women into the byre, where it is leant against the wall near the corner in which the ancestor shrines are kept. Taking a calabash of porridge and a pot of soup from among those which were placed in front of the stick, the daughters of the deceased enter the byre and feed the shrine three times. They are followed there by those of their neighbors who have brought offerings of food, which they have cooked in the house, each woman flicking a portion onto the bamboo three times.

When the shrine has been placed in the byre and given its first food offerings, the women all retire to the main room of the house to feast. The food is divided in the following way. First, there is "the food for the washers of the stick" (*daa suori saab*), that is, for the wives of the burial group; then "the food for the whitewashers" (*yoo guorbe saab*), for the fellow clanswomen of the widow; and, finally, "the food for the spectators" (*zingurbe saab*). Each group receives a dish of porridge and a small pot of beer. The women who bathed the stick each pour a little beer on the floor three times before passing the calabash to the old woman who has supervised them. Then the rest of the beer is drunk by women who have no husbands, excluding those belonging to the lineage that has suffered the loss. When the food and drink are finished, the women are asked about the dead man's debts, just as the men are similarly questioned in the rituals concerned with the settlement of his estate, which follow immediately afterward.

THE SETTLEMENT OF THE ESTATE

Whereas the bathing of the widow is done by her fellow clanswomen and the washing of the stick by the burial group, the last part of this ceremony, the rites in the dead man's room, are carried out by men of his patriclan sector, together with the senior man among the gravediggers and representatives of the mother's patrilineage. These rites are a continuation of those performed immediately after the burial itself, but there are some significant variations. Most obvious of these is the way that the mixed group that met at the orphans' meal has now split into men and women, each conducting their separate rites.

In the half-light of the dead man's room the spectators sit with their backs to the mud walls, while three men squat around the small pot of beer that is used for ritual occasions. These three represent the mother's patrilineage, the burial group, and the funeral group. The last two are of course members of other lineages of the dead man's patriclan, or of the linked clan among the LoDagaba.

On one occasion when I was present, neither of the representatives of the first two groups had turned up, and clansmen from lineages other than the deceased's, who were also sister's sons of the clans in question, were asked to act instead. "Take the beer for your mother's house," they were told.

The representative of the reciprocal funeral group first grasps the pot of beer and pours some of its contents into his own calabash. He empties this into the calabash of the person sitting next to him, who pours it back again into his. This act is then carried out by each of the other two persons in turn. In the usual course of events it is forbidden to drink beer that has been poured from one calabash to another, so that this manner of acting is a deliberate reversal of normality. The three men drink the beer that they have treated in this way, as may any orphan present who does not belong to the deceased's lineage (since for the deceased's lineage this beer is "dirt"). The dregs from the pot are poured into a calabash held jointly by the three men and then thrown across the floor, so that the whole room is dampened. By this act the dead man's room becomes cool again after the heat engendered by the death.

The representative of the reciprocal funeral group leaves the room to fetch the quiver, which ever since the burial has remained hidden under the granary and which contains some arrows, twenty cowries, a hoe, and various other objects of iron. With it he brings half of the fowl slaughtered on the temporary shrine during the proceedings of the previous day, the other half having been taken by the grave-diggers. The quiver and the carcass are laid in the middle of the floor, where the dregs of the beer have been swilled. The ritual officiant, a senior member of the funeral group, calls upon one of the joking partners of the deceased's matriclan to come forward; for his participation again has the effect of making the objects of property cool, that is, safe for those who inherit. The officiant addresses the joking partner and asks, "What matriclan did the dead man belong to?" When he has been told, he says, "Shake the quiver." The man does so, and the leader asks, "What do you see?" To this the joking partner gives a set reply, "An axe, a hoe blade, a knife, a chisel, a needle, twenty cowries, and forty arrows." The question is repeated a second time, and the same answers are given except that the number of arrows is now increased to one hundred. At the third time of asking this is further raised to two hundred. The same question is asked of a member of the funeral group, who is here known as *sããbie,* father's child, a term indicating distance within the kin group, as distinct from *mabie,* mother's child, which emphasizes closeness. The same answers are given except that the number of arrows is raised still

higher. Then the whole rite is repeated once again for a representative
of the dead man's matriclan (*beltaaba*). In these ritual contexts such
an individual is also known as *gbanggbaataaba*, the literal meaning of
which is "fellow slave."[2]

To understand the replies about the arrows it should be remembered
that these possessions, like the beer that was drunk earlier in the ceremony, are identified with the dead man himself. The increase in the
number of arrows corresponds with the three main stages of a man's
life, child (*bie*), young man (*pol*), and elder (*nikpēē*). This retracing
of the steps in the dead man's life is emphasized by using the quiver
that was made for him as a young lad, when he was given his first real
bow. Once again it is a matter of "taking out the dream."

When the questioning is finished, the representative of the funeral
group gathers up the quiver and carries it away to its hiding place until
the final ceremony. With it he takes the carcass of the fowl, to which
he is entitled as the man who lays down the quiver (*lo' dielo*).

In the corner of the room there stands more beer, which is kept in
one of the earthenware stew-pots normally used for cooking soups and
relishes (*zier duli*). During the entire course of the funeral ceremonies,
such pots are referred to as vats (*siung*), the large containers in which
the brewing itself takes place. This usage may be a standardized exag-
geration of the kind employed in dedications to shrines when the sacrificial sheep is referred to as a cow. On the other hand, it is when the
beer is brewing outside in the vats that the ghosts of the dead are supposed to come to drink, and these large pots therefore acquire a special
association with the shades. Since they are too large to be moved, the
cooking pots, which are roughly of the same shape though much smaller
in size, are perhaps substitutes for them.

The joking partner goes over to the pot and pours a little of its
contents on the floor. This is a regular feature of all beer-drinking
among the LoDagaa. Before touching the liquid himself, a man will
first pour a little on the ground as an offering to the Earth shrine as well
as to any other supernatural agencies who may have helped in producing the grain to brew the beer or in getting the money to buy it.
Then a representative of the funeral group walks over to the vat and

---

[2] The word has no immediate connotation of slave status, but refers to a matriclan member who is not a full brother, and in fact the people I have seen fill this role
have also belonged to the reciprocal funeral group. The explanation of this usage is
of some relevance to my general theme, but owing to its complex nature, it is better
dealt with when I come to consider the system of inheritance, by which time the
reader will have a greater acquaintance with some of the associated institutions.

fills one small pot and two calabashes, which he hands to another member of the same group. The man carries these containers into the open courtyard outside the room, deliberately slopping the beer on the ground as he goes. When he gets there, he puts them down in one corner, saying as he does so, "This is for the xylophone players, this for the Earth shrine."

Inside the room the officiant turns to the senior man from the deceased's lineage, who has so far taken no part in these proceedings except to see that all the correct rites are performed. He addresses the elder, saying:

You bore a child who came and helped you, but death came unexpectedly
Yi doona a bie ko wa wiia yi, titshe ka kũ ma in naboo yaara

and killed him, so that now he's in the vat. Therefore I say what I am saying to you,
wa ko, ko le be a siung puo. Alena n yil ka n yil ko,

regard your child.
nyãã fu bie.

To this the lineage elder replies:

We bore a child who came and helped us, but death came unexpectedly
Ti doona bie ko wa wiia ti, ti a kũ le wa i a naboo yaara

and killed him. Take him and do what has to be done to make all well.
wa le koa. Fun de tun ka in vla.

What the elder asks the funeral group to take (in the last line quoted above) is the beer, which is also the dead man. Just as the animals acquired by him and slaughtered to his name, the tools of his economic pursuits, and his close personal possessions are all in various contexts identified with the deceased, so here the beer brewed from the grain he has grown is the dead man. He lies in the vat (*o bin a siung puo*).

The officiant repeats his speech, addressing in turn the chief mourner, who was here the brother of the deceased (*yeb*), the deceased's fellow matriclansmen (*beltaaba*), and lastly the member of his mother's patriclan, to whom he says, "Regard your sister's son" (*arba*).

Three ordinary beer pots are then produced for the assembled company. Although these are already full, they are topped up to the brim with the remnants of the beer from the cooking pot. These three pots, though drunk by all fatherless men present at the ceremony, are given separate names: the beer for the mother's patriclan (*ma yidem dãã*); the beer for the waist (*sie dãã*), a reference to the aches that farming brings and hence, presumably, to those who farmed with the dead man; and the beer for the contributors (*tshier dãã*), since in earlier times men gave a little grain to brew the beer for the dead man's rites, instead of contributing cowries as they nowadays do. However, although the pots are given these separate names, they are in fact drunk by all those present entitled to drink funeral beer. The dregs are not drunk by the man who pours the beer, as is normally the case, but are again swilled across the length of the floor.

When the beer is finished, inquiries are again made about debts. After this the widows return on a visit to their fathers' compounds to collect grain for the final ceremony, if it is planned to hold it that year. This grain is used to brew the beer that is drunk when the widows have been finally bathed and their innocence established.

These rites in the dead man's room conclude the ceremony of the Bitter Funeral Beer. It is bitter in that the loss of the dead person is still felt by the bereaved. He has not finally been aggregated to his ancestors, and his social personality is in the intermediary state universally associated with ghosts and revenants. This ceremony prepares those connected with the deceased by social ties for his final disappearance from the material world and for his installation as an ancestor; prepares them for a relationship in which the ties are no longer corporeal but supernatural. To this end, further measures are taken to secure a smooth distribution of such of the dead man's roles as he can no longer fill and such of his property as he can no longer enjoy. The widows, still contaminated with his body dirt, are further cleansed; his ancestor shrine is being created. If we may judge from the emphasis it receives, this concluding ceremony of the Bitter Funeral Beer prepares for what is, with the exception of the remarriage of the widows, the most dangerous aspect of the process of readjustment, namely, the reallocation of the dead man's property.

CHAPTER XII

From Ghost to Spirit: The Final Ceremony

Maintain a mourning ostentation,
And on your family's old monument
Hang mournful epitaphs, and do all rites
That appertain unto a burial.

Much Ado About Nothing (IV, i)

The last of the series of funeral ceremonies takes place, supplies of grain permitting, after the first harvest following the burial. This ceremony is known as the Cool Funeral Beer (*Ko Dãã 'Baaro*), and it brings to an end the period of transition between life and death. The dead man is finally placed among his ancestors, while the bereaved return to the community from which they have been partially separated. The long mourning is ended by the creation of the ancestor shrine and by the final redistribution of the dead man's rights and duties among those who survive him.

On the first day, the Day of the Funeral Beer (*Ko Dãã Bibiir*), the stick for the ancestor shrine is cut and carved, and then brought to the vicinity of the dead man's house. The next morning, the Day of the Widows' Dispersal (*Poobe Yaaro Bibiir*), the shrine is carried into the byre and placed near those of the other ancestors. On this day, the widows are finally purified from their contact with the dead man; they are tested once again to see whether they have committed adultery since his burial and are released from their coital obligations to him, though not from their procreative ones, which they continue to owe him until death, or until the bridewealth given on his behalf is returned to his lineage. On the third day, the Day of the Children's Ordeal (*Bi Pol Bibiir*), the children are tested for responsibility in their parent's death and are formally shown the men who stand in the position of classificatory "fathers." After this certain of those present go into the dead man's room to perform the series of rites that concern the redistribution of the property. The Cool Funeral Beer is thus very similar in general outline to the previous ceremony. Both consist essentially of three phases: the installation of the shrine, the bathing of the widow, and the settlement of the estate.

The initial act is again the brewing of the beer, which is begun two days before the opening of the ceremony, and once again the xylophone is played continuously throughout this period. The beer is brewed right outside the compound, not in the open courtyard as is usually the case. From one standpoint this way of doing things constitutes one of the many reversal customs found in funeral ceremonies and especially in the worship of the ancestors. But it has further, more specific, meanings, which are connected with the eschatology of the LoDagaa.

As in so many societies, death is seen not only as the end of the mortal life, but as the beginning of a journey to another country, the Land of the Dead. However, the dead man does not immediately set out to join his forebears, for major changes of status require a transitional period of adjustment. Moreover, since the performance of funerals and ideas about the fate of the soul in death appear always to involve some ethical or moral judgment of the deceased's past life, time is required for the assessment to be made and for any necessary atonement to take place.

During this liminal period the status of the dead man is in transition. He has as yet no permanent shrine, nor is he considered one of the ancestors; he is a *nyāākpiin,* a wraith, a revenant, a visible ghost, rather than a *kpiin,* a true ancestral spirit. As far as mundane affairs are concerned, his estate is as yet undivided, and his control over the sexuality of his wives has not yet been broken. In many contexts he continues actively to fill his earthly roles. Indeed, his social personality persists as long as his personalty remains intact.

This transitional stage in the social system is reflected in his spatial position between this world and the next. He is neither wholly of one world nor entirely of the other. Between the first and last of the funeral ceremonies he is thought of as inhabiting the treetops. From here he returns to the vicinity of the compound only during the actual ceremonies. One such occasion is the day before the final funeral ceremony, when the spirits of his agnatic ancestors come to bathe the ghost in the beer that stands in the vats outside the house. The ceremonial performed by the living is re-enacted by the dead.

Were the vats in their usual position, the ghosts would have to re-enter the compound itself, an event that the LoDagaa take many precautions to prevent, especially during the hours of darkness. The night before the final ceremony, in particular, is spoken of as an evil time, since it is the last visit of the dead man to his house before journeying to the Land of the Dead. And as physical proof of this nocturnal appearance, the inquirer is told, there are the hairs that the ghost is supposed to leave in the beer.

In preparation for this visitation, a fowl is slaughtered earlier that day over those of the dead man's clothes that have been left hanging on the wall of the house since the time of the burial. This sacrifice can be seen as the final separation rite, which frees the ghost for his journey to the Land of the Dead. This apparel, being impregnated with the dirt of the dead man's body, is regarded by the LoWiili as too dangerous to be handed over to another person and is left to disintegrate where it hangs. Among the LoDagaba, however, although the garments are still considered unsafe for any member of the dead man's patriclan, they may be taken by someone from the linked clan, the members of which stand at a social distance sufficient to neutralize the mystical dangers that would attack closer kin.

Among the LoDagaba, a further ceremony is performed before the final funeral in connection with the dead man's membership in the Bagre society. There are, in fact, a series of such rites. On the day after the burial, members of the linked clan bury the gourd (*tshiili*) in which a senior member of the society keeps his special Bagre medicine. The burial takes place in an anthill, like that of a child who dies and returns three times; it is thought that the ants will entirely destroy the corpse and thus prevent the sprite from coming back again to plague the parents. The same idiom of utter and complete destruction is appropriate in the Bagre context as well.

Bagre members are subsequently called to attend the Diviners' Beer, which, as I have mentioned, differs from the ceremony that is given the same name among the LoWiili. At the Bitter Funeral Beer, which for senior members is held not at the beginning of the rains but at the time of a certain Bagre ceremony known as *Bag Sebr*, the same persons come together once more; on this occasion, too, they divine in the Bagre manner and end by arranging the date of the final funeral to coincide with a later Bagre performance, *Bag Puru*. At this last ceremony, the senior members take the dead man's cowry container and divide up the contents, as well as the cowries that the kin throw for them. The goatskin bag (*bagtshuur*), which has been hanging on the compound wall, is taken down and ripped in half. A special beer (*Gan Dãã* or *Bagtshuur Dãã*) is brewed for the occasion, usually the day before the beginning of the final funeral itself. If the deceased has acquired much wealth, either through his membership in the society or else by sprite divination, animals may also be killed to his name and the flesh shared among the initiates present at the time. Such an offering is not primarily a recompense for services rendered, but rather a recognition of the wealth the dead man had accumulated by divination. Indeed, membership of the Bagre society brings wealth not only because of the opportunity it offers to practice divining, but also because, by participating in the entrance rituals, existing members (especially the senior ones) can derive benefits from the dues and supplies provided on the neophytes' behalf.

THE FIRST DAY: THE CREATION OF THE FINAL
ANCESTOR SHRINE

As with the previous ceremonies, the Cool Funeral Beer begins on the day of the week on which the burial itself took place. The day dawns to the sound of the wailing of women and the shooting of guns, and the dead man is again mourned as at the funeral itself.

The main activity of this day is the carving of the ancestor shrine (*kpiin daa,* the spirit's stick), a wooden figure some two feet long, with a rounded knob for a head and a straight body forking into two legs. The shrine is said to be "cut" by the senior son of the dead man (that is, the eldest son of his senior wife), and in this task he is assisted by the eldest son of the next senior wife. In fact, the actual operations involved in the creation of the shrine are performed by a member of the reciprocal funeral group who is also a matriclan joking partner, but they are done in the name of the sons of the dead man. The senior son brings a black cock, the second son a hen; and a party of men drawn from the lineage, from the burial group, and from the funeral group set off for the bush in search of the wood for the shrine. A man (*daatshiero*) previously selected by the diviner cuts a branch from a tree. (The tree is also specially chosen, either by the diviner or else by the joking partner mentioned above.) In one LoWiili case I knew of, the person selected was a "sister's son"; he climbed the tree, put a rope around the branch, and hacked it off. "A sister's son is afraid of nothing" (*arbile be zore bumzai*), I was told.

Led by the funeral group, the party sacrifice the black cock at the foot of the tree, pour a libation of funeral beer, and then drink what remains in the pot. As in the sacrifices to the provisional shrine, the fowl is not allowed to flutter, but is held until it dies. At other sacrifices, the fowl is cast aside while still alive, because the way it dies determines whether or not the shrine has accepted the offering. The beer used in these offerings is also of a special kind, since no yeast has been added to it.

The wood for the shrine must on no account be allowed to touch the ground before it enters the byre, and the branch has therefore to be cut down from the tree with great care. The senior son has to stand under the branch, tug with the rope, and then catch it when it falls; if he fails to do so, people will say the branch is not his father, and they will have to start again. When this work has been safely accomplished, the branch is covered with a cloth or smock and carried near to the house of the person who will shape it into an ancestor shrine. Ancestor shrines always have to be wrapped up in this way whenever they are taken from the darkness of the byre to some other dwelling. When this is being done, they must be carried on the shoulder, never, as ordinary objects are, on the head.

Before the branch is taken over by the carver, another fowl is killed and the blood allowed to drip onto the bark. Porridge and beer are brought along, and some of this is fed to the embryonic shrine, the remainder being left for the carver. Each stage in the creation of the ancestor figure is marked in this same way. For the shrine is intensely dangerous and is described as an evil thing (*bum faa*) that might mystically seize upon (*nyoona*) those who come in contact with it.

The man who has cut the branch from the tree approaches the woodcarver (*daapieno*), also chosen by divination, and informs him that the dead man's patriclansfolk (in fact, the members of the reciprocal funeral group) have brought the stick for him and placed it outside his house. This is a further indication of the dangerous nature of the shrine. The woodcarver is not shown where it is, but has to search for it himself; having found it, he takes it to the shade of a tree, where he sits down with his adze to shape the wood into the stylized form of a human being.

That evening, when the carver has finished his work, the eldest son comes and carries the stick to the vicinity of the house, putting it down where the path leading to the natal home of the dead man's mother is crossed by another track. As I remarked in describing the disposal of an infant's corpse, crossroads provide a most suitable location for a separation rite in that they are inevitable points of dispersal. When the eldest son puts down the shrine, beer, porridge, soup, and a hen are brought out from the deceased's compound. The carver kills a fowl upon the shrine and makes the shrine an offering of food and beer. The housepeople then throw grain and other produce of the fields. The offerings of food, as in the other sacrifices that have marked the various stages in the making of the shrine, belong to the carver himself. But now he ceases his association with the shrine, which is taken over by members of the reciprocal funeral group on behalf of those of the deceased's patrilineal kin who continue to inhabit the same compound; for it is in their byre that the figure will be placed. Hence, quite apart from indicating a stage in the creation of the material correlate of an ancestor, this rite separates the carver from his handiwork, since his own soul might have passed into the work during the creative process.

When the woodcarver has finished his task, the shrine is returned once again to the patriclan. This handing over is marked by the killing of another fowl. These sacrifices on the path to the dead man's mother's home are a reaffirmation of matrilateral ties at the very moment when the shrine is about to be accepted as part of the sacra of the patrilineal group. It acknowledges the continuing importance of extraclan kinship even in the context of an ancestor cult that is patrilineally controlled. Moreover, the fact that the stick has rested on the ground at this point lies behind the frequent use of crossroads as an alternative altar for sacrifices to the ancestors, especially ancestors whose shrines are some distance away from a man's present home.

The shrine is carried to the vicinity of the compound by the eldest son, but it is taken to the house itself by one of the daughters of the lineage. When the house is reached, the women walk around the figure three times before leaning it against the wall beside the opening to the byre and the ladder that leads to the roof. The rites now carried out are a repetition of those performed around the provisional shrine during the second phase of the Bitter Funeral Beer. A member of the burial group takes porridge, beer, and a fowl, provided on behalf of the eldest son by the reciprocal funeral group, and offers them to the shrine. Throughout this ritual the ancestor is given food that has been fully prepared, whereas at the earlier ceremonies the sorghum flour was simply mixed with beer or water to make the brose that women serve when time is short, a dish looked upon with much less favor than porridge (*saab*). When the fowl is killed, the women burst out weeping, and crops are dropped from the roof by the chief mourner. Beer is provided (a pot for men and a pot for women), food is offered to the shrine by daughters and others, and the ceremony is at an end for that day.

THE SECOND DAY: THE BATHING OF THE WIDOWS

The following morning the members of the burial group return to the compound, and another fowl is killed. The shrine is then washed, crops are dropped from the rooftop, and food is offered to the shrine as at the previous ceremony. But before the shrine is taken inside, the widows are first bathed and then tested by means of a ritual meal that they share with the dead man's shrine. This is part of a sequence of rites that brings to a consummation all the various ceremonies concerned with the purification of the widows.

First of all, the widows are bathed as in the post-burial rites and at the Bitter Funeral Beer. Indeed, the rites on these three occasions are virtually identical, save that the progress toward complete separation of the conjugal pair is marked by dressing the women in different clothes. The widows, then, are led behind the house and bathed. Great care is taken not to let the water fall in their eyes; for this water has been defiled by the husband's dirt that remains on the widow's body, the dirt that is so dangerous to her should she enter upon another sexual union. Next, her head is shaved (a frequent rite of separation), and the hair thrown on the midden, which stands near the house; but this time no whitewash is daubed on her body. Finally, she puts on the clothes proper to an adult woman and discards the widow's weeds she has worn for so long. Her patriclan "sisters" provide new perineal bands sewn from goatskin (*gammie*), and the bands she has been wearing now become the property of the old woman who has organized the bathing rituals.

Goatskin bands are the appropriate dress for a married woman, though nowadays clothes of foreign manufacture, African or non-African, are often worn over the traditional costume. But like the corpse earlier in the ceremony, the women are not only dressed, they are dressed up. The widow has beads hung around her head and neck, and is attired in a man's smock and a red fez. On top of her head she carries a "shrine basket" (*tiib pele*), a small square basket that women always take with them on journeys to hold their personal shrines, their money, and possibly a few groundnuts to eat when hungry. I have also seen some widows with their faces powdered white, grasping a knife or dagger in one hand and carrying a spare cloth over their shoulders. This is the dress in which the Bagre neophytes appear when, at the end of the long series of initiation performances, they make their first appearance in public by parading through the market place at the ceremony known as Bagre Bells (*Bag Gbelme*).

I have remarked that when the corpse is dressed up in a similar manner, this is done partly to honor the deceased and partly to demonstrate a change in status. The same may be said about the dressing up of the widow: she, too, is being honored for having successfully emerged from her various ordeals (although the last of these is yet to come), and her status is also undergoing a change as she reaches the end of the period of mourning. Furthermore, there is the reversal theme that runs through the rituals concerning the disposal of the dead; as one LoDagaa said in reply to my queries about the widows' use of male dress, "A funeral is different." But in addition to these factors another element is present in the rites. As a later stage in the ritual makes clear, the widow herself undergoes a burial service as a homeopathic protection against her late husband. She is dressed up as if she were herself the corpse.

Attired in this way, the widow is led to the front of the house, where the shrine rests against the compound wall. During the earlier bathing rituals, she had been tested by being fed by the whitewashers; she is now given a meal to eat jointly with her husband's shrine. My account of this ritual is taken from a LoDagaba funeral near Tom, but it appears to be similar in every major respect to what takes place among the LoWiili.

The ritual was carried out by two old women from the widow's patriclan (*poghsããmamine*). First of all, they tied gay-colored head-bands around her head; the plain grass band acquired after the burial had been removed during the bathing. A woman's stool, distinguished from a man's by having four legs instead of three, was placed in front of the shrine, and the old women took the widow by the arm, stood her in front of the stool, and made her flex her knees three times as if she were going to sit down. Only on the fourth occasion did they actually permit her to do so. The old women then took porridge, water, soup, and flour water, mixed them in one calabash, and stirred the ingredients together three times with a wooden spoon. On the fourth stir the widow herself assisted the old women. Having first fed some of this mixture to the shrine, the whitewashers approached the widow and handed her a morsel of porridge, which she raised to her mouth three times and finally threw on the shrine. She repeated this action three times in all and then did the same with some meat from another pot. In doing this the widow took care not to drop food onto herself; for if she did so, it is feared she would die. For the same reason, when the meal was over, the old women carefully wiped her mouth clean. The widow was then raised to her feet in the same manner as she had been sat down; only on the fourth occasion did she actually stand upright.

Attention has already been drawn to the two main aspects of these rites. In the first place, they constitute one of the principal separation rites of the whole funeral performance. When the husband dies, both he and his widow are placed on the margin of social life. The subsequent rituals complete the husband's departure from this world and establish him in the next, finally separate the husband and the wife from each other, and return the widow to the life of the community. The bathing is concerned with the second of these themes, the dressing up with the third, and the ritual meal with both the second and the third. For at her husband's death the wife becomes a young girl again, and she is fed like a child, a person entering a community for the first time. After passing through the various ages of woman, she becomes an adult once more, having sloughed off all personal associations with her dead husband.

A second aspect of both the whitewashing and the feeding rites is that they are also ordeals that test the widow to discover whether by adultery, witchcraft, or other means she has had anything to do with her husband's death. If one feeds the ancestor, one must have no blame in his death; for hostile acts and the provision of food are incompatible, as the obligations of a host make clear in this as in so many other societies. For, as I have emphasized, it is those most intimately connected with him who are the likeliest to have come into conflict—suppressed or overt—with the dead man, and therefore to have wished him harm. Consequently, all close bereaved have to undergo an ordeal, which serves a dual function. First, the test amounts to a social recognition of the hostile element within such relationships. When the actors perform these rituals they are giving conscious expression to this component, that is, to the suppressed hostility thought to be a possible cause of the death they are mourning. In this concrete fashion they are acting out their guilt feelings in socially standardized ways. Not only is the person who successfully undergoes the ritual himself relieved of guilt; he is also cleared in the eyes of the community. Second, in addition to having this effect of personal catharsis and collective exculpation, the ordeals serve as mechanisms of social control in a rather different sense. From the standpoint of the community, they provide a sanction against the suppressed tension within a domestic group breaking out into overt conflicts. They cannot prevent, but they do limit, the damage to the nuclear units of social life.

The next part of the ceremony includes a final testing of the widow as well as a reassertion of the continuing interests of her natal patrilineage, even though she is to be inherited leviratically. The particular example I give is a LoWiili one, and it begins with the woman's "burial." A male member of the widow's patrilineage brings a cloth, which four women from the same patriclan (her "fellow daughters" and her "father's sisters") hold over her and wave slowly up and down, singing:

Sontshi yaarbe,

Sontshi yaarbe,

Be dong ter mena,
They had me as a wife,

ka le wuni me.
and it grieved me so.

Pogh kuor paala nuo be in nuo.
The happiness of a marriageable widow cannot last.

Biu na vier e be lon ler ngmãã
Tomorrow will come, and they'll hit me with an old axe.

The cloth they hold was likened by the LoDagaa to that which covers the funeral stand; indeed, the widow actually stands on the place where the corpse rested when it was brought out of the house. The widow is undergoing a separation from her husband, a burial of their inter-personal relations. When she has been cleared of complicity in his death, she is then at liberty to enter into sexual relations with another male without fearing the wrath of the dead man, who has by now begun his journey to join his forebears in the Land of the Dead. But these rites of purification and separation are performed not by her husband's but by her own patriclansmen, who come to bury their own daughter. A woman's position as wife-mother in one lineage and daughter-sister in another involves a conflict of roles that can never be finally resolved once and for all. At this moment, her position lies in the balance between these two clusters of roles, since she has been freed from the particular individual who had control over her as a sexual partner and not yet attached to another. Her patriclan takes the major part in this separation, for they are concerned that no responsibility for the death should be laid at the feet of their "daughter." Should she be held to blame, the husband's lineage could refuse to accept her as a leviratic spouse, and until expiatory rites had been performed, she would remain in danger from the anger of her dead husband. So that whereas her spouse's agnates do take precautions in the matter, her own patrikins-folk have the major part to play in clearing their "daughter."

The role of the widow's patriclansfolk at the funeral emphasizes the fact that, even after her marriage, rights and responsibilities continue to be vested in her natal kin group. That she is no mere chattel of her marital lineage can be seen from the words of the song they have just sung. The widow's "sisters" claim that she has been badly treated by her husband's kin; the use of the plural *be,* rather than the singular *o,* is significant here in indicating that this is a collective rather than a personal matter. That is to say, the maltreatment is not attached to any particular husband-wife relationship. From time to time, most women marrying away from their natal kin feel themselves to be strangers in a hostile land and harshly done by at that. By giving expression to these recurrent feelings, the women's patrikinsfolk show that they are still concerned about their "sister's" welfare and are ready to come to her aid if she is not treated in a fitting manner.

The same theme is yet more strikingly demonstrated in the next part of the ritual. While their "sister" is undergoing the mock burial, the male members of her patrilineage sit under a nearby tree. When the rite has ended, they get up and seize any fowls they can from the outskirts of the dead man's compound. Then they call the widow and question her privately about her chastity since her husband's death, for they want to see her name free from any possibility of scandal.

When the widows have each been questioned by their own kin, they are subjected to a similar but more elaborate ordeal in front of the husband's kinsfolk.[1] This second declaration is public and has strong supernatural sanctions. Once when I was present, a widow stood upon the dead man's grave and swore that she had been faithful to him since the day he died, a procedure that is not encouraged because of the possibility of breaking the pot with which the tomb is closed. More usually a small pile of soil is made where two paths cross, and the oath is made upon this altar to the Earth, which also represents the grave itself. The Earth shrine is situated in a central grove, but domestic sacrifices to the Earth may be performed at any place by scraping together a little soil.

The widow is then called over, and she comes forward holding twenty cowries and a guinea-corn stalk, supplied by her patriclansfolk, and this she sticks in the pile of earth. Accompanying her is one of her "father's sisters," who carries a small pot of beer on her head. One of her "brothers" now interrogates her for all to hear, asking whether she has slept with any man since her husband's death. In reply the widow makes a public declaration of her fidelity, affirming that her late husband treated her well, and that if any of his agnates wishes her as a

---

[1] I have seen these two rituals combined when only one widow was involved.

wife, let him take the twenty cowries she holds out. On one occasion, I saw the widow throw the cowries on the ground saying, "If there is anyone here who can look after me as well as my husband did, let him pick up the cowries. If not, give me the money back again."

The attitude that the widow now expresses toward her marriage differs radically from the one attributed to her by her patrikinsfolk shortly before. For despite the difficulties of married life and the gratitude she feels for the support of her paternal kin in times of adversity, a woman among the LoDagaa, as in most societies, prefers to reside as a wife than as a sister. An older woman likes to live with her sons, and to do so she must be acceptable as a leviratic spouse by a member of her late husband's lineage. In any case, a husband is deemed a more suitable source of support than a brother, and the acceptance of these cowries ensures that a widow will be provided for by her late husband's kin. Even for a widow not contemplating leviratic marriage, the promise of such support is desirable, especially when a rejection of the cowries would suggest that she had a hand in her husband's death.

The cowries are accepted on behalf of the dead man's lineage by a specific person. However, this does not mean that the widow will eventually marry that man, but simply signifies an acceptance by the husband's lineage of her conduct up to date. She is cleared of blame for her husband's death and is free from any charge of unexpiated adultery either during his lifetime or during his transformation into an ancestral spirit. She is accepted once again as a spouse of the lineage, which is turn reaffirms its responsibilities for providing her with food, medicine, and shelter. During the next few months she may in fact choose a man outside the kin group as husband; there is no restraint on her in this respect. But if she does marry elsewhere, the bridewealth contributed on behalf of the dead man has to be returned in full.

When she has made her declaration, the widow bends the guinea-corn stalk until it snaps. As it breaks, the woman who has accompanied her dashes the pot of beer on the ground as an offering to the ghost of the dead man. Nothing is said at the time, and no action is taken irrespective of whether or not the stick breaks cleanly. But in fact this act is held to be the final proof of the widow's innocence. A clean break means she has remained chaste since the burial and has had nothing to do with her husband's death. The sticking of the guinea-corn stalk in the pile of earth is equivalent to swearing an oath to the Earth shrine. In effect the widow is saying, "If I have done wrong, may the Earth punish me." Retribution for any offense she may have committed is placed firmly in supernatural hands. The dead are also involved; the offering of beer is made quite specifically to the deceased, and the small pile of earth outside the compound, a substitute for the grave, can also serve as an altar to the ancestors. Indeed, the whole ceremony is reminiscent of the funeral speeches made during the burial service, when the dead body is addressed by friends and by lovers.

The final rite[2] in the complex centering upon the bathing of the widows emphasizes even more clearly the conflicting aspects of the social personality of a married woman who is sister in one lineage and wife in another. By her husband's death she is placed in an intermediary position, which results in a formal restatement, in dramatic form, of the rights and duties held by members of the two kin groups in respect of her and, conversely, of her privileges and obligations with regard to them.

The widow's "brothers" have been present since the bathing of the widows and sit together in a group, armed with their bows and arrows. These men are the male lineage members of the woman's own generation, those in a position to make use of the bridewealth she has brought in, which is theoretically confined to members of the same generation; it is these persons who are most concerned in the material consequences of the transfer of the woman's sexuality.

Earlier in the ceremony, when the "burial" of their sister was over, these men jumped up and seized some chickens belonging to members of the dead man's compound. Now, too, when the pot of beer has been dashed to the ground and the clanswomen of the widow start loudly hooting their approval of her innocence, the "brothers" again try to seize what fowls they can lay their hands on. This time they set off home, taking with them both the fowls and the widow herself. Meanwhile the female members of the dead man's own clan sector—that is, the women who have married elsewhere and who have a joking relationship with their brothers' wives—sing out to the widow as she departs, "You are ours, you are ours." A "brother" of the dead man runs after the widow's party and starts to remonstrate with her kin, but he is permitted to bring her back only after making a gift of twenty cowries to his "brothers-in-law" and allowing them to keep one of the guinea-fowls and one of the chickens they have seized. This fowl is known as the brother-in-law's fowl (*dakye nuura*), the name also given to the one that may be brought to the burial service by these men, the in-laws who have given wives to the deceased. Just as the widow gives twenty cowries to

2 Although I speak of this as the final rite, I once saw it performed before the questioning of the widows about their sexual relations; and on another occasion it took place after the meal that usually completes the day's activities.

the dead man's lineage, so her brothers demand the same amount from that group. In both cases the transactions between the wife-giving and the wife-taking groups serve to redefine the dead man's network of affinal ties and to emphasize its continuing nature. For these exchanges demonstrate that the handing over of rights in the widow to the levir is not merely a matter of automatic inheritance, but that her kin have direct interests in the transfer, for which they claim a token bridewealth.

These relationships between the groups are inevitably ones that tend to bring them into conflict, because at times both parties have opposing interests in the same individual. These contrary interests are given dramatic expression in the attempt of the widow's patrikin to take her back to her natal home, and particularly in the element of limited force that characterizes both the seizure of the chickens and the abduction of the woman. The rites thus enact a situation of conflicting interests in a woman, a situation that resembles that found in the practices characterizing the mother's brother-sister's son relationship in many patrilineal systems (Goody [1959a]), as well as the custom of so-called marriage-by-capture (Hertz [1960], p. 150; Radcliffe-Brown [1950], p. 49). This institutionalized threat of "divorce-by-capture" is an example of a similar mechanism at work.

A brief account of this part of the ceremony as carried out by the LoDagaba will bring out the similarities between the societies in their treatment of rights in women as well as confirm some of the points already made. I shall begin at the moment when the brothers seize (*faana*) the widow and pretend to take her home. What happens goes something like this. One of her late husband's sisters calls out, "We don't want the woman, but leave us the child," while another shouts "Leave the child behind. It hasn't yet learnt to feed itself." I have already remarked that such comments form part of a more inclusive joking relationship between a wife and her husband's "sisters." Here, however, I want to call attention to the specific content of the exchange, which constitutes a further recognition of the distinction between the procreative and coital aspects of a woman's sexuality. As female lineage members, the "sisters" are not primarily interested in the woman as a sexual object, but rather in her offspring, who are members of their own patrilineal descent group.

The widow and her party do not get far before one of her husband's "brothers" runs after them, catches them up, and begs her to come back, offering to pay (*yaana*) for her once again. Only a token amount of twenty cowries is handed over, for in fact leviratic rights are transferred with the original bridewealth payments. Nevertheless, the extraction of a further sum for the retention of their "sister" by the late husband's lineage emphasizes the jural ties that continue to exist between a woman and her natal patriclan.

When the widows are brought back to the compound, they lead their agnatic kinfolk into the section of the house allotted to them for their domestic tasks. Here the food and beer prepared from the grain they have collected from their kin are laid out and divided into two parts, one for the widows' own "brothers" and one for their "husbands" (*sir kuorbe*). With this meal, the bathing of the widows is finally brought to an end; they will indeed return home with their kin at the conclusion of the ceremony, but only as visitors, not as residents.

After the Dispersal of the Widows, the wives of the deceased are free to sleep with other men. Unless the bridewealth is repaid, any children a widow bears are children of the deceased. If she marries leviratically, either she may accept the designated heir to the dead man's sexual rights, that is, his nearest kinsman of the same or alternate generation, or she may marry any other of his patriclansfolk, provided he is of the right generation. I have known of several cases when a widow "married" the son of an agnatic "sister" of her late husband. But such a union is better described as widow concubinage; for in neither community do the offspring belong to the same patrilineage as the *genitor*, nor can he make a claim for adultery. Indeed, a union of this kind is not dissimilar to cohabitation with any other outsider, except that the late husband's patrilineage would be more chary of attempting to force a "sister's son" to return the bridewealth.

In the case of a true leviratic marriage, the future husband gives one of his "elder brothers" a hundred cowries (*pogh kuor koba*) to offer to the widow; by taking these, she accepts him as a husband. However, before he can take her as a wife, both of the intending partners have to be bathed. The new husband sends the widow's agnatic kinsfolk a fowl, known as the "room fowl," and this is killed at her father's shrine to the beings of the wild, the shrine that protected her as a child and helped her to grow into a woman. In addition, he sends 140 cowries for the women who bathe her, and a guinea-fowl for his future mother-in-law. When this rite has been performed, the new husband is jurally entitled to claim for adultery (*paa libie*, vagina money), but the children still belong to the man on behalf of whom the bridewealth was paid, that is, to the dead man.

The ceremony of bathing and dressing up finally establishes the surviving spouse in a new role. Each change of social position has to be marked in some visible, though not necessarily public, manner. There are a number of ways of accomplishing this end. The stages of a woman's life are marked not only by changes of a physiological order, but also by changes of dress. A man who has killed a human being or slaughtered one of the larger animals is set apart by having to observe certain prohibitions and by being accorded various privileges. Some of these prohibitions and prerogatives have an idiomatic connection with the role itself, as, for example, the freedom of homicides to eat the flesh of the vulture, an animal that itself consumes the flesh of man and is tabooed to all other categories of person. Other such special forms of acting appear to designate a class of persons, without having any particular connections, either with the role itself, or with other networks of meaning associated with ritual acts or cosmological ideas. They appear simply as emblems, whose association with the object or person in question is validated within the one context alone.

A man who has lost his wife acquires certain prerogatives that mark him off from other members of the community and indicate that the role of widower is visualized as permanently assigned, whereas the role of widow tends to be allocated to a woman only for the duration of the funeral ceremonies.

A widower can build himself a special type of room on top of his house, known as a *bopie*. This is constructed by first filling in the dead wife's room with rubble and then building another on top, so that the entrance leads directly onto the flat roof. This custom varies somewhat from clan to clan. Among the Kusiele patriclan of Lawra (LoSaala), a man must have lost three wives before the room can be built. In some patriclans in Tom (LoDagaba), a man can make himself such a room without his being a widower, by claiming to be building for a forefather who was. A further prerogative obtaining in the settlement of Tom is that only a widower can sit upon the large wooden mortars to be found in the open space in front of the house, or upon the stones used as a cooking place. Moreover, only a widower can own such a mortar; they cannot be owned either by women (they are seen as part of the "fixtures" of the house), or by men who are not widowers. If a man who is not a widower needs a mortar, he selects a suitable thorn tree and asks a widower belonging to the same patriclan to come and make the first cut with the axe. Even then, the widower is said to "own" the mortar, although his kinsman has full use of it. Another privilege of widowers is that like women they are allowed to pick up cats. Cats (*diu baa*, literally "room dogs") are not thought of as domesticated in the same way as other animals; indeed, they move from the house to the woods with considerable ease. Moreover, they are mystically dangerous animals, believed to possess medicine (*tĩĩ*), that is, to have extraordinary powers, and in general they are associated with women.

I am uncertain of the geographical extent of the observance of these various prerogatives. They were not put to me as distinctive of a clan or a locality, but I did not in all cases make the inquiries necessary to ascertain their distribution. However, their common characteristic is plain; widowers are permitted to perform certain actions that are closely associated with women. The loss of a wife places a man in a special category in which the differences in behavior of men and women tend to be broken down. I suggest that this is a social recognition of the fact that the widower may have to take over the domestic activities of the dead woman, especially with regard to their children. He is now the sole remaining parent, and if the children are young, he has to see that they are fed. If he has no wife or daughter-in-law, he may even have to cook for himself.

The actions characterizing a widower thus fall into the first category of role behavior mentioned above; apart from their obvious function as status emblems, they appear to have specific metaphoric meanings. A further point to note is that these customary acts are all prerogatives; the prohibitions have to be observed by other members of the community who do not belong to this particular class. In general the LoDagaa appear to associate special statuses with the freedom to perform acts otherwise forbidden. They rarely make use of the alternative device, often found in centralized societies, of hemming in special roles with added taboos that the ordinary person is not required to observe, a device that serves, in part, to legitimize the office in other people's eyes. But then among the LoDagaa such positions hardly carry the concrete prerogatives of high offices of state, prerogatives that help to offset the disabilities often imposed upon the incumbents.

Since I have discussed the status of a widower in this context, it seems appropriate to mention here some other details of the sequence of post-burial rites for a woman, especially in view of the close parallel they offer to those I have described for a man.

A woman's shrine is treated in much the same way as a man's. The women from the burial group bathe the stick, their husbands kill a guinea-fowl upon it, the women burst into lamentations, and the chief mourner scatters crops (for a wife, too, has had a hand in producing these, since it is she who plants and helps to harvest them). The eldest daughter breaks one of the dead woman's pots and one of her calabashes at the foot of the shrine, and the shrine is then carried into the byre.

The daughters feed their mother's shrine, and drink is provided for the onlookers and participants. Then the wives of the burial group take a cloth into the byre to wrap the shrine, and also a wicker frame (*zong*), normally used for carrying firewood, to convey it to the dead woman's natal home. With the eldest daughter in the lead, they bear the shrine slowly, without looking back, taking at the same time a guinea-fowl, porridge, soup, a small pot of beer, a bunch of guinea-corn heads, some groundnuts, and twenty cowries. The cowries are spoken of as *poo tshera libie*, bridewealth money, and the sum explicitly represents a further and final installment of the bridewealth at the time when the dead woman is taken back to her father's house for the last time.

When the women arrive at the father's house, they lay the shrine against the wall. The deceased's natal lineage kill the guinea-fowl they have brought on the stick and scatter the crops over it; the women who have accompanied the daughter do the same with a guinea-fowl and some crops that are provided by the father's kin. The shrine can now be placed in the byre near the shrines of the dead woman's paternal ancestors.

When the women return, those who have whitewashed the husband at the earlier ceremonies, the husband's "father's sisters," proceed to do so again, thus finally inducting him into the status of widower. He is bathed in a similar way to the widow, standing on the mat on which he and his wife slept together. As they shave his head and wash his body, the old women really come into their own and assert their ritual authority over the male sex. They bring oil to anoint his body, and when this is done, new clothes, a quiver, a bow, and some beads to dress him in.

When they have finished bathing him, the senior whitewasher takes a calabash of water, into which some medicine has been mixed, and leads the widower to the foot of the ladder going up to the roof; here she sprinkles some of the mixture on his feet and on the bottom steps of the ladder. She climbs up to the roof, sweeps his path clear of groundnut husks, and descends into the dead woman's courtyard; then she goes into the sleeping room itself, sprinkling water on the doorway and on the husband before they both enter. Other women bring porridge, soup, and a pot of beer into the room, and the whitewashers take a little of each, pouring it upon the floor "to make the place cool." The husband, who is sitting on a stool at the side, is given food and drink, and the rest is eaten by any of the women present who have themselves been widows. As they are finishing, the ritual leader tells the other women to hurry, saying "Make haste. He wants to go and collect white ants to feed his chickens." And the husband is led outside the house, just as he had been led in, and then dismissed from the proceedings to carry on with the jobs a man has to do.

In the dead woman's room, the women proceed with the ceremony, which corresponds to that performed around a man's quiver. More food is brought in, and a small pot of beer, some soup, and some porridge are placed in the middle of the room. Each of the women who have washed the stick (*daa suorbe*, the wives of the grave-diggers) takes some food and throws it on the floor. Another small pot of beer is brought in for the whitewasher (*yagrguori*), then a larger pot for the spectators (*zingurbe*). A dish (*laa*) is brought into the room, the one used for covering the top of the pot in which a woman keeps the left-over porridge soaking in water. In the dish are a needle (*pĩĩ siera*) for mending gourds, a calabash (*ngman*), a ladle (*suule*), a porcupine quill (*siɛ̃ pĩĩ*) for making mats, a knife, an eating bowl, and some cowries. And across the mouth of the dish lies a broom (*saar*) and a stirring stick (*vuur*).

The old woman conducting the ceremony, the husband's "father's sister" from a different lineage, then tells her assistant, who in this case came from the dead woman's own patriclan, "There is a Naayiili child," Naayiili being the name of the clan. "We went to beg her to come here to fetch us water. Now she is no more, but those are her things. What shall we do with them?" The dead woman's kinsfolk reply, "Take them and do whatever is best, then give them to us." A matriclan joking partner lifts the pot four times, twisting it about in her hands as she does so; then, placing the pot on the ground again, she puts in her hand. "What's there?" asks the leader of the ritual. She replies, giving the names of the items I have just listed. The same actions are repeated by the dead woman's reciprocal funeral group (*sããbir*, her "father's children"), next by her co-wives (*sir poo*), and finally by the husband's reciprocal funeral group (*lo' dielo*).[3]

Then all the objects are emptied from the dish, and the cowries, which stand for those that the dead woman has accumulated by brewing beer and trading, are collected together with the left hand. The same four representatives are asked to count, and, as with a man's arrows, the numbers are grossly exaggerated and increase with each speaker. After this inquiries are made about the debts.

The money in the pot is divided among the four representatives,

---

[3] The corresponding actors at the funerals of LoDagaba women were the *lonluorbe* (joking partners), *sããbir* (the dead woman's linked patriclan), *yentaaba* (co-wives), and *gbanggbaataaba*. It is these last who differ from the persons engaged in the LoWiili ceremony, although the difference may be more apparent than real. The term *gbanggbaataa* refers in this context to a fellow matriclanswoman (or rather, as I will explain later, a member of the matriclan that stands in a reciprocal funeral relationship to that of the deceased's) who belongs to an outside patriclan. This is the person who takes a woman's pot and a man's quiver, and while I am not sure of the specific implications of the difference, it appears to reflect the greater emphasis that the LoDagaba place upon uterine inheritance.

except for twenty cowries, which are put back in the pot, together with the neck (*nyũũ*) of the guinea-fowl that was earlier slaughtered on the shrine. The contents of the pot are emptied out, and it is filled with water, which the daughters are made to drink. The pot is eventually sent to the dead woman's natal home, since they will know to whom it belongs; among the LoDagaba, it will go to a member of the same reciprocal matrilineal group that in a man's case takes the quiver (e.g., SomDa and KpoDa).

Not only the daughters but all the children are initiated into the status of orphans, of being without a mother. There is no "ordeal of the children" (*bi pol*), but *laa yaghl saab,* the "porridge for taking down the pot," is made, and the children are fed with this and a soup cooked without condiments. The daughters have their "mothers" pointed out to them and are told, "See your mothers who have come to the funeral. If you need leather waistbands, then go to them. If you need ingredients for soup, then go to them."

The recognition of orphanhood, like the recognition of the role of the widower, begins at a much earlier phase of the funeral ceremonies. There is the orphan's meal (*kpielo*), held immediately after the burial, and before this the children of the dead woman are sometimes fed at the foot of her funeral stand.

In the case of an infant still nursing at the mother's breast, special measures have to be taken. On the day of burial, women come and place the child on the dead mother's knee, resting her arm on the infant's shoulder. Some of the women call out "Take the child," and others "Leave it." If the child tries to get down and the mother's arm falls off the shoulder, all is well. But if the dead person still clings to the child, then a joking partner has to be called to throw ashes, to play with those involved, and then to remove it from its mother. At this point the dead woman's mother takes the child back with her to where she is living, for it is thought that the orphan cannot prosper if left in the father's house with only a co-wife as proxy parent. When she returns home, the maternal grandmother puts some earth (*tenggaan tene,* the Earth shrine's earth) into a calabash of water, drinks a little herself, then feeds the child. By these actions the infant is said to be thrown upon (*loba*) or given to (*den ko*) the Earth shrine of the locality where it lives. If the child is a girl and grows to a marriageable age, then before her marriage takes place a sacrifice should be offered to the Earth; this should also be done for a boy when he returns to his father's kin. Should this sacrifice be omitted, the child continues to be a child of the Earth shrine (*tenggaan bie*) where he or she has been brought up, and remains in effect an attached member of the mother's lineage. Indeed, even if the infant has not been formally presented to the Earth shrine, when the father's agnates come to take the child away, they must bring some guinea-corn and a fowl to "take out the *kpielo*," the orphanhood. Otherwise future misfortunes are liable to be attributed to this omission.

THE THIRD DAY: THE SETTLEMENT OF THE ESTATE

The third and last day of the final ceremony begins with a repetition and elaboration of the rites in the dead man's room that took place after the burial and again during the performance of the Bitter Funeral Beer. My accounts of these earlier ceremonies were based upon the LoWiili, and in order to bring out a number of differences between the two communities I shall describe a LoDagaba version of the rituals concerning the redistribution of property.

The reader will have observed how during this whole series of ceremonies two aspects of the dead man's life are stressed above all others: first, the roles he plays as husband-father and, second, those he fills as hunter-farmer. The first set are connected primarily with the reproductive processes, the second with the productive. The ceremony I have just analyzed concerns the man's role as husband, and the orphans' meal, which I consider in the coming section, has to do with his role as father. The present ritual sequence centers upon his activities as hunter and farmer, and serves three purposes, which the LoDagaa would describe as celebrating the dead man, "taking out the dream," and "making the place and the property cool."

The first act is to bring in the beer made from the dead man's own guinea-corn and to lay it before those who have assisted in the ceremonies. Four pots are brought into the room, and these are spoken of as: *dãã suo,* "the washing beer," used for bathing the ancestor shrine; *yir dãã,* "the house beer," for the members of the linked patriclan sector; *sããbe dãã,* "the fathers' beer," for the members of the father's matriclan; and *gbanggbaataaba dãã,* "the fellow slaves' beer," for the members of the deceased's own matriclan.

The names given to these pots are somewhat different from those used by the LoWiili, who generally speak of the pots as the beer of the mother's patriclan (*mayidem dãã*), the beer of the patriclan (*sããyidem dãã*), and the onlookers' beer (*zingurbe dãã*). These two last are probably to be identified with the contributors' beer (*tshier dãã*) and the waist beer (*sie dãã*), mentioned in the account of the Bitter Funeral

Beer. From one point of view, the names by which the pots are called does not greatly matter, since each is consumed by everyone attending the ceremony with the exception of lineage members and men with living fathers. But from another, the differences with the LoWiili are significant. In both communities there is a pot for the patriclan (*yir*). Among the LoWiili, one of the other two pots is allocated to the mother's matriclan, whereas no mention is made of this among the LoDagaba; there, indeed, a man's mother's patriclan plays little part in the whole ceremony. Instead, the beer is allocated to his own and his father's matriclan, to the first of which his mother's full brothers would of course belong. The personnel involved in each case are very much the same, but in the first greater emphasis is on the set of patriclans, and in the second on the set of matriclans. I would add that the situation differs somewhat from many similar variations between the two communities, as when, for example, the same names are given to the parts of an animal but the actual mode of distribution is different. In the present case, the differences are explicit rather than implicit. However, once again they appear to be related to two interconnected aspects of these rituals, differences in the contributions to and expectations from the funeral ceremonies.

The special pot of "washing beer" is kept covered with a calabash, which a joking partner fills and throws across the floor of the room, "to make it cool." He carries the remainder outside, slopping it as he goes, and pours it over the kitchen midden (*tampur*) for all "makers of things" (*bum ngmiere*).

When he returns, an elder of the reciprocal funeral group, which in this case is a sector of the linked patriclan, asks:

"Why do you do that?" (*Buono?*)

To which the others reply:

"The blacksmiths, the xylophone players, the funeral chanters, the basket makers, the potters, it's for them." (*Zemberdem, gobr,*[4] *langkuone, pewuobe, dongmiere, be lo so.*)

The rite of pouring the beer is very similar to the one held at the Bitter Funeral Beer, which I have already described, but without offering any explanation for it. The main theme has to do with the dead man's role as a farmer in a society which, though it would commonly be described as "undifferentiated," "homogeneous," or "characterized by mechanical solidarity," is nevertheless dependent upon various

---

[4] *Gobr* means left-handed men and here refers to the fact that a man must have control of both hands in order to play the instrument; the term is also applied to diviners.

specialized activities such as the preparing of iron and the divining of mystical troubles.

Man's main activity is farming, and throughout the funerals his achievements in this sphere are emphasized. I have given some examples of songs celebrating these skills. In addition, the corpse is littered with the produce of the fields, thrown from the rooftop by the chief mourner and hung on the stand by other kin. Now the beer in which he is washed is identified with the dead man, since it is made out of the grain he grew himself. "It's because he's a farmer," the LoDagaa say when asked about this custom.

But man as a farmer is supported by a number of other roles, and at his death a formal recognition is made of the division of labor that has rendered possible his own way of life. "You take, and let us take too," the leader says, invoking as a group past xylophone players and others with special accomplishments. Then part of the remainder of the pot is used to fill a tiny calabash, which is handed round among those present. The dregs are emptied out into one of the smaller pots employed for ritual purposes, and this is later used for washing the ancestor shrine. In other words, the small pot of beer is divided among the living, the long dead, and the newly deceased.

When the beer has been drunk, attention is turned to the man's quiver, which is here associated with his activities as a hunter and warrior. Inside the quiver are placed the various iron objects connected mainly with his role as farmer, which in both communities are handed over to his sons. The reciprocal funeral group bring the quiver into the room, and, as at the earlier ceremony, a matriclan joking partner is asked what he sees, and a similar series of answers are given. The ritual is repeated for the representative of the reciprocal funeral group, usually a matriclan joking partner as well, who is known in this context as the *logh dielo*. But unlike the Lo Wiili, the LoDagaba do not normally ask questions of the fellow members of the dead man's matriclan (*gbanggbaataaba*), because, it was explained to me, they already own the property.

The rites that follow are specifically concerned with the distribution of the movable property of the dead man. When the heir comes from the deceased's own compound, as for example when a full brother inherits, the elder of the reciprocal funeral group is called forward and is asked about the dead man's wealth. "How much does it amount to?" he is asked. To this he replies "Five," a standardized answer that deliberately understates the number of cowries left by the deceased. In fact about two thousand cowries are brought into the room, and the joking partner takes some of these to share with his fellow matriclansmen, leaving the rest to be divided among those of the dead man's own matriclan who are present. The main body of the inheritance remains within the household, and its distribution is discussed no further. The joking partner has now made the property safe, and the position of the heir as member of a property-holding corporation has been publicly affirmed by the division of the token cowries among those of his matriclan who attended the ceremony.

Should there be no person from the compound eligible to inherit, then the movable property is taken by an heir outside the patriclan, one of the deceased's matriclan, the members of which are referred to in this context either as *gbangdiru* or as *mwo puo nibe,* people from the bush, that is, those who are not from the patriclan (see p. 355). As so often in LoDagaa terminology, the "bush" (*mwo,* literally "grass") is here contrasted with the "house" (*yir*) or "room" (*diu*), the distant with the close at hand. If the heir comes from the patriclan, he is known as the *yir* (or *diu*) *puo dire;* since the core of the compound is agnatic, these words refer to patrilineal relationships.

If the property is to leave the compound, then the eldest member of the deceased's matriclan to be present is called forward and told, "Take a look at the empty room." However, some of the dead man's money is nevertheless brought out, and the officiant declares, "The person of yours (*fu nir*) that died owned five cowries." Again the joking partners and matriclansmen withdraw a token amount. Then the eldest matriclansman is shown the domestic animals belonging to the dead man and is told, "This is the animal he owned." The person addressed in this manner is not in fact the actual heir; usually, if not always, he is a member both of the deceased's matriclan and of the linked patriclan sector performing the reciprocal funeral services. Such a man is considered to be in a good position to act as a witness for the inheritor himself, because he forms a bridge between the agnatic and the uterine ties of the deceased, here pulling in opposite directions. The understatement of the amount of the inheritance gives a dramatic form to the reluctance, inherent in the social situation, that the agnatic core of the living-together group displays toward parting with property belonging to one of its members, even though that property is vested in the alternative set of descent groups.

The cooling of the property by the joking partner may be seen as a standardized projection of the feelings, anticipated and actual, that the process of inheritance arouses. As in the redistribution of the sexual rights in the widow, there is the double problem of enacting these feelings and of ensuring some form of social control over the disruptive tendencies that the situation holds. In both cases the problem is met by a complex funeral ritual that is very sensitive to changes in nuclear situations such as the alignment of the holder-heir relationship. Thus the whole of the ritual dealing with the distribution of movable property is absent from the LoWiili ceremony, since among the LoWiili movable property, like real property, is inherited patrilineally, so that the particular conflict situation does not arise.

The actual removal of property does not take place at the final funeral ceremony. Not before a month has passed is the heir called over, and when he comes (with his joking partner), he is told, "See the empty room." To which he replies, "Even if there are only five cowries, let me see them." He now enters into his inheritance, which includes obligations to the dead man's children (of which he is the matriclan "father"), as well as rights to his wealth.

The cooling of the dead man's property does not conclude the rites in the room. As at the previous ceremony, the "beer in the vat" is shown to the "father" and to other representative persons, who are made to knock on the pot and repeat, "You are my child. I thought you had come to help me. Now you are in the pot." When this rite is finished, the debts of the deceased are formally discussed for the third and last time.

The entry of the shrine does not always occur at a fixed point in the ceremony. Among the LoWiili it tends to be early in the day, whereas among the LoDagaba it is usually last of all. But it seems convenient to describe the ceremony at this point.

The shrine is bathed in the same way as at the Bitter Funeral Beer; the women break into lamentations, the chief mourner drops grain and other crops from the rooftop, and the onlookers throw money on the shrine. The four whitewashers pick up the stick and carry it horizontally into the byre as if it were the corpse. Daughters and neighbors provide food for the dead man, and beer is provided for the participants and the spectators. The women then perform their own parallel ceremony of the room as at the Bitter Funeral Beer.

When the ancestor's shrine is taken into the byre, it is placed slightly apart from the other shrines and is described as uneasy (*ur*, "scratchy," "uncomfortable," the same word that was used earlier of the house). Offerings of beer and fowls are not yet made to the new shrine. This is done only at a later sacrifice, made by the agnates and known as the Beer of the Entry of the Stick (*Daa Kpiero Dãã*), when the shrine is aggregated to the shrines of other ancestors. Such a sacrifice is made either at the annual offering to the household shrines (*Bagmaal Dãã*), or else when the house is afflicted by some misfortune which the diviner relates to the dead man. I have been told that if the offering is made before the year is out, only two fowls are required, if later, a domestic animal; but in fact the timing and nature of the sacrifice depend very much upon the livestock the dead man has left behind him.

THE THIRD DAY: THE ORDEAL OF THE CHILDREN

When the elders of the patriclan sector emerge from the dead man's room, the final ritual of the funeral ceremonies takes place. During the Ordeal of the Children (*Bi Pol*), the offspring are tested and cleared from complicity in their father's death and then shown the men who stand in the position of classificatory "father" to them.

The children of the dead man are called together and are seated on a log drawn up in the open space in front of the compound. Nearby, in a group, sit their "fathers," members of the dead man's matriclan. The leader of the ritual (a member of the reciprocal funeral group and also of the same matriclan as the deceased and hence himself a classificatory "father" of the children) takes some of the sodden malt grains from which the funeral beer (*ko dãã*) has been brewed, and smears them between the toes and behind the ears of each child. As before, this beer is regarded as the dead man himself; drinking it is an act of communion, but is also equivalent to taking an oath that one has not caused the death, just as a person accused of witchcraft is tested in a similar manner by being given some earth and water to drink.

The officiant next takes a bunch of guinea-corn heads that come from the dead man's granary and beats them three times on the ground in front of the children. Walking anticlockwise, he then circles the log three times, dropping some of the grains here and there as if he were sowing, an action that refers to the fact that the children have now taken over from their father the responsibility for carrying out the productive tasks of the household. An assistant takes a cock purchased with money provided by the "fathers," slits its throat, and follows the ritual leader around the children, allowing the blood to drip onto the grain that has been scattered.

After this the children are fed in the same manner as the widows earlier in this ceremony. Three times they are offered flour and beer, but on each occasion they refuse; on the fourth they accept, but spit out the food and drink upon the ground. The leader makes three pretenses at pulling the children to their feet and finally does so, saying, "Stand."

The senior son is then given the axe and hoe belonging to his father, the same implements that were used in the rituals performed in the dead man's room. In addition, he is offered the roasted leg of the fowl used in the rite. All these gifts he accepts with both hands outstretched. Now that the innocence of the children has been proved, into their hands are placed the tools of production and the emblems of their orphanhood.

The contributions of cowries mentioned above are made by the matriclan "fathers" of the deceased. All the "fathers" who contributed "the matriclan twenty" toward the burial expenses are invited to this ceremony and asked to give a further twenty. Among the LoDagaba a similar contribution may also be made by the other matriclans (either Some or Da) belonging to that group, the same group who together share in the meat of the Cow of the Rooftop; again the distribution of meat is correlated with the contribution to funeral expenses.

Out of this money, a hundred cowries go to purchasing the cock that was used in the ceremony. Another hundred cowries are given to the officiant, who is also handed the "bitter quiver," together with the "bitter arrows" it contains. "Bitter quiver" is the name given to the quiver used in the rites in the dead man's room. It was these rites that made the property safe for redistribution to the heirs, and in this subsequent phase of the ceremony some of the objects left by the deceased are actually handed over to the inheritors. The officiant picks up the hundred cowries he has been given, takes out a handful, and places the rest in front of the eldest son. The remainder of the cowries collected from the "fathers" is gathered together and redivided amongst the "sons." Here the matriclan of the dead man deliberately create and then disperse a fund out of which they make a gift to the children. This transaction resembles the treatment of the twenty cowries hidden in the quiver, when the "fathers" again appear to be giving their blessing to an alienation of some of their corporate funds to the "sons"

The bitter quiver is collected by the eldest of the "fathers," together with a leg of the cock, and a sum of money, which varied from twenty to five hundred cowries. Emptied of its special contents, which have been made safe for the sons of the dead man, the quiver is now sent to matriclansmen outside the patriclan and later returned to the house.

Meanwhile, the rest of the cock, apart from the legs (one of which is given to the eldest son, and the other kept with the quiver), is made into a stew to accompany a meal of porridge cooked from guinea-corn flour, which is again taken from the dead man's own granary. This food is used for another orphan's meal (*kpielo*), the counterpart of the one held the day after the burial, and any man who has lost his father may partake. Finally the "fathers" are given a pot of beer to "put them on the road." Once again emphasis is laid on the significance of losing a parent; but whereas the first occasion confirmed the children in their new status as orphans, the weight here falls upon their position as classificatory "sons" of a large category of classificatory "fathers." In this respect, as in many others, the final ceremony is the integrative phase of the funeral.

Before they eat this meal, and while they are still sitting on the log, the children are formally shown their classificatory "fathers," that is, the members of the deceased's matriclan. These are also the men who, through their representative, have tested the children, just as it is her "father's sisters" that test the widow. Special recognition is sometimes given to the nearest of the kinsmen referred to as "fathers," and I came across an instance of a man's best friend bringing him a cock to present to his late father's full brother who was in the process of assuming the role of proxy parent. However, essentially this ceremony is concerned with the whole category of "fathers" rather than with one particular individual. Pointing to the group sitting opposite, the leader of the ritual says: "There are your 'fathers.' If you see one of them carrying a log, then take it along for him. If on your way home one of them asks you for the 'father's leg' (*sãã gber*) of the animal you've killed in the hunt, don't refuse, saying you have a 'father' in the patriclan sector (*yir puo sãã*). Let him take the leg. He can't eat it in the bush, but will bring it to your house and show it to your lineage 'father.'" At the end of his speech, the officiating "father" pulls the children up one by one by their right hands, pretending to do so three times before they are finally put on their feet again.

This speech may seem a rather oblique expression of the relationship of "son" to "father"; its significance depends upon a recognition of the part played by the "father's leg" in the whole complex of property, which at this point provides definite links between the domestic role of the father and the supernatural role of the ancestor. It has already been noted that a hind leg of any animal killed either at a funeral or at any sacrifice to the ancestors is allocated to the "father"; the meat is given jointly to the ancestor concerned and to his "brothers" upon earth. This mode of distribution is characteristic of sacrifices to the ancestors as distinct from those made to other shrines, and it accords with the way in which the flesh of wild animals is divided up among kin. Two legs of the animal are given to the hunter's father, who can sell the meat and buy hoes to cultivate the land. In pre-Colonial times, hoes were of great economic importance owing to the difficulties of iron-working and the fact that it was a specialist craft. I was told about some farming groups in the days before the coming of cheap metal of European origin, who passed around one hoe between their members, each of whom farmed with it for short, intensive stretches at a time. The purchase of these tools was an expensive business, since the extraction of iron from the low-grade laterite ore found in the locality was a long and difficult process. It was the father's job to accumulate enough money to keep the members of the group in hoes and thus to provide the means to preserve the continuity of the productive process, just as he had to supply the bridewealth necessary to maintain the reproductive one. For this purpose, saving money was as important as saving seed.

Even in the old days the father did not necessarily use all the money obtained from selling his part of the hunter's kill to purchase hoes. For the "father's leg" is also regarded as a return for providing his children with food while they are young and with the means to gain their own living when they are old enough to farm. While the son is farming with the father, he is supposed to bring to his parents the gains he has made by any economic activities; the father has the right to all the son's earnings. In practice, however, a wise man takes only a small proportion of what he is shown and leaves the rest for his son; otherwise he runs the risk that the boy might employ one of the few sanctions available to him and run away. And a father is reluctant to let this happen, for although a man in the prime of his life is able to support himself and his family, in old age he is almost as dependent upon the labor of his sons as they in their youth were upon him. The father would gain nothing by pressing the son too hard, for the latter could easily find an alternative place to live. In patrilineal systems, the matrilateral tie offers a solution to, and a control upon, conflicts within the father-son relationship. If the child regards himself as being badly treated, he can always run away to his mother's kinsfolk, among whom, as the offspring of a female member of the descent group, he is certain of a welcome. Migration to join agnates or other kinsfolk farther afield is another possibility; there is constant movement taking place into less populated areas. Today the most prevalent method of escape is to sell one's labor in the southern part of the country, where paid work is plentiful.

If a youth leaves home to work as a wage laborer in another part of the country, on his return he should bring to his father a cloth, a smock, and a certain amount of salt, all items of foreign provenance. In addition he should show him all the money he has earned. But here, too, the wise father will take only a little for himself, and this amount is again known as the "father's leg."

For the LoDagaba, among whom wealth is transmitted matrilineally at death, this institution of the "father's leg" provides a method of transferring property from father to son. When the father has received a certain amount of money or goods in this way, he may show his son one of his cows, declaring before witnesses that the youth may keep the animal in return for all he has done for his father. The cow remains in the father's byre until his death, when it will be taken by the son, not by the inheritor. But if the LoDagaba father does not do this while he is alive, the son has no claim after his death. "Father and son," it was explained to me, "eat together in life but not in death" (*sãã ni bideb, be long dire ni nimir titshe be be long dire kũ*). As the later chapters will show, this difference in the possibility of contracting a debt is of fundamental significance in the comparison of ancestor worship in the two communities.

Two other aspects of the ritual of showing the children their "fathers" require some further elucidation. The first of these has to do with the existence of reciprocal services within the set of matriclans, and the second with what I refer to as double or duplicating kinship.

The first of these institutions exists only among the LoDagaba. It will be remembered that when they divided the flesh of the Cow of the Rooftop (or the Matriclan Cow), the various clans and subclans concerned grouped themselves in pairs. KpoDa and SomDa, for example, are said to "have the same rooftop" (*be long garo*). But I was often told that formerly these pairs of matriclans were much more closely interlocked, that not only did they eat (*di*) food together, they also inherited (*di*) certain items of each other's movable property, and especially that they could take each other's widows in leviratic marriage and that they would be given the other's "bitter quivers" (*be long pogh kuor ti long gbang ti long 'yere logh*). It is also said they tested each other's children (*KpoDa na pol SomDa bibiir*). In other words, they took over certain of each other's exclusive rights, those rights that are especially likely to prove mystically dangerous to close kin of the deceased, and at the same time they performed ritual services on each other's behalf.

This type of inheritance of movable property and of each other's widows has disappeared, if it ever obtained. For although it is still said in Tom today that a man of the KpoDa matriclan can marry the senior widow of a SomDa man if both belong to the same patriclan sector, I know of no recent case in which this has happened, and any such claim would in practice be strongly resisted. Among the LoDagaba, however,

KpoDa do test SomDa children. It is a SomDa man who brings the cock for the ceremony, but a KpoDa will kill it, speak to the children, and show them their KpoDa "fathers." KpoDa also take the bitter quiver containing the arrows, although it is eventually returned to a member of the dead man's own matriclan and patriclan, so he may guard the house (*gũ a yir*). A man has an obligation to carry loads for any one of his "fathers," who include all members of the paired matriclan; he must also allow such a man to take the "father's leg," although, as in the case of the quiver, this will eventually be returned to the "father within the house," to whose significance in these rites I will shortly return.

This complex of services is essentially similar to the cathartic assistance rendered by funeral groups, burial groups, and joking partnerships in the critical situations in which they emerge. And like these forms of assistance it is part of the network of reciprocal services between the constituent units that maintains the wider social system.

The speech telling the children of their duties toward their classificatory "fathers" brings out the second aspect of these ceremonies that requires some further explanation in order to make more intelligible the rites I have just described. In a system of double clanship, the classificatory usage of a kinship term such as "father" has two possible sets of referents, the patrilineal and the matrilineal descent groups. Among the LoDagaa, any member of the next senior generation of one's patriclan is a "father," and so also is any member of one's father's matriclan. Any such person can say of a man, "I begot him." But clearly the man most closely identified with the dead parent is one who is "father" both in agnatic and in uterine terms, who is a member of the next senior generation of one's own patriclan and who also belongs to the father's matriclan. Hence the importance in these ceremonies of the person who occupies a kinship position on both counts, patrilineal and matrilineal, and whom I refer to for convenience as the double (or duplicate) father, mother, brother, or sister.

In the speech in question, the children are told that not all members of the father's matriclan stand in the same position to them, that the *yir puo sãã*, "the father in the house," is of greater importance than the *mwo puo sãã*, "the father in the bush." Whereas the latter category consists of all members of the father's matriclan outside the patriclan, the former (at least among the LoDagaba) includes all those within, and especially, of course, the dead man's full brother, the kinsman most closely identified with him. I have added the parenthetic qualification about the LoDagaba because these overlapping kinship categories are of somewhat greater significance there than among the LoWiili. If a LoDagaba other than a duplicate brother of the dead man (that is, a man belonging to the same patriclan and the same or reciprocal matriclan) marries his widow and wishes to be recognized as *pater* of her children, then he is required to send the original bridewealth to be divided among these kinsfolk; whereas the duplicate brother need not. Again, it is to the duplicate brother that the "bitter quiver" is returned after it has circulated among more distant kin.

Among the LoDagaba, throughout the funeral ceremonies, the Bathing of the Widow is also carried out by women standing in an exactly similar position. It will be remembered that the women who take part in these rites are drawn from two categories of persons known as *poghyaataaba* and *poghsããmamine,* which I have translated as "sisters" and "father's sisters" respectively, indicating that these persons were members of the widow's patriclan. The term *poghsããmamine* means literally "the woman's father's mothers"; just as a person refers to his mother's "brothers" and "sisters" as his *mamine,* his "mothers," so, too, he can speak of his father's matriclan "brothers" and "sisters" as his father's "mothers." But here the group reference of the term is neither completely matrilineal nor completely patrilineal; it indicates neither the members of the father's mother's patriclan nor the members of the person's own matriclan, both possible interpretations, but rather the members of his own patriclan who are also of the same matriclan, hence the duplicate "father's sisters."

Among the LoWiili, on the other hand, the same person is usually spoken of as *sãã pure,* which is the usual term for the father's sister in a purely patrilineal context. Once again, the LoWiili place less stress on matrilineal bonds. Here they tend to replace the duplicate by the patrilineal "father's sister." A similar transposition occurs in the persons who carry out the ceremony of Testing the Children. Among the LoWiili, this ritual is conducted by a duplicate father, a member of the same patriclan (although of the reciprocal funeral group) and of the same matriclan as the dead man. Among the LoDagaba, there is a slight but characteristic shift, and the person who performs this rite has to be a member of the reciprocal matriclan of the dead man and outside his patriclan. Both these ceremonies are carried out by "fathers" (*sããmine*) of the dead man, but in each case this role is a little differently defined. There are a number of other differences that follow the same pattern. In the matter of funeral contributions we have already seen how the matriclan is replaced by the "matriclan within the patriclan," i.e., the duplicate clansfolk. With regard to the contributions to and division of the funeral meat, as well as the inheritance of the senior widow, the "bitter quiver," and the dead man's clothes, the LoDagaba institution of reciprocal matriclanship is absent from both LoWiili theory and LoWiili practice. The nature of these differences is complex, but their general pattern is clear enough, and this I have tried to bring out in Tables 5 and 6.

I have written of the LoWiili situation as one of change. It is a truism to remark that no social system is completely static; quite apart from the stability of external forces, human or physical, no system of transmission ensures a complete repetition of the cultural equipment of the society from generation to generation. Among the LoDagaba, too, there appear to have been certain changes in the function of the reciprocal matriclans, not to mention developments in the wider political domain. However, among the LoWiili, changes in the social system are occurring over a wider area than among the LoDagaba. Whereas formerly the social organization of the two communities seems to have been fairly similar, the LoWiili are now moving away and showing definite differences. The nature of this move, and the fact that these differences are comparatively recent in origin, can be illustrated by comparing accounts of how inheritance worked in the past and what happens today. A striking instance of this is the history of Wurader's quiver.

TABLE 5.—THE ROLE DIFFERENCES IN LoDAGAA FUNERAL INSTITUTIONS

Institution	LoWiili	LoDagaba
Testing the children	Duplicate "father" in reciprocal funeral group	"Father" in reciprocal matriclan and outside patriclan
Inheritance of clothes	Destroyed	Linked patriclan
Matriclan funeral contributions, sharing of meat	(a) Duplicate "fathers" (b) Duplicate "brothers"	(a) Matriclan "fathers," including members of reciprocal matriclans (b) Matriclan "brothers"
Whitewashing widows	Patriclan "father's sisters"	Duplicate "father's sisters"
Levirate	Patriclan "brothers"	Duplicate "brothers"
Inheritance of movable property	Full brothers, then sons	Full brothers, then sister's sons
Inheritance of land	Patriclan members of farming group	Patriclan members of farming group

TABLE 6.—DIFFERENCES IN FUNERAL INSTITUTIONS AMONG THE LODAGAA

		Dealt with by		
Institution	*Patriclan*	*Duplicate clanship*	*Matriclan*	*Reciprocal matriclan*
Testing the children		W (reciprocal funeral group)		D (outside patriclan)
Inheritance of clothes*				D (linked patriclan)
Matriclan funeral contributions, sharing of meat		W	D	D
Whitewashing widows	W	D		
Levirate	W	D		
Inheritance of movable property	W		D	
Inheritance of immovable property	W, D			

W = LoWiili
D = LoDagaba   * Among the LoWiili, clothes are destroyed.

Some thirty years ago, when Wurader, father of the late Chief of Birifu, died, a member of his own matriclan (KpoDa) took Wurader's bitter quiver, together with a leg of the cock and twenty cowries (among the LoDagaba this would have been a member of the reciprocal matriclan). After being passed to various members of his matrilineage (*ma per*), presumably as a sign that one of their number was dead, the quiver was sent back to Wurader's own compound, where it was given to Doeri, an illegitimate child of his patrilineage and a member of the same matriclan, a person, therefore, who was a duplicate "brother" to the dead man. In 1950, when Wurader's son Gandaa died, his quiver was hung in the long room of his house after the funeral; although the heir declared his intention of sending it around the matrilineage, it was still there when I left a year after the final ceremony, and I doubt whether anyone will do anything more about it. Like the personal effects hung on the wall of the byre, it will probably be left there to rot.

In every field, then, the increased emphasis on patriclanship among the LoWiili has been accompanied by a weakening of the ties based

upon matrilineal descent. Indeed, it is perhaps surprising to find matriclan "fathers" pointed out at all in the final ceremony, since they have
little significance in the social system. For whereas among the LoDagaba
the term *yir sãã,* "house father," denotes a member of the father's matriclan who is also a member of his patriclan, the phrase among the
LoWiili more usually indicates any member of the patriclan of the same
generation as one's father. Nevertheless, in the present LoWiili ceremony the reference is definitely to the duplicate father.

The reason for the persistence of this institution lies perhaps in the
more permanent nature of fatherhood so defined. In due course a man
loses his own parent, and eventually all his agnatic "fathers," the patriclansmen of the first ascendant generation, die off, even though the
relationship is continued on the supernatural plane. But the fund of
matrilineal and duplicate "fathers" is never-ending, because any member of a self-perpetuating clan can play this role.[5] Consequently,
throughout a man's life he is subordinate to a living father. Although
one may be an orphan in the sense of being without parents, one can
never be without classificatory "fathers" or "mothers" in a society in
which such labels are attached to the entire membership of self-recruit-
ing groups. By this device, the kinship relationship is not allowed to
die; it is perpetual in the sense that one continues to fill the role of
"child," "father," "mother's brother," and so forth, from the moment
of one's birth until the day of one's death. Even then the ancestor cult
gives an added immortality, or anyhow extrahuman persistence, to
these relationships.

Nevertheless, although the matriclan among the LoWiili is certainly
not functionless, it seems likely that further changes will continue to
take place and that the role of patrilineally defined kin will increase
at the expense of those defined by matrilineal or by duplicate kinship.
For these changes appear to be associated with changes in the system
of inheritance, in the way in which property is transmitted between the
generations, changes that have not yet had their total effect upon the
other institutions of the society. It is this process of intergenerational
transmission that we shall examine in the following section.

[5] Since the matriclans are only four in number, and even these are linked together in various ways, a man is bound to have a "duplicate father" alive, that is, a
member of his own patriclan and his father's matriclan. This, I suggest, is one reason
for the disparity between the large number of patriclans and the small number of
matriclans.

Property

The Merry Bells: Intergenerational Transmission and Its Conflicts

> Writing as I do by the light of a later knowledge, I suppose I
> should have seen nothing in this but the world's growing pains,
> the disturbance inseparable from transition in human things. I
> suppose in reality not a leaf goes yellow in autumn without ceas-
> ing to care about its sap and making the parent tree very un-
> comfortable by long growling and grumbling—but surely nature
> might find some less irritating way of carrying on business if she
> would give her mind to it. Why should the generations overlap
> one another at all? Why cannot we be buried as eggs in neat
> little cells with ten or twenty thousand pounds each wrapped
> round us in Bank of England notes, and wake up, as the sphex
> wasp does, to find that its papa and mamma have not only left
> ample provision at its elbow, but have been eaten by sparrows
> some weeks before it began to live consciously on its own account?
>
> BUTLER, *The Way of All Flesh*

In analyzing the mortuary institutions of the LoDagaa, we have found
that the main concern is with the reallocation of the rights and duties
of the dead man among the surviving members of the community. This
redistribution is part of the more general process of transmitting the
cultural equipment of a specific group from one generation to the next.
Given stability in the external situation, the continuity of any social
system depends largely upon the ability of the adult members to transfer
the particular cultural tradition of the system to the following generation, a tradition that includes a heritage of both customary behavior and
material property.[1]

The major part of this social heritage is passed on in the process of
what Durkheim called socialization, that is, education in the widest
sense. In the course of this process, which varies widely in the formality

---

[1] Although these crucial transfers may also occur laterally, in the end they must
take place between generations; I therefore refer to the process as one of intergenerational transmission.

of the methods used, in the time spent, and in the degree of specialization involved, the young learn something of the general ways of acting appropriate to members of the community at large, such as the use of a communal language, as well as special forms of action proper to certain persons but not to others—to a son, for example, but not to a father. It is these clusters of customary ways of acting appropriate to specific social persons that are known as roles. In this sense roles are necessarily exclusive; for the concept has to do with differential behavior, defining the positions of actors in relation to one another. Hence roles involve the relationship of two or more persons and can be defined in terms of the mutual expectations that the parties have of one another. In legal and jural contexts these expectations are expressed as the rights of one side and the correlative duties of the other.

The new entrants into the society not only learn about the behavior of others and thereby acquire some idea of the totality of social actions, but also receive direct induction into specific roles. For example, the educational process itself demands special behavior from the "learner" toward the "upbringer," that is, the socializing agent or "tutor." In this relationship the learner is inevitably placed in a subordinate position, since, however carefully the tutor may tread, he has always to correct the mistakes of the learner. Moreover, the process normally continues over a considerable span of years, the acquisition of the society's cultural equipment being a lengthy and often arduous business. All this means that the relationship can be expected to yield signs of covert tension and often of overt conflict of the kind so vividly described in *The Way of All Flesh*. In varying degrees, the Pontifex situation is a universal aspect of socialization.

Within the body of social conduct and material possessions that forms the cultural heritage, there are components of two differing kinds. If I pass on to my son the language I speak, I in no way diminish my own holding of social equipment; indeed, in a sense I augment the value of my stake, because I increase the number of persons with whom I can freely communicate. With material goods this is not so. If I hand over to my son the right to cultivate four acres of my eight-acre plot, I thereby diminish my holding by half. Hence there is an important distinction to be made between the transmission of information, either in the process of socialization or in other communicative situations, and the possession and transfer of relatively exclusive rights. Items of culture of the former kind give rise to conflicts over transmission, but only in a very limited sense to conflicts over possession. The aim is to pass on such items to the junior generation within a short space of time, and although the process inevitably creates some friction, nobody loses by the actual business of giving. On the other hand, this is only true of the transfer of exclusive rights if the process is one of exchange, and in intergenerational transmission such return transactions are minimal.

It is not only property rights that display this characteristic, but all rights of a relatively exclusive kind. Within this general category, one most important group consists of sexual rights, either in men or in women, though it is usually the latter that have the greater social significance. Whereas property rights are the basis of the productive process, sexual rights form the basis of the reproductive one, two essential aspects in the maintenance not only of a particular social system but of the human species in general.[2]

The similarities of certain property and sexual rights have led to lengthy discussion about whether "wives are to be regarded as property" (see Herskovits [1952], p. 316). Rights of sexual access, like property, are certainly exclusive in character and are often considered as rights *in rem,* since they are held "against the world" (Radcliffe-Brown [1952b], p. 33). A further similarity lies in the multiplicity of interests that may develop both around the sexuality of men and women and around objects of property. These points have led writers like Lévi-Strauss ([1956] p. 283) to treat marriage as an exchange of women between males, and as essentially similar to the transactions that involve material objects. There are two reasons why the treatment of womankind as a "commodity submitted to transactions between male operators" (*ibid.,* p. 284) pushes the resemblance too far (unless, of course, the woman is a slave and hence stripped of rights). First, in most if not all cases, a woman's natal kin retain some legal or jural interest in her even after she is married; as in the case of many property transactions

---

2 The importance of these twin processes was noted by Marx and Engels. In the Preface to the first edition of *The Origin of the Family, Private Property and the State* (1884), Engels writes: "According to the materialistic conception, the determining factor in history is, in the final instance, the production and reproduction of the immediate essentials of life. This, again, is of a twofold character. On the one side, the production of the means of existence, of articles of food and clothing, dwellings, and of the tools necessary for that production; on the other side, the production of human beings themselves, the propagation of the species. The social organization under which the people of a particular historical epoch and a particular country live is determined by both kinds of production . . ." ([1942] p. 5). In his introduction to Renner's *Institutions of Private Law,* Kahn-Freund writes in a similar vein: "All economic processes . . . are themselves part and parcel of the social processes of 'production' and 'reproduction,' of the maintenance of the human species. Legal institutions can and must be understood as the tools used by society in achieving this ultimate aim. They are cogs in the mechanism of the production, consumption and distribution of the social product" ([1949] p. 5).

in non-European societies, the complete alienation implied by our concepts of "gift" or "sale" is rarely involved. Second, the woman differs from property in that she herself is and never ceases to be a right- and duty-bearing persona, who is generally endowed with rights both in respect of her affines and in respect of her natal kin.

Although property and sexuality are often linked to specific roles and offices, we may nevertheless treat the modes of conduct attached to social positions as a third category of rights of an exclusive kind. By the term office, I mean to imply a superordinate role, access to which is deliberately restricted. All roles are to some extent exclusive; a person cannot fill the roles of mother and daughter in respect of the same individual. But whereas, given certain restrictions such as sex and age, it is the lot of most members of a particular society to fill roles, only a few have the opportunity to occupy an office, so that the attainment of office is likely to give rise to a wider range of conflicts. Every male in a society can look forward to the possibility of becoming a father, but not all can act as chief.[3]

As I have already remarked, the transmitting of the cultural heritage in the process of upbringing creates friction between members of different generations; so also does the transfer of exclusive rights lead to tension. But the very fact that these particular rights—property, sexual rights, and roles and offices—are all relatively exclusive raises additional problems over both their possession and their transmission. Since the rights represent restricted resources, some categories of persons are necessarily excluded from their enjoyment, and the consciousness of these differences creates tensions between the haves and the have-nots. The relationship between the possessors and the non-possessors is never immutably fixed, even when the resources are vested in an exclusive social group. Everywhere there is some resort to unauthorized as well as authorized modes of transfer, usurpation taking the place of succession, and theft of gift. Or the holder may voluntarily divest himself of his rights, by abdication or by prestation. But the fact of death makes some attempt at a system of authorized transfer inevitable for every society.

The persons between whom an authorized transfer is made may be prescribed in advance, as in many systems of monarchical succession, or they may be specified only at the time of transfer, as in the selection

---

[3] In general, offices have specific names or titles and definite rites of induction. The distinction that I use between roles and offices serves simply to point to the different sorts of conflict over possession and transmission that such positions may involve and needs considerable refinement before it can become a satisfactory analytic tool.

by horoscope of a new Dalai Lama. Clearly, there are some advantages in a rule of inheritance or succession that selects the heir in advance, since some of the inevitable uncertainties associated with the transfer of property or office are thereby lessened. On the other hand, the very existence of an heir apparent encourages the kind of tension between the incumbent and successor that marked the relationship of Prince Hal with his father and culminated in his overhasty assumption of the crown.

> Thy wish was father, Harry, to that thought.
> I stay too long by thee, I weary thee.
> Dost thou so hunger for mine empty chair
> That thou wilt needs invest thee with my honours
> Before thy hour be ripe? . . .
> Thou hast stol'n that which, after some few hours,
> Were thine without offence; . . .
> Thy life did manifest thou lov'dst me not,
> And thou wilt have me die assur'd of it. . . .
> Then get thee gone, and dig my grave thyself;
> And bid the merry bells ring to thine ear
> That thou art crowned, not that I am dead.

> (*2 Henry IV,* IV, v)

A rule of inheritance or succession usually designates either a multiplicity of possible heirs, or else a single line—that is, one or more categories of social persons, sometimes rank-ordered for eligibility, sometimes not. Conflict is therefore likely to arise among those expecting to benefit from the transmission of property or office. In its most extreme form this situation results in a history of bloodshed as with Gloucester's efforts to be crowned Richard III over the dead bodies of his kinsmen, efforts to which he was urged on by his ambitious Duchess:

> Were I a man, a duke, and next of blood,
> I would remove these tedious stumbling-blocks
> And smooth my way upon their headless necks.

> (*2 Henry VI,* I, ii)

In most cases the transfer of rights between the holder and the heir occurs only after the death of the holder, and so, as the dying Henry pointed out, for those near to the deceased the funeral is a time of rejoicing as well as of sorrow. However, in some societies these anticipatory tensions are mitigated by the transfer of rights to the heir before the death of the holder, as happens when one generation of Nyakyusa collectively hand over chiefship and land rights to their sons (Wilson [1951], pp. 19–31), or when Irish farmers pass on the control of the farmstead at the time their children marry (Arensberg [1937]). As Shakespeare's account of Lear's bitter experience reminds us, such procedures are likely to reduce the tensions of the young at the expense of increasing the problems of the old, since by this process the senior generation undergo a social euthanasia before their physical death. For one thing, the transfer of rights often involves a spatial separation from the property itself, as among some European peasant communities, when the aged parents move into the smaller house beside the main farm.

Similar arrangements obtained in thirteenth-century England. Homans points out that "often an heir did not have to wait for the death of the last holder before obtaining the tenement: while the last holder was still alive he handed it over to the heir" ([1941] p. 144). In some areas, at least, this settlement appears to have been made at the marriage of the heir, whereupon the husbandman's old father and mother would retire to a cottage in the yard of the farmstead and depend upon the new holder for the provision of food, shelter, and clothing. In his admirable account of the social organization of villagers under the open-field or champion economy, Homans sees this particular system as correlated with the impartible inheritance of land, which is in turn associated with the stem-family as distinct from the joint-family. He further connects this mode of inheritance, though this time implicitly rather than explicitly, with the existence of the custom whereby a man hands over his farm to the heir before his own death, thus allowing the heir to take a wife. Among the possible motives for such an arrangement, he suggests "the desire for a grandson, the desire to see the son settled in life, the desire to be rid of the responsibility for the tillage of the tenement, and perhaps the fear of what the neighbors would say if the son were kept waiting beyond what was considered a proper age" (*ibid.*, p. 156).

This transmission of basic resources between the living is found not only in Western Europe, but also under very different sets of conditions. The Fulani father gradually hands down his herds to his sons (Hopen [1958]; Stenning [1959]), and a similar situation has been reported by Gray from the predominantly agricultural MBugwe of Tanganyika:

> A young man brings his wife to live in his own small house at his father's homestead. As his younger brothers come of age they are likewise given small houses at the homestead, to which they bring their wives. After the eldest son has been married for a few years (this period varies from 2 to 10 years) he exchanges houses with his father. The small house is enlarged at this time, but is never made quite as large as the original parental house. The son also takes over

a portion of his father's cattle when the exchange of houses is made.
. . . If there are more sons the exchange process continues: the younger sons in turn move into the somewhat larger house that had been occupied by the father and receive a share of the cattle, while the ageing father moves down the line, ending up in the small house of his youngest son, bereft of most of his cattle ([1953] pp. 234–35).

Although the elder son is favored so far as the inheritance is concerned, the younger son also receives some compensation for taking care of the parents in their old age (*ibid.*, p. 242); to this link between preferential ultimogeniture and *pre mortem* inheritance we shall return in a later chapter.

These examples show that even transfers made to the heir within the lifetime of the holder must be seen in the total context of intergenerational transmission. In the last analysis all such transactions, including the dowry given to a woman at marriage, can be considered as advance payments on the material heritage, and, whether they occur *post mortem* or *pre mortem*, they can all be thought of as made *propter mortem*. The same is often true of bridewealth payments when contributions are made by other members of the same property-holding group. As Homans suggests, when a man passes on his property at his heir's marriage, he arranges at one blow for the continuance of both his line and his estate. Under a bridewealth system, he provides for the continuity of his human heritage at the expense of his material one.

If we regard the "motives" that Homans assigns to *pre mortem* inheritance as social consequences, "latent functions," then cross-cultural evidence appears to lend some support to his suggestions. But from the standpoint of the present discussion there seems to be one important omission. Despite the difficult situation in which the parental generation may be placed when they hand over their property to their heirs,[4] such a system nevertheless wards off the threat of the following generation and consequently diminishes in certain important respects the tension that develops between holder and heir. This assumption, which is of obvious relevance to the present study, could be tested by examining the mortuary institutions in a number of societies. For when the advancement of the heir depends upon the death of the holder, a causal relationship is often presumed to exist between the interests of the heir and the death of his benefactor. The transfer of rights before death alters this state of affairs, and the funeral ceremonies, beliefs in the

---

[4] As Homans observes, the problem receives an excellent treatment in Robert of Gloucester's thirteenth-century version of the Lear story (even more emphatic in this respect than Shakespeare's version) and also in Mannyng's *Handlyng Synne*.

afterlife, and the worship of the ancestors might then be expected to display significant differences, for example, in the degree of elaboration given to mortuary institutions and in the attitudes to death and the dead.

The particular character of the social situations with which we are dealing thus stems from two main sources. First, the role relationships within which the exclusive rights will be transmitted are specified in advance; the transfer is basically non-testamentary. Second, the transfer takes place within the framework of the inheritance situation and thus differs in major respects from those transactions of relatively exclusive rights that we speak of as exchange or gift. For the transmission of the rights in no way involves an alienation from the corporate unit consisting of holder and heir. And although the heirs have duties toward the holder, there is no definite concept of reciprocity or roughly equivalent return implied in the transmission. As we have seen in discussing the LoDagaa funerals, in these communities debts in the strict sense can be incurred only outside the holder-heir situation.

A categorization of the ways in which relatively exclusive rights may be transferred is given in Table 7. It should be added that this is intended simply as a preliminary attempt to formulate a number of interrelated categories in order that the position of the LoDagaa may be examined within a broad comparative framework.

TABLE 7.—THE AUTHORIZED TRANSFER OF RELATIVELY EXCLUSIVE RIGHTS

	Propter mortem			*Other transfers (gift, exchange, etc.)*	
	Recipient specified in advance				
Donor-recipient relationship	By prescribed rule (e.g., primogeniture, succession of next junior in organization)	By choice of present holder, incumbent, etc. (e.g., testament)	Undesignated at time of death, i.e., no heir apparent	Prescribed	Voluntary

The category of acts with which I shall be most concerned falls within the first of these columns, namely, prescribed transfers made "on account of death"; for it is such transfers that involve anticipatory conflicts between holder and heir and between the prospective heirs themselves.

I should add here that prescriptive rules for the transfer of relatively exclusive rights, especially offices, may of course be modified by the use of other principles of selection. For example, further criteria of choice may be introduced so as to exclude persons who are considered physically or mentally incompetent from filling important positions in the social system. Or the successor may be chosen from a pool of "heirs" provided by the ruling dynasty, thus doing away with the concept of heir apparent. Under this procedure, office passes between members of the royal kin group, but by election rather than by proximity of kinship. The combination of the prescriptive and elective elements is most marked under the system of tanistry that obtained among the Irish, Gaels, and Ashanti, as well as in the Near East.

The classification of prescribed transmission is further broken down in Table 8, in which I also include unauthorized transfers, since these are a direct function of the more general have and have-not situation.

TABLE 8.—THE TRANSFER OF RIGHTS BETWEEN ROLES

Type of exclusive right	Authorized transfer (prescribed, propter mortem)	Role relationships	Unauthorized transfer	Role relationships
Property	Inheritance	Holder-heir	Theft	Holder-thief
Sexual	Levirate, etc.	Husband-levir, etc	Adultery, Incest, Abduction, etc.	Cuckold-adulterer, etc.
Roles and offices	Succession	Incumbent-successor	Usurpation	Ruler-rebel

As an illustration of the need for such conceptual distinctions in sociological analysis, I would refer briefly to the transmission of rights over women among the LoDagaa. As in many other communities, one of the main subjects for conflict between adjacent generations is control of the sexuality of women. When we compare the situation of the son and sister's son, however, one important difference stands out. The son may be jealous of the father's sexual rights over his wives, but the situation is not radically altered by the death of his "rival," since marriage and intercourse with these women is always condemned. No authorized transfer is possible. However, the sister's son who coveted his uncle's rights when he was alive can in fact marry his mother's brother's widow, the woman who may have been acting as his female parent figure if he has been living with his mother's people. The situation of the full brother introduces one further variation: not only is he permitted to marry his brother's wives, but he actually inherits these women by a leviratic rule. These three situations may generate three distinct types of tension over sexual access: The first, tension over illegitimate possession, arises from the desire to acquire an object that is absolutely forbidden; the second, straightforward tension over possession, arises from the desire to acquire an object that is forbidden only because it is in someone else's hands; and the third, anticipatory tension, adds to the elements present in the second type the knowledge of the non-possessor that he is the person destined to fill the possessor's role.

This example, the transfer of rights over women among the Lo-Dagaa, points up some of the wider implications of the attempt to distinguish between various elements involved in the process of intergenerational transmission. It suggests, for instance, that although Freud's treatment of father-son hostility in terms of the Oedipal complex is of great value to the comparative sociologist, he cannot hope to bring all his data on intergenerational tensions under this one rubric. For although Freud's formulation accounts for certain aspects of the son's jealousy of the father's rights over women, it neglects the envy aroused by the possession of other exclusive rights. It has been argued that these latter conflicts between father and son derive from the primary sexual one. But this proposition receives little confirmation from other sources. The sociologist cannot adopt so monistic a frame of reference, when observation shows how the focus of envy shifts in accordance with changes in the distribution not only of rights over women, but also of property and other rights.[5]

Moreover, the Freudian approach fails to distinguish between tensions arising out of possession on the one hand and transmission on the other. Yet the "Prince Hal complex" differs from the Oedipal complex not only because it centers upon office rather than women,[6] but

[5] Fromm makes a similar point in his discussion of the Oedipus story, when, after pointing out that Freud interpreted the myth solely in terms of the jealousy of the son for the exclusive sexual rights of the father, he comments, "There is no indication in *Oedipus at Colonus* that the hostility of Oedipus' sons against their father has any connection with the incest motif. The only motivation which we can find in the tragedy is their wish for power and the rivalry with their father" ([1959] p. 437). The sexual rivalry between father and son is seen by Fromm as one aspect of a wider conflict, properly called Oedipal, "the rebellion of the son against the pressure of the father's authority—an authority rooted in the patriarchal, authoritarian structure of society" (*ibid.*, p. 446).

[6] In an interesting discussion of Shakespeare's *Henry IV* and *Henry V*, Ernst Kris suggests that the Prince's rejection of the court is connected with the fact that the King had himself acquired the throne by rebellion and by regicide, by killing his second cousin Richard II. In his theoretical treatment, Kris sees the Oedipal con-

also because it concerns transmission rather than simply possession,[7] since it occurs within the context of the holder-heir situation. What I wish to emphasize is that the Oedipal situation, in the sense Fromm gives the phrase ([1959] p. 446), must be considered within the context of the entire process of intergenerational transmission and is, indeed, one of its inevitable outcomes. Tension and conflict between adjacent generations follow from the necessity of equipping the new entrants to fill existing roles and from the fact that in all human societies this occurs, to a greater or lesser degree, within relationships defined by bonds of kinship.

The holding of exclusive rights, then, gives rise to the general problem of possession, the tension between the haves and the have-nots. But when the future holder or holders are specified in the corpus of social norms, the problem of the anticipated inheritance is brought into being and leads to further forms of conflict, those between the holder and the heir, the incumbent and the successor, the spouse and the levir, as well as those between the prospective heirs themselves. It is these transmission conflicts, particularly those over property, that are of central interest to our present study.

---

flict in the play as "incomplete," since women do not enter into the picture. Prince Hal is contrasted to Hamlet, in whom "the oedipus is fully developed, centering around the queen" ([1948] p. 502). It seems to me that this approach, too, fails to give sufficient independence to the varied sources of intergenerational conflict.

[7] The fact that for the young child transmission conflicts are not of course differentiated from possession conflicts does not, I think, affect my argument.

CHAPTER XIV

Property

Well, some people talk of morality, and some of religion, but give
me a little snug property.

EDGEWORTH, *The Absentee*

In the last chapter, I gave a brief outline of the main categories of relatively exclusive rights, the modes by which they are transferred and the
tensions to which they give rise. In examining the funeral ceremonies
of the two LoDagaa communities, we saw that the main differences in
the possession and transmission of such rights lay in the field of property. It has already been indicated that the persons involved in upbringing or socialization are virtually the same in both communities,
since there is little difference in the composition of households (Goody
[1958]). With regard to offices, the communities differ hardly at all,
either in the custodianship of the Earth shrine, or in the leadership
exercised by elders within the patrilineage. In the modes of inheriting
sexual rights there are again only slight differences. Thus, in the sphere
of relatively exclusive rights, it is basically in their property relations
that the LoWiili and the LoDagaba are to be distinguished from one
another. In this chapter, I want to discuss property as an analytic concept for comparative studies, particularly in relation to full systems of
double descent like that of the LoDagaba.

THE CONCEPT OF PROPERTY[1]

In sociological as in legal writings the term property has been applied both to the material objects said to be owned as well as to the

[1] My main sources for this and subsequent sections are Wesley Newcomb Hohfeld's *Fundamental Legal Conceptions* [1923] and C. Reinold Noyes's *The Institution
of Property* [1936]. Two good statements by anthropologists are to be found in A. I.
Hallowell's "The Nature and Function of Property as a Social Institution," in *Culture
and Experience* [1955], and E. A. Hoebel's "Fundamental Legal Concepts as Applied
in the Study of Primitive Law," *Yale Law Journal* [1942]. The work of Sir Henry
Maine, Sir Paul Vinogradoff, and John R. Commons is also of special relevance to a
comparative study of the institution of property.

rights held in such objects. A yet wider usage appears in some anthropological writings. Lowie ([1928] p. 1), for example, employs the phrase "incorporeal property" to cover any assets that have exchange value, including rights in magical formulae that are the subject of market transactions.

Today most legal writers apply the term property to the rights in the objects as distinct from the objects themselves, and this is the sense in which I shall use the word here. It is important for the comparative sociologist to draw a distinction between material objects and property, between land and land tenure, women and rights in women. Unless he does so, it is difficult for him to give full appreciation to the variety of interest that may arise in this connection, and to the way in which this bundle of rights (to use Maine's phrase) is distributed among various persons in different positions in the social system.

From the standpoint of this definition, the distinction between corporeal and incorporeal property is, as Hohfeld pointed out, a false one, in that both terms refer to rights, which are necessarily incorporeal. But if we accept this, how then are we to distinguish property from other relatively exclusive rights?

In his book *Legal Foundations of Capitalism* (first published in 1924), Commons differentiates between two kinds of property,

> both of them invisible and behavioristic, since their value depends on expected activities on the commodity and money markets. One of these may technically be distinguished as "incorporeal property," consisting of debts, credits, bonds, mortgages, in short, of promises to pay; the other may be distinguished as "intangible property" consisting of the exchange-value of anything whether corporeal property or incorporeal property or even intangible property. The short name for intangible property is *assets*. ([1959] p. 19.)

Commons's definition runs up against difficulties when applied to non-industrialized societies. The determination of value by reference to market transactions can be effectively utilized as a distinguishing criterion in Western societies, in which a wide range of rights in goods and services are exchanged in this way, but for the comparative sociologist such an approach has its weaknesses. Polanyi and his collaborators have insisted that "the categories and definitions of modern economies are not applicable to cross-cultural studies" (Fusfield, in Polanyi, Arensberg, and Pearson [1957], p. 353), and in the present context there are three specific reasons for these difficulties. First, there can be exchange without "markets," whether this term be understood in the economist's sense of a price mechanism or in the comparative sociologist's sense of "a meeting place for the transfer of goods from one set of hands to another" (Neale, in *ibid.*, pp. 357–58); second, the circulation of objects in different non-communicating systems of exchange often makes it impossible to translate the objects of one system into the "currency" of another (Steiner [1954], p. 120); and third, certain goods and services may be excluded altogether from the system of exchange.

This last situation applies in general to rights over women in contemporary Western society, although there are some obvious exceptions; in many simple and in some "archaic" societies, land is yet more strictly *extra commercium*.[2] The LoDagaa, for example, never exchange rights in land. Some years before the Second World War, the Gold Coast Government wished to construct an agricultural station in the northwest of the country, and they chose an area of land near Birifu on which some LoDagaba compounds stood. The inhabitants were persuaded to move to another site and were offered monetary compensation for their land. Although they agreed to move, they refused to accept the money on the grounds that they could not sell land: that was a sin. Such a transaction was incompatible with their idea of the inalienability of land rights, an idea that carries the supernatural sanction of the Earth shrine. When I was in the area some fifteen years later, the local government accounts for the district still carried over from year to year the original sum set aside to pay for the rights acquired. Although land is certainly not a free commodity among the LoDagaa, its value cannot be determined by exchange transactions, since it is transferred only by inheritance or else by gift or loan between kin.

The rights over goods and services discussed above are simply part of the category of relatively exclusive rights, any of which may be the subject of exchange transfers; but exchange is only one of several ways of determining the value of the rights and not the most relevant for present purposes. Instead of attempting to define property with reference to the mode of transfer, it seems preferable to concentrate upon the object of the right.

In his study *The Institution of Property,* Noyes comes to a similar conclusion, that alienability is an inadequate criterion for differentiation and that "the only satisfactory basis of distinction between property and other rights is that the former cover all interests of whatever nature in appropriable material and quasi-material objects and that they are strictly limited to such" ([1936] p. 435). This leads him to define property as follows:

> any protected right or bundle of rights (interest, or "thing") with direct or indirect regard to any external object (i.e. other than the

---

[2] See Vinogradoff [1922], II, 206 *et seq.*, for a discussion of "the lingering influence of tribal institutions on the law of the classical period."

person himself) which is material or quasi-material (i.e. a protected process) and which the then and there organization of society permits to be made the object of that form of control, either private or public, which is connoted by the legal concepts of occupying, possessing or using. (*Ibid.*, p. 436.)

Basically, therefore, we are dealing with rights and duties in relation to material goods, goods whose characteristics—their scarcity and the fact that persons or groups claim relatively exclusive rights over them—signify that they are valued. The definition of property revolves essentially round the problem of exclusion. As emphasized by Hohfeld and others, we are not dealing with rights of a person over a material object, but rather with rights between persons in relation to a material object. A man without social relationships is a man without property.

To clarify this concept of property we may turn to Hallowell's helpful discussion of the problem, in the course of which he isolates four variables: (1) "the individuals or groups of individuals in whom rights and privileges, powers, etc., are invested and those who play the correlative roles in the operation of the whole complex schema of relations"; (2) "the nature and the kinds of rights exercised and their correlative duties and obligations"; (3) the "social sanctions which reinforce the behavior that makes the institution a going concern"; and (4) "the things, or objects, over which property rights are extended" ([1955] pp. 241, 239, 244, and 242). These four variables provide a useful basis for the cross-cultural analysis of property as well as of other types of exclusive rights. In the following sections of this chapter they will each be separately discussed and elaborated.

THE PARTIES INVOLVED

The idea of a simple relationship of two parties in respect to objects of property needs some modification if we are to include not only material objects, but also what Noyes refers to as "quasi-material" objects or "protected processes" such as debts and copyright. In the case of these indirect interests in material objects, it is useful to introduce some concept of a personal or impersonal fund mediating between person and object; such a fund Noyes describes as "a legally segregated organic grouping of property interests to which persons are attached by means of offices—that is, places or *rôles* existing apart from the persons—which are occupied independently of their relations to other such groupings" ([1936] p. 469). Noyes's formulation corresponds closely to the traditional concept of a corporation; indeed, he goes on to claim that the law deals with a corporation not as a group of individuals, not as an artificial personality, but as a fund.

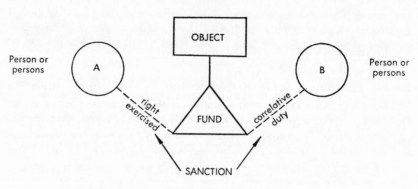

FIG. 8.—The property relationship.

If property is a right between persons in respect of material or "quasi-material" objects, it follows that every right involves a correlative duty. Correlative duties need to be distinguished from concomitant ones. If I have the right to expect my father to provide the bridewealth for a wife, then he has the *correlative* duty to find such a sum. On the other hand, I may have the *concomitant* duty of helping him on the farm.[3] As I have argued in connection with the analysis of the relationships between the mother's brother and the sister's son, the sociologist needs to examine any specific claim in terms of the total nexus of rights and duties obtaining between the persons in question (Goody [1959a], p. 70), which means that both correlative and concomitant aspects should be taken into consideration.

Rights are of course invested in individuals, but a number of persons may hold similar rights in respect of the same object. Moreover these rights may be held as against one person or "as against the world," the distinction often made between rights *in rem* and rights *in personam* (Radcliffe-Brown [1952b], p. 33). However, like other concepts adopted from Roman law and applied to the legal institutions of quite different societies, the term has suffered many changes of meaning, past usages often remaining attached to present definitions. This situation has led some recent writers in the field of jurisprudence to abandon this terminology altogether, as having no fixed meaning.

A preferable distinction is that made by Hohfeld between multital

---

[3] A similar point has recently been made by Gouldner, who discusses the importance of distinguishing between a situation of complementarity, the presence of a right and a correlative duty, and one of reciprocity, the presence of a concomitant right and duty ([1960] pp. 168–69). In most analyses of exchange transactions it is also useful to specify whether the return act is equivalent in kind and in degree. Only equivalent return would I speak of as reciprocal in the strict sense.

and paucital rights, which comes close to some usages of *in rem* and *in personam,* respectively. A multital right "is always *one* of a large *class* of *fundamentally similar* yet separate rights, actual and potential, residing in a *single* person (or single group of persons) but availing *respectively* against persons constituting a very large and indefinite class of people." A paucital right in his definition "is either a unique right residing in a person (or group of persons) and availing against a single person (or single group of persons); or else it is one of a *few* fundamentally similar, yet separate, rights availing respectively against a few definitive persons" ([1923] p. 72). What, therefore, I refer to as exclusive rights are in general multital rights. However, property is an aggregate of rights and duties, which may be split up into various interests, and certain of these interests may be paucital in kind.

The most obvious of the situations in which types of material object are differently treated, and one found in a wide range of societies, is the division into objects exclusively associated with either men or women. Attention has already been drawn to the existence of such sex-linked property among the LoDagaa, and it is clear that the allocation of property to the sexes is intimately connected with the division of labor and with the productive system as a whole.

THE NATURE OF THE RIGHT

In discussing his second variable, the rights themselves, Hallowell refers to Hohfeld's ingenious categorization of legal relationships (i.e., whether a particular right is a privilege, a power, etc., a distinction that relates to the kind of coercion exercised by one party over another). This method of analysis had already been recommended to anthropologists by E. A. Hoebel [1942],[4] but without much result on the empirical level. For present purposes this schema is of peripheral importance.

Another distinction to be made within the over-all body of rights is functional in kind. As has often been remarked, "ownership" does not refer to one single right but to what Maine referred to as a bundle of rights. Applying this idea to the English feudal system, he described the kind of complete ownership known as the feodum or fee as consisting of a "long succession of partial ownerships" ([1883] p. 344). This breaking down of the monolithic concept of ownership has been fruitfully applied to non-Western societies by Malinowski, Gluckman, and others.

---

4 See also Gluckman ([1955] pp. 166–68).

For general analytic purposes, the complete property is divided up into different "bundles" by different authors. Hearn [1885] distinguishes the right to possess, to use, to produce, to waste (use up), to dispose, and to exclude. Noyes divides "the functional relations of direct property in material objects into three component elements; control, use and return" ([1936] p. 512); when a fund intervenes between person and object, that is, when the property interest is indirect, the component elements are two, control and return, i.e., rent. Goodenough examines Truk corporations in terms of provisional and residual title, the corporation being the residual title holder in relation to its members ([1951] p. 42); this roughly corresponds to the customary dichotomies between present use and ultimate control, between possession and "ownership."

With regard to the multiplicity of possible rights and duties that may be developed around them, objects of property have certain similarities with the sexuality of men and women. For example, the rights held over a married woman do not consist merely in one general right of ownership. In many cases, both a girl's guardian (or the group into which she was born) and her husband (or the group into which she marries) have rights and duties in respect of the same person; these are differentiated in her roles as daughter-in-law–wife–mother on the one hand and as daughter–sister–father's sister on the other. Thus, in relation to the persons who hold them, these rights in women are divided into two main interests or bundles. If some other aspect of the relationship, such as the content of the right, is considered, then a different subdivision must be made, into coital, procreative, and domestic rights, for example. In different societies, marriage, the relatively enduring union of man and woman in sexual partnership, is characterized by the transfer of distinctive clusters of rights and duties.

This method of analysis into functionally defined clusters cannot be so usefully applied to the comparison of systems of property, because, apart from the broad categories of use and control, property rights are subject to so much variation. For example, if we are examining the degree of control vested in each level of the series of more inclusive groups that emerge in the context of land tenure, the situation would need to be redefined for every society. In theory it would be feasible to list all possible rights in property and to plot these on a grid against the relevant social roles and groups. But whether this technique could lead to anything more than a methodical description of particular systems is open to doubt. At any rate, for the purposes of comparing the LoWiili and the LoDagaba, it is not the functional classification and distribution of rights that are of major importance; the similarities in the economic system and in the organization of social groups mean that the manner of holding property is approximately the same in both communities. The difference comes not in the modes of tenure as such but in the transmission of rights.

The method by which the title is entered into and broken off is an intrinsic part of the definition of the right itself and has already been briefly discussed. A detailed treatment is, however, required (because of the importance of the subject both in the present study and in comparative investigations generally), and I shall give further consideration to this topic in the next chapter. Although one of the advantages of using modes of transmission as a variable is that they can be treated in a relatively precise way, the terms often used are subject to some ambiguity, which has concealed certain of the interesting problems involved.

THE SOCIAL SANCTION

In dealing with the third variable, the nature of the sanction that upholds the right, I employ the categorization made by Radcliffe-Brown ([1952a] pp. 205–11).[5] He distinguishes three kinds of rights: legal, jural and moral. A legal right, in the narrow sense in which the term is here used, is a right that can be defined and upheld only by the decision of a tribunal backed by a monopoly of force; it is therefore dependent on the existence of a centralized political system. A jural right is a right that is enforced by self-help or other recognized forms of overt counteraction; it is brought into play by a breach in behavior that calls for some kind of action even in the absence of specifically legal institutions. A moral right is a right to which only diffuse sanctions are attached. Ritual sanctions of different kinds are often found associated with the legal, jural, and moral sanctions; among the LoDagaa, the ancestor cult reinforces the moral "privilege" of an individual not to be killed by another member of the patriclan, whereas the Earth cult supports his privilege not to be killed by a fellow member of the parish.

There is of course a considerable degree of interdependence between the nature of the right, its sanction, and the person or group in whom it rests. Indeed, the analysis of the total complex of such rights and the way in which they are exercised, upheld, and breached within a particular society constitutes in effect the analysis of the formal structure of the social system itself.

[5] This classification stems from the work of Durkheim [1933], Fauconnet ([1920] pp. 12 *et seq.*), and Hartland ([1924] pp. 137 *et seq.*).

OBJECTS OF PROPERTY

The purpose of trying to analyze the concept of property is to clarify
our thinking about this body of rights and to establish a limited series
of categories that can be taken as variables in comparative sociology.
Apart from the modes of transmission discussed in the next chapter, it
is the last of the four aspects of the relationship isolated by Hallowell,
the material objects themselves, that is of particular importance in this
respect, since it is with reference to them that the concept of property
has been defined.

As a starting point for our discussion, let us return to the situation
among the LoDagaa. Attention has already been called to the fact that
the central difference between the LoWiili and the LoDagaba lies not
in the presence or absence of unilineal descent groups, or in the economic system as such, but rather in the mode of transmitting property.
Among the LoWiili, all property is inherited within the patriclan;
whereas among the LoDagaba, houses, compound shrines, land, and
the instruments of production are transmitted patrilineally, but movable property—that is, livestock, grain, and money—is passed down
within the matrilineal descent groups.

This splitting of the objects of property into two major categories
characterizes not only the LoDagaba, but many of the societies in Africa
that have two sets of unilineal descent groups (Goody [1961a]). If we
examine the other six groups of fully corporate double descent systems
in Africa (listed in *ibid.*, Appendix), fully corporate in the sense that

TABLE 9.—THE ANALYSIS OF PROPERTY

The parties involved	*The nature of the right*	*The object of the right*	*The nature of the sanction*
Having the right	How entered into and how broken off	Productive resources	Legal
			Jural
Having the correlative duty	Use, control (return)	Dwellings	Moral
		Objects of produc- tion, including the accumulated wealth and the objects into which this has been converted	Ritual
	The concomitant rights and duties		
		Personal effects	

both sets of unilineal descent groups are property-holding, a similar division appears to obtain in the societies with agricultural economies. By the phrase similar division, I do not simply refer to the fact of splitting the property between two lines, since this is true by definition, but rather to the manner in which the rights in the objects are grouped together. For rights in land are vested in one set of descent groups, and wealth in the other. In most cases, land is held exclusively by one group, and wealth by the other. However, among the Nuba, where most land is vested in the patriclan, certain types of plot may be held by the matriclan (Nadel [1947; 1950]); while among some Ada and Abam groups of Ibo in Eastern Nigeria, farming land is often held by the matriclan, although the compounds and surrounding land are subject to patrilineal transmission (Forde and Jones [1950]). However, in the other African cases, immovables appear to be vested in one line, movables in the other.

The nature of this division is not accidental, but related to the existence of a double set of unilineal descent groups. In order to maintain territorial continuity for either set, land used for residential purposes, and to a lesser extent land used for farming, herding, or hunting, must be vested in one particular line. If, therefore, in addition to this association of locality with one set of descent groups, the other set are also to be property-holding corporations, then houses, their sites, and, in most instances, other types of land will fall in one bundle of property, while movables are likely to be allocated as a totality to the alternative line.

There is yet a further similarity in the property relationships of these full double descent systems. Not only is there a general subdivision along the lines of movable-immovable property, but the immovables are mainly vested in the patrilineal descent groups, and the movables mainly in the matrilineal ones. Even in the case of the Ada, house sites are transmitted within the patriclan; consequently the agnatic descent groups are always localized, and the matrilineal groups necessarily nonlocalized. Thus when the movable objects are transferred between generations, they pass between members of different exogamous groups, which are also different local groups, except when the holder-heir situation falls upon close collaterals such as full brothers.

This passage of goods can clearly be viewed as a mode of establishing or continuing ties between the relatively discrete local segments of descent groups, a function that may be served not only by transactions in property, but also by the transfer of other exclusive rights, in the sexuality of men and women or in offices. Indeed, any communicative act between individuals or between members of different groups can fulfill a similar function, but transactions in exclusive rights, particularly, of course, those that relate to enduring resources, have an intrinsic capacity for promoting what may loosely be called solidarity, because of the ease with which they give rise to relationships that persist over time. I mean by this not only that the exchange itself may establish or strengthen a continuing relationship, but that the expectation of that event at some future date may have a similar result, resembling the lasting character of the creditor-debtor relationships in some societies (e.g. Arensberg [1937], p. 173). For the wider social system, the effectiveness of anticipatory ties of this kind is increased when a general rule specifies the roles between which transfer is to take place, as in the case of a rule of inheritance. However, reference to the holder-heir situation serves as a reminder that the counterpart of the stronger ties is the anticipatory tension to which such specification gives rise.

The transfer of sexual rights may lead to results similar to those achieved by property transactions; some prescriptive marriage systems provide a permanent framework to the relationships between members of discrete exogamous groupings, while institutions such as the levirate may perform a similar function within. And the persistence of such relationships built around the transfer of relatively exclusive rights is again accompanied by anticipatory tensions. Systems of affinity do not of course invariably indicate a specific bride or category of brides in this way. More often a wider choice is allowed, which permits of three possibilities, the reaffirmation of a perpetual relationship, the continuation of a temporary alliance, or the creation of a new coalition. Indeed, in Western Europe, the contracting and the dissolving of marriages between royal houses as well as among the landed nobility was a political mechanism of first importance, as is evident from the plots of Shakespeare's historical plays.[6]

[6] For example, in *3 Henry VI* (III, iii), the Earl of Warwick is sent by Edward IV to the French King

> to crave a league of amity
> And lastly to confirm that amity
> With nuptial knot.

To this stratagem the exiled Margaret objects, claiming that Edward's motive in making such a proposal is solely political, springing from the need to bolster his position not only abroad, but also at home.

> For how can tyrants safely govern home
> Unless abroad they purchase great alliance?

The property arrangements involved in such marriages were often considerable, since land and goods could be transferred both to and through women. This aspect of affinal relationships is well illustrated in Homans ([1941] pp. 144 *et seq.*); Holmes [1957]; Stone ([1961] pp. 182–206); and Habakkuk ([1950] pp. 15–30).

The third type of exclusive rights, those relating to offices, are less frequently transferred between members of different groups, but in the form of polydynastic succession such transactions are not uncommon. The rotation of an office among a number of segments means that a larger group will be interested in the occupancy and also helps to distribute power between a number of more or less equal claimants. Among the Gonja of Northern Ghana, for instance, the paramountcy passes in turn among the rulers of the territorial subdivisions of the state, thus helping to maintain the internal unity of this sparsely populated kingdom.

This particular example of the Gonja state brings out a further aspect of the transfer of exclusive rights between members of different groups. While such transactions resemble other forms of social action in establishing or maintaining external relationships, they also constitute distributive as well as communicative acts. The rotation of the paramountcy between the subdivisions avoids the creation of a hegemony of one such subgroup over the others. The transfer of movable property between dwelling groups has a similar leveling effect.

Although I have so far discussed the division between movable and immovable property in double descent systems only, this dichotomy is not of course limited to such societies. In many other types of social system, a similar division is found, between *mobilia* and *immobilia*, *alod* and *feud*, land and chattels, the heritable (hereditament) and the non-heritable, the real and the personal, the formal and the informal. These categories of property are distinguished in that they are distinctively treated, frequently being subject to different rules of inheritance, just as they are in full double descent systems.

Such a dichotomy is characteristic of many early European societies, the transmission of movables being allowed to members of both sexes, with women being excluded from the inheritance of land (Vinogradoff [1926], p. 5). The well-known code of the Salic Franks concerning the inheritance of private property (*de alode*) declares that daughters cannot inherit land. Other Frankish and Lombard laws include similar prohibitions. Norse law also put men and women on the same footing in respect to all forms of property equated with "movable money" (*Lösöre*), but placed men in a privileged position with regard to land. It was the Church that favored bringing the transmission of the two categories of property into line, both in respect of the capacity of women to inherit and in respect of the alienability of land, since the Church stood to gain by the increased allocation of property for ecclesiastical purposes. This idea had its effect in England as early as Anglo-Saxon times, and it is significant that bookland, which was held by the possessor with a right to leave it to whom he wished, was originally granted only for religious ends.

This view of the Anglo-Saxon situation rests largely upon Vinogradoff. John has recently argued somewhat differently. Written charters, the instrument by which bookright was created, were introduced into England by churchmen in the second half of the seventh century. Based upon the Vulgar law of the late Roman Empire, these charters were used "to secure and protect *ius ecclesiasticum,* to match the eternal endurance of their Church with permanent and enduring endowment for their churches" ([1960] p. 24). This endowment consisted largely of grants to *feorm,* alienated royal services and food rents, which were obtained from the king. Such rights were normally held under a precarious tenure that made the transfer of land—as distinct from other property (*feoh, sceatt,* and *irfe,* which, in this context, meant movables, cattle, and money)—dependent upon the king's pleasure. The *ius perpetuum,* the rights in perpetuity granted by the written charter, made the property secure, in theory, from possible claims by the donor's successor; "the rights of free disposal and testament were merely concomitants of the creation of a perpetual tenure" (*ibid.,* p. 39).

The two views are not in complete contrast, since the creation of perpetual tenure was also a way of legitimizing the process of alienation. Both authors agree that by means of the written charter, that great property-holding corporation, the Church, succeeded in altering the legal system to its own advantage, and in a way that was to have important consequences for the aristocracy of early England. From an analytic point of view, the charters may be said to have accomplished their aim by approximating rights in land to those in movables.

Noyes suggests that in certain respects these two categories of land and movables had "their common source" in the distinction between *familia (res mancipi)* and *pecunia (res nec mancipi)* made by early Roman society ([1936] p. 83). But the problem raised by this dichotomy is not merely a question of the historical derivation of specific legal concepts from archaic societies, since, as we have seen, a similar distinction is made in many simple communities. We also require an explanation in terms of the social implications of this division; for, as Vinogradoff points out, "A totally different set of interests is connected with *immovable* property: here the rights and interests involved are clearly of a more permanent character, and in many cases extend beyond the isolated individual" ([1920] I, 274).

The basic distinction between movable and immovable property lies in the difference between land and other material objects. Man is a land-based animal, and most of his social relationships have a terrestrial framework. Land is consequently the focus of a multiplicity of interests. Contiguity, for example, is everywhere a criterion of eligibility for membership in significant social groups. Furthermore, in settled societies, a hierarchy of interests can be built up more readily in land than in other objects of property that are simpler to divide. Property in land is characteristically distributed in a series of aggregates of rights, known as estates of interest, held by different holders or holding groups in the society, and different segments of a lineage of varying orders of inclusiveness may have different interests in the same territory. So important are these rights in land that, as we have seen, they are subject in many non-European societies to inheritance but not to alienation. Only rarely can they be sold, and, as in Northern Ghana, the undesirability of alienating rights of an alodial kind is often buttressed by strong ritual beliefs. Similar restrictions were found in early English society. I have already mentioned that in order to consolidate their position with regard to their holdings, the Anglo-Saxon Church had to employ new instruments of social change in the shape of written charters to land, thus substituting "a form of property, similar to that known to Roman law, for the landownership restricted by tribal custom" (Vinogradoff [1929], p. 36). This was part of the more general problem that faced Anglo-Saxon society, one of adapting traditional forms of organization to the new ecclesiastical institutions. But the introduction of bookright was limited to "the highest class of society, and the most superior kind of right" (John [1960], p. 61), and restrictions on alienation persisted in other forms of tenure.

Of the thirteenth century it has been said that "on many manors land could be alienated only for the lifetime of the holder of the land, or for the lifetime of those to whom it was alienated" (Homans [1941], p. 197). Alienation of land was in some cases against the interest of the lord to whom the tenant owed services; indeed, he could prevent any such transfers from taking place, since they took the form of a surrender into the lord's hands before the hallmote, followed by a regrant. But these restraints on the alienation of peasant holdings "outside of the blood" are also an index of the fundamental importance of land as a source of livelihood.

In other social strata, however, restrictions on alienation may be more directly connected with the holding of a particular office or with the maintenance of high status. Under mortmain, for example, the holding reverted to the lord at the death of the tenant; again, the system of entail prevents the splitting up of an estate, since no one person in a line of heirs is absolute owner. It is worth noting that in Western societies today there are still great differences in conveying and establishing title to land as compared with other objects of property, in which possession alone may in some cases be sufficient proof of ownership.

The multiplicity of interests that land involves fall under two main headings, interests in land as a locality and interests in land as an economic resource. In speaking of land as an immovable, it is primarily the first of these sets of interest to which we refer. Interest in land as a locality includes both residential rights, which largely determine the composition of domestic groups, and political rights, which largely determine the composition of more inclusive territorial groupings. Apart from these interests, there is the economic aspect of land, the contribution it makes to man's livelihood, and this is a factor that clearly differs according to the type of productive system. In agricultural societies, land is the basic economic resource. In hunting, gathering, and herding societies, rights over land also have a fundamental significance for the economy. In most simple societies, such rights form part of a common fund of groups of kin between whose members they are transmitted from one generation to the next.

Thus the dichotomy found in double descent and other systems between land rights and other property is related not only to the land as locality, the movable-immovable distinction, but also to the difference between the basic productive resources and non-productive objects of property. In other words, we have also to deal with "a distinction between personal goods and the property forming the economic basis of existence for the family which is strongly expressed in early law" (Vinogradoff [1926], p. 2).

To take a specific example, in early Roman law a firm distinction is said to have been drawn between *familia* and *pecunia*. The *familia* included rights not only in those objects that were tied to the land, but also in those that were essential for the purposes of production, land, buildings, beasts of burden, implements, and seeds, as well as the laborers who were employed on the land; in other words, it comprised the plant or *instrumenti fundi*. The *pecunia*, on the other hand, consisted of the herds, excluding the beasts of burden (Noyes [1936], p. 89).[7] The difference between these types of property is reflected in the modes of possession and transmission. It appears that the *pecunia* was the first category of objects to be transmitted by testament and hence could be disposed of more flexibly. This differential treatment is quite compre-

---

[7] *Pecunia* from *pecus*, a herd, is later associated specifically with money; chattel, cattle, and capital are all etymologically derived from a common root.

hensible, since such property can be alienated without damage to the productive resources around which the corporation is organized, a fact that also applies to the rule in early Germanic law whereby movable property could be dispersed by transmission through both sexes, but land was retained in male hands.

The relationship of the dichotomy between *familia* and *pecunia* to the question of mobility was clearly understood by von Ihering, when he wrote in his study of the history of Roman law, "The *familia* is fixed, stable, continuous; the *pecunia* is passing, changing, floating."[8] But that this is not simply a division between movable and immovable is indicated by the fact that the implements of production are also included "as part of the *fundus* which could not be detached from it at random" (Vinogradoff [1922], II, 200).[9] We are here faced with a separation between those objects of property that are essential for carrying on the productive process and those that are not.

The relevance of this distinction in the present context is brought out by a consideration of the one African case I know of a full double descent system in which land does not form the direct source of livelihood. I refer to the Herero of Southwest Africa, who have a pastoral economy. From the standpoint of the productive system, land tenure is not of primary importance. Indeed, apart from the definition of tribal boundaries, rights in land are little developed. The productive resources are the herds, the gourds, and the pails for holding milk, all of which are vested in the matriclan. The patriclan, which again serves as the core of the local group, has its own property, largely devoted to certain ritual purposes, the most important being the worship of the ancestors, so that the property includes sacrificial animals and various sacred objects (Vedder [1938], p. 195; Gibson [1956]).

The distinction that obtained in early Roman society between the *familia* and the *pecunia* is not so clear in pastoral societies, partly because the basic means of production act as a store of wealth in addition to being the main source of food. In agricultural societies like the LoDagaa, the two are usually differentiated in a more emphatic way. For where the seasonal nature of agricultural activities is very marked, the produce of the fields has to be stored away and rationed until the next harvest. Then the crops that remain, the surplus of production over the year's consumption, are turned out of the granary to be exchanged

---

[8] "Die *familia* ist das Feste, Beständige, Dauerhafte, die *pecunia* das Vorübergehende, Wechselnde, Flüchtige" [1894], p. 51; see also von Ihering [1875], II (ii), 157n.

[9] "There are definite indications of a similar view in Greek law, although it was not neatly reduced to a formula as in the French *Code Civil* under the heading of *immeubles par destination*" (*ibid.*).

for other goods and services, and in this way perishable foodstuffs are turned into more durable commodities. By throwing large feasts, or by more direct forms of gift, food may be translated into hierarchical position of either a permanent or a temporary kind, that is, into rank or prestige. By transactions of a different kind, the produce of the fields may be translated into other commodities, and especially into the most generalized of all, money. These commodities can then be employed in their turn to acquire rights in persons, most commonly sexual rights, which are obtained by the transfer of bridewealth or of groomwealth.

Of course not all objects used in bridewealth transactions are created anew in this way. When the objects are durable in kind, they can be used in a continuing series of marriages, their progression being in the opposite direction to rights in men or women, those received when a member of one sex marries being set aside until a member of the opposite sex is ready to take a spouse. Nevertheless, since the objects employed can also be used in other transactions, and since there is often a disparity between what is received and what is given, the pool of goods used for bridewealth requires to be supplemented from out of the productive surplus.

Among the LoDagaa this process of transferring the produce of the fields into more permanent commodities works in the following way. When the harvest has been gathered in and laid out to dry on the rooftop, the central granary is emptied of grain and smoked out to free it from vermin. Last year's grain is put aside to be eaten, taken to market, or brewed into beer for sale. The first call on the cowries received is to replace the instruments of production, the hoes, the axes, and similar equipment necessary to make a living. Of the remainder, some money is used to buy clothing for members of the household, and some is hidden away until there is enough to purchase a goat, a sheep, or a cow, known as the Beast of the Hoehandle. As explained in the account of the funerals, it is expected that every self-respecting man will have acquired such an animal by the time he dies.

For the LoDagaa, livestock are basically repositories of wealth. Their meat is of course consumed when animals are slaughtered, either in blood sacrifice to supernatural agencies or in the similar offerings made at funerals. But cattle are not employed for traction, neither is their dung much used for manure nor their milk for food. Indeed, among the LoDagaba and elsewhere in this region, the cattle are often tended by Fulani strangers, who have a right to the milk and the manure as long as they provide the owner with a return on his investment in the shape of an increasing herd.

The distinction between the productive resources and the commodities acquired with the surplus produce is less clear in the case of herders like the Herero, among whom any increase is automatically reinvested in the undertaking. But the grouping together of the herd and the apparatus of production in opposition to the ritual paraphernalia and the "sacred cattle" set aside for sacrifice (that is, for consumption) points to a similar, if not identical, dichotomy to that which is so widespread among agriculturalists. That the distinction *familia pecuniaque* relates to differences between productive resources and consumer goods rather than simply to differences between *immobilia* and *mobilia* is indicated not only by the Herero case, but also by early Roman law, in which, too, the major productive resource, the land, is associated with the tools of production, the *instrumenti fundi*, in one bundle of property, the *familia*. And a similar situation obtained in medieval England. In the champion country, where the farm holding usually went to a single son of the deceased, the goods and chattels were customarily divided among the widow and children, after the best beast had been given to the lord as a heriot, and the second best to the parish priest as a mortuary. However, a certain number of tools required for husbandry and housekeeping were retained by the heir for working the family holding.[10]

That a very similar grouping is made by both the LoDagaba and by the LoWiili was seen in the account of the funeral ceremonies. The hoe, the adze, and the other objects that are brought into the dead man's room when his debts are determined are formally handed over to the eldest son so that he may take over the responsibility for production. It is these same objects a father gives to his son if and when the young man starts to farm on his own during his parent's lifetime. Nor is this a "symbolic" act alone, for, in earlier times, metal objects were a most valuable commodity.

Apart from sacrifices to spiritual beings, the main use of cattle is in bridewealth payments. How closely their employment for this purpose is related to the basic economic activities is seen from the fact that when a son goes out to farm on his own, his father is no longer responsible for providing the bridewealth should he wish to get married.

---

[10] "Sometimes the best example of each kind of tool was expected to go with the holding. These were the *principalia*, in English the heirlooms. (*Loom*, in Old English, meant *tool*, any tool.) Sometimes a list of the *principalia* was inscribed on the court roll when a man inherited a tenement and was given seisin, as at Wotton Underwood, Bucks., in 6 Edward II, where the *principalia* on a holding of a messuage and somewhat more than five acres of land included a coulter, a plowshare, a yoke, a cart, an axe, a cauldron, a pan, a dish and a cask" (Homans [1941], pp. 133–34).

The interrelationship of the productive and reproductive processes is clarified by considering a young man's farming obligations. Among the LoWiili, he has to farm for his father during the father's lifetime, unless the latter has set him up on his own as the result of a quarrel; he has no independent property in land until his father's death, but each year he can ask to be shown a part of the main farm where he can cultivate subsidiary crops such as yams after he has put in a normal day's work on the joint fields. The produce of such a plot of land belongs in effect to the young man, although if he sells any of the crops he has grown, he should show the money to his father, or father's brother, who will take out a certain amount, "the father's leg," and leave the rest to be consumed (*di*, eaten) by the son; this is his *peculium*.

The LoDagaba recognize a similar obligation for a young man to farm for his father, who must in return provide the son with food and bridewealth for the first wife. The small plot, however, is given greater importance among the LoDagaba, and a young man may start such a farm on a fertile patch underneath a tree without even asking his father. And apart from farming both for his father and on his own behalf, he has an additional obligation to take farming parties to his mother's brother, who provides him in return with the bridewealth for his second wife.

Although it might appear from the young man's standpoint as if he were acquiring his bride by the fruit of his own labors, out of the surplus of production over consumption, such is not in fact the case. The sums demanded are considerable in relation to what a man can set aside and even to what is acquired by inheritance. The full bridewealth payment amounts to between 10,000 and 20,000 cowries, two or three cattle, and, among the LoWiili, a sheep. The average holding of cattle in 1948 was four per compound, or two to every five persons (Goody [1956a], p. 29).

The difference, of course, is made up by the circulation of goods through other bridewealth transactions; the cattle brought in when a young girl marries are sent out again for her brother's bride. But the objects used in marriage transactions are not kept solely for such purposes; for example, part of every bridewealth payment is offered to the ancestors. So that as a result of expenditure on this and other transactions, the common fund requires constant augmentation by investment of the surplus of production over consumption.

In this manner, rights over money, cattle, and women enter into the same cycle of exchange; the ends of production are interchanged for the means of reproduction, but the means of production themselves are kept outside the system of exchange. And although for the LoWiili these two types of property are vested in the same set of unilineal descent groups, they are nevertheless distinguished in terms of the kinds of transaction to which they may be subjected.

In this last section we have been concerned with the categorization of objects of property in terms of the two, often overlapping, dichotomies between movable and immovable goods on the one hand, and capital and consumer goods on the other. But frequently the consumer goods themselves are further differentiated, and a category of personal effects is set aside from the bulk of the deceased's possessions, like the paraphernalia of a married woman in English law. These personal effects are often treated differently from other objects; in some societies they are considered particularly dangerous to the near kin and have either to be destroyed or else transmitted to persons more distantly related to the dead man. However, these are problems that relate to the subject of the next chapter, the manner of transmitting property, rather than to the objects of property themselves, and it is to a discussion of the variables involved in this process that we shall now turn.

CHAPTER XV

Inheritance

The brothers remained alone and at first just looked at each other.
"There you are," Pavel finally began; "there's today's youth for you! There they are—our heirs!"
"Our heirs," repeated Nikolai with a dejected sigh . . . "You know what I kept thinking of, Pavel? I quarreled with Mother once. She shouted, didn't want to listen to me. I finally told her, 'You really can't understand me; we really belong to two different generations.' She was terribly offended, but I thought: What can one do? It's a bitter pill—but it has to be swallowed. So now our turn has come, and our heirs can say to us: 'You really aren't of our generation—swallow the pill.' "

TURGENEV, *Fathers and Sons*

There are a variety of methods of acquiring or relinquishing exclusive rights. In this chapter, however, I am mainly concerned with what Commons [1959] calls "authorized transactions"—that is, legitimate transfers—and particularly with those that are required in order to perpetuate "going concerns" over time. To confine the area of discussion in this way is not to deny the part that other transfers play in human societies. Social scientists have sometimes been accused of concentrating upon the element of order to such an extent that they neglect the role of brute force, that is, of illegitimate force. There is some validity in this criticism; on the other hand, one can only discuss illegitimate actions against a background of the legal and jural norms. One can only examine the exercise of unauthorized power in the context of legitimate authority, as Weber was well aware. But however this may be in other cases, here, at any rate, the attention given to authorized transactions is less a reflection of a conservative philosophy than a matter of practical convenience.

The most important form of authorized transaction for the present study is inheritance. In the past, aspects of the system of transferring property have tended to be dealt with piecemeal, and in an attempt to avoid this danger it seems worthwhile to give brief consideration to the other modes of acquiring, and relinquishing, such rights.

It should be remarked at the outset that no method of transferring rights necessarily entails physical change of possession (*traditio*). The transmission of property is a transfer of rights and not necessarily of the goods themselves. Nor, of course, do all physical changes of possession involve transfers of rights. As von Ihering remarked, "The commerce of exchanges, looked at from the legal point of view, is not a circulation of objects; it is a transfer of rights."[1] But although in analysis it is often necessary to distinguish between "possession" and "ownership," in custom they are usually identified. The handing over of some physical object, like a ring at marriage, may publicly announce the transfer of rights and duties, even though the object delivered has no intrinsic connection with the property or the person in relation to whom the right exists.

METHODS OF ACQUIRING AND RELINQUISHING RELATIVELY EXCLUSIVE RIGHTS

By the Creation of New Rights

In industrial, archaic, and simple societies, a distinction is often made between ancestral and self-acquired property.[2] Many African societies distinguish property brought into being by an individual from that which a man controls by virtue of his membership in a corporate group, and each category may be subjected to different rules of inheritance. The Tallensi, for instance, distinguish in this way between patrimonial property (*faar*) and individually acquired property (Fortes [1949], p. 157). This distinction is sometimes linked with the whole set of ideas relating to ancestor worship and to the human personality. For example, the LoDagaa regard objects of a man's own creation as being imbued with his personality (*sie*, soul); they are saturated with his body dirt, and ritual precautions have therefore to be undertaken before these objects can enter into any interpersonal transactions.

A similar distinction is that made between a man's personal resources and the property he controls as the incumbent of an office, a corporation sole. Weber regarded the "complete separation of the property belonging to the organisation, which is controlled within the

[1] "Der Tauschverkehr, mit juristischen Auge angesehen, ist keine Circulation der Sachen, sondern eine Ubertragung von Rechten" ([1875] II, 435).

[2] For a discussion of this distinction in Ancient Greece, see Vinogradoff [1922], II, 201.

sphere of the office, and the personal property of the official, which is available for his own private uses," as being one of the main characteristics of the rational-legal authority found in bureaucratic systems ([1947] p. 304). Similar, if less developed, institutions are to be found with types of "domination" that Weber would certainly have designated as "traditional," for they appear whenever the regalia of office is distinguished from a man's private property. Among the Gonja of Northern Ghana, crown property (which, as in Ashanti (Busia [1951], p. 73), included the widows of the chief) was transmitted to his successor, who because of the rotational system was always a distant kinsman; his personal wealth, on the other hand, followed the usual rule of inheritance and went to his close relations. But of course the distinction between personal and corporate property is never absolute in the long run, since when self-acquired property has once been inherited, it tends to become absorbed into the familial resources and transmitted according to the same rules.

New rights are established not only by the creation of new objects but also by priority of claim, as for example when a LoDagaa moves into an uncultivated area that is not in practice subject to the ritual jurisdiction of an Earth priest. In this case, the newcomer himself acts as the intermediary with the Earth and hands down the office to his descendants, who acquire not only rights of ritual jurisdiction, but also rights to cultivate the land.[3]

In many societies the creation of new objects of property is found side by side with its mirror opposite, the deliberate destruction of existing ones. Clearly, if the basic productive resources are subjected to such a process, the group itself may no longer be able to continue its way of life. It is therefore consumer rather than capital goods that we may expect to find treated in what Lowie called this "economically imbecile" way ([1948] p. 147).

Goods are, of course, destroyed during the owner's lifetime as well as at his death; the potlach is at once a destruction of property and a translation of the rights in it into rank and prestige. But here I am principally concerned with destruction at death, an institution that was widespread in both aboriginal America and pre-Christian Europe. Most frequently it is the category of personal effects that is treated in this way; indeed, they are often seen as harmful to the surviving members of the community. As I have remarked in connection with the funeral cere-

---

[3] In many villages in medieval England, new land acquired by clearing (*assarts* or *riddings*), or by any other method, did not have to be transmitted according to the usual rules of inheritance (Homans [1941], pp. 132, 195).

monies, this custom reflects in an extreme form the dangerous character of all inherited rights;[4] for the destruction of part of the heritage was there interpreted as indicating an institutionalized reluctance to transfer the dead man's rights to the survivors, which in turn constituted a social projection of the guilt feelings generated within the holder-heir situation. The reluctance is the greater the closer the association of the object with the deceased. The LoWiili usually leave the dead man's smock and hat hanging on the wall of his byre, so that with time they eventually fall to pieces. The LoDagaba give the hat (*sapiu*) and the bag of woven grasses (*kor*) in which a man used to keep his clothing to the members of the linked patriclan. They say that if these objects remained around the house, the children or other close kin might catch sight of them and be reminded once more of their grief.

From the actor's point of view, goods are destroyed not only because they are dangerous to the survivors, but also because of the related idea that the holders of rights continue to maintain these interests even in death. In order to cater to the dead man's needs in the other world, certain of his possessions are often buried with him. The institution of lavish grave-goods, especially widespread in Ancient Egypt and in pre-Christian Europe, was also a means of celebrating the status of the deceased, as excavations of Pharaonic tombs and Viking ship-burials vividly attest.

The account of the Arabian traveler Ibn Fadlan, written about 921, describes a similar destruction of property in a Russian boat-funeral, which included the sacrifice of the deceased's concubine, whose body was later burned on a huge pyre.[5] The killing of persons, often of low or servile status, is reported from the mortuary ceremonies of many parts of the world; such persons form part of the property that a man still clings to after death.

The same account of early Russia tells us that the whole of the personal property was divided into three equal parts; one part went to the family, the second was used for making clothes and other ornaments for the dead, and the third was spent carousing on the day when the corpse was cremated. A similar tripartite division is found in Germanic law and formed the starting point of the inheritance rules for personal property that persisted in England until 1857. Under the English open-field system of champion agriculture, when the holding was inherited by a single son, the goods and chattels were first subject to various deductions for the lord, the priest, and the heir, and the remainder was

4 On this subject, see Adam [1935].
5 See the German translation by Togan [1939], pp. 85 *et seq.*

divided into three equal parts, of which one went to the widow, one to the sons and daughters who did not inherit the land, and one to the dead man himself. This last the deceased could bequeath as he wished, and "the dead man's part" often fell to the Church. The medieval Church claimed the right to protect and execute the dead man's will, which was properly made only in the presence of the parish priest (Homans [1941], p. 134).[6]

By Force

It is necessary to consider forceful acquisition even when limiting the discussion to authorized transactions, since, in the absence of any developed political system, the seizure of property is often a legitimate way of redressing wrongs, at least in the eyes of one of the parties concerned.

The LoDagaa distinguish between three kinds of transfer of possession by physical force, two of which are, in effect, authorized modes of transmission. Seizure (verb, *faa*) is the appropriation of the property of an enemy, conceived of as counteraction for a wrong done by a member of another group; successful robbery of this kind may be celebrated at a man's funeral by slaughter of a cow. Theft (verb, *zu*), on the other hand, is the acquisition by force of property held by those standing in a friendly relationship to one's own group, an act that is most strongly condemned. It is said that formerly a persistent thief would have his fingers chopped off by his own kinsmen. Snatching or "ritual stealing" (verb, *ara*) falls somewhere between these two; a man can snatch only from his mother's agnates, who put up a token resistance to the attempt, but take no counteraction when it succeeds.

By Alienation

Apart from the creation of new rights and the appropriation by force of those that already exist, rights may be the subject of authorized transfer either by transmission between persons within the inheritance situation or else by alienation. Alienation here is a residual category that includes all transfers outside the holder-heir relationship. When agnatic inheritance occurs, a father does not alienate goods by passing them to his son, since the latter would in any case inherit them at his death.

Permanent alienation of relatively exclusive rights, as distinct from the temporary kind involved in lending and borrowing, in leasing and renting, takes a variety of forms, which may be thought of under the following headings:

6 See also Vinogradoff [1920], I, 275.

(1) Barter: the permanent alienation of rights in return for a variable quantity of other objects of property, agreed upon at the time of transfer.

(2) Sale: the permanent alienation of rights in return for a variable quantity of the most generalized commodity, money, agreed upon at the time of transfer.

(3) Gift exchange: the permanent alienation of rights the return for which is unspecified at the time of transfer, either because the quantities are traditionally established, or else because they are determined by the recipient.

(4) Donation, or "free" gift: the permanent alienation of rights with no expectation of return either in goods or in services.

Transactions of the first three kinds do not necessarily diminish the estate to be handed on to the coming generations, since even if the basic means of production have been alienated, they can be acquired again by reversing the exchange. With donation, which is admittedly the limiting case, the position is different; from the analytic standpoint it comes closest to inheritance, and yet should usually be distinguished from it as a form of alienation.

Among the LoDagaba, relatively exclusive rights are transmitted between adjacent generations both by inheritance and by donation, or, at any rate, by non-reciprocal forms of gift exchange. Rights in livestock are in principle transmitted by inheritance to the sister's son, but a man may also give his son a cow in return for receiving the "father's leg"; this latter is a gift transaction, since it alienates rights over the property of the matrilineal corporation.

This mode of transmission, by gifts *inter vivos* between father and son, is of considerable importance in societies with matrilineal descent groups, particularly where a man's sons are living patrilocally.[7] Good-enough indicates one of the functions of such transfers in his account of the Pacific island of Truk, where the institution appears in a more

---

[7] For example, among the Navaho (Kluckhohn and Leighton [1946], pp. 60 *et seq.*) and the Ashanti (Busia [1951], p. 43). Of the Ashanti, Busia writes "A man was permitted by custom to make a gift of part of his farm to his son. This was valid if it was made in the presence of witnesses, and if the gift was acknowledged by the offer and acceptance of *aseda* (token of thanks) in money or drink. But the gift was subject to the approval of the maternal kinsmen, who were thereby deprived of part of their inheritance." That this custom is not simply an aspect of recent changes of a more general character can be seen from Bowdich's account of his stay in Ashanti. He observes that matrilineal inheritance is "universally binding" (although it is through the King that the dead man's gold dust is distributed), but that "this law is sometimes anticipated, by a father presenting his children with large sums of gold just before his death" ([1819] p. 254).

radical form and where even some productive resources are transferred in this way.

In actuality very little property remains to be inherited on the death of an individual or of a corporation. The practice is to make a *niffag* [a gift expecting no return of goods] of most of one's property to one's children when they reach adulthood. As long as one lives, then, one has the rights of a residual title holder. As a man gets older and is no longer vigorous he continues to receive his share of the produce, while the responsibility for working and maintaining the property rests with his children. *Niffag* thus constitutes a sort of old age insurance, and gives legal sanction to the dependence of the aged on their children via the obligations of the provisional to the residual title holder. ([1951] p. 46.)

As with similar institutions characteristic of many patrilineal societies (in particular the "ritual stealing" by the sister's son from the mother's brother), the effect is to alienate property from the main line of inheritance which falls within the corporate descent group. Such transactions reinforce certain strategic extraclan ties that are traced through the parent or sibling other than the one through whom descent is reckoned, ties that may provide a man with considerable assistance in times of need.

In non-literate societies with established rules of inheritance, oral testaments that take effect at death can serve a very similar function. Indeed, among the Ashanti, wills have been described as "a form of inchoate gift that takes effect on death" (Matson [1953], p. 224). Analytically, both modes of transmission provide standardized ways of alienating property from the corporate group. However, normally the individual is not free to make such gifts or testaments except with the approval of other members of the group, who are called upon to act as witnesses (Busia [1951], p. 125).

It should be added that even where testamentary inheritance is the established practice, it does not necessarily follow that a man has free disposition of all his property. Under the French *Code Civil*, for example, no person can make a will depriving his children of their legal share; and although in other Western societies the written codes make no specific provision for the widow and children, failure to do so would certainly run contrary to widely held moral norms.[8] For a Roman

---

[8] In English Law, the Inheritance (Family Provision) Act, 1938, confers upon the High Court the power to order payments out of a testator's net estate upon an application on behalf of his or her dependents. The dependents of a man are defined as a wife, a daughter who is unmarried or incapable of maintaining herself, an infant son, or a son who is incapable of maintaining himself. In making an award, the Court must take into account the testator's reasons for not providing for his dependents.

citizen to make a will against the interests of a son or grandson, he had formally to disinherit the heir (*exheridatio*), a right that is comparable to the *ius necis,* the right of the father to put the son to death (which was in practice rarely resorted to).[9]

I encountered several cases among the LoDagaa of a man's attempting to bequeath his property in ways opposed to the rules of inheritance. Among the LoWiili, one elder, Bōyiri, who had sent his eldest son out to farm on his own, told me that when he died, the son would get nothing more from his estate. However, other members of the descent and local group were quite definite that the ways of the ancestors could not be abandoned like this; for no man had the power to disinherit his children. In no instance that I heard of did an oral will prove an effective instrument for bypassing the authorized heir. Alienation occurs *inter vivos,* but not by oral testament.

By Inheritance

From the standpoint of this study, the most important method of acquiring property is by the process of inheritance, "the entry of living persons into the possession of dead persons' property" (Cole [1932]). When there are prescribed rules, or even expected modes of inheritance, the transfer of property to the heir at the holder's death must be looked at in the context of the total transactions between the persons involved; often there may be very little left to hand down by the time death occurs. In other words, we must consider transfers of property from holder to heir during the holder's lifetime as well as after his death. Moreover, transfers of property also involve transactions from heir to holder; for, as we shall see later, sacrifices to the ancestors are intimately connected with the inheritance of property. We therefore need a more inclusive term for the whole process of intergenerational transmission of property (or what we may call corporate transmission, since holder and heir constitute what is, in many senses, the basic corporate unit of

---

[9] In Ancient Greece the bequeathing of property by will, the introduction of which was attributed to Solon, was conditional on the absence of children (Vinogradoff [1922], II, 212). Vinogradoff relates the development of testamentary inheritance in Rome to the system of agriculture, which was based upon plough farming and the cultivation of grapes and olives; this he maintained "did not favour either the growth of joint families or the formation of fixed holdings" ([1920] I, 292), but rather individual property in small farms. The hypothesis is worth testing on a wider front. However, it appears that in the Far East intensive systems of agriculture are not necessarily inconsistent with the presence either of joint-families or of corporate descent groups. To account for testamentary succession, in the sense of free disposition, it would seem necessary to take into account other social changes, such as access to alternative ways of earning a living, developments in technology, especially in literacy, as well as changes in the political system.

the society), and I propose to refer to this process as the process of devolution.

The reader will notice that I use the term inheritance in a wider sense than some writers, indeed to include what Maine would have called perpetual succession. Thus I speak of the process of devolution that occurs at the death of a member within a Joint Undivided Family (i.e., a kin group in which property is jointly held) as inheritance, since this event is bound to involve some readjustment in the distribution of rights and duties, whether or not these are jointly held. Moreover, most non-industrial societies devolve property within such joint ownership groups, holder and heir usually working together with the lands or herds that will eventually be transmitted between them. However, there is often an important distinction to be made, on both the societal and the individual level, between cases in which property is inherited within the work group and those in which it is inherited outside.

This point raises the desirability of further clarification of the concept of the corporate group. In earlier publications I have used the term to mean a property-holding group, or the group within which property is transmitted, and I have spoken of a major unilineal descent group as corporate if such activities took place among its members. Although this usage is, I believe, more useful for analysis than other current sociological uses, it may still be somewhat ambiguous, because, in addition to the inclusive corporate group, we usually need to isolate three further groups. These are the group that holds effective joint rights over the property, the group that works the property, and the group within which the property is normally inherited. Such groups may, and often do, overlap; but a recognition of the possibility that they are distinct in some situations helps to clarify certain problems in the analysis of corporate groups.

Rules of inheritance may take a wide variety of forms, but there are a number of general elements that enable us to simplify the discussion. In the first place, I shall be dealing with inheritance between kin. Benedict [1936] noted that in simple societies the most important economic rights were transmitted between consanguineal kin to the exclusion of the spouse, even in "bilateral" systems like those of Samoa, Kwakiutl, and Ifugao.[10] The statement does not of course hold for the

10 Inheritance of the basic property between kin is of course a prerequisite for the maintenance of corporate (property-holding) unilineal descent groups. Benedict called indirect attention to this point when she wrote: "This fact of the primary rights of the consanguineal kin to economic goods, to the exclusion of the spouse, makes clan institutions, either matrilineal or patrilineal, not a catastrophic change in social arrangements, but an ever-recurring possibility" ([1936] p. 372).

major literate societies. In Babylonian law, in the legal codes of Ancient Egypt, Classical Greece, and Rome, and in the Hebrew, Hindu, and Moslem codes, the widow inherited a portion of the property at her husband's death. Or, rather, she acquired rights to certain parts of the conjugal estate that had been established at marriage and that she and her kin had in fact helped to set up by the marriage endowments. For conjugal inheritance appears closely correlated with the dowry proper, both of them involving the transmission of property between the sexes.

The establishment of a conjugal community of property[11] may be looked upon as one of several methods of providing for the widow. For although in most simple societies no marital inheritance occurs, the society has the alternative of arranging for her destruction or for her support, and in the latter case responsibility falls either upon her husband's or upon her natal kin. Indeed, the provision of such support is in many cases an integral aspect of the levirate and the related institution of widow inheritance; the custom of "marrying" a grandfather's widow, for example, usually has more to do with the supplying of food and shelter than with the exercise of sexual rights.

The second restriction I place upon the data is in concentrating primarily upon the way in which property passes *between* rather than *within* the generations. A limited degree of lateral transmission between siblings is provided for in most systems, and I do not wish to minimize its importance in relation to the central theme of this analysis; relationships between siblings are often strongly influenced by considerations of property.[12] However, such lateral movement as occurs may be regarded, for present purposes, as preliminary to the essential downward transfer to the junior generation, anyhow as far as the transmission of enduring goods is concerned.

With regard to other categories of exclusive rights, it is possible entirely to confine their transfer to members of the same generation,

[11] To use Kephart's phrase ([1938] p. 6). Another method of providing for the widow is the practice whereby the dower is set up as an independent fund for the wife-daughter in anticipation of her widowhood. On this subject, see Maine [1875], pp. 306 *et seq*.

[12] Lowie tends to treat this subject in terms of the stages in a society's development, the primeval unity of the sibling group being disturbed at a later stage by the interpolation of property considerations: "The bond between siblings, which among simpler peoples is one of the strongest conceivable, is often overshadowed by envy when property has advanced to a prominent place, hence the animosities to be observed in sophisticated societies among the closest relatives" ([1950] p. 155). But conflicts between brothers over the distribution of material goods are by no means confined to "sophisticated societies."

and notably in the case of kinship roles and sexual rights. The fact of generation usually enters into the definition of close kinship relationships in so basic a way that only in a limited sense can these roles be taken on by members of adjacent genealogical strata. It is true that among the LoWiili, people will say of the eldest member of a group of fatherless siblings that "he has now become the father" (*o lieba sãã*). But this statement refers to certain very restricted aspects of the elder brother's role in the household and in no sense alters his kinship status with regard to members of the lineage belonging to other households. Nor would his younger brothers even address or refer to him as "father"; the usage is openly metaphorical.

Again, in many societies with agnatic inheritance, rights over women do not pass between adjacent generations, but either laterally or between alternate ones; such is the case among the LoDagaa. The rule against inheritance of widows between close agnates of adjacent generation can be considered a device to protect the dwelling group from anticipatory conflicts over women; it means that the death of the father provides no sudden reversal of the "incest" taboo on his wives. On the other hand, in some patrilineal systems, of which the neighboring Dagaba are one, the lineal principle overrides these considerations and permits a son to marry his father's wives, although even here the biological mother is excluded from the inheritance.

Theoretically, it is possible to transfer rights over women (or men) entirely by a system of lateral transmission, since the life cycle allows them only a limited span, while of course providing for the continuous creation of such rights with each new generation of women. But usually with objects of property, and always with the basic means of production, such as land, the situation is different; the demands of "perpetual" or long-term inheritance mean that provision must be made for vertical as well as horizontal transmission. Indeed, logically, the former is "essential," the latter "optional." And so, to simplify the ensuing discussion, I shall concentrate primarily upon vertical inheritance. Even this I shall further restrict to downward transmission. For in the long run the passage of property to ascendants goes against the general line of human traffic; it is but rarely done, and then only as a temporary measure. Indeed, there is often a specific prohibition upon the upward movement of goods by inheritance. Paulme writes of the Dogon of West Africa, "les biens ne remontent pas" ([1940] p. 349), and in medieval English law, it was said that a man could not be both lord and heir of the same piece of land, and that an inheritance, like a heavy body, cannot fall upwards (Holdsworth [1923], II, 191).

HOLDER-HEIR RELATIONSHIPS

Rules for the transmission of property are often identified with rules for the membership of descent and kin groups. For example, rules both of inheritance and of unilineal descent are usually classified as patrilineal and matrilineal, whereas in fact these words are differently employed in the two contexts.

In speaking of unilineal descent, I refer to those groups whose membership is based upon the sibling bond, i.e., groups that recruit members of both sexes.[13] The rules defining membership of a unilineal descent group show the following two characteristics:

(1) They exclude the transmission of rights of membership through one sex, through one element of the sibling group.

(2) They allocate these rights of membership to persons of each sex, to the entire sibling group.

Moreover, so far as the entry into and the organization of unilineal descent groups are concerned, there are only two alternatives, patrilineal or matrilineal.

Rules for the transmission of property differ from rules for the membership of unilineal descent groups. As the result of the sexual division of labor, certain objects of property are often identified with, employed by, and transmitted between the members of one sex only. Hence rules of transmission have always to provide for the fact that property is vested *in* both males and females, and must therefore be transmitted *by* both sexes. In other words, the situation is complicated by the presence of a further variable, the sex of the parties between which the transfer occurs. This variable takes three possible forms:

(1) Homogeneous or monosexual transmission: the transfer of rights between members of the same sex, male to male, female to female.

(2) Diverging transmission: the transfer of a person's rights to members of both sexes, male to male and female, female to male and female.

(3) Cross-sexual transmission: the transfer of rights between members of opposite sexes, male to female, female to male. There are two variants of this type:

(a) Irreversible cross-sexual transmission: i.e., rights held by females can be transferred to males, but those held by males cannot go to females.

---

13 In the present context, I explicitly exclude from consideration single-sex or compromise kin groups, since they give rise to different, though related, problems. For a discussion of single-sex groups, see Southall [1959] and Maybury-Lewis [1960]. Compromise kin groups are partially recruited by criteria other than unilineal descent, e.g., by locality or by affinity.

(*b*) Two-way cross-sexual transmission: rights can be transferred both from male to female and from female to male.

It is clear that each of these methods of passing property *between* persons of the same or different sex may also take place *through* persons of different sex. In the usual terminology, inheritance may be either "patrilineal" or "matrilineal." But, as we have seen, there are a number of important differences between handing down the membership of unilineal descent groups and passing on rights over property. It therefore seems preferable to restrict these two words to the descent situation and to use the more general terms agnatic and uterine to describe the alternative means of transmitting property through one sex or the other.[14] By doing this it is possible to make a clearer distinction between descent and inheritance variables and to recognize, for example, that agnatic modes of inheritance are found not only in association with patrilineal descent groups, but also in the absence of such units (i.e., in "bilateral" societies).[15]

To put this another way, the property of both males and females may be transferred *directly* to ego's children, or *indirectly* to the children of ego's sibling of opposite sex. Direct transmission of property between males is agnatic, and between females uterine; indirect transmission between males is uterine, and between females agnatic.

The different possibilities arising from a combination of the *through* and *between* variables for cases in which a man is transmitting the property are listed in Table 10. But each society has to make arrangements for the property of both sexes, so that a further set of combinations is involved. Moreover, as in the case of the LoDagaa, not all of a man's property may be transmitted in the same way; land, in particular, is often subject to a special set of rules. Hence, when we are defining any actual system of inheritance, we need to specify to what bundles of rights a particular mode of transmission applies. To do this is sometimes quite a complicated process, as will be seen from the following chapter.

For example, if we look at homogeneous inheritance in terms of these two variables, namely, the sex of the persons involved and the

[14] Medieval lawyers described inheritance of the first type as *per virile secus,* and I have elsewhere used the term virilineal (and uxorilineal) to denote this method. But in current anthropological usage the term agnatic has often appeared to duplicate "patrilineal," and it therefore seemed more economical to make use of it in this context.

[15] In the text, I refer sometimes to patrilineal inheritance. By this I mean a system in which the holder-heir relationship is located within the patrilineal descent group; it is simply agnatic inheritance in the context of unilineal descent groups.

TABLE 10.—HOLDER-HEIR RELATIONSHIPS, MALE TRANSMITTING

PERSONS BETWEEN

PERSONS THROUGH	Homogeneous	Diverging	Cross-sexual
Males (agnatic; direct)			
Females (uterine; indirect)			

Heavy lines indicate relations of kinship. Dotted lines indicate passage of property.

direction of the transfer, agnatic or uterine, it can be seen that there are four general possibilities for the transmission of rights in a social system: (1) between males, through males (agnatic); between females, through males (agnatic); (2) between males, through females; between females, through females; (3) between males, through males; between females, through females; and (4) between males, through females; between females, through males.

It would seem that of these possible systems only the second and the third are at all widespread, since, in the vast majority of cases, almost universally, female property is transmitted to full siblings and children and not to a brother's children. In other words, whereas transmission between males may be either direct or indirect, transmission between females is largely direct, an imbalance that seems related to the different roles of the sexes in the reproductive process. Indeed only when the female members of a patrilineal corporation are able to hold the group's basic property will it be necessary to prescribe indirect (agnatic) inheritance for women in order to prevent the dispersal of the property. This does occur in contemporary Buganda, where transmission of a woman's property to her brother's daughter is a function of the ownership of the patriclan's land by both sexes. Sex differences also appear to account for the absence or relative infrequency of other possibilities, such as the combination of uterine and diverging transmission illustrated in Table 10.

I have tried, for reasons I have mentioned, to separate systems of inheritance from systems of recruitment to unilineal descent groups. But while no one-to-one correlation exists, there is clearly a certain correspondence between rules of transmission and rules for the membership of kin groups, between homogeneous (or monosexual) inheritance and unilineal descent groups, between diverging inheritance and "bilateral" systems, and possibly between cross-sexual inheritance and alternating kin groups of the kind reported for the Mundugumor (Mead [1935], pp. 176 *et seq.*). To take the first of these rough correspondences, homogeneous inheritance is the only method that ensures continuity between a unilineal descent group and a fixed estate, if either the male or the female members are regularly scattered through exogamous marriage. On the other hand, the same system of inheritance can be employed to give continuity in the male line when there is no organization of unilineal descent groups, but rather a system of stem-families, or alternatively joint-families centered upon a core of male agnates, such as existed in various parts of Europe.[16]

However, in order to ensure continuity under these conditions, assuming the absence of a prescribed marriage arrangement, yet a further restriction is required, namely, that the property essential to the perpetuation of the group be kept in the hands of one sex only. I have already commented upon the institution of sex-linked land among the Salic Franks. Similar provisions exist in many agricultural societies, and indeed one of the great problems of Islamic law is the fact that the system of diverging transmission that it supports creates difficulties in this very area, particularly when the basic resources are of a fixed rather than a movable kind.[17] A number of societies that have adopted Moslem law, such as the Nupe of Northern Nigeria and the Kabyles of North Africa, have tended to exclude land from the property to be divided between the members of both sexes (Nadel [1942], pp. 173, 181; Letourneau [1896], p. 331). Indeed, Trimingham ([1959] p. 129) points out that in West Africa, Islam has had an influence on the law relating to land only in urban centers and heavily populated rural areas,

---

16 See Jolliffe [1933] and Homans [1941], as well as other authorities mentioned later in this chapter.

17 Although the difficulties are greater when the basic resource is land, the diverging succession that Moslem law prescribes may be resisted by pastoral peoples as well. Of the Gwandu Fulani, Hopen writes: "Quite apart from their aversion from paying death duties herdsmen do not favour the Maliki system of inheritance whereby a daughter receives one-half of a son's share. Cattle are traditionally the property of men and any system whereby women acquire animals is regarded with disfavour" ([1958] p. 139).

such as parts of Futa Jalon and Bornu. In this respect, the Islamic code is adapted to urban and to pastoral conditions rather than to agricultural economies; in fact it is becoming more widely applied only in those places where the influence of Western Europe has led to a predominantly cash economy and to the fragmentation of land holdings.

An alternative means of preventing the alienation of resources in a system of diverging transmission is to prescribe endogamous marriage. In the Old Testament, the daughters of Zelophehad are said to have come to Moses with the request that they not be excluded from inheriting the property of their father because of their sex: "Why should the name of our father be done away from among his family, because he hath no son? Give unto us therefore a possession among the brethren of our father" (Num. 27:4). Moses took their argument before the Lord, who ordained that it should be so. Sometime later the elders came to Moses and pointed out that if a woman now married a member of another tribe, and had no brothers, then the inheritance would be lost to them. As a result, an additional rule was promulgated to prohibit out-marriage in cases of this kind.

> And every daughter, that possesseth an inheritance in any tribe of the children of Israel, shall be wife unto one of the family of the tribe of her father, that the children of Israel may enjoy every man the inheritance of his fathers.
> Neither shall the inheritance remove from one tribe to another tribe. . . . (Num. 36: 8–9.)

I shall later discuss the general connection between diverging transmission and in-marriage.

Objects are sex-linked when they are vested in and transmitted between members of one sex only, a matter that tends to be determined by the sexual division of labor. Thus, cooking pots are often transmitted only between women, weapons only between males. However, the division of labor is not the only relevant factor. In matrilineal systems with uxorilocal marriage, land may be transmitted between women, even though it be exploited by men; for the women are the representatives of the descent group that remains on the estate belonging to the matriclan corporation. It is they who provide the descent core of the local group. Among the LoDagaa, mortars are vested in widowers, and in some societies, such as Dahomey, rights in women may be held by other women (Herskovits [1938], I, 319–21; Bohannan [1952]).

With regard to sex-linked property, one final point requires some comment. The protest of the daughters of Zelophehad was not directed against the failure to divide the property among all members of the sibling group, females as well as males; it was made in order that women should be granted residual rights in their paternal estates, so that the property would become theirs in the absence of any male children, rather than fall to any more distant male kinsfolk. In other words, so far as property considerations were concerned, the unity of the sibling group was given greater significance in relation to outsiders than the linking of property to one sex only. Whereas the daughters did not otherwise share their father's estate, in the absence of brothers they had a prior claim over male collaterals, acting, as it were, in a representative capacity.

Maine compares a woman's role in this respect with certain other legal fictions that simultaneously provide a man with an heir to his property and a worshiper at his shrine; among the various mechanisms he discusses are adoption, the levirate, procreation through the wife by means of a proxy husband, the purchase of slaves, and the system of "appointing" a daughter whose son can inherit ([1883] pp. 90 *et seq.*). In this last instance, commonly discussed in early Hindu law books, the daughter herself has no rights to the property, but her son acquires a claim through the submerged rights of a female member of the sibling group. This mechanism is similar to the one I have suggested as the explanation of the ritual stealing by the sister's son in societies with corporate patrilineal descent groups (Goody [1959a]). Maine regards inheritance by the son of an "appointed" daughter as connected not only with the residual inheritance by daughters in the absence of males, but also with the ultimate admission of female descendants to a share in the inheritance (*ibid.*, p. 108). He sees the connection as being evolutionary in kind.

However this may be, the important point here is to recognize that in systems of homogeneous inheritance between males, a balance has to be made between giving consideration to the claims of close kin, including females, and tying the estate to kin more distant but of the same sex as the deceased. The LoDagaa give preference to collaterals of any degree, rather than transfer male property to females. In medieval Europe, in the Mediterranean area, and in India, even productive property is generally retained within the sibling group, despite differences of sex; and this residual inheritance by women of the major resources is usually combined with the passage of a portion of the movable property to the daughters by diverging transmission. These differences in property-holding and transmission appear to be correlated with other important differences, such as the structure of unilineal descent groups (Goody [1959a], p. 83).

PARTITION

In discussing the ways in which property is transmitted to the junior generation, I have already touched upon the question of which members of the sibling group are the beneficiaries. In homogeneous transmission, property is transferred between members of the same sex; in diverging transmission, to members of both sexes. There are, however, two further important factors involved in the transfer of property to the next generation. First, there is the general question of whether or not the property is partible or impartible, whether the estate is kept as a single unit or divided among the possible heirs. And, second, there is the question of whether the property, unified or divided, is distributed among the sibling group by equal or unequal division; i.e., in impartible systems, whether all or one of the siblings takes over, and in partible ones, what differences there are among the various portions (equal or unequal division).

Let us first consider impartible inheritance. One type of such system is that associated with the domestic organization that Maine ([1883] pp. 232 *et seq.*) referred to as the House Community, the Joint Undivided Family. All the members of the junior generation hold approximately equal rights in the common fund to which they contribute by their labor and draw upon for their support. Equality in respect of the basic resources is as important here as the unitary nature of the holding. It is particularly important, since, as Maine himself noted, the impartibility of these joint-families is often a relative matter, the group tending to split after a certain number of generations (*ibid.*, p. 240).[18] And when fission occurs, all male members are equally entitled to share in the joint estate.

But not in all impartible systems are rights equally distributed among the sibling group. More usually one specific heir carries on the family estate, a procedure that was prevalent in parts of medieval Europe. In England, for example, side by side with the gavelkind of Kent,

---

18 He notes that both among the Southern Slavs as well as in India, joint-families, composed of the descendants of a dead ancestor, are interspersed with "natural families," composed of the descendants of a living man. While he tends to consider this in long-range evolutionary terms, he also sees that time factors may be important here over a much shorter span, and he ends up by suggesting that the differences between these forms of domestic group correspond to phases in the developmental cycle. "The family, when it does not dissolve by the swarming off of the children, expands into a house community; the community (though not as often as in India) breaks up into separate natural families. The process, for all the evidence before us, may have gone on from time immemorial" (*ibid.*, p. 244).

the Celtic areas, and parts of East Anglia, primogeniture, known as Borough French, and ultimogeniture, Borough English, were practiced throughout the Midlands. Property, at least immovable property, was treated like office as indivisible. Nor was this arrangement limited to the upper levels of society alone, although there it had a particular importance, since the possession of lands was often a prerequisite for the holding of office. Attention has already been drawn to the importance of impartible inheritance in the open-field agriculture of the champion country. Here the complex system of village farming appears to have militated against land and farm implements being equally divided among the sons, a procedure that would have led to inequalities in the agricultural units. Such a prospect not only met with objections from fellow villagers; it also would have greatly complicated the whole system of services to the lord of the manor, services that were charged to particular tenements held in villeinage (Homans [1941], pp. 199–200).

In impartible inheritance of this kind, the excluded siblings have two alternatives in front of them, either to stay in a subordinate capacity, or to quit and make a living on their own. The first of these eventualities results in a situation akin to that of the Joint Undivided Family, except that the sons other than the main heir have restricted rights in the estate. They cannot of course lay claim to an individual share of the basic estate, since the productive unit is considered to be an organic whole and incapable of partition. But although the impartible property may be vested in one person for certain limited purposes, the other members of the sibling group have the right to derive a living from it. Sometimes, however, their rights are even further restricted. For example, under the champion system of medieval England, a son who did not inherit his father's land could stay on in the same household in which he had grown up, but he could not take a wife. No land, no marriage, Homans remarks ([1941] p. 137), a rule that had fundamental implications for medieval demography as well as for the whole domestic organization. It was, however, consistent with the cardinal principle of the social organization "that a family holding ought to descend undivided, generation by generation, from one representative of the blood of the holding to another" (Homans [1941], p. 138).

The other alternative is for the non-inheriting males to leave the family estate and establish themselves on their own. But in this they are not left entirely to their own devices. Some compensation in cash or other movables is usually provided for those who leave to make a living elsewhere, whether on new lands or in a new occupation.[19] Like

[19] This occurred in the settlements made among the aristocracy of eighteenth-century England at the marriage of the eldest son. "Their essence, so far as the pro-

the women who leave on marriage, the men, too, have their "portion." It is here that the distinction between movables and immovables, between consumer goods and productive resources, is relevant. To distribute consumer goods does not diminish the basic estate; it is to the productive resources, and particularly land, that the rules of unigeniture mainly apply.

In medieval England, in feudal tenures as well as among the peasantry of large parts of the Midlands, primogeniture was the rule as far as the productive resources were concerned. However, elsewhere in the champion country, Borough English or ultimogeniture obtained. Frazer has tried to trace a connection between ultimogeniture and swidden, or slash-and-burn agriculture ([1918] I, 481), an association that Leach also notes for the *gumsa* Kachin ([1954] p. 260). However, ultimogeniture is certainly not confined to societies with a shifting agriculture; for it obtained widely in medieval Europe under the name of *droit de mainteté* and *Jüngstenrecht,* and it is often found in African societies, particularly when the fission of joint households occurs during the lifetime of the father, leaving the youngest in possession at his death. Vinogradoff points out that this type of inheritance is also associated with fixed holdings, especially among small European peasants "exploited by lords." When only one of the sons could inherit, the strongest of the non-inheriting sons was sent out "into his own independent walk of life, either as a settler under new conditions on reclaimed land, or as an occupier of a deserted holding, or as a sergeant or bailiff, later as a labourer seeking wages" ([1920] I, 286), while the youngest, the *astrier* who remained behind by the hearth or *astre,* took over the family holding.[20] The hypotheses are not inconsistent, for there is a common element behind shifting agriculture and impartible medieval holdings, namely the existence of alternative land or jobs for the non-heirs. Indeed, unless such alternatives are present, complete primogeniture or complete ultimogeniture are hardly viable systems.

In other systems of unigeniture, the heir was not particularized to the same extent, but was selected either by the holder or by the siblings themselves. Such was the case in eastern parts of Norway,[21] where the

---

vision for the children was concerned, was that the family estate remained intact in the hands of the eldest son, and the younger children were provided for by burdening the estate" (Habakkuk [1950], p. 15).

[20] Maine's explanation is similar, but characteristically places greater emphasis on parallels with Roman institutions. "The home-staying, unemancipated son, still retained under Patria Potestas, is preferred to the others" ([1875] p. 223).

[21] In western Norway, a family holding was partible, though often held in common by a group of heirs.

peasants set great store on holding the ancestral property together and felt that the *gaard* or farm ought not to be parceled into smaller holdings. In the case of several heirs with an equal claim on the property, they generally agreed among themselves who was to remain in charge; the rest were given money or helped to start a new farm. But the payment of such a sum did not deprive those who left the homestead of all interest in the property; this remained the "family farm," and if the heir wished to dispose of it, he could not simply go into the market and look for the highest bidder. Under the system of *Odal* inheritance, he had first to offer the estate for sale to his own relatives, who could buy it at four-fifths of the market price.

Systems of inheritance of this kind, which confine the inheritance of the impartible estate to only one member of the sibling group, are associated with the stem-family (*Stammfamilie*), called by Le Play *la famille-souche.*[22] This type of domestic organization has been characterized by Arensberg in the following words:

> Through matchmaking and other mechanisms such restriction of inheritance to a single heir in each generation often became standard, acceptable, even ideal. The household and lands remained a stem or source of new heirs and new emigrants in each successive generation; a long line of holders kept the homestead in the line or stem; it even, usually, carried the name of the farm as a family name. Each generation knew a three-generation household of retired parents, heir and his spouse (either a son or a daughter might get the land as heir of the intact holding and Norman-French primogeniture and estate entail was merely one version of such custom). Each generation knew new waves of brothers and sisters, noninheriting children who must go out into the world to "make their fortunes" elsewhere, on new farms, in marriages outside, in the apprenticeships leading to artisan or other work in the cities. ([1960] p. 67.)

Partible systems, like impartible ones, also vary in respect of the equality or otherwise of the shares allocated to the junior generation. First, there is the question of whether or not women are included in the division of property, and if included, whether their shares are equal to those of their brothers. In Moslem codes, for example, women are given half a man's share. As I have mentioned earlier, the solution adopted

22 "Cette organisation associe aux parents un seul enfant marié. Elle établit tous les autres avec une dot, dans un état d'indépendance que leur refuse la famille patriarcale" ([1874] I, 367). The author favorably contrasts this type of family with the joint-family (*la famille patriarcale*) on the one hand, and *la famille instable* of industrial societies on the other.

here is bound up with the nature of the productive resources, with the system of local groupings, and with the types of marriage permitted.

Second, there is the question of whether or not the brothers have equal shares, and here there are a number of similarities with impartible systems. Under the Kentish custom of gavelkind, the holder's property was divided equally among the heirs at his death. But in systems of equal partition, the timing may vary considerably. Among the LoDagaba, the actual division of land often takes place before the father's death, so that the sons are able to establish their own fund of movable property that will be safe from the father's matrilineal heir. Among the LoWiili, on the other hand, the brothers often continue to farm together after their father's death. The only difference between such a household and a Joint Undivided Family in Maine's sense is that among the LoWiili each man has the right to leave when he wishes, taking with him his share of the joint estate.

Indeed, in discussing the Kentish institution of gavelkind, Jolliffe suggests that it was a modification of an earlier system of joint holdings, a hamlet community of co-heirs that was held together by the exigencies of working the land with the "great plough" and its team of eight oxen ([1933] pp. 19 *et seq.*). For instead of the compact villages and open fields of the champion region, Kent was a country of enclosed "woodland" agriculture, similar to the parts of England and Wales that remained Celtic; it was farmed by hamlet communities, with "each group of cultivators converging upon its single field of arable, and farming it with its own resources of wood and pasture" (*ibid.*, p. 17). Whereas the champion country was marked by systems of unigeniture, the woodland country was characterized by gavelkind, by equal division deriving from equal rights.[23]

When the property is not divided equally between the male siblings, then partible inheritance bears some resemblance to the systems of unigeniture present in medieval England. However, these more widespread customs associated with partition are inevitably preferential rather than complete forms of the institution, for the total exclusion of males from certain rights to the basic resources of the domestic group is compara-

---

[23] Although in England there was a close correlation between champion agriculture, unigeniture, and the stem-family on the one hand, and woodland agriculture, equal rights, and the joint-family on the other, Homans points out that the same is not true of other parts of Europe. In Russia, agriculture of the open-field type was associated with joint-families, among whom the available land was periodically redistributed (Homans [1941], pp. 119, 206–7). This situation serves as a reminder that productive systems and modes of inheritance, although obviously interconnected at many points, must be given a certain independence as variables.

tively rare. Preferential treatment for the eldest son requires little explanation, since it is he who so frequently takes on some of the responsibilities of the dead father. As regards the other main form of partition, preferential ultimogeniture, we have already noted, with reference to the MBugwe of Tanganyika, how this is closely connected with providing for parents in their old age; the last son, who remains in the house, gets preferential treatment at the death of the aged father whom he has had to look after. An additional point of interest in this connection is that the MBugwe place great emphasis on raising cattle, a form of property that is easily divided, often during the lifetime of the parents; similarly, among pastoral peoples that divide up the herds during the lifetime of the parents, it is also usually the youngest son who remains at home.[24]

TABLE 11.—PRIMOGENITURE AND ULTIMOGENITURE

	Complete	Preferential
Primogeniture (Senior right or Borough French)	Exclusion of younger siblings from inheritance	Custody of father's rights on behalf of sibling group
Ultimogeniture (Junior right or Borough English)	Exclusion of elder siblings from inheritance	Transfer of residuum of father's rights after other members of sibling group have received a share during his lifetime

These two forms of preferential unigeniture are not necessarily exclusive, and in some societies both the eldest and the youngest sibling are favored in different ways. Among the LoWiili, the sons nearly always farm with their father until his death, when it is the eldest who steps into his shoes; although in economic matters he takes over only for such time as the sibling group continue to work as a productive unit, and not after they have split up. As I have noted, *post mortem* transmission of this kind may increase intergenerational tension, but it solves an important problem of old age; the fathers cling to their property until they die and hence are automatically provided for by the heirs, who are working with them. A LoDagaba father, on the other hand, encourages his sons to farm on their own, so that when he dies there will be less

---

[24] The association of preferential ultimogeniture and *pre mortem* inheritance in pastoral societies was noted in the eighteenth century by the Oxford jurist Sir William Blackstone, when he dismissed as apocryphal the idea that the last son was favored on account of the shadow of illegitimacy that the supposed existence of the "droit du Seigneur" threw upon the eldest (Maine [1875], p. 222).

common property for the matrilineal heir to take out of the compound. In effect, the father does what we have seen happen in some matrilineal societies; he divests himself of some of his wealth during his lifetime by alienation to his sons. But when the father permits his sons to make separate farms, he retains the youngest to work with him. Here again residual ultimogeniture is a type of provision for old age. The special obligations of the youngest son to his parent are buttressed by additional rewards out of the inheritance, and there is a recognized advantage to be derived from continuing to farm with the father.

Ultimogeniture performs a similar function among the Kachins. According to Frazer, it is because he acts as "the natural support and guardian of his parents in their old age" ([1918] I, 481) that the youngest son in that society inherits the dwelling and consequently the custodianship of the shrine of the household ancestors. Chiefship, among the Kachins, is transmitted in a similar way, but since office is generally indivisible, it is subjected to complete rather than to preferential ultimogeniture.

The systems of transmitting rights, particularly the inclusive process of devolution, are related to the general mode of livelihood, as well as to the particular manner of exploiting the basic resources. But the relationship is a complex one, and as the LoDagaa case makes clear, the systems of transmitting relatively exclusive rights may vary although the economy itself remains constant. This set of variables has received relatively little emphasis from comparative sociologists since the work of the great figures in comparative jurisprudence, Sir Henry Maine, Sir Paul Vinogradoff, and others in that tradition. I have therefore tried in these last three chapters to elucidate the major types of transmission, drawing attention to the fact that each of these ways of organizing the intergenerational transmission of relatively exclusive rights throws the main weight of the holder-heir situation upon a different relationship, thereby setting up different tensions in the social system.

In the light of this generalized discussion, we can now turn to a detailed treatment of inheritance and succession among the LoDagaa. I have mentioned earlier that there is reason to believe that in both communities people who have moved into the area, or who live adjacent to groups with different systems, have changed their customary methods of inheritance. The analysis of the factors behind such changes is a problem of considerable interest; but here I am primarily concerned with other aspects, the social consequences of adopting one system as against another, since it is these that bear upon the examination of the differences in funeral customs and ancestor worship in the two communities.

CHAPTER XVI

Succession and Inheritance Among the LoDagaa

> Society not only continues to exist by transmission, by communi-
> cation, but may be fairly said to exist in transmission, in com-
> munication.
>
> JOHN DEWEY

Among the LoDagaa, transmission of relatively exclusive rights, whether in social position, sexual objects, or material goods, usually occurs only at the death of the holder. There are two exceptions: first, when the property is handed down to the sons for bridewealth payments and, second, when a father expels his son from the farming group while he is still alive. Otherwise old men hold onto their rights in office, women, and property until the day they die, and in so doing they are firmly supported by the cult of the ancestors, even in the eyes of the coming generation.

The process of transmission, which begins at death, is a gradual one, for the dead man retains many of his rights until the final ceremony has been performed. As a ghost (*nyāākpiin*), he continues to hold some of the exclusive rights he held in life; it is only when he becomes an ancestor spirit (*kpiin*) and takes up permanent residence in the Land of the Dead that these rights can be taken over by the heir. Even then the dead man retains certain of his former interests, and he is still the social father of any children born to his widows who have been taken in leviratic marriage. In a yet wider sense, the process of transmission is never complete, since the dead ancestors continue to belong to the same corporation as their living descendants; indeed they are its most important members. "All guinea-corn belongs to the ancestors," one is told. So, too, do cattle. And the whole system of sacrifice to one's fore-bears is linked, by the LoDagaa themselves, to the perpetual nature of claims upon property.

In this chapter, I shall examine the ways in which the three main categories of rights—rights to social position, to sexual objects, and to material goods—are transmitted in the two communities. When a society is described as having an inheritance system of a certain type (e.g., agnatic), it is the transmission of the rights of the male members that is usually meant, and it is this that I shall first consider.

SOCIAL POSITIONS

Offices

Under the heading of social positions, I wish to discuss not only what are usually called offices, but other roles as well. For offices, superordinate roles of a restricted kind, cannot be rigidly separated from other social positions; among the LoDagaa, there is a continuum between the role of father in the domestic group and that of elder (*nikpēē*) of the lineage, from the actors' as well as from the analytic point of view. While each man in his day can become a father and each an elder, not all become head of the whole lineage. The role thus begins to take on some of the characteristics of an office.

However, if the term is used in a stricter sense, it can be said that the only distinct office among the LoDagaa, before the coming of the British administration, was that of Earth priest or custodian of the Earth shrine, known to French writers as the Master of the Earth. There were, in addition, other specialized positions, more vaguely defined than this. The Master of the Wilds or Bush (*wiosob*) still exercises some ritual jurisdiction over collective hunts, but there is no formal induction as in the case of the Earth priest. The role of Master of the Wilds, which has a very limited importance, appears to be handed down, together with the shrine to the Wilds, to the next head of the compound in which the shrine is kept. Some other named positions reflect a person's competence in a specialized activity; a good shot with the bow is known as Master of the Bowstring (*tamyuur na*), such a man formerly playing a leading part in war. Some of these roles are limited in number; for example, when the Bagre ceremonies are held in Birifu, each patriclan sector in the parish provides one senior representative to act as officiant. Other occupational roles such as that of diviner are restricted only by the fluctuating demands of the inhabitants. Although there is some tendency for such activities to be taken up by junior members of the same household, there is no prescribed system of transmission.

Custodian of the Earth shrine. The office of custodian of the Earth shrine tends to be vested in both the patriclan and the matriclan of the putative founder of the settlement. In other words, the holder of a position should belong to the same matrilineal and patrilineal groups as the previous incumbent, another instance of the duplicating kinship so common among the LoDagaa.

In Tom the successor should be a member of the Nambegle patriclan and of the Some matriclan, and in Birifu of the Yongyuole patriclan and the SomDa matriclan. However, in Birifu the office has for many years passed between patriclans, although always within the SomDa matriclan. First of all, a member of the Baaperi patriclan took office as a sister's son of the previous holder. More recently, the late chief of Birifu, a member of the Naayiili patriclan, became the custodian. He had claimed a distant "sister's son" link with earlier officeholders, although this was never spelled out to me and was described only in terms of ties of matriclanship.[1]

In the case of the late chief of Birifu, the channel of matriclan relationships appears to have been used as a means by which the most powerful patriclan, in terms of the new secular office of chief, also drew to itself the most important ritual office. Formerly this acephalous system worked on a balance of power, a segmentary opposition among the constituent segments of the community, and any superior status that the descendants of the first arrivals in the parish may have had lay only in their custodianship of the Earth shrine. The introduction of chiefs by the Colonial administration has tended to alter this rough balance of relatively equal parts, and in many communities in the area the office of Master of the Earth has either diminished in importance, or has been taken over by the chief's patrilineage. These developments repeat the history of many centralized states in this region; in parts of Ashanti the office of chief and Earth priest appear to have been combined in one, whereas in conquest states like Gonja and Dagomba the office was retained by the autochthonous peoples, but given much less significance (Rattray [1932], pp. xiv *et seq.*).

The death of the custodian is marked by funeral rituals of a special kind, and a new incumbent should not be installed for a considerable time. During the intervening period, which may last some three years, performances at the shrine are carried out either by one of the elders who stands in the correct relation as regards clanship, or else by the assistant who wields the sacrificial knife. Neither Birifu nor Tom had a custodian proper during my stay; both communities were engaged in the long search for a new priest that ends only after many consultations with diviners. For few men are anxious to accept the responsibility of maintaining the well-being of the parish that this office entails; a

[1] For a fuller treatment of these points, see Goody [1956a], pp. 96–98.

mistake in the ritual procedure may mean death. Indeed, the installation ceremony is marked by a vivid display of institutionalized reluctance on the part of the new priest at having this position thrust upon him.

Chiefs and headmen. Today, in addition to the Earth priest, most parishes have a "chief" and one or more "headmen," paid from local government sources. Their authority varies greatly in different villages. Gandaa, the late Chief of Birifu, had been a strong ruler; but the larger part of my stay there took place during the interregnum that followed his death, when there was little or no centralized authority. His successor, one of his educated sons, has filled the position in much the same way as his father did. In Tom the chief carried little or no weight, and the headman of the southern part of the settlement who came from the patrilineage of the custodians of the Earth was in fact a figure of greater importance than his official senior.

Rules of succession to the new chiefship have a measure of flexibility. Since they are required to participate in meetings at the administrative headquarters, which lie at some distance from their own villages, chiefs who suffer from any infirmity are under strong pressure to give up their offices. In the early days, government officers asked each chief to name his successor, and the nominees were duly written down in the District Record Book. In most instances, chiefs appear to have nominated their sons. However, the person named in this way did not necessarily succeed. The father might be dismissed for some misunderstanding or misdemeanor, or the inhabitants might refuse to accept the successor. In the latter case, the elders of the settlement would usually be asked to select another chief; for the administration was concerned to have persons who would be "followed." Indeed, during the 1930's the administration sometimes tried to achieve this end by running elections, the inhabitants being asked to drop a stone in the box of the candidates whom they favored. However, the principle of father-son succession to these offices had been generally accepted by that date, and the people usually seem to have chosen on this basis.

Roles

The social positions considered here involve a somewhat different set of rights than are elsewhere discussed in this chapter in that only to a limited extent are they exclusive in kind. Since I have briefly discussed the transmission of other roles already, I shall concentrate mainly on kinship roles.

There is a great variation in the extent to which different societies perpetuate particular kinship roles by systems of prescribed transmission. In most instances roles of this kind are filled in the normal course of the domestic and reproductive cycles—a man becomes a "father" when his wife bears him a child—but in addition all systems provide for the transfer of some relational roles at death, even if only to allocate proxy or foster parents to orphaned children. The most complex form of this institution is found in the so-called "positional succession" of East and Central Africa. It is reported, for example, of the MBugwe of Tanganyika that "when a person dies a member of the same lineage is designated to take his place in the kinship structure. The substitute assumes most of the kinship relations of the dead person and also, in the case of a married person, his affinal relations" (Gray [1953], p. 233). A more limited form of the same mechanism is found in the institutions of the levirate and sororate, which will be treated in the following section. The MBugwe (and other East African peoples) are exceptional in that they not only replace parents, husbands, and wives, but also transmit the role of child.

The LoDagaa transmit the father's role in accordance with their system of double clanship, and I have already discussed this in some detail, pointing to the differences that appear when the matrilineal descent group is fully corporate. The role of mother, however, is not formally transferred to another person in the same way. When the mother of an unweaned child dies, the infant is taken to be cared for by the maternal grandmother until considered strong enough to return to the father's house. No question arises if the children have already been weaned; they remain in the house and are looked after by a co-wife, a classificatory "mother."

Although the role of a dead child is not transferred to another living member of the community, the next full sibling to be born is regarded in a certain sense as taking the place of the one who has died. A male child who dies and later returns to his mother's womb to be born again is called *Der*, with the name of his father preceding it. All in all, these forms of positional inheritance of kinship roles are very limited in scope when compared to the institutions of some central Bantu peoples.

The headship of the compound falls to the next senior male inhabitant, seniority here being defined first by generation and then by birth order, except in the case of paternal siblings; as I have explained, the senior member of the sibling group is the eldest child of the senior wife. The same system of reckoning applies within the patrilineage. However, the position of lineage head is not defined in any very formal way; the eldest member will be called on by other members of the group to take part in various activities, and if he is infirm, they will automatically go to the next senior.

There is no distinct head of a clan sector. By definition this unit lacks a genealogy, so that when it is necessary to calculate seniority, this is done by birth order. Among the LoWiili, the opinion of the eldest of the heads of the constituent lineages may carry more weight than the voice of the others, but only in an informal way. Among the LoDagaba, the lineages are numerically smaller and do not constitute organized segments of the clan sector in the same way; here it is even less appropriate to speak of the head of a local clan sector, and headship at the lineage level is also more vaguely defined than among the LoWiili. One reason for this indefiniteness is the greater emphasis on duplicate kinship and the less extensive development of specific genealogical ties. When the classificatory boundaries of kinship terms are provided by both patrilineal and matrilineal descent groups, it can be seen that in many cases a person whom one calls a "father," because he is a member of the senior generation of one's lineage, will also be a "brother" or a "mother's brother" if he is a member of one's own matriclan. Within the elementary family such relationships are automatically kept in line by the rules of exogamy. However, beyond the families of orientation and of procreation, the complexities of the system encourage fluctuating authority relationships, so that persons who occupy a leading position in one set of circumstances may well be of less importance in another.

WOMEN

Among the LoWiili, rights over the widow are inherited within the deceased's patrilineage. Only members of the same or alternate generations can marry her without repayment of bridewealth, and a further restriction prevents elder "brothers" from marrying the widows of junior siblings.

Earlier we saw how a widow is tested for complicity in her husband's death; if she comes through this ordeal successfully, a representative of the lineage accepts the twenty cowries that she offers. By this gesture, the lineage acknowledges its responsibility for the future maintenance of the woman. But she has not yet been inherited as a sexual partner; this only happens when she herself accepts a hundred cowries (*poo kuor koba*) from a lineage member in proper standing, a gift that she has the right to refuse. Even after she has taken this sum, her offspring are still considered to be the social children of the dead man. However, the new husband of the inherited spouse retains any bridewealth that may be received from the marriage of the female children he begets, a right that carries with it the concomitant duty of providing the bridewealth for any male child. In addition, if a man should die without a son and subsequently have a child begotten to his name by the levir, then it is the levir who must supply the boy with the grain and livestock necessary to prepare an ancestor shrine for his *pater*; for *genitor* and offspring farm together and constitute a single productive unit.

If a LoWiili widow marries anyone other than a member of the dead man's patrilineage, then this group are entitled to demand the return of the whole of the bridewealth so far paid. If this is not forthcoming, as sometimes happens, particularly when the new husband is a sister's son, then any children born of this union belong to the dead man.

Among the LoDagaba, the inheritance of widows differs in a number of ways. First, a man can marry the widow of his senior as well as his junior brother. Second, the patrilineal descent group within which widows are inherited is the clan sector rather than the lineage, a transposition found in many other social situations. Third, restrictions upon inheritance within the patriclan apply not only to adjacent generations, but also to anyone who is not a member of the same matriclan as the dead man. In other words, the levir is defined by duplicating kinship.

There are two further restrictions. If a man has slept with his brother's wife, he would put himself in danger of mystical retribution were he to marry his widow or inherit his property; for his action may have been the cause of the death. He has broken the basic norm of clanship. Nor can a man inherit his brother's widow or goods if he eats the produce of the dead man's fields that is thrown over the corpse and over the ancestor shrines. For these crops have become contaminated with the dead man's body dirt, and to eat them is to eat one's brother; only joking partners and others who do not stand in such a close relationship to the deceased can take the growing things thrown during his funeral ceremonies.

From members of the patriclan or the matriclan of the deceased who are not duplicate kinsmen and who wish to marry his widow, the first bridewealth payment is always demanded, even from the heir to the dead man's movable property. In order to establish himself as jural father of the children, a sister's son has to pay the first bridewealth payment to the patriclan sector of the deceased when he marries his widow, although he is excused the second payment of cattle. This first payment, which consists of cowries, is taken by members of the same matriclan and patriclan as the dead man, his duplicate "brothers," who also call in the sister's son as the heir to the movable property. They show him the bridewealth that he has paid, and then divide it up among those present, saying, "This belongs to all of us matriclan members" (e.g., *Some zaa dibno*; *dib* is from the root *di,* eat).[2]

A further complication appears to have existed among the LoDagaba in the past, owing to the system of reciprocal matrilineal groups. But since this is a matter that also concerns movable property, I shall discuss it in a later section. However, I should make it clear at this point that even if one matriclan (e.g., KpoDa) formerly inherited from its reciprocal group (SomDa), apparently, in the case of the widows, the heir had to be a member of the same patriclan as the deceased. In short, among the LoDagaba, leviratic rights are vested in agnates of the deceased who also belong to the same matriclan (or possibly in the past the reciprocal matriclan); that is, they are defined by duplicate clanship. Among the LoWiili, they are transmitted between agnates, but only between those of the same or alternate generations.

PROPERTY

The Means of Production: Land, Tools, and Labor[3]

The land tenure system of the LoDagaa can be visualized as consisting of three levels of rights and duties. The duty of ritual supervision in relation to the Earth cult is vested in the custodian of the Earth shrine as representative both of the patriclan and matriclan of the first settler and of the inhabitants of the parish as a whole. Rights in unused land belonging to the members and duties of ritual supervision in relation to the ancestor cult are vested jointly in the lineage, with the elder sometimes acting as the representative of the other members.[4] Rights of tillage and duties of ritual supervision in relation to

---

[2] In some cases the sister's son is only asked to pay the relatively small amounts required to make a sacrifice of a fowl to the dead man's ancestors and other payments of a ritual kind. But the offering of these "bitter cowries" is essential if the sister's son is to be recognized as the father of the widow's offspring (see Goody [1956a], p. 49).

[3] In the sense in which I am using the term, rights to labor are not strictly property rights and should therefore have been discussed in an earlier section; however, the particular forms of work I am dealing with here are bride services, which are difficult to separate from other marriage prestations on the one hand, and the whole productive process on the other.

[4] In my earlier monograph on the LoWiili [1956a], I wrote of the rights of bestowal held by the lineage elder in a representative capacity. Among the LoWiili, where land is not plentiful, this statement applies to land that has been abandoned by a lineage member, and in such cases the elder acts as administrator in consultation with the interested parties. I know of no similar cases among the LoDagaba of Tom, since land is easily available; areas of bush are spoken of as belonging to a particular patriclan, and the members of the local sector are mostly free to farm where they will, although they usually mention what they intend to do beforehand.

farm shrines are vested in the senior member of a farming group on behalf of the other persons belonging to the productive unit.

The first two levels of rights and duties are transmitted along with the social positions to which they are attached, and this I have discussed in an earlier section. I am here concerned with the transmission of tillage rights, which depends upon two variables—the type of land and the relationship within the farming group. As far as the land itself is concerned, rights are differently distributed depending upon whether or not it is permanently farmed. Bush land is usually cultivated for four years and then left alone; land in swamps and in the immediate vicinity of compounds is planted every year. Inheritance of land under swidden cultivation is not of great significance, since within a short time particular plots revert to bush once again. More important is the fact that a man is entitled by birth to farm any uncultivated land owned by the patrilineage (or clan sector among the LoDagaba), a right that has the effect of adjusting holdings, within limits, to the size of the component households and is thus similar in function to the annual redistribution of land that occurs in some more intensive systems of agriculture.

The inheritance of specific farming rights has much greater significance in respect of land that is permanently cultivated, and there is some difference here between the two communities. Compared to the LoDagaba of Tom, the LoWiili of Birifu have little bush nearby, but have more land under continuous cultivation, in swamps, on river banks, and around the compounds. Land under continuous cultivation is inevitably subject to a more precise system of transmission, the general principle behind which is equal division between the surviving sons, although this is modified in some situations. But the rich land immediately around the compound or on the site of a ruined house is divided on a different basis from the remainder, by a method Gluckman discusses under the heading of the "house-property complex" ([1950] pp. 193 *et seq.*). Equal shares are allocated to each group of full siblings, so that inheritance is *per stirpes* rather than *per capita*, the stocks in question being the maternal cells of a polygynous household.

Gluckman has called attention to the widespread distribution of the house-property complex in Africa, which he sees as associated with patrilineal descent groups that have father-son inheritance. He suggests that the absence of this institution in certain West African societies, namely Tallensi, Ibo, and Dahomey, is connected with the presence of lateral transmission; when the property first passes to brothers, the estate can "not be divided into sections passing directly to groups of sons demarcated by their mothers" (*ibid.*, p. 199). Among the LoDagaa, both institutions are found together. Brothers inherit specific rights to land from one another, but only if they are farming together. On the other hand, "house-property" inheritance also occurs, but only in relation to the small area around the homestead. The inhabitants themselves connect the operation of this system with the fact that portions of this land are allocated to each wife, so that she can plant vegetables among the growing crops sown by her husband. Although a son does not necessarily inherit the exact patch that his mother cultivated, his rights of tillage in the vicinity of the house are seen as deriving from the privileges allotted to her.

The second main variable determining the transmission of land is the structure of the productive group. Among the LoDagaba, a man will send out his senior sons to farm on their own, so that they may build up a fund that his heir cannot touch when he dies (Goody [1958]). When a person does this, he is said to cut (*ngman*) land for his sons, since only brothers can divide (*puon*); it is only after the holder is dead that the farm can be finally split. However, a man may become the proxy-parent of the young children of a dead brother who had been farming on his own; but although he will take over his brother's land, the children will lay claim to it when they become adults.

The land a man holds is not divided immediately after he dies. Indeed, among the LoDagaba, the division cannot take place until the heir, if he comes from outside the patriclan sector, is called to collect the wealth to which he is entitled. Until he does so, the produce that is grown there belongs to the heir rather than the sons, although in practice few would attempt to assert such a claim, and fewer still succeed in enforcing it.

For some years after the father's death, then, brothers often continue to farm together. Indeed, unless a man has children old enough to help him in the heavy tasks that farming involves, he will rarely attempt to set himself up on his own. And therefore when any split occurs, either by "cutting" before the father dies or by "dividing" afterwards it usually does so between groups of full brothers; for only in this way can they establish an effective unit of production.

In theory, land cannot be permanently alienated from the corporate group. But it is possible for a man to obtain permission to farm a piece of land by asking (*zele*) the holder, who retains the critical right to gather nuts from the shea trees growing there. The farming rights granted in this way may be deliberately restricted by a specified time limit. On the other hand, the grantor, after discussing the question with other members of his lineage, may declare, "I cut and give you" (*n ngman ko*), in which case no such restriction is implied. Land is sometimes granted in this way to a sister's son, particularly to a man who has lived with his mother's patrikinsfolk since childhood, and it would be unthinkable for these rights to be withdrawn. In fact, such land gradually becomes included in the patrimony of the grantee, so that although rights in land, apart from a temporary usufruct, cannot be alienated, time slowly brings about a *de facto* change in the situation.

There are two other matters of inheritance that are closely linked to the basic productive resources and their exploitation, namely, tools and labor services.

The most important of the tools, the *instrumenti fundi*, is the hoe used in farming; together with other iron implements, it is handed over to the eldest son during the final ceremony in public recognition of his new status of being without a father. As with land, the transmission of rights in these tools is similar in both communities.

Labor services among the LoDagaa are of three kinds: those owed to the farming group (i.e., one's own unit of production), those owed to in-laws, and, among the LoDagaba, those owed to the mother's brother.

Only the second category is subject to inheritance. A man has to take parties of his friends and kinsmen to farm for his father-in-law during the first few years of his marriage; he is also required to bring people to repair the roof of his mother-in-law's room. If the bride's father dies, these services are inherited "within the house," and the son-in-law farms for a "brother" of the deceased. Among the LoWiili the "brother" is defined by agnatic kinship alone. Among the LoDagaba he is a duplicate kinsman of the dead man, a brother both in patrilineal and in matrilineal terms. This is the same person or category of persons that inherits the widows, the house timbers, and the bitter quiver. But he takes over these rights on the understanding that he will look after the house and care for the children, and most of the in-law farming is allocated to the children remaining in the dead man's house.

The economic significance of these services can be considerable. One homestead in Tom, inhabited by a widow and her young children, largely depended upon such help to cultivate their fields. This case was exceptional, but many men who have little permanent assistance on their farms receive important aid from the labor brought in by the marriage of their daughters.

Dwellings

In African double descent systems, land for house sites, and in most cases for farming, is inherited agnatically, and so, therefore, are the compounds. Both the LoWiili and the LoDagaba are similar in this respect; houses are inherited by the next senior member of the dwelling group, in the sense that he takes over the religious duties associated with the headship of a compound, and in particular the custodianship of the ancestor shrines kept in the byre.

Within the compound, each married man has his own quarters, and the material out of which these are constructed belongs to him. If he decides to build on his own, he will break down his rooms, so that he can use the heavy posts and beams to construct his new house; for suitable wood is scarce and the preparation hard. The value placed upon these timbers, which are also inherited agnatically, is one of the factors making for a very close relationship between the physical layout of a compound and the composition of the household that occupies it.

Personal Effects

Before dealing with the main body of objects of production, I want to refer briefly to a category of goods that the LoDagaa set aside for special treatment, the personal effects of the dead man.

These objects are the "bitter quiver," also known as the "ancestor's quiver" (*kpiin lo'*), and some items of the deceased's apparel. The clothes are thought to be impregnated with his body dirt and are therefore dangerous to close kin; so they are allocated to the reciprocal funeral group. The LoWiili reject these goods even more firmly, and the funeral group hangs the dead man's smock, hat, and other personal items on the wall of the byre, where they will eventually fall to pieces under the force of the heavy storms of the rainy season.

The bitter quiver is a man's emblem, the epitome of his role in the sexual division of labor. First of all, it is taken by a member of the reciprocal funeral group, who hides it away during the intervals between the ritual sequences. At the ceremonies in the dead man's room, this group returns the quiver, filled with the iron tools that are to be handed over to the sons as well as with the "evil arrows" (*pīī faa*), those that have been rendered especially dangerous by contact with human blood. The removal of the arrows by the various joking partners is said to "cool" the harmful objects, so that they may be taken by the rightful heirs. Formerly, among the LoDagaba, the quiver and arrows were then taken by members of the reciprocal matrilineal group outside the dead man's patriclan (*mwo puo sãã*) and finally returned to one of their number within the patriclan (*yir puo sãã*, a duplicate father), who took it to "protect the house" (*gũ a yir*). Among the LoWiili, the matriclan of the dead man took the place of the reciprocal matrilineal group.

Nowadays, however, the quiver appears to be left in the dead man's room, hanging unused upon the wall.

The "bitter bow," the one that has killed a man, is not inherited in the same way; it is usually broken in half and the pieces aggregated to the homicide relics of the patriclan.

Besides these dangerous weapons, a man also has a "cool bow" or hunting bow (*tam 'baaro* or *wie tam*), a cool quiver, and cool arrows. The LoDagaba allocate these weapons to the heir, but he normally leaves them in the house for the sons. The effect of this practice is that in both communities the basic hunting equipment, like the tools required for farming, is transmitted to the sons and thus remains within the productive unit.

Among the LoDagaba, a gun is normally taken by the matrilineal heir, since it is presumed to have been acquired either through uterine inheritance or with money made out of farming. But a man may also accumulate money from the payments made to him by clients who visit a medicine shrine (*tiib*) installed at his house, or who want him to set up a similar altar in their own compounds. If a gun is purchased out of these funds, it remains in the house, like the shrines themselves and any other objects acquired with money that the shrines have earned. Indeed, all ritual objects remain within the house, and so, too, do the xylophones and the smithy, both of which have a quasi-ritual status by virtue of their associations with the Earth.

In addition to these personal items of the deceased, a token quantity of the movable property is also treated in a distinctive manner. At the time when the LoDagaba arrange for the division of the wealth, the joking partner is required to take out a small amount to make the remainder safe for the inheritor; here again there is a partial rejection of the objects of property. On this same occasion, some of the cowries are distributed among those of the matriclansfolk of the deceased who are present; this is not alienation, but rather an expression of the joint rights of the matriclan in each other's property.

The LoWiili also attempt to make the property safe for the heir. In one instance I knew of, the dead man's paternal brother took sufficient cowries out of his property to buy a fowl to kill to the newly made ancestor shrine. In many other cases, the first sacrifice to a dead man's stick is carried out for the selfsame reason.

Objects of Production

An examination of the system of inheriting movable property among the LoDagaa brings out two main kinds of differences, those between the communities themselves and those between the sexes. For although we have so far limited our discussion to rights held by males, there has in fact been little or nothing to add on the subject of rights held by women. When a woman dies, there is no transmission of rights in office, or women, or land; for what limited interests she does have in these derive from membership of her natal descent group, in which she ranks as a jural minor. A certain continuity is given to the peripheral role of lover and co-wife in the funeral speeches; a man who is well satisfied with the manner in which his bereaved son-in-law has conducted himself may suggest that he court another daughter to replace the wife he has lost; and although the role of daughter is perpetuated in the ceremony of the Testing of the Children, there is no formal handing over of the role of "mother."

But women sometimes hold considerable rights in movable property, rights that are the subject of intergenerational transmission. As I have remarked, these rights are transmitted between uterine kin. A woman's sex-linked property, her cooking utensils and clothing, are taken by her uterine sisters and her daughters. During the course of the burial service itself, some of the dead woman's pots and calabashes are brought out of her room, carried around the stand, and then broken into pieces in front of her; these utensils are known as the "outside things" (*yuon bume*), and a few of them, including the dish (*laa*) used in the cere-monies in the room, are saved and given to her full sister, together with the sum of twenty cowries. Her grinding stone (*nier*) and her other pots and pans are "room things" (*diu bume*) and normally go to her daugh-ters. But wealth—that is, any cowries and livestock she may have accu-mulated by trade or other means—is considered to be linked to the male sex and passes to her uterine brothers and her sons. These men, how-ever, may employ this property for the benefit of their sisters and may occasionally give some to the husband "on account of the hoe," that is, because he has farmed for the food she has eaten. This one-way cross-sexual transmission prevents any accumulation of inherited wealth in female hands. Over the generations capital can only be accumulated by males.

It is the inheritance of property between males that is the major difference between the two communities. We have already seen that among the LoWiili movable property is inherited among agnates, first by full brothers and next by the senior son of the dead man, that is, by the eldest son of his senior wife, although all the other sons are entitled to a share of their father's wealth.

Among the LoDagaba, the movable property consists of livestock, money, farm produce, and, formerly, male slaves; it often includes cloths, guns, and other manufactured goods, if these have been purchased with wealth obtained by inheritance or by farming. Such property is inherited according to uterine ties, and nowadays preference is usually given to close kin in the following order: full brother (*yeb*), maternal half brother (*yeb*), mother's sister's son (*yeb*), sister's son (*arbile*), and sister's daughter's son (*yong*).

Agnatic transmission is explicitly rejected. It is said that "a child cannot 'eat' (inherit) his father's things," and "a child 'eats' with his father during his lifetime but not after his death." This system is maintained not only by strong religious sanctions associated with ancestor and matriclan shrines, but, as we shall later see, by the principle of reciprocity as well.

In theory, the main inheritor is entitled to take all the movable property other than the "personal effects." Although this is his entitlement, in few cases would an outside heir actually remove all these objects from the dead man's compound, and the way he behaves in respect of the children distinguishes a good or generous man (*ni vla*) from a bad or ungenerous one (*ni faa*).

A generous man leaves everything in the house, taking with him only a handful of guinea-corn and other crops. The animals stay in the byre, and if the children want to buy anything, they ask the heir, and he points out one which they can sell. When they have sold the animal, they bring him the money, and he takes out a handful of cowries, saying, "Keep the rest for looking after the cows." In other words, he presents them with the equivalent of a Cow of the Byre (*zo naab*) for taking care of his property.

The stereotype of a hard man, on the other hand, is one who carries everything off to his own compound, even the contents of the granary. If there are small children left, the mother herself is forced to beg food for them from her own brother, an act that strengthens the ties between mother's brother and sister's son. There is no specific ritual sanction against taking all the property in this way, but a general feeling prevails that some harm is bound to come from ungenerous actions. "If you take the property away ('eat') too quickly, you'll meet an early death." (*Ka fu di fõ, fu na nyããna ti kpi.*) And apart from these supernatural dangers, diffuse moral sanctions also come into play; an inheritor who empties the granary and takes away all the livestock gets himself a very bad name. Indeed, in parts of the area, especially in the LoDagaba settlement of Kwõnyũkwõ, I have often been told that the heir has in fact no right to take away the fowls and the guinea-corn, and in practice these remain in the compound. For the grain is required for feeding the children, and the chickens for performing the sacrifices essential to their spiritual well-being.

The reasonable man acts in a manner that falls somewhere between these two extremes. But how a person will behave in these circumstances is thought to depend very much on how he himself was treated at the death of his own father. "If someone drags you over the sand," I was told, "you'll do the same" (*nisaal na vub biiri puo, fu minga vub biiri puo*); in other words, if you have been dragged over stony ground—that is, treated badly—in respect of your father's property, you will do the same when you come to inherit. The principle of reciprocity tends to perpetuate harsh or generous behavior, just as it perpetuates the system of inheritance itself. If a man's father's wealth has been inherited by someone other than a close agnate, he himself will insist upon his rights, even though, as is perhaps increasingly the case, he may express disapproval of the system of uterine inheritance. Marriage to the father's sister's daughter gives teeth to the business of literally "getting one's own back," since a man's son becomes the heir of his father's inheritor, and the operation of reciprocity, or its counterpart in negative acts, the *lex talionis*, is brought very near to home.

The least that a reasonable inheritor will leave in the byre is a cow, a sheep, and a goat. These animals are said to belong to the dead ancestor and may be killed to the shrine should any misfortune of a mystical kind be attributed to his spirit. But although it is the agnates of the dead man who have to perform the sacrifice to his ancestral shrine, the actual donor of the animals is the sister's son, a member of the same wealth-holding corporation as the deceased.

In fact a reasonable inheritor behaves in the same way as a reasonable father. While his father is alive, even if they are not farming together, the son has an obligation to show him the *kaper*, the surplus guinea-corn left in the granary, and by extension any crops that remain unconsumed at the end of the year. This he can do either with the produce itself or with the money he gets by selling it. In theory, all this belongs to the father, but the reasonable man will take out only a small quantity, the "father's leg," and leave the rest.

The heir will act in the same way; for he, too, is a classificatory "father" to the dead man's children, since he belongs to the same matriclan. He is a classificatory "brother" of the deceased as well as a sister's son. At the final ceremony he sits among the "fathers" when they are formally pointed out to the orphans. Later on he is called to see his heritage, which includes some of the dead man's responsibilities as well as his property. While the children ought to show him the surplus grain for three years (a term is placed upon their filial duties), the heir has the responsibility of finding them the money and cattle they need for their first marriages.

The same situation exists among the LoWiili, but in this context fatherhood, like inheritance, follows agnatic rather than uterine ties. Although property passes to full brothers and then to sons, there is an important sense in which the sons continue to enjoy their patrimony only by permission of the patrilineage "fathers." And these are the men whom they should consult when wanting to dispose of money and cattle, either by sacrifice or by marriage.

Although among the LoDagaba it is the matriclan that is visualized as the property-holding group, the effective range of inheritance today consists of persons tracing their descent in the female line to a common grandmother, a unit that has no individual name but is described by the technical term *ma per* (literally, the mother's stem).[5] Within what is in fact the matrilineage of greatest extent, the limit of uterine ties genealogically reckoned, property is first inherited laterally, that is, between "siblings," then lineally, but never in an upward direction. *Ma be dire bie,* a mother cannot inherit from ("eat") a child.

The members of this shallow matrilineage hold definite rights in each other's property even while the holders are alive. If a man can persuade his mother's brother to let him have some piece of property, it cannot be held a debt. Indeed, if he is hungry, he may even go to his uncle's granary and take some grain, an act forbidden to a son. Should the uncle remonstrate, the man can reply, "It's my mother's things I'm eating," a metaphor that stresses once again the fact that consumer goods are vested in the female line. Indeed, the word *di,* which I translate as both "eat" and "inherit," applies only to consumer goods or objects of production; one does not "eat" immovable property.

So, although there is always a main heir, other members of the matrilineage may effectively assert claims to parts of the property. Certainly if such a person has borrowed anything from the dead man, there is no question of repayment. The same is true, though to a lesser extent, of members of the more inclusive matriclan. Clansfolk have certain shadowy claims on the property administered by any one of them, which are in a sense a corollary of the duty of helping each other in times of

[5] As I have earlier pointed out, in other contexts *ma per* may refer to the group of full (and sometimes uterine) siblings; like the patrilineal equivalent *yir,* the order of segmentation of the group implied depends upon the particular situation to which the speaker refers.

difficulty. These matriclans are non-localized, having no segments with a territorial focus, so that their importance as social units relies heavily upon their property-holding character. The duty of providing hospitality for visiting clansmen, which is one of the main situations that bring into play the large dispersed clans found among the Akan- and the Mande-speaking peoples, can be seen as the limiting case of joint rights over property.

In the past, the LoDagaba say, joint rights were held by even larger groupings. I was repeatedly told that in the days of the grandfathers of living elders, a dead man's property was inherited by members of the reciprocal matrilineal group when there was no full brother or sister's son. Only in recent times, people say, have specific matrilineal ties been traced for inheritance purposes beyond this limited range. Previously it was KpoDa, for example, who constituted the residual heirs of a SomDa who had no close uterine kin. Even so, not any KpoDa could inherit, but only those who belonged to the same patriclan sector. In other words, except when the uterine half brother or the sister's son inherited, the property remained within the patriclan.

These reciprocal matriclans were said to "eat together" (*be longna di*), a phrase that is understood metaphorically to mean that they inherit each other's wealth. They do in fact share in the flesh of the Cow of the Rooftop together, and I have heard it said that in inheritance as with funeral meat Some and Da form a kind of dual division within which, but never between which, the transfer of wealth is possible.

Yet more common than the assertion that these groups acted as residual heirs is the statement that among the LoDagaba they tested the orphans, inherited the senior widow, and also took the "bitter bow," though this weapon was returned to a fellow matriclansman within the house. Indeed, the reciprocal matriclans still test the orphans, take the bow, and share the Cow of the Rooftop together. The exchange of this particular set of services seems explicable in terms of our earlier analysis. For it would appear that such persons inherited these rights and carried out these duties because they were thought to be dangerous if left to the more immediate kin. The reciprocal groups took over those roles of the deceased that would have been unsafe for the less distant "brothers," just as a linked patriclan sector performs other highly charged tasks for the dead man's kin during the course of the mortuary ceremonies. In the context of these dangerous activities, dangerous because the passage of property coincides with the death of the holder, outsiders take on the role of "father" to the children and "husband" to the widow.

What from the actor's standpoint is seen as the rejection of dangerous goods and services can also be regarded as the maintenance and creation of wider social relationships. One of the positive functions of uterine inheritance in double descent systems of this sort is that it counters the exclusive tendencies of the localized patrilineal groups. With a limited number of matrilineal descent groups, the cross-cutting bonds are given an extensive spread; this is yet further increased by combining these groups into reciprocal pairs and achieves its maximum possible expansion in the moiety organization, vague as this is.

Nowadays reciprocal groups of matriclans play little part in matters of inheritance, but people often relate themselves to one another on the basis of these matrilineal groupings. In some contexts the extent of the actual passage of property is less important than the presence of a concept of corporate ownership: the idea that an outside member of a reciprocal matriclan has the right to take away the bitter quiver, circulate it among other representatives, and eventually return it to one of his number in the dead man's patrilineage, so that he can "look after the house." Concrete transfers of property between reciprocal matriclansmen could never have played a very large part, since in the first place such people were only residual heirs, inheriting when there were no full brothers or sister's sons. And, furthermore, there existed a number of mechanisms by which property was diverted away from kin outside the patrilineal descent group.

These same considerations apply to the matriclans themselves, a fact that bears directly upon this problem of the actual, or hypothetical, narrowing of the range of uterine inheritance. For, on the one hand, the matriclans are regarded in speech as having joint rights in each other's property; "This woman is your wife," I was told when I was visiting a village for the first time and the inhabitants discovered I belonged to the Some clan. On the other hand, there are two facts that stand opposed to the conception of corporate ownership. First, property has in general to be administered by a single member or a relatively small group. Second, today at least, the transmission from holder to heir usually takes place within a fairly narrow radius. Implicit in the whole situation lies a potential conflict between the idea of joint ownership and the operation of a next-of-kin principle of selection, between the claims of a single individual and those of the corporate group as a whole.

This contradiction, particularly noticeable in uterine systems, leads to a certain degree of fluidity, even at the present day. It is not always the closest matriclansman who inherits, in the absence of a uterine brother or child of a uterine sister. Various sorts of pressures may disperse the wealth more widely, such as a pre-existing debt with a distant matriclansman that is canceled at death, the known poverty (or state of wifelessness) of a fellow clansman, and sometimes the tenuously based demands of the "white man's chiefs." Indeed, a similar ambiguity exists about the past, for I have occasionally heard it maintained that inheritance was formerly narrower than it is today. Such differing interpretations of the past depend to some extent upon the particular hopes and fears of the speaker; nevertheless, it is generally held that in earlier times a greater emphasis was placed upon distant rather than close uterine inheritance.

It is possible, then, that the idea held by most LoDagaba that the range of inheritance in the past was less circumscribed than it is today may reflect a basic contradiction in the working of large-scale corporate kin groups. This does not mean that such changes as the people describe may not have actually occurred in the recent past. If it is correct to regard wide-ranging corporate ties as an instrument of social control, and one that is of particular significance in acephalous societies, then the emergence of a centralized system of government could well lead to such ties being given less emphasis. The difficulty with this plausible hypothesis is that the inhabitants refer these changes to a period before, or perhaps coincident with, the effective establishment of the colonial regime in the area, a process that began about 1910.

Although such influences appear to have a similar effect on other uterine systems, I do not think these changes can be accounted for in terms of external pressures alone. There are other factors to consider. The opposing forces we have noted operating within the structure of corporate descent groups are capable of making a whole series of possible adjustments of limited stability, and between any of these possibilities the system may oscillate for mainly internal reasons. The present and past situations of the LoDagaba may thus represent two of a number of possible states of the system.

The emphasis on the corporate, as distinct from the next-of-kin, aspect of inheritance appears in other matrilineal systems. Of the Akan-speaking Akim of southern Ghana, M. J. Field writes that no one succeeds automatically as in Europe, but an heir is selected by the lineage elders at a post-funeral meeting held to settle the affairs of the dead man ([1948] pp. 113 *et seq.*). Among the neighboring Ashanti, property is commonly vested in a lineage segment known as the *yafunu*, from among whose members the heir is chosen (Fortes [1950], pp. 257–58, 271–72). A more striking case is that of the Plateau Tonga of Northern

Rhodesia, among whom it is considered inappropriate for the full
uterine brother

> to perform the purification of the widow or to succeed to his posi-
> tion. A sister's son or a sister's daughter's son (who ranks as brother)
> is a suitable choice, but the most desirable is a classificatory brother
> or a classificatory sister's son from another womb, for such a suc-
> cession strengthens the links between the different members of the
> group and hinders a splitting into independent segments based on
> womb membership. (Colson [1955], p. 38.)

The attribution of a cohesive force to the wide circulation of a man's
goods at his death is not simply the sociologist's invention; it is recognized by the Tonga themselves. For "if a womb is repeatedly forced to
provide its own successors, its members will feel that they have been
rejected by the rest of the matrilineal group" (*ibid.*, p. 38).

Colson also notes two other points concerning Tongan inheritance
that support the analysis I have offered here. First, she comments upon
the difficulties involved in making the dogma of undifferentiated obligation within the matriclan square with discrimination in favor of close
kin (*ibid.*, pp. 38–39). Second, she remarks upon the growing tendency
to reduce the range of possible heirs.

I have already remarked that changes of the kind reported by Colson
for the Tonga, and by the LoDagaba for their own society, could have
resulted from the take-over by a centralized government of the wider
problems of maintaining law and order. But there are also more immediate factors at work. Among the LoDagaba, the transfer of wealth
outside the living-together group to distant uterine kin is based upon
a recognition of reciprocity, so that what is lost in one transaction can
be regained at the next. Large inequalities of fortune render such a
mode of inheritance difficult to work, because they upset the operation
of equal exchange; and nowadays people are more likely to hold on
to wealth, since they can do more with it.

Moreover, not only are these systems of "distant" inheritance based
upon reciprocity, and hence threatened by big differences of wealth;
they also involve a certain "leveling" of existing inequalities within
the society. By this I mean that since the rights of distant kin are dependent upon the corporate character of the wider descent group, their
recognition may involve a plurality of heirs rather than a single
claimant. Of the Tonga we read that "All members are held to have
the right to receive a share of the estate when someone dies. If the estate
contains only a few cattle, one may be assigned to a representative of
each womb with the proviso that he must share the increase with other
members of the womb" (Colson [1955], p. 38). Leveling mechanisms of

this kind are widespread in non-industrial societies[6] and often constitute an important element in accusations of witchcraft and sorcery. They tend to inhibit the retention of resources in narrow family groups and are in many ways destructive of the sort of accumulation of property in individual hands upon which depends the development of privately owned ("capitalist") mercantile and industrial enterprises, together with associated phenomena such as wage labor. A partial exception here is to be found in certain types of peasant agriculture and family industry that can be operated as joint concerns. But, in general, contemporary economic changes lessen the importance of these types of leveling mechanisms (although there is often an increase in their importance at the governmental level), especially with regard to the corporate character of wide descent groups and the claims that members have one upon another.

Changes in range of uterine inheritance can then be seen partly as an effect of certain problems inhering in the organization of large-scale corporate descent groups and partly as an effect of political centralization and increased differences in wealth. But there is yet a further aspect to the whole problem of transmission among the LoDagaba, quite apart from the narrowing range of inheritance and corporate ties. For when there is no full brother, the LoDagaba make considerable efforts to prevent all the property from going to the nearest heir, the sister's son, and thus from leaving the compound. We have already seen that the widows, the house timbers, the bride services, and the bitter quiver are not taken by the nearest heir, the sister's son, but by a matriclan member from the deceased's own patriclan, a person who is in fact a more distant kinsman in uterine terms. Here the sister's son has nothing to say. With regard to the main body of movable property, he has; but even so there are a number of ways of seeing that part of it stays within the compound.

I have already discussed the function of gifts *inter vivos* between father and son as a method of keeping property within the compound. There are three other methods commonly employed: arranging for one's son to marry one's sister's daughter, incorporating the fatherless children of one's daughter, and, formerly, purchasing a slave.

When a man marries the daughter of his father's full sister, the off-

6 Such mechanisms might also have been called redistributive, but Neale has used this term to denote redistribution through a central agency without any implication of equality of treatment: "The produce of the group is brought together, either physically or by appropriation, and then parcelled out again among the members . . . there is no implication of equality of treatment, fair shares, or payment for value. The social pattern is characterized by centricity—peripheral points all connected with the central point" ([1957] p. 223).

spring of this union belongs both to the same patriclan and to the same matriclan as his grandfather; he is the sister's son of his grandfather's sister's son. If we refer to Figure 9, we see that when A dies, his son B cannot inherit his wealth, but his sister's son, D, can. On the other hand, if B marries his cross-cousin, E, then the offspring, C, would at least be entitled to divide the property with the sister's son. By this arrangement, "the house remains a house" (*a yir tshaan yiri*). When a man asks his sister to let her daughter come and marry his son, he says, "I want her to come and wash the sores on my back" (*N bobra ko wana pegh n zukur natir*). By these words he means that since his own daughters will all marry and leave the house just as his sister has done, there will be no one left to look after him in his old age unless the sister persuades her daughter to come and wed his son.

The situation among the LoDagaba emphasizes what some recent analyses of cross-cousin marriage have tended to overlook, namely, the varied functions of unions between close kin. A father encourages such a marriage—indeed, the return of the eldest daughter was one of the unstated implications of his sister's marriage; and he does so partly to strengthen kinship ties, partly for reasons of reciprocity (it is an obvious way of liquidating a bridewealth debt), and partly to prevent his wealth from leaving the compound.

The LoWiili, too, welcome such marriages. The return of a woman's first daughter to marry into her patrilineage is regarded as part of the original marriage transaction; a wife is thus provided for a member of her patriclan. But among the LoDagaba such unions have a further function in that they also supply the father-in-law with a possible heir. It is not surprising, therefore, to find that the LoDagaba place more stress upon this institution. In Birifu (LoWiili) it was several months

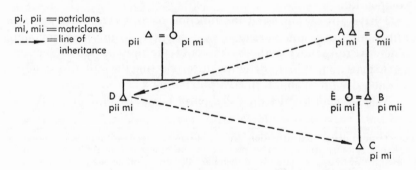

Fig. 9.—Father's sister's daughter marriage in a double descent system.

before I first heard patrilateral cross-cousin marriage expressed as an ideal union, whereas in Tom (LoDagaba) my attention was constantly being drawn to its advantages.

At the beginning of the century, a closely related method of keeping property within the compound was by the purchase of male slaves. A slave automatically belongs to the patriclan and matriclan of his master. He cannot, however, take over his property, for he belongs to a special subsection of the matriclan whose members are unable to inherit from persons in the other subsection. These subsections are usually indicated by the suffix *zie,* red, which is added to the clan name; the non-slave section is referred to as "black" (*sebla*). Slave and non-slave sections can intermarry. However, this fact is more or less irrelevant to the LoWiili, among whom the named matrilineal groups are not generally held to be exogamous, although in neither community do men marry close uterine kin. Like the matriclans themselves, the slave and non-slave divisions are recognized in both communities but play only a minor role among the LoWiili.

In his account of the neighboring peoples in the Ivory Coast, Labouret writes of the division into slave and non-slave groups as evidence of a dual organization unrelated to slavery itself ([1931] p. 244). Such was not the case among the LoDagaa,[7] where there was a definite association between these divisions and slavery proper. For example, when the Cow of the Rooftop is slaughtered during the LoDagaba burial rites, no member of a slave subsection can go up on the roof to share the meat, unless he is called to do so by one of the non-slave matriclansmen; instead, slaves are given the neck (*nyũũ*) as their portion. That they were not allowed to join in the division of the meat was associated with their inability to inherit, and this in turn was traced to their slave origin. In fact, members of such groups, other than those who have been purchased as slaves or are the children of female slaves, are ordinary citizens and inherit among themselves in the normal manner. Although these groups perpetuate slave origin in the uterine line, servile status itself ceases after the first generation; indeed, the offspring of male slaves are no longer slaves in any sense, for neither status nor origin is transmitted in the male line.

A slave was virtually bound to marry a daughter of his master's sister, and since he addressed his owner as "father," he in effect contracted a marriage with the "father's sister's daughter." In this case, too, such a

---

[7] I did find another dichotomy between Some and Da, who in certain contexts act as each other's slaves; but this is a division between, not within, matriclans (see p. 356).

union is said to strengthen ("build up") the house, because the wealth is then retained within the dwelling group. For the offspring of such a union would belong to the patriclan and matriclan of the man who purchased his father and could therefore be his father's master's inheritor. The male children begotten by a slave may inherit rights over their own father in this way, since slaves are acquired with wealth and subject to similar forms of inheritance. With regard to the property a slave acquires, this is taken by his son, but the bridewealth of a daughter begotten by a slave goes to her father's master, the man who paid the bridewealth for her mother.

Although male slaves continue to belong to the patriclan of their purchaser, they are equated with money and may be inherited by the sister's son. A female slave, on the other hand, is virtually equated with a wife and is inherited in the same way, i.e., by a duplicate clansman of her purchaser. Indeed, I was once told that female slaves are no different from any other women, for "don't you buy (*daa*) them all?" However, a female slave is in fact known as a slave; the children belong to the appropriate section of her purchaser's matriclan, and she herself suffers all the disabilities of being kinless. Although her offspring are not slaves in the full sense, they have no mother's house. I was present at the funeral ceremonies of one such man, Katu, the offspring of a female slave, and his property like his mother was taken by double clansfolk. The explicit reason behind this was that since he had no mother's house, he could not have inherited from his maternal uncle; hence his sister's son was given no say whatever in the distribution of the property. Another way of putting this is to say that since Katu's father owned his mother, his clansfolk owned the property of the offspring.

The fourth way of retaining wealth inside the compound is by "institutionalized illegitimacy." A fatherless child (*yirbie,* literally, a house child; LD *dondorle,* literally, a small door, i.e., a junior segment) belongs to the same patriclan and matriclan as his maternal uncle and may inherit from him. Among the LoDagaba, however, the practice is disapproved of by the LoPiel of Tom and approved of by the LoSaala and the LoPiel of Kwõnyũkwõ. The reason for the disapproval of some of these groups may rest on the fact that wealth is retained within the patrilineal corporation only by the retention of rights over women, by rejecting the exchange of rights between these corporations that marriage involves. But my material does not indicate any explanation for the differences.

With slight variations in form, each of these four methods is widely used among human societies. Of the frequency of gifts *inter vivos* as a method of alienation I have already written; its counterpart in societies with corporate patrilineal descent groups is the transfer of property from a mother's brother to a sister's son by "ritual stealing" and by other means such as the gift of a Cow of the Byre.

Kinship marriage is also often used as a way of retaining property within a particular kin group, either to a cross-cousin, especially the father's sister's daughter as among the LoDagaba, or else to a parallel cousin, especially the father's brother's daughter as in many Islamic communities. In societies with patrilineal descent groups, this type of parallel-cousin marriage is simply a form of endogamous union such as the daughters of Zelophehad were enjoined to practice when they asked for, and were given, a share in their father's inheritance (Num. 27:1–3; 36:1–3).

Israel also provides examples of the use of slaves to perpetuate a patriline and prevent the dispersal of property. When Seshan begot no sons, he gave one of his daughters as wife to his Egyptian servant, and her son, Attai, was reckoned as a patrilineal descendant of his mother's father (I Chron. 2:34–36; Patai [1959], pp. 225–26). The children born of a concubine were also given full status and could inherit their father's property. In a number of cases a barren wife would use her own slave girl to bear children on her behalf. Sarah gave her handmaid Hagar to Abraham, and she bore him a son, Ishmael (Gen. 16:1–3). That in these unions the handmaid is a substitute for her mistress is seen by the statement of Rachel when she offers her maid Bilhah to Jacob: "She shall bear upon my knees, that I may also have children by her" (*ibid.*, 30:3).[8]

The fourth method of acquiring offspring, by the birth of "illegitimate" children to one's daughter, is not, I believe, found in ancient Israel, and it would run counter to the great emphasis placed by Middle Eastern societies upon premarital chastity, an attitude that is brought out clearly in many marriage rites. However, a parallel mechanism exists in the institution whereby a woman marries a free man, often bringing him to live at her father's home in uxorilocal residence, while at the same time her paternal kin retain rights to the offspring. The Old Testament, for example, records that the children of Barzillai were named after their mother's father, Barzillai the Gileadite (Ezra 2:61; Neh. 7:63), and they were presumably entitled to inherit his property.

In the earlier discussion of systems of inheritance, we saw how the

[8] For the connection of the knees with generation in this and other Mediterranean societies, see Onians [1954], pp. 174–86, 491.

last two devices, breeding through slaves and through unmarried daughters, could be employed either to increase the numerical strength of a kin group or, more specifically, to provide a man with an heir, that is to say, a closer heir than would otherwise be at hand, and usually a person to whom he would stand not only as benefactor but also as upbringer. The same is true in some of the examples drawn from Biblical sources. But the LoDagaba have a dual system of inheritance, and the devices elsewhere employed as "perpetuating mechanisms" are here used as "circumventing mechanisms," their purpose being to prevent, or at least to limit, the transfer of movable property from the house. In the case of father-son gifts, the wealth of the matriclan is alienated, with its permission, to the succeeding generation of agnates. But the other mechanisms are not of this type; they provide a close duplicate kinsman who will take precedence over, or at least share with, the outside heir. Indeed, the same function was also performed by the reciprocal matrilineal groups. Although conceptually they extended the range of heirs, in fact they served to restrict inheritance to duplicate clansfolk. This effect was achieved by widening the corporate group to such a degree that there was almost bound to be a possible heir among a man's agnatic grandchildren, even in the absence of a patrilateral cross-cousin marriage.

In the last analysis, these various mechanisms are dependent upon the concept of corporation, the idea that all members of the matriclan are entitled to share in the dead man's property. They do not narrow the range of uterine inheritance as such; rather, they employ the idea of joint rights to keep part of the property in the local patrilineal group, property that would otherwise have gone to an outside heir.

The existence of rights held by members of the whole clan in the property administered by each individual is at once the strength of the corporate ties and the subject of internal disputes. Not only will the sisters' sons struggle against one another (*tag ta*), they also have to contend with their fellow matriclansmen in the house. The result is usually a division of the spoils. But the situation is one that sets a premium upon possession and gives rise to disputes that could formerly be settled only by a measure of self-help. Nowadays, the struggle among those who consider they have claims on the property has to take a less violent course, although mystical aggression is a potent supplement to judicial proceedings.

The important question that the use of circumventing, as distinct from perpetuating, mechanisms brings to mind is this: Why not do away with the system altogether and adopt agnatic inheritance?

Many LoDagaba today are conscious that their mode of inheritance is out of keeping with the agnatic emphasis of Western European systems. But the problem is no new one, although in some ways it has been aggravated by current changes; it is inseparable from double descent systems as well as from some matrilineal ones. I develop this point in the final chapter, but here I want to try to establish the fact that the problem has long been present in the system. The existence of the circumventing mechanisms supports this contention, but more significant is the evidence that emerges from an examination of the concept of uterine inheritance among the LoDagaba; for such an examination shows how these conflicting attitudes are embedded in the very way the people themselves conceive this method of transmission.

The word for matrilineal inheritance is *gbang,* and the inheritor is called *gbangdiru,* the consumer of the *gbang.* But the term is only used when the property passes outside the house. If the inheritor is a full brother or a sister's daughter's son, he is not called by this name; he is the "heir in the room" (*diu puo dire*), not an "heir in the bush" (*mwo puo dire*).[9]

Now, during the ceremonies in the dead man's room, the fellow members of one's matriclan, and in particular those located outside the patriclan (i.e., the heirs in the bush), are known by a rather similar name, *gbanggbaataaba.* *Gbanggbaa* means "slave" from *gbang,* a slave raider, and *taaba* means "fellows," so that the literal translation of the word is "fellow slaves."[10] The LoDagaa recognize a connection between *gbangdiru* and *gbanggbaataaba,* and the latter was sometimes explained to me in terms of the first. "*Gbangdiru* is when your *gbanggbaato* eats." No one could elucidate the reason behind this usage in any greater detail, but it appears to be connected with the fact that in areas with uterine inheritance of movable property, it is a fellow matriclansman, and specifically the mother's brother, who is able to sell you into slavery. A person therefore has this power over the man who may inherit from him and the woman whom he would like to see married to his son. On this interpretation, matriclansmen would be "fellow slaves," because they can sell one another, though, of course, they would do so only in extreme circumstances.

---

[9] The reader will have noticed how the LoDagaa continually contrast the house and the bush (or wilds), farming being identified with the one and hunting with the other. The Earth shrine, patroness of cultivated lands, likewise stands opposed to the shrine to the Wilds, and at times the ancestors to the beings of the wild.

[10] The second syllable may possibly derive from *baa,* a dog; but see p. 356 for an alternative connection with *gbaa gbong,* to gamble (throw cowries).

But there is another possibility. I have mentioned earlier that the groups who gather on the rooftop to eat the cow killed to the dead man's name are often spoken of as those who, in the very widest sense, have joint rights in one another's property. Slave subsections do not foregather with their "masters." Equally, members of the vaguely defined matrilineal moieties Some and Da do not join in the distribution of each other's meat. In other words, they act as if they were one another's slaves, and on these occasions there is a good deal of joking on this score. On this interpretation, a "fellow slave" would mean a person outside the house who was in a position to take your property, that is, an heir in the bush rather than a duplicate clansman of the dead man. Moreover, a slave is also a "bush (or roadside) person" (*mwo puo nir, sor puo nir*); he stands contrasted to a man of the parish (*tengbir*), as the form of his burial makes quite clear.[11]

I am not certain whether *gbang,* matrilineal heritage, and *gbang,* slave raider, are truly homonyms; there may well be semantic differences that I was not able to detect. But this association between slaves and outside inheritance was certainly made by some LoDagaa. There is, moreover, a third word that resembles these in several ways; it is the word for gambling, *gbong.*[12] Gambling consists of throwing cowries in a similar way to that used to confirm divinations; as elsewhere games of chance and techniques of augury have much in common. In this context the cowries used are known as *gbongbie,* rather than by the usual name of *libie, bie* being a diminutive; to throw cowries is *gbaa gbong.* There was little play during the period of my field work, since it was forbidden by law, and this would have made difficult the recovery of any gaming debts, which were often large and might include a person's wife and children, who thus became slaves. But gambling was still vigorously carried on at the funerals of old men as a way of "taking out the dream," and from the evidence of these ceremonies it would appear to have been much more prevalent among the LoDagaba with their uterine inheritance, though it occurred in both communities.

I do not wish to place too much emphasis on the similarities between these words; on the other hand, each of the activities to which they refer involves the transfer of movable property outside the *yir,* the house or patriclan, and, by implication, into the bush. Moreover, although all three activities are perfectly legitimate in the strict sense, they are never-

---

11 The burial I refer to in the text was of a man of the parish who had been sold into slavery and then returned to his native settlement without being ritually released from his previous status.

12 *Gbang* and *gbong* appeared to be alternatives.

theless only half approved, only partly countenanced. The LoDagaa were quite explicit about the evils of gambling, and the older men often remarked that the great blessing of European rule—they were frank about its curses, too—was that it put an end to this, to the activities of slave raiders and to the famines that had led to the selling of kin. Uterine inheritance was in many ways a similar kind of activity. When I was watching the gambling at Katu's funeral, one man got annoyed with another of the players and said, "You got rich through inheritance," implying that he had not worked for it with his own hands. This was taken as a bitter insult. The word used for inheritance was *gbang*, the transfer of uterine property outside the house. Had it happened within the house, which is what the circumventing mechanisms try to ensure, the half-disapproving term would not have been used. The property would have been taken by a duplicate clansman, probably a member of the same or alternate generation to the dead man.

The way in which the LoDagaba conceive uterine inheritance outside the house can be seen from the pejorative implications of the word *gbang* as well as from the existence of well-entrenched circumventing mechanisms. The evidence suggests that these concepts and institutions are not of recent development, but have long been present in this community. The further implications of this conclusion will be developed in the final chapter.

Inheritance, the subject of the present chapter, is of key importance to the whole study; for, as I have indicated, many of the important differences between the two communities are related to the transmission of property at death. I have shown how a man's roles, women, and property are redistributed when he dies and have drawn attention to the differences that obtain among the LoDagaa. In the next section, I consider the final stage of a man's translation into ancestral spirit and the ways in which the relationship between the living and the dead is influenced by these differences in the transmission of man's worldly goods.

PART FOUR

The Ancestors

CHAPTER XVII

The Eschatology of the LoDagaa

The eyes are not here
There are no eyes here
In this valley of dying stars
In this hollow valley
This broken jaw of our lost kingdoms

In this last of meeting places
We grope together
And avoid speech
Gathered on this beach of the tumid river.

ELIOT, *The Hollow Men*

THE CONCEPT OF THE SOUL

In the whole nexus of beliefs and practices associated with the dead, the central concept is that of the soul. For present purposes, I understand by "soul" the dictionary definition of the English word: "An entity conceived as the essence, substance, animating principle or actuating cause of life . . . separate in nature from the body and usually held to be separable in existence" (Webster). Although the difficulties involved in translating complex notions of this kind can hardly be overestimated, the evidence does appear to support Tylor's contention that these opinions are "world-wide" ([1920] I, 429). After a careful survey of concepts of early European and Near Eastern societies, Onians concludes: "It is remarkable that, with slight variations in detail, the same basic conceptions of the body, the mind and the soul which can be traced in our earliest evidence for the Greeks and Romans and the Celtic, Slavonic, Germanic and other 'Indo-European' peoples are to be seen also in early Egypt and Babylonia and among the Jews" ([1954] p. xvii). Furthermore, the "doctrine of the soul" is as much a characteristic of advanced societies as it is of the "lower races"; quite apart from its intrinsic association with all varieties of religious belief in the modern world, in the shape of the mind-body dichotomy not only is this concept built into our folk beliefs through the language we employ in everyday life, but it is very much a part of current controversy in the philosophy of science (Ryle [1949]; Feigl [1958]). The dualistic concept of the human personality still remains the "world knot" of Schopenhauer, "truly a cluster of intricate puzzles—some scientific, some epistemological, some syntactical, some semantical, and some pragmatic" (Feigl [1958], p. 373).

Although there are difficulties in subscribing to the evolutionary implications of Tylor's thesis, to the idea that all spiritual beings arose from this one source, there can be little objection to his assessment of the doctrine of the soul as central to religious beliefs in the restricted sense. For it is this notion that provides the cognitive basis for the transformation of a human being into an ancestor, that supplies a thread linking the Land of the Living to the Land of the Dead. As Rose remarks of the Roman *anima*, it "is the 'breath' of the living as much as the soul . . . of the dead" ([1930] pp. 133–34); it is the element of the human personality that persists after the body itself has decayed. Although it is possible to construct a system of beliefs in an afterlife on the basis of the notion of the resurrection of the whole body, in practice this concept is an accompaniment rather than an alternative to the doctrine of souls.

Not only is the notion of the soul intrinsic to beliefs in an afterlife; it is also closely linked to ideas about the mystical interaction of living persons. For the conception of a spiritual entity separable from its material frame is the basis of many beliefs about witches. The LoDagaa maintain that it is the witch's soul that goes out at night to meet in coven and attack its victims, while the witch's body lies in a deep slumber upon its mat of woven grass. When the sudden death of an apparently healthy person is attributed to witchcraft, the LoDagaa explain that witches attack not the flesh itself, but the soul's flesh, which they gradually but persistently gnaw away. Thus the soul is thought of as having substance like the body. Witches in their nightly peregrinations catch hold of the souls of their victims, tie them up so that they cannot escape, and slowly consume them over a period of time. This materiality persists even after the soul is transformed to spirit. When the LoDagaa recount nightmarish experiences in which they have seen visions, the ghosts of certain acquaintances, they speak of having been slapped across the face or of other tactile sensations.

Apart from its association with beliefs in an afterlife and the activities of flying witches, *les mangeurs d'âmes*, the concept of the soul is also implied in ideas of transmigration and transmutation. In the strict sense, transmigration or metempsychosis, the passage of a soul at death to another body, is not found among the LoDagaa. However, the beliefs that surround the death of young infants and the complex concept of the spirit guardian (*siura, sigra*) display a number of similarities; for, in their different ways, they both provide for the continued representation of the dead among the living. Some account of the former set of beliefs has already been given. A person's spirit guardian may be discovered for him at the "outdooring" three or four months after birth, or as the result of some sickness during childhood, or at initiation into the Bagre association; the procedure is for a diviner to be consulted and asked to reveal the nature of the child's tutelary. Often the guardian turns out to be a grandfather or another forebear of that same generation, and after a sacrifice has been made, the child may be called by the person's name; but the connection between the two is one of close association rather than identity, and it is not thought that the soul of the ancestor enters into the living.

Transmutation, the belief that a being can transform himself, or be transformed, into another animal or person, also depends upon the notion that some enduring element remains throughout these radical changes in outward appearance; the belief is not uncommon among the LoDagaa, and men who possess the proper medicine are said to change themselves into animate—and sometimes inanimate—objects, in order either to defend themselves from attack, or, more frequently, to attack others.

Tylor not only pointed to the importance of the concept of the soul as a separable entity; he also offered an explanation for the fact that the idea is so widely, indeed universally, distributed. In the first place, he deliberately sets aside the hypothesis that these beliefs could have diffused from one source. He sees these doctrines not as a degenerate result of contact with the "higher races," but as "answering in the most forcible way to the plain evidence of men's senses." His explanation is best given in his own words:

> It seems as though thinking men, as yet at a low level of culture, were deeply impressed by two groups of biological problems. In the first place, what is it that makes the difference between a living body and a dead one; what causes waking, sleep, trance, disease, death? In the second place, what are those human shapes which appear in dreams and visions? Looking at these two groups of phenomena, the ancient savage philosophers probably made their first step by the obvious inference that every man has two things belonging to him, namely, a life and a phantom. These two are evidently in close connection with the body, the life as enabling it to feel and think and act, the phantom as being its image or second self; both, also,

are perceived to be things separable from the body, the life as able to go away and leave it insensible or dead, the phantom as appearing to people at a distance from it. The second step . . . is merely to combine the life and the phantom. As both belong to the body, why should they not also belong to one another, and be manifestations of one and the same soul? ([1920] I, 428–29.)

In the earlier chapters, I associated the belief in the survival of phantoms after death and in the body-soul dichotomy with the contradiction between the continuity of social systems and the mortality of their personnel; in individual terms, such beliefs help to fill the breach made in a person's network of relationships by another's death, as well as providing the living with some consolation for the mortality of their bodily frame. Tylor's explanation is not inconsistent with this view, for although he stresses physiological factors, he does not ignore social ones. Moreover, it seems reasonable to conclude that the remarkable and detailed similarities in beliefs about the ghost-soul to be found so widely in human societies should be connected with the need for having some sort of conceptual framework for these phenomena.

Whether or not a modified version of Tylor's explanation is considered acceptable, we must certainly recognize the central importance of the dualistic view of mankind in the beliefs and practices of peoples throughout the world, at all known stages of development. Without an appreciation of the doctrine of the soul, the mortuary institutions of the LoDagaa, or of any society, would be difficult to understand.

THE SOUL IN LODAGAA RITUAL AND BELIEF

The LoDagaa perceive a human being as composed of a soul (*sie*) clothed with a skin or body (*yanggan*). This soul is similar in appearance to the body and has the same organs, except that "the eyes are not here," for they are without pupils. The breath (*nyovuor*), which in some contexts can be translated as life, is often spoken of in the same way as the soul. It is said of both that they quit (*yiina*) the body at death. But the two concepts should not be completely identified, for whereas it is possible for the soul to be separated from the body even before death, a person continues to breathe until the last.

Although it is usually the soul alone that is thought to continue its existence after death, I have also heard people tell stories about how the body itself died and rose again. In one case, a certain man who was much preoccupied with the subject of death—he was the senior grave-digger in the neighborhood—told how he had once found that the stone slab that rests on top of the grave had been moved; he poked a stick down the hole and found that the whole body had disappeared. Another man present told a similar story; and a third recounted how one day a stranger was traveling to Nandom, when he met an old man riding upon a donkey. He greeted him, passed the time of day, and went on to the town. When he got there, he asked after the old man's housepeople, and learnt that they had just had a death in the house, the death of the very person he met on the road. He said nothing at the time, but sometime later when he was drinking beer at the same house, he told the old man's kinsmen of his encounter. They went immediately to examine the grave and found his body had disappeared. Not only that, but his donkey too was missing.

A number of stories of this kind circulate among the members of any LoDagaa community. And they refer not to the temporary manifestations of souls or ghosts, but to instances in which the actual body is thought to die and come to life again. It should be noted that persons to whom this happens do not reappear to their kin, but only to strangers. Moreover, they do not hang about their usual haunts, but go off to distant places, such as Kumasi. Such stories appear to reflect concern about, and to offer an explanation for, the dissolution of the human body after death.

In general, the LoDagaa adopt a unitary concept of the soul, but the unity embraces some considerable diversities. One man maintained that the soul consists of three elements, which he described to me in the following way:

Soul I is the one that leaves the body at night when a man dreams and that in its wanderings may become the prey of a malevolent witch. For although witches are loosely said to eat human flesh, their victims display no visible signs of an attack; when questioned about this matter, an elder explained that it is the flesh of the soul they consume, and this in turn causes the body to pine away. I have also heard it said that another person's soul may enter the body when it is in this dissociated state and in this disguise commit an act of witchcraft, which may thus be blamed upon the wrong "person."

Soul II is the one that becomes first a ghost (*nyããkpiin*), and then a spirit (*kpiin*) that journeys to the Land of the Dead; for it remains intact even in face of the attack of witches.

Soul III is the shadow (*dasule* or *'baaro*) that accompanies the body wherever it goes and disappears at death.

Although it was only on this one occasion that the idea of the plurality of souls was spelled out with such precision, passing references to such a belief are not uncommon. Indeed, this reduplication serves to rationalize a number of the difficulties to which the concept of the soul gives rise, difficulties that are the very stuff of religious controversy, at least among the specialists. The doctrine explains, for example, how it is that the soul can proceed on its way to the Other World if it has been badly damaged by malevolent attacks. But it also raises other problems, further ambiguities, as do all human conceptions of the immaterial. Thus, although the body is said to be the proper dwelling of the soul, this is clearly not so as far as the shadow is concerned. During the ceremony known as "sweeping the soul," which induces a wandering soul to return to its abode, its resting place is sometimes spoken of as a room of the house; to those who inquire about such matters, this ritual can be explained as referring to the shadow.

A wandering soul is visible only to certain diviners known as *sie nyere* or *nyããkpiin nyere,* finders of souls or ghosts. These diviners are not concerned with the nightly exits of the soul that occur while the body sleeps. It is absences that may prove permanent that they investigate and attempt to cure; they diagnose the trouble and propose a specific course of action, which usually involves the ritual I have mentioned above.

Soul and body can be in a state of disassociation for as long as three or four years before a person dies. At first the separated soul is known as a "white soul" (LD *si pla*). In this condition, the finder of souls, gifted with second sight, sees the soul as the man's double, but with the hair shaved back a little at the temples, and the widow's peak, which is itself spoken of as the shadow (*dasule*), cutting in toward the crown. The thinning of the hair is a sure sign of approaching death; as we have noted, a funeral is marked by shaving the heads not only of some of the bereaved, but of the corpse as well. When the hair is seen to thin like this, the only action that can save the man is the performance of the ceremony known as "sweeping the soul," which can prolong the person's life for a further stretch of time.

When the soul is seen to have the hair shaved right back to the crown, death lies very near at hand. In this extreme condition, the soul is usually known as a "black soul" (LD *si sebla*), but sometimes it is already referred to as a ghost (*nyããkpiin*). It is thought to be particularly drawn to funerals, where it takes up its position at the foot of the funeral stand, sometimes causing the structure to sway a little. If people see the stand move in this way, they know that some person is at the point of death. It is this attraction of black souls to the vicinity of corpses that necessitates all the many and various precautions taken to

ensure the safety of these souls during the course of the funeral ceremonies and especially the measures used to ward off the ghosts of those
already dead.

Only prompt action can save a person in this condition. The ceremony performed is similar to that for a white soul except that the sacrifice is heavier; for a "black" or dangerous animal (LD *dun sebla*) has
to be killed, that is, a sheep or a dog. In both rites a black fowl and a
guinea-fowl are used, and the sacrifice is made to the ancestors (*kpiin*),
or to the beings of the wild (*kontome*), or at any other shrine as indicated by the diviner.

Although these two rituals are referred to as "sweeping the soul"
(*be pire a sie*), they are really attempts to sweep away the dirt of the
body, that is, to purify the skin, so that the soul may once again enter
its abode. For when the soul quits the body, it leaves the skin all dirty,
leaves it like the sloughed-off skin of a snake (*fofur*). A sacrifice must
then be made to cleanse the body, so that the soul can re-enter. The
altar chosen is usually the patriclan shrine itself, but in some instances
another important shrine belonging to a member of the sector may be
used. The occasion is a strictly private one, attended only by the affected
person and a close agnatic kinsman, who carries out the performance.
I was present at only one such ceremony, the circumstances of which
I shall relate.

A youth returned from working in the South and was told that
during his absence someone had reported seeing his soul in the market
place. This person told how one day, in the midst of the crowded
market, he had seen a figure whom he had taken for the lad in question.
Wanting to greet the boy on his return, he stepped up to him and found
himself speaking to another person altogether. It was a soul, a white
soul, that he had seen. When he spoke of the matter, one of the boy's
kinsmen consulted a diviner, who prescribed the usual sacrifice. In
fact, this precaution is sometimes taken for a man returning to his
native parish after a long absence, whether or not his soul has actually
been seen.

In this instance, the shrine to which the sacrifice was made was the
clan shrine, situated in the long room of the senior house of the lineage.
It consisted of a branch, embedded in the ground, which divided into
three smaller branches with a large gourd resting in between; hanging
from the rafters above were a number of smaller gourds, a collection of
skulls of animals, and a variety of scarcely distinguishable objects
covered with grime and cobwebs, among which I discerned some porcupine quills and a small cylinder made of cowries threaded tightly to-

gether. At the foot of the branch lay a heap of blackened objects including several of the small carved figures known as *baatibe*. From this
pile the boy's "father" took the broken fragment of a large pot and
untied a marrow-shaped gourd (*kuor*) from the shrine and poured some
black powder into the sherd. With the blade of his knife he then dug
a small hole in the ground in front of the shrine. He took a pot of
water and dropped into it some dried fragments of the spiky grass (*kalinyãã*) that is used during the burial service to expel wandering souls
from the tomb.[1] The water from the pot and the earth from the hole
were mixed together into a ball of mud, and the medicine itself was
sprinkled into some of the black greasy by-product of the fat (*kã*) made
from the nut of the shea tree.

He took up his knife again in one hand and with the other shook
an iron bell (*gbelme*) of the type used for calling upon the beings of the
wild, recounting at the same time the story of what had happened.
When he had finished, he slit the throat of a young chicken and threw
it on the floor. It fluttered feebly and eventually came to rest belly
downward; the offering had been refused. He spoke once more, saying
that if the shrine accepted the next fowl, he would arrange for all the
goods that the youth had brought back from the South to be carried in
and placed at the foot of the shrine. This procedure is the usual one
adopted in such circumstances; for shrines have claims upon the wealth
that a man has accumulated as the result of their protection, just as they
have claims upon the persons whom they have saved from sickness or
from death. Moreover, the major shrine of the patriclan has a special
claim upon a man, as we saw in connection with hunting and warfare;
the "sweeping of the soul" after a person has returned from working
abroad bears a general similarity to the sacrifices carried out after a man
or an animal has been killed with the help of the clan arrow poison.
Therefore, in making this promise, the officiant was engaging to carry
out no more than the usual procedure adopted on these occasions.
Addressing the shrine, he said, "If it is on account of this that you refuse
the chicken, then take the next one." The second chicken came to rest
on its back; now that the gift of greeting (*bun puru*) had been accepted,
the main sacrifice could be carried out.

The "father" told the youth to approach the shrine and, taking
some of the grease with which the medicine had been mixed, drew a
line from the nape of the boy's neck over the top of his head and down

---

[1] Human souls are also allergic to ashes, which make hot things cold, and to
brooms, which sweep away dirt.

to the tip of his nose. The same act was repeated on the guinea-fowl, after which some of the medicine was forced down its gullet. Three pebbles had been placed in the pot of water, and the "father" bent down to take them out, clenched them in his fist, and thumped the boy three times on the small of the back, the shoulders, the head, and the chest. The boy then took the pebbles one by one, put them in his mouth, and spat them into the small hole in the ground in front of the shrine. The "father" cut some pieces of hair from the boy's head and dropped them in the same hole. Next he took dried herbs from the shrine and gave some to the boy. They both extended their hands three times toward the hole and on the fourth occasion let the herbs fall among the hair. The "father" then bent low over these objects and breathed on them three times; the youth followed suit. The "father" coughed into the earth; the boy did likewise. Finally, they both spat there, filled in the hole with the soil that had been removed, and pressed down the earth with their feet, each action being repeated three times.

The "father" turned around, seized the guinea-fowl by the legs, and beat it on the ground three times; the boy did the same. Taking hold of both the black chicken and the guinea-fowl in one hand, the "father" brushed the youth from head to toe. Once again he addressed the shrine, calling first the name of his own father and those of the ancestors of the patrilineage, then asking the forefathers who brought the shrine there to continue to watch over the well-being of their descendants. "We want no more funerals. Take this soul into the room and let it remain in the house." When he had finished speaking, the officiant sacrificed the black fowl. With the medicine he drew a single line across a gourd bowl, which is later used for preparing the chicken that the two will eat. Finally, the boy was bathed three times, and some of the feathers from the fowls were tied around his ankle.

It will be remembered that feathers are twisted around the ancestor shrine when it is taken inside the byre at the third and fourth funeral ceremonies. At every sacrifice some of the tail feathers of the chicken are stuck in the blood that has been allowed to drip upon the shrine itself. However, in the sacrifices made during the entry of the ancestor shrine and the "sweeping of the soul," as well as during the similar rites performed for some of the bereaved, the feathers plucked from the sacrificial animal are deliberately tied around the shrine in the one case and around the sufferer in the others. It is possible that the metaphoric meaning of this act is the same in both cases and that the spirit of the ancestor is being made to enter its material counterpart, the shrine, just as in the other ceremony the soul is encouraged to return to the body.

The difficulties involved in reconciling the presence of the spirit in the shrine with its journey to the Land of the Dead are solved by means of the concept of the multiple soul.

The metaphoric significance of the ceremony itself is straightforward enough. Purification is achieved by the transfer of dirt to other material objects and in particular to the sacrificial scapegoat, the guinea-fowl. The soul is then restrained from leaving its proper dwelling place for a period of three years by the mimetic rite of burial in a hole near the shrine; for the three stones representing the three years were likened to the stones placed on top of a grave. But this act should also be linked to the burying of three stones from the Earth shrine in the entrance of the byre to protect a new house from harm and especially to the use of these same stones in taking precautions against possible suicide. On both these occasions, exuviae of the body are enclosed in a hole as part of the restraining process.

Purification is an act of separation, of disassociation, but the cleansing is usually achieved only by transferring the impurity to another object or a different medium. In other words, cleansing oneself of spiritual impurity is treated in the same way as cleaning the dirt from the body. Indeed, as in our own usage of the word "dirt," physical impurity and the consequences of transgressing certain moral norms are all included in the one concept. The use of the scapegoat is merely one means adopted to rid oneself of "dirt" and is common to a number of rituals. In sweeping a man when his soul quits the body, and in sweeping the Earth shrine when a suicide has been committed in the parish, the fowls and the dog act as scapegoats. I have been told that formerly when a young man's soul departed, a ritual specialist might attempt to localize it in one of his domestic animals. If this operation is successful, the beast dies, but the youth retains his life (*nyovuor*). "When the cow expires," it was explained, "it is you yourself who die." Three days afterwards, the youth would have to undergo the ritual of sweeping. If the soul was black, the client had to tread a dog to death; the corpse of the animal took away the dirt, so that a new soul could enter the body of the youth.

Such are the rituals performed when a man's soul is thought to leave his body, in an attempt to bring it back to its proper dwelling place. In the case of a married woman, a sacrifice has first to be carried out at her natal home and then subsequently at her husband's house, so that her wandering soul will return to the room she lives in. If these performances are unavailing and the patient dies, then the soul begins its second existence as a spirit and starts its journey to the Land of the Dead.

At death the soul becomes a ghost (*nyããkpiin*), which, like an errant soul, is visible at certain times to certain people; only after the shrine has been created at the final ceremony does it become a spirit proper (*kpiin*). At burial the body is consigned to the earth, while the soul escapes. As the grave is closed, precautions are taken to prevent other souls from entering there. The ghost cannot as yet proceed upon his way to the Land of the Dead, for he has neither completely relinquished his human roles nor yet acquired his supernatural one. But he no longer dwells in his house, and any effort to return there is discouraged by the survivors. His most personal possessions are sent away, so that he will not be tempted to return for them, or else hung on the wall of the byre, so that if he does come back, he will not enter the compound itself. During this transitional period the ghost lives in the treetops, waiting until he is released by the final ceremony to go and join his forebears.

The ghost returns to the vicinity of the compound during the various funeral ceremonies. At the last of these, he is bathed in the funeral beer by his ancestral spirits, after which his shrine is carved and carried inside the byre, while the spirit sets off on the journey to the Land of the Dead. Thus a ghost becomes a spirit only when the funeral ceremonies are fully completed. As a ghost, he wanders about the earth and still retains his rights in women, goods, and positions. When he becomes a spirit, he relinquishes all specific claims, although as an ancestor he continues to hold certain general rights in the worldly property of his descent group.

The Land of the Dead lies to the west, the direction of the setting sun, and on his journey there the spirit arrives at a river, which is crossed by a ferry. It is for this crossing that friends provide the fare of twenty cowries at the time when speeches are made to the dead body. Up to this point, the crossing of the river, the beliefs I have described are widely held and often referred to, though obliquely rather than directly. Furthermore, it is generally acknowledged that the passage of the River of Death is an ordeal that not only tests but also punishes wrongdoers, excluding certain sorts of sinner from the Land of Ancestral Spirits (*kpime tiung*), the Country of God (*Na'angmin tiung*). But there is considerable variation in the way different people elaborate these beliefs, and the account I give below is that of a person who, although quite a young man, was particularly well-informed in all matters of ritual and ceremony.

The Journey. On the way to the River of Death you meet the One-Breasted Woman (*bir gō*). She runs after you and tells you who was responsible for your death. If you get angry and want to return to kill the person concerned, she'll joke with you to make you laugh. Once you do this, that's an end to it. For you can never return to earth (*tenggaan tiung*, the country of the Earth shrine). But if you don't laugh, the witch will die. The One-Breasted Woman will help you; she'll kill the witch, for she is the child of God (*Na'angmin bie*). Once the witch is dead, he'll catch you up on the road and you'll both travel along together. Otherwise you carry on alone until you come to the river.

If you've led a good life, then when you get there you'll go straight across. If you've done wrong, when you enter the boat you'll drop through the bottom into the water. So people go across singly, lest they get involved in someone else's troubles. If you fall in the water, you won't drown, but will just have to go on swimming for a long, long time; it'll take you some three years to cross. You'll suffer a great deal on the way and you'll have nothing to eat.

If you owe anything to a person who is still living, you'll have to wait there for him and pay him when he comes. If you've stolen anything, you'll have to wait until your friends are all gathered at the bank. Then when the owner arrives, the ferryman'll say, "Here's the man who stole from you." And you and all your friends will feel great shame. If a man asks you for something and you say you haven't got it when you have, you, too, will have to wait for him at the river's bank.

The Punishment of Witches. On the left-hand side there's another river, known as *sor man*, the Witches' River, that only witches go to. But here they can't cross by boat, for there's no ferryman. A leading witch (*sor na*) stands on the bank and shows you what suffering you must endure. He forces you to eat yourself. First he'll take a bite from the muscle of your left arm; you'll have to eat the rest, right down to the fingers. The same thing happens with your thigh. Then he pushes you into the river to make you swim across, but the water is full of pepper and so wide that the journey takes three years. You see the other bank very near you and think that you'll soon reach it. But you go on swimming for a long, long time, two whole years, and still you don't get there. At the end of the next year, you finally reach the far bank. When you get to the Land of the Dead, all the people will see the arm and leg you've eaten, and they'll know you're a witch.

The Land of the Dead. When you arrive at the Land of the Dead, the old spirits (*kpime kora*) show you difficult tasks which you've never seen before. They'll make you sit in the sun on top of a withered tree. You'll sit there for three months. But the sun isn't like the sun here, for they say it is very close at hand. If they hang meat outside, it'll roast.

If you had a good heart (*pu pla sob*, literally, a person whose belly is white), you'll sit there for three months; if you had an evil disposition (*pu byuur sob*), for six months; if you were a thief, for five months; if you told lies, for four months; if you were a witch, for three years; if you were a rich man,[2] for three years.

After this is over, they'll make you farm as you never did before; the length of time you spend doing this depends on how hard you worked during your lifetime. Meanwhile the women make things. If you took part in fighting, they will find a man stronger than you to fight with, and the length of this again depends on how much you fought during your lifetime.

The Judgment. Then they'll divide the women and their progeny. They'll sit all the women separately; the children of one woman and all their progeny will sit together. They'll count how many bad people there are in each group. If they see that there are a thousand witches among your group, or a thousand thieves, or a thousand liars, then to that woman and her progeny they will give all the bad things in the country, everything that brings pain. Salt water will be their only drink. The people will claim that their wickedness comes from the woman, that her heart was not good. To the woman of good disposition, and to her children, they will give good things, pleasant things—good food and plenty of rest.[3]

Once the men have been separated out, they don't have to farm any more. They just think what they want to eat, and they get it. But those who have been evil must ask God. They ask him, "Why do you make us suffer?" And God replies, "Because you sinned on earth." And they ask, "Who created us?" To which God replies, "I did." And they ask, "If you created us, did we know evil (*yil faa*) when we came or did you give it us?" God replies, "I gave it to you." Then the people ask God, "Why was it you knew it was evil and still gave it us?" God replies, "Stop. Let me think and find out the answer."

God thought for a thousand years and came back; they were still suffering. He said, "The things we were talking about, I want you to tell me of them again." They said, "Why did you say you would make us suffer?" He replied, "Because of the evil deeds you've done." They said, "Who made us that way?" And he replied, "I did." And they said, "Then we can't have done wrong. If you have a child and give him something bad to keep, then whatever he gets hold of as bad as that, it's your fault. So you can't make us suffer." When they had spoken in this way, God put an end to their suffering and set them to farm to get food.

Beliefs in a future life display many remarkable similarities throughout the world, so that an explanation of the LoDagaa concepts should also apply to a wide range of other societies. For we are dealing with a

[2] *Na*, the word now used for chief; the implication here is that you must have treated others badly in order to be well-off yourself.

[3] The literal meaning of *pieno*, which I have translated as "rest," is "lying"; it can refer to sexual intercourse.

set of standardized conceptual adaptations to universal human situations. Here I want to discuss three main features common to a large number of societies, the journey to the Land of the Dead, the River of Death, and the idea of retribution.

(1) *The Journey*. Death is a separation; social separation, a process that runs parallel to the separation of the soul from the body, is envisaged in physical terms and takes the form of a long journey to the west. The setting of the sun has a general association with the extinction of human life. It forms one of the set of metaphors that occur over a great range of societies, that body of "non-logical" associations out of which much ritual thought is built. Their wide distribution is due primarily to the inevitable character of these associations and to their adequacy in organizing certain experiences common to the human situation.

(2) *The River of Death*. The belief in a river which divides the Land of the Living from that of the Dead and across which a spirit has to be ferried bears a remarkable resemblance to Greek and other mythologies, so that the view of many early writers, that such similarities could only have arisen by diffusion from "higher cultures," is quite understandable. But even if such a hypothesis were acceptable, and there are a number of reasons why it should be rejected, this would leave the core of the problem untouched, that is, why in so many societies we should find the Land of the Living separated from the Land of the Dead by a river or similar stretch of water.

I suggest that this feature of the topography of the Other World, the interpolation of another element between the two firmaments, emphasizes the discontinuity between the worlds. Moreover, in this part of Africa all journeys of any length include the crossing of a river, and at most times of the year this can be done only by canoe.

The payment of the ferryman with the only cash at one's disposal stresses the fact that the journey is one way, that death is irreversible. Many societies have stories telling of exceptions to the rule, how this man penetrated to the Land of the Dead and returned to tell his tale, how that man was resurrected from the dead. These tales help to explain how man acquired knowledge of the Other World, and hence hope for the future, despite the irreversibility of death. In the origin myth of the LoWiili, recounted during initiation to the Bagre society, it is told how one of the two first men climbed up into the sky to visit God and was there taught by him how to reproduce his kind. Apart from this, I know of no accounts of visits to the Other World. The dead themselves cannot go back to punish those who killed them; this is done by the One-Breasted Woman. Temporary absence from the social group may be explained as a visit to the beings of the wild who live in the woods, hills, and streams, but not to the Country of God, whose habitat is as remote as he from the affairs of men. God created man and showed him how to create himself; but all other arts man learnt from the beings of the wild, who continue to interest themselves in all that he does. God, on the other hand, is remote and distant, the denizen of another world.

(3) *The Idea of Retribution.* Following Burton, Tylor classified "pictures into which this world has shaped its expectations of the next" into two, the first based upon the "continuance-theory," the second upon the "retribution-theory"; he further suggested that in the evolutionary sequence, the retribution theory developed out of the continuance theory ([1920] II, 75). Future life as a reflection of this present existence was superseded among higher societies by the idea of the other world as a compensation. This distinction between the religions of literate and non-literate societies has had wide currency in the field of comparative religion, and religions of conversion are sometimes thought to hold a monopoly of ethical ideas, including that of personal salvation.

The LoDagaa beliefs lend no support to Tylor's evolutionary sequence, nor even his classification. I do not wish to imply that these people are oppressed by the idea of retribution in the next world, for they are not more affected by this notion than contemporary Europeans. Indeed, although I had encountered the custom of giving cowries to the corpse at a relatively early stage in my field work, it was not until much later that I recorded a detailed account of ideas about the future life. But although it would be an error to overemphasize the importance of such beliefs, either in our own society or among the LoDagaa, the idea of retribution is certainly present. The Land of the Dead is sometimes referred to by the LoDagaa as *ngmalugetiung,* the land of wood-chopping, for this is an extremely onerous task and hence one that serves as an appropriate punishment for wrongdoers. Indeed, I would suggest that retribution is to some degree an essential feature of all beliefs in a future life. For whether the Other World is seen as a continuance or as a reversal of this, its whole conception must necessarily reflect the ideas of the living, ideas that are always tinged with moral undertones, even if they fail to make explicit provision for a judicial process in the Land of the Dead. In other words, the idea of rewards and punishments after death appears to be an inevitable extension to the supernatural plane of the system of social control that obtains upon earth, no less so if the next world is seen as making up for the inadequacies and inconsistencies of this.

However, even if my argument concerning retribution does not have general validity, the LoDagaa evidence nonetheless runs counter to the general hypothesis of Tylor and of those more recent writers who have supported him. I make this point because of some of the implications that accompany this assumption, namely that among non-literate peoples the beliefs in a future life in some way lack a moral and ethical content.[4] Among the LoDagaa, at least, both funeral ceremonies and beliefs about life after death reflect the moral judgments made in the society and need to be examined within the context of the total system of social control.

Looking at this system as it operates among the LoDagaa, we can see that a person's misdeeds are punished in different ways according to his position in the life cycle. If we consider only the social pressures exercised by those in superordinate positions (that is, if we deal with authority, rather than with the influence of the peer group and others of equal status, or with "control from below"), we can categorize the following three methods of reward and punishment according to the agent involved.

First, there is the authority of the living over the living. Until adolescence, domestic authority is largely vested in the father or guardian. In certain respects, punishments and rewards are distributed by the father as long as he is alive; hence, the crucial importance of having or not having a father. One may include here the whole question of the treatment accorded to a person at his funeral: that is, the differential forms of ceremony including special burials and the creation of the ancestor shrine, all of which involve moral and ethical judgments by the surviving members of the society.

Second, there is the authority of the dead over the living. At the death of the father, a man comes under the direct aegis of his spirit; indeed all men at all times are subject to the authority, sometimes capricious, of the ancestors.

Third, there is the authority exercised by other spiritual beings over the dead, which reinforces the whole system in a variety of ways. On the plane of supernatural beliefs, there is the revenge against witches and the punishment meted out by the ferryman to debtors, thieves, and those who refuse legitimate requests; later there are the punishments and rewards distributed by God in the Land of the Dead.

For the LoDagaa the idea of retribution and its obverse, that of sal-

---

[4] For example, James writes: "Generally speaking, however, death is not an initiation into a fuller life in a progressive sequence. Rather is it a mutilated existence, a shadowy reflection of this life, with no idea of rewards and punishments based on ethical conduct" ([n.d.] p. 131).

vation, is an extension of the system of social control into the Land of the Dead. Indeed, the continuance and retribution theories are not alternatives, but complementary to one another. Retribution is in itself an aspect of continuity, a projection of the moral and jural norms onto the supernatural sphere. On earth, some offenses are dealt with by supernatural, or rather by diffuse, sanctions alone; the murder of a clansman is mainly left in the hands of the ancestors of the descent group. And it is not only those offenses subject to supernatural sanctions during the lifetime of the offender that are punished after his death, but other infringements of the moral and jural code are similarly treated. The idea of supernatural retribution reinforces the moral code by the belief that death itself provides no end to the system of rewards and punishment; often, indeed, it serves to adjust the inevitable differences between ideal and actual patterns of behavior.

"Looking at the religion of the lower races as a whole," wrote Tylor, "we shall at least not be ill-advised in taking as one of its general and principal elements the doctrine of the soul's Future Life" ([1920] II, 21). His opinion is backed by the considerable weight of evidence that Frazer later gathered together. For while it is possible to conceive of an Other World independent of the idea of a future life for the inhabitants of this, in fact the two notions always seem to accompany one another. Thus in practice the dualistic concept of man is a universal accompaniment of the belief in spiritual beings, and hence a fundamental component of any religion. According to Tylor, "the doctrine of a Future Life as held by the lower races is the all but necessary outcome of savage Animism" (*ibid.*, II, 1). He offers no other explanation of this institution, and it is to be assumed that he regarded the belief in the afterlife and in spiritual beings as deriving, in the last analysis, from the explanation of perceptual phenomena.

While there is much to be said for the "physiological" account of the universality of the body-soul dichotomy, it appears inadequate as an explanation of the beliefs and practices that relate to the spiritual world. Indeed, as far as beliefs in the soul and its future life are concerned, it seems possible to regard them both as an outcome of the dissonance created by the consciousness of a continuing social system staffed by a mortal personnel.[5] In terms of specific function, the belief in a future life may have a number of facets. It may act as a mechanism to adjust differences between the ideal and the actual, and especially to compensate for the deprived positions of special categories of persons,

---

[5] For a discussion of the importance of "cognitive dissonance," see Festinger [1957].

such as the poor or the aged. Like other supernatural beliefs, it may serve to reinforce the system of social control and place it past human questioning. It may assist the readjustment of the bereaved and thus reduce the sense of loss. This belief performs all three of these functions among the LoDagaa. Yet, as I have remarked, it would be wrong to place too much stress upon the part played by this notion in social life as a whole. As in our own society, internalized reactions, public opinion, and jural and legal sanctions are all of greater importance in the system of social control, and the Hawthorne effect produced by ceremonial has perhaps as great a consequence for the adjustment of the bereaved.[6] Our interest in these phenomena centers primarily upon the relationship of the doctrine of the soul to concepts of the future life and the importance of these beliefs as a background to the worship of the ancestors.

[6] In the important researches carried out at the Western Electric Company's Hawthorne works, output increased however the experimental conditions were varied; all changes improved the "mental attitude of the workers." For a summary of this work, see Homans [1947], pp. 448–60.

CHAPTER XVIII

Diis Manibus

Religion prescribes that the property and the worship of a family
shall be inseparable, and that the care of the sacrifices shall always
devolve upon the one who receives the inheritance.

CICERO, *De Legibus*

Associated with those notions of the dualism of man and of his persistence after death that seem to be found in the beliefs of all societies, even
in the folk-beliefs of contemporary "secular" societies, there is another
widespread, if not universal, social institution, the cult of the dead.
For whenever beliefs in a future life are incorporated in standardized
practices, such as the custom of placing some of the dead man's property
in his grave, then the cult is present. The European habit of laying
flowers upon the grave is another such practice, but one that borders
on a simple commemorative rite; like the insertion of memorial notices
in *The Times,* it does not necessarily involve any specific concept of
survival.

The cult of the dead as manifested in the custom of tending the
grave shades imperceptibly into the worship of the dead (Crooke [1908]).
By "worship" I understand the sorts of activity to which Frazer referred
when he defined religion as "a propitiation or conciliation of powers
superior to man which are believed to direct and control the course of
nature and of human life" ([1935] I, 222). Such acts of propitiation
include sacrifice (food offerings and especially blood offerings), libation
(offerings of drink), gifts of other material objects, prayer (verbal offerings), and the "payment of respect" by other forms of gesture. Thus the
worship of the dead implies not only the idea of survival, but also the
active participation of the dead in mundane affairs. It is their intervention, in the past or in the future, that requires the living to pro-
pitiate the dead by the offer of goods, services, words, and other gestures
to secure their favor.

As an example of the propitiation of the dead, there is no clearer case than that chosen by Tylor, namely, the hagiolatry of the main Christian sects. He points out that "although full ancestor-worship is not practiced in modern Christendom, there remains even now . . . a well-marked worship of the dead. A crowd of saints, who were once men and women, now form an order of inferior deities, active in the affairs of men and receiving from them reverence and prayer" ([1920] II, 120). And he goes on to point out how these figures in the Christian pantheon were often specific replacements for local deities or the patron gods of specialist groups.

In considering the various forms of ritual and belief surrounding the dead, we need to distinguish two further dimensions: namely, the inclusiveness of the cultus and the relationship between the living and the dead. By inclusiveness, I mean simply the numbers and status of those members of the population who become the subject of these rites when they die. In Christian countries, for example, ministrations at the grave are practiced in the large majority of deaths, but other forms of honoring the dead are accorded only to a few. Saints, like heroes, are a small and select company, and the "benefactors" of colleges who are celebrated by feasts, portrait, or prayer are likewise but a small fraction of all the colleges' alumni. Clearly, the choice of which people are to be included in the pantheon of the sect, state, or corporation is related to the acts and status of these persons while alive. And even in societies where most men become ancestral spirits capable of receiving the offerings of the living, their status on earth may still affect the nature of the worship. For example, in many societies with centralized institutions and an inclusive system of ancestor worship, the spirits of dead kings have to be propitiated on behalf of the whole chiefdom or nation in order to ensure the continuing well-being of its inhabitants. Among the Ashanti (Busia [1954], pp. 201 *et seq.*) and the Ba Thonga (Junod [1927], II, 372–428), ancestor worship faithfully reflects the system of political stratification.

The inclusive type of cultus, in which the large majority of the dead are celebrated, requires further differentiation, since it may vary in respect of the degree of individualization entailed in the treatment of the dead. They may be dealt with collectively, as in the services conducted upon All Souls' Day, a time devoted to a general intercession for, and commemoration of, the faithful, whose souls in the Other World can be helped by the prayers of the living. Or they may be individually named and celebrated, as when a Chantry mass was endowed for the soul of a particular person. Clearly, a relevant factor here is the nature of the shrines at which the dead are commemorated, whether these are collectively or individually designed, a Tomb of the Unknown Warrior or a Chantry chapel; in the technology of ancestor worship, which played a considerable part in the early history of art, there is often a link between collective shrine and abstract form, between individual altar and human figure.

The second main dimension concerns the nature of the relationship between the living and the dead. When the Chinese offer prayers to the souls incorporated in memorial tablets, there is a link of kinship between the congregation and the dead, a connection that is lacking between the Christian saint and his diffuse crowd of worshipers. It is for the former type of cult, in which the living and the dead are kin one of another, that we shall reserve the phrase "ancestor worship."

Even in ancestor worship in the strict sense, the relationship of living to dead has a number of modalities that must be disentangled if we are to establish any correlations between religious systems and other aspects of the social order. In the first place, it is often necessary to distinguish between the relationship of the dead ancestor with the person who conducts the ritual, the officiant, on the one hand, and the person who provides the offering, the donor, on the other. As the LoDagaba material demonstrates, these relationships by no means always coincide. Furthermore, the officiant-ancestor and the donor-ancestor relationships display several alternative possibilities. As I have mentioned earlier, various writers in the field have remarked that the typical congregation of the ancestral cult is a unilineal descent group, a clan or lineage. But one also finds practices consistent with our definition of ancestor worship in "bilateral" societies, that is, societies in which unilineal groups are absent. In Polynesia they appear in association with the type of group Firth refers to as a ramage [1957]; and they are found in societies like that of the Gonja of Northern Ghana that lack any boundary-maintaining kin groups, at least in the domestic domain. Nevertheless, it is the lineage group organized around a unilineal genealogy that provides the typical congregation in the worship of the ancestors, and this type I shall speak of as manes worship.

Unilineal genealogies, in the restricted sense in which I use the phrase, possess the characteristic that their span varies according to their depth, a feature that arises from the way they act as the framework for a lineage group, as a mnemonic of existing social relationships. The genealogy of a ramage may work in a roughly similar way, although here kinship is never the only criterion of group eligibility. And even in societies without these kinds of kin group, the genealogy still bears a close relationship to the network of immediate kinship ties.[1] The fact that genealogies provide a calculus for the system of social relationships means that they are constantly in the process of change; for memory is continually reinterpreting the information stored there in accordance with changing social pressures. The part of a genealogy that is remembered tends to be what has social significance at the moment of remembering. The introduction of writing, however, radically alters the process of the intergenerational transmission of culture; society now no longer depends only upon oral mediation, which of necessity is limited to face-to-face situations. And when the genealogy gets written down, it cannot continue to have the immediate link with contemporary social groups that it had before. The lists of names recorded in the Book of Numbers and in Chinese genealogy books may once have served as such a reference; but their very preservation deprives them of the flexibility necessary if they are to serve as a guide for relationships that are bound to change with time. But like Burke, Debrett, and the *Almanach de Gotha,* they may still assert personal claims to high status, often of an antiquarian kind.

In the remainder of this chapter, I shall be concerned with the analysis of ancestor worship among the LoDagaa. But my intention is not to provide a comprehensive account of this institution, for to do so would require a treatment of other aspects of the religious system with which the ancestors are often connected. What I wish to do is to give the reader a broad picture of how a sacrifice to the ancestors takes place, so that he can understand the crucial differences between the two societies. These differences concern the relationship between the donor and recipient in blood sacrifice and closely correspond to differences in the kinship position of the holder and the heir.

THE SHRINES

The ancestor shrine is a creation of the funeral itself. During the third ceremony, a provisional shrine is made from the wood used for bows and then is placed in the byre of the dead man's compound; at the final ceremony the permanent shrine is carved and also put in the byre beside the anthropomorphic figures of earlier ancestors. This piece of forked wood is known as the spirit's stick (*kpiin daa,* from *kpi,* to die),

---

[1] A pedigree, as distinct from a genealogy, traces a line of filiation. The pedigree of a European royal family does not serve primarily as a reference for group organization or kinship orientation. It is a charter to office and to other rights; the longer the pedigree, the more imposing and the more effective it is as a device for legitimizing both the office and the officeholder.

or alternatively as the father's stick (*sãã daa*); since the word for "stick" is usually dropped, the shrine is often spoken of simply as "spirit" or "father."

Not every male is entitled to a shrine, but only those who have children born to their name, since it is the child that is said to carve the ancestral figure for the parent. A child is born to a man's name when the bridewealth for the mother has been given on his behalf. The bridewealth cowries are laid at the foot of the ancestor shrines of the husband's compound before they are taken to the bride's patrilineage, so that the dead will watch over the rights in a woman's procreative powers that this payment secures and help them to prove a profitable investment.

It is sometimes said that if a man has no son, a daughter can make the shrine instead. But on this question I found some disagreement, and in every case I encountered in which a daughter was said to have done this, it turned out that she had a younger brother on whose behalf she was acting. As a result, I assumed that only a male child could carry out this task, an opinion that was confirmed by the statements of many informed persons. On the other hand, it cannot be denied that the other belief is also current, and I was told that a "brother" of the dead man would help the daughter find what grain was required for the food and beer used in the performances; such assistance is considered to be the particular responsibility of the man who has taken his "brother's" wife in leviratic marriage and who, therefore, might yet provide him with a male heir. Although the idea that a daughter could have a shrine made for her father was less widespread among the LoWiili than among the LoDagaba, I do not have enough information to be able to link this difference with the inheritance of property and the organization of descent groups.

Not only men who die childless, but also those who have suffered an evil death are denied an ancestor shrine, unless the sin that has been committed is first expiated by the prescribed sacrifices. Atonement for offenses against the Earth shrine can be made by an appropriate payment of cowries and sacrificial animals; on the other hand, the killing of a fellow clansman is an offense against the ancestors that cannot be forgiven, and a shrine is never carved for a man who kills his father or his brother.

A woman who has left children behind her also has a shrine established to her name, one that is similar in form to the provisional shrine provided for a man at the Bitter Funeral Beer. At this intermediate ceremony a woman's stick is taken into the byre of her husband's house and leant against the wall. At the Final Ceremony it is carried in solemn procession to her father's house and placed near the shrines of her patrilineal forebears. The progress of a woman's married life is marked by the gradual extension of privileges in her husband's patrilineage, but the last rite of the funeral places her once and for all among the dead of the lineage into which she was born. However, if she is survived by a son, another shrine will be carved to her name and placed in the byre of her marital home, so that he will have some means of communicating with her. Although I encountered no instances of a woman's receiving an individual sacrifice from her son, both sisters and wives of the lineage would receive part of the offerings made to male ancestors or to the collective dead.

In most LoDagaa clans the ancestor shrines are placed in a corner of the byre, but one clan has a different type of shrine. Among the Tiere or Tiedeme the usual wooden figure is carved, but is then thrown away into the midst of a thicket; in its stead a piece of slate or flat rock is stuck in the earth by the entrance to the house, and it is on this stone that sacrifices are made (Plate 15).

CUSTODIANSHIP OF THE SHRINES

The duty of creating a man's shrine falls upon the eldest son of his senior wife; he it is who provides the cock that is sacrificed when the branch is first cut from the tree. In this task he is assisted by the eldest son of the second wife, who supplies a hen for the same series of rites.

The senior son is said to "own" (*so*) his father's shrine. However, so long as a full brother, the inheritor of the deceased's estate, remains alive, the son cannot remove the shrine to another house. But if there is no such close "father" alive, a man can take the shrine with him when he builds himself a new compound. Should it happen that the eldest son of the second wife also wishes to build a house of his own, then he takes with him the provisional shrine of his dead father.

The logic of this concept of seniority derives from the fact that the group of siblings in the patrilineage is differentiated by maternal filiation. In polygynous households the continuous process of fission of domestic groups organized around an agnatic core centers in the first place upon the mother. From an early age, the group of agnatic siblings born of a polygynous father is differentiated both in its food supply, especially during the period of oral dependency, and in its physical location; for young children either sleep in their own mother's room or on the section of the flat roof above it. Later on, the group is similarly divided over the inheritance; for within the patrilineage only full siblings take precedence over sons, and in the house-property complex the farm immediately adjacent to the compound is divided between the groups of full siblings as distinct stocks (*per stirpes*). When the split in the sibling group occurs, whether it happens before or after the death of the father, it is expected that full siblings will remain together, an expectation that is reflected in the order of inheritance. The way in which the duties involved in creating a man's shrine are divided between the eldest sons of the two senior wives again stresses this differentiation into matrisegments, and it is on this basis that the dwelling group will eventually split. The creation of two shrines during the funeral ceremony provides both groups with their own altars for the byre, inside which are kept not only the household's capital of livestock, but also the sacra through which communication with the ancestors is maintained, an anthropomorphic shrine for the senior son and a provisional one for the next in line.

The custody of ancestor shrines is in the hands of the head of the compound. He it is who must address the ancestors in prayer before anyone can make an offering to them. These compound shrines usually represent the dead members of a lineage segment. If the occupants of a house are not all descended from a single ancestor whose shrine they possess, then the two sets of figures are kept slightly apart, so that sacrifices can be made to each group separately.

A situation of this kind existed in one compound in Tshaa, Birifu, known as Wakara's house from the name of the man who built it. Most of the men living there were descended from Jipla, a son of Kontshol, the founder of the lineage (Figure 10).

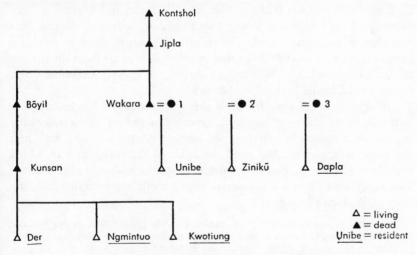

FIG. 10.—The genealogy of Jipla's descendants (1).

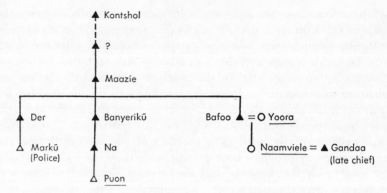

FIG. 11.—The genealogy of Puon's ascendants.

In addition to these descendants of Jipla, a young man called Puon also lived there, in a part of the house that had a separate entrance.[2] Puon was said to be descended not from Jipla but from another son of Kontshol, whose name no one could remember. This failure to recall the name seems to be connected with the fact that the ancestor in question does not form a point of bifurcation, and the genealogy is apparently in the process of "telescoping," or contracting, an adjustment that must occur continuously if a fairly stable population is to maintain lineages of a relatively constant depth (Evans-Pritchard [1940], p. 199; Peters [1960], p. 32). The agnatic grandchild of Kontshol was called Maazie, and he in turn was Puon's father's grandfather (Figure 11).

This residential pattern came about because Puon's father, Na, had died when his son was still a young lad, and Puon and his mother had been cared for by agnates living in a neighboring house. At the time Na's house was abandoned, the ancestor shrine of Maazie was also brought over to Wakara's house and stood slightly apart from the shrines of Jipla's descendants. When Na's shrine was carved sometime later, it was placed in the byre near Maazie's.

When a house is abandoned in this way, a sacrifice has to be made to the shrines to discover their willingness to be moved. Sometimes they express their refusal by rejecting the chicken offered to them, and then the wooden figures are left amid the ruins of the compound in which they dwelt (Plate 13). But in the present case the ancestors gave a favorable reply, and the figures, covered with a cloth, were carried into the byre of Wakara's house.

2 LoWiili houses formerly had no entrances on the ground floor except into the byre itself, and access was by means of ladders to the roof. But nowadays it is not unusual for the wall of the open courtyard to be constructed with a gap in it; in Puon's case the outside wall had simply never been completed.

At the beginning of 1950, one of Wakara's sons, Zinikū, separated from his brothers and built himself a house about a hundred yards away, using for this purpose the supports and rafters from his old rooms. Since he was the son of a junior wife, he could not take away his father's final shrine, so the provisional one was carried off to the byre of the new dwelling. Had Zinikū been the head of the compound, he would have taken all the shrines with him, except those of the fathers of the men remaining behind in the old house.

Two years later, Puon, who now felt himself able to act as the head of a compound, also constructed a house for himself and his mother on the exact site of his father's home, and the ancestor shrines were then taken back again. Thus the temporary fusion of the residential units was followed by fission, re-establishing the earlier distribution of homesteads. I should add that apart from the religious grounds for returning to ancestral sites, there are other reasons why people prefer to build on the slightly higher land that the ruins of a compound provide; for one thing, it is drier during the rainy season.

A further example of the way in which residential fission determines the custodianship of shrines is provided by another group of Jipla's descendants, who lived in a compound close by Wakara's (Figure 12).

In 1949 all the descendants of Ziem and Der were living in one compound. The following year Sue and Nyengmaa built themselves a house of their own and took with them the shrines of Lompo, Ziem, and Jipla. The year after, Tīīnyue moved into a new house, taking his father's shrine with him and leaving only the offspring of Wuntuo living in the original compound.

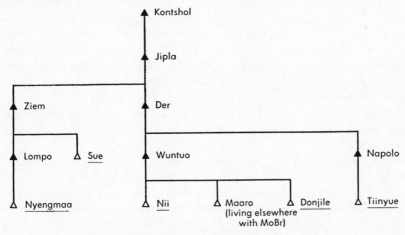

FIG. 12.—The genealogy of Jipla's descendants (2).

In some cases it proves ritually inadvisable to move the ancestral figures. This happened to Lugber's shrine. His son Baare took over the house at his death, but died soon after, leaving only his own young son, Tatuur, who was taken in by a neighboring kinsman. The shrines were carried off to the kinsman's house, but a subsequent misfortune to the family was traced by the diviner to the fact of their transfer. The ancestors were said to fight (_ziora_) with the inhabitants, and the shrines were therefore taken back to the site of Lugber's house, where they lay exposed to the elements in the middle of a field. It is of course still possible for Tatuur to sacrifice to his agnatic forebears, and when he builds himself a house of his own, the ancestors will doubtless agree to be taken there.

Among the Tallensi, the custodianship of the shrines coincides with the distribution of authority within the lineage; their handing over in itself confers a lineage position upon the holder. There is no such close overlap among the LoDagaa. The byre of the senior member of a lineage does not necessarily contain the shrine of the founding ancestor. Although the elder may make an attempt to move it, mystical trouble is often traced to this disturbance, and the shrine has then to be returned to its original resting place. But even if it is not kept in his house, the senior member is still responsible for seeing that the proper ceremonies are carried out, and it is he who addresses the founder's shrine at any sacrifice made on behalf of the lineage as a whole.

Ancestors are neither remembered nor worshiped forever. Unilineal genealogies are reference systems for social groups that have to maintain a fairly constant strength, if only because they function in reciprocal relationships with other similar groups. The turnover in the membership of descent groups means that the genealogy is continuously extending itself in depth. But the optimum span of the genealogy, which depends directly upon its numerical strength, is held constant by the demands of reciprocity, even in conditions of an increasing population. Consequently, "telescoping" and similar devices are necessary to maintain the balance. Genealogies, as distinct from pedigrees, are characterized by continual shrinkage, and in an oral tradition the simple process of forgetting destroys links in the chain that are no longer required.

In a very similar way the shrines themselves, the objective correlates of the ancestors, are also gradually eliminated from the scene as new ones come into being. Although it is difficult to observe this process in action during a period of field work, it is clear how it might occur. In the house of Zengmaa, in the LoDagaba settlement of Tom, two groups of shrines stood separately in the byre; one consisted of those forebears whose names were remembered, the other of the unknown dead. Zeng-maa maintained that were he to build himself another house, he would take with him only those shrines he could definitely associate with named ancestors; it would be dangerous to take others you did not know about. In this way shrines that are not significant to the genealogy around which the lineage is organized would be automatically eliminated.

Apart from being abandoned when their names are forgotten, ancestor shrines also disappear from natural causes. If fire destroys them, only shrines known to belong to a particular ancestor are remade, and then not until a diviner has confirmed the advisability of doing so. White ants are the most likely source of danger; as time goes on, the wooden figures get smaller and smaller as the termites gradually eat into them, and once again no replacement is made unless it is known which ancestor the shrine represents, and then only if the ancestor continues to be of some social significance.

The market at Tom, known as *Zeng daa,* was called after the man said to be the original founder of the present village, although his name no longer appears in current genealogies. One day when I was walking around the senior house (*yikpēē*) of the lineage, I asked to see Zeng's shrine. "*Zeng in tan,* Zeng is earth," I was told. "The white ants have eaten the shrine. He has no place at which we can make offerings." The shrine gradually disintegrates into dust; at this point the worship of the Earth and the worship of the ancestors merge into one.

Men's ancestor shrines are created and kept by their direct agnatic descendants; in this there is no difference between the two communities. The accumulated shrines provide a material counterpart to the patrilineal genealogy; both maintain a rough relationship with the composition of the lineage itself by means of similar processes of telescoping.

OCCASIONS FOR SACRIFICE

In discussing "ancestrolatry" among the BaThonga of southeastern Africa, Junod distinguishes several kinds of offering to the ancestors, whether they are national or familial, whether simple or sacramental,[3] whether or not bloodshed is involved, and finally whether the offerings are made regularly or in special circumstances.

It is with this last distinction that I am primarily concerned. As with the ceremonies we discussed earlier, sacrifices, especially those performed at regular intervals, may be set within the cycles either of cosmic

[3] Sacramental offerings are always ordered by the diviner and accompanied by a special prayer called *tsu* (Junod [1927], II, 390).

or of human time. The aspect of the cosmic cycle of greatest relevance here is the seasonal rhythm of production; other important offerings of this regular kind occur at set stages in the life cycle and are mainly centered upon the physical and social processes of reproduction.

In the majority of non-industrial communities, the big seasonal ceremonies take place at the beginning and the end of the productive season. At the Rogation festival the community begs the assistance of spiritual beings in the coming season, while at the Thanksgiving ceremony it rewards them for their help. The second occasion is generally the more important of the two, occurring as it does at a time of plenty, when enough food is available for feasting and drinking. Festivals for the spirits of the dead therefore tend to take place at the end of the productive season, particularly in those collecting and agricultural societies in which the seasonal nature of the productive process is most marked.

Some of the main factors influencing food production are climatic, and in the savanna belt of West Africa the amount and timing of the rain are particularly critical. Factors relating to the climate are generally ones that affect the whole, rather than a part, of any local community, all of whose inhabitants are visited by a good or a bad harvest at one and the same time. Consequently, ceremonies that relate to the major turning points in the business of food production tend to emphasize communal rather than sectional interests.

The LoDagaa lack any specific planting ritual, but they have two post-harvest ceremonies, the Earth Shrine Festival (*Tenggaan Dãã*) and the General Thanksgiving Festival (*Bomaal Dãã*).[4] At the first of these, each compound in the ritual area contributes grain for a general sacrifice at the Earth shrine. The second ceremony is carried out by the local descent group or a subsection of it. Fowls are killed at all the shrines in the farm and in the house, and new crops are often offered at the same time. The practice varies with the patrilineage, which of course forms the widest congregation in terms of the worship of specific ancestors. In some groups, all the ancestor shrines from each of the compounds are brought to one house, where the offering is made in the presence of the body of its members. In other instances, representatives of the lineage may gather at the shrine of the founding ancestor to perform a more esoteric rite (Goody [1956a], pp. 68 *et seq*.). But in both these cases the thanksgiving sacrifice to the ancestors provides a focus of great importance for the religious activities of the lineage.

----

4 *Dãã* means beer, which is an essential component of any major festival. *Bomaal* (LD *Bagmaal*) means "shrine offering." I have often translated *bo'or* (LD *bagr*) as "mystical trouble," but here, like the cognate Tallensi term *boghar*, it also refers to the shrine itself. *Tiib* is the usual word for shrine.

The important stages of the individual life cycle—those associated with the turnover of personnel, namely birth, marriage, and death—are all marked by performances connected with the ancestors, although not in every case are these sacrifices in the strict sense.

A member of the lineage first sees the light of day in the very presence of the ancestor shrines; for when a woman feels the pangs of birth she is taken into the byre to bear her child under their aegis. Soon after the birth a chicken known as the Fowl of the Breasts (*Bir Nuo*) is sent to the mother's natal home for sacrifice to her own patrilineal forebears; for it is believed that her milk will begin to flow only if this is done. When the child reaches the time for his "outdooring," at the age of three months for a boy and four months for a girl, some patriclans consult a diviner about the spirit guardian. Although a variety of supernatural agencies may serve in this capacity, the diviner often selects an ancestor of the lineage whose name the child takes.

In initiation ceremonies to the Bagre society, the ancestors again have their part to play; at the opening rite in the whole complex sequence (*Bag Puru*), the officiants go to the byre of the main compound of the lineage, pour water over the shrines, and address the ancestors. Later, when a young man arrives at the age of marriage, the bridewealth cowries are first placed in front of the ancestral shrines before being carried to the bride's patrilineal kin, since it is they who will assist the new wife to bear children for the lineage. The ancestors have vested interests in the rights over both her coital and her reproductive services. Any child born of that woman is a member of the lineage, no matter who the *genitor*; the man on behalf of whom the bridewealth was paid remains the *pater* of all the children she bears until the bridewealth is returned to her paternal kin. When these rights, jointly acquired by the living and dead members of the lineage, are infringed, as when adultery is committed, then an expiatory sacrifice has to be made to the ancestors.

It should be noted that the LoDagaa do not categorize sexual offenses in the same way that Euro-American societies do. In the first place, the categories are tied to the system of descent groups. There are thus three main types of heterosexual offense: sleeping with a clanswoman, sleeping with the wife of a clansman, and sleeping with other married women; these offenses I refer to as "incest," "group-wife adultery," and "adultery."[5] In the last two cases the adulterer is required to provide an animal to be killed in expiatory sacrifice to the husband's ancestor shrines, but an offense against a female member of the group

[5] For a general discussion, see Goody [1956b].

("incest") necessitates no such payment. If it occurs before the girl's marriage the affair is not treated in a serious manner. To sleep with a "sister" after her marriage is a different question. A man who commits such an offense cannot partake of the flesh of the Bull of Childbearing, part of the second bridewealth payment, when such an animal is sacrificed to the ancestors. To do so would be to have one's cake and eat it; it would contravene the demands of reciprocity. Except in this case, sexual offenses after marriage are reckoned to be offenses against the ancestors of the husband, not against those of the bride.

"Group-wife adultery" not only requires but demands a sacrifice, although in such a case the whole matter is settled as privately as possible. In sacrifices for adultery both within and without the clan, the meat is consumed by the members of the lineage whose rights have been infringed, but the husband himself cannot participate. To eat the flesh of an animal killed for a sin committed by one's wife might be taken as condoning the offense, and even as profiting from it.

The offense of adultery may be avoided if a fowl is sacrificed to the ancestors before the woman and her paramour sleep together, but this situation can of course arise only when the couple have the husband's approval in their action. There are two possible circumstances in which such approval might be forthcoming. First, if the failure to have children is attributed to sterility on the husband's part, then the wife may select one of his lineage "brothers" with whom to have intercourse. The responsibility of the spouses is determined in the following fashion: the parties are each made to urinate on some grains of guinea-corn; if a person is sterile, it is thought that the grain he has watered will not germinate. The second situation is when a man permits his wife's lover, if he is a friend, to have intercourse with her. In both cases a fowl must be killed to the ancestors before intercourse takes place, otherwise the husband would be obliged to claim the "adultery" payment.

Marriage involves sacrifices to the ancestors other than those arising out of the breach of relatively exclusive sexual rights, as is shown by the fact that one of the cattle received as bridewealth for a daughter has to be slaughtered to the founding ancestor of the lineage. This is the Bull of Childbearing, which is killed either at the shrine of the lineage founder himself, or else at the shrines in the girl's own compound; in the latter case it would be accompanied by a request that the animal be given to the apical ancestor, although it may be offered in the first place to some closer forebear. This sacrifice is one at which the elder of the patrilineage acts as officiant, and the flesh is distributed among all the patrilineage members, with the exception of those who have committed "incest," i.e., those who fail to observe the major premise of the marriage arrangements—that a man cannot have as sexual object both his own "sister" and someone else's. A portion of this sacrifice is also given to the other lineages in the clan sector.

References to the expiation for adultery and to the Bull of Childbearing lead to a consideration of the category of occasional sacrifices, those that occur not on regular occasions but at unpredictable times, especially when someone is ill. For although there is a general obligation to give the Bull of Childbearing to the ancestors, the transaction rarely, if ever, takes place until some misfortune has happened to remind the living of what they owe the dead. For example, when a child falls ill, the compound head consults a diviner, who may relate the sickness to a failure to kill such a bull when it was first sent by the wife-taking in-laws. The sacrifice may then be carried out and the matter repaired; if the sickness continues, a diviner is consulted again in an attempt to get to the heart of the matter.

A man has an obligation to offer the ancestors part of the goods he acquires not only by incoming bridewealth payments, but also by inheritance, farming, hunting, wage labor, and other economic activities. But these offerings to the ancestors are rarely, if ever, made when they first become due. What happens is that if a man finds himself in a situation of anxiety and is unable to deal with it by the other techniques available to him, he will consult a diviner, who shows him which of the supernatural agencies is responsible for the misfortune that has come about. If the client has been a successful farmer, it is likely that the soothsayer will tell him that the ancestors are angry because they have not yet received a portion of the gains that are their due.

An account of one such sacrifice will bring out some of the points I have made. When Diiyir's young son died in Tshaa, Birifu, a diviner traced the cause of the death to Diiyir's failure to offer a farming sacrifice to his own father, Der; he had also made money by grave-digging and had given nothing to the ancestors. This omission Diiyir quickly corrected to prevent further misfortune. Several months later he called his "father," Bõyiri, to come and sacrifice a sheep to his grandfather, Bazio; a diviner had announced that he, too, was angry at receiving nothing, although he would have been given a leg of any sacrifice made to his son, Der (Figure 13). Bõyiri came to perform the sacrifice, or rather to address the shrines, bringing with him a lineage member of junior generation, Dire, to cut the throat of the fowl killed on the altar before the main offering was made.

The Bull of Childbearing and a proportion of the animals acquired

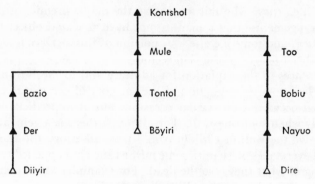

FIG. 13.—The genealogy of Diiyir.

by other means should be given to the ancestors, but their descendants on earth withhold such offerings until some specific occasion arises. In a sense, most occasional sacrifices to the ancestors are unfulfilled obligations. It is the failure to fulfill an obligation that is thought to anger the dead man and cause him to take retaliatory action, which is often capricious, cruel, and out of proportion to the offense. Even the very first sacrifice to a particular ancestor is of this retrospective kind. When the shrine is taken into the byre at the last funeral ceremony, it is set apart from the other figures, being finally placed among them at a later rite performed by the heir. But often nothing is done until the dead man reminds the living of their duty by causing some misfortune, the reason for which is later revealed by the diviner.

Sacrifices to the ancestors, which consist in rendering unto them what is their due, can hardly be thought of as a gift. I have earlier defined a gift as a transaction between members of different property-holding corporations; yet it is mainly between the living and the dead members of such groups, persons who have joint rights in each other's property, that sacrifices are made. Moreover, most of the sacrifices that the Lo-Dagaa make to specific ancestors are expiatory in form, fulfilling neglected obligations and offering to the spirits what was already owed them for other reasons. Indeed, every man at all times lies under an obligation to the ancestors. From the general point of view he can never repay the weighty benefits he has received from his forebears, and on the particular level there is always some service to the dead that he is behind with.

But apart from these rituals of affliction, there are other situations when the notion of the exchange of services implied in the phrase *do ut des* is more appropriate. For regular sacrifices often consist in asking and thanking the ancestors for specific favors. And sometimes occasional sacrifices, too, consist of small offerings accompanying a request, and a conditional promise of a larger reward should the request be met. One form taken by such conditional promises is the invocation against another human being. I speak here of rogation (and thanksgiving) sacrifices in order to distinguish them from expiatory or demand offerings, which are a response to affliction. The distinctions are shaded among the LoDagaa, but the people do differentiate between sacrifices that are initiated by the ancestors and those that are set in motion by the mouths of men and are in this sense voluntary.

There is a further point that needs making here. General explanations of sacrifices are often capable of being disproved by particular examples. The root of the difficulty here lies not so much in the explanations themselves, but in the category of actions they are trying to explain. If the over-all category of sacrifice is broken down, then different explanations can be found to apply to different types of offering.

SACRIFICIAL ROLES

In most sacrifices, not only among the LoDagaa but in a wide range of societies, four main roles are distinguishable:[6]

(1) The donor, who owns the offering; in rituals of affliction he is sometimes distinguished from the person suffering the misfortune.

(2) The officiant or speaker, who addresses the shrine; I also use the phrase "ritual leader," since "priest" tends to imply a full-time specialist.

(3) The sacrificer or assistant, who wields the knife and supervises the cutting up of the meat for distribution.

(4) The recipient, the supernatural being to whom the offering is made.

The recipient is of course indicated by the diviner, and in the present analysis it is his relationship to the donor that is of the most significance. The officiant may vary, and the determining factor here is the kind of animal offered to the shrine. Domestic animals, like wild animals, are divided into "white" and "black," a dichotomy that has been noted in several other ritual contexts during the course of this study. The black domestic animals include the cow, the sheep, and the guinea-fowl; the white comprise the goat and the fowl. What is black is "dangerous," and sacrifices of these animals involve the whole lineage, usually being

6 See the articles on "Sacrifice" by Rose and others in Hastings's *Encyclopaedia of Religion and Ethics* (1908).

carried out by the elder himself. Fowls and goats may be killed by the compound head at the ancestor shrines that come under his custodianship, and no outsider need be informed. Typical of this latter form of sacrifice is that in which a man offers his father a hoeing fowl (*kuur nuo*) when he has achieved success in farming or in some other activity.

The difference between these two types of sacrifice was brought home to me in Birifu one day, when I was visiting a lineage head whom I knew well. I arrived at his house and found him in the process of offering a goat to the founding ancestor. Apart from his son, who was acting as the sacrificial assistant, no one else was present. I could not at first reconcile this esoteric performance with the often-repeated maxim that "A sacrifice to a grandfather belongs to everybody" (*Sāākum bo'ore, ni yo'o so*). Then I realized that Bōyiri was acting as head not of the lineage but of the compound, as custodian of the shrine. Had he been making the sacrifice in the former capacity, the meat would have had to be shared among all the members of the lineage. As a compound head, he could sacrifice a fowl or a goat to the shrines standing in his byre without calling upon outside assistance.

The lineage head should officiate when any "black" animal is offered, although he may delegate this task to another member. Other persons in the lineage may attend these sacrifices, but they do so as individuals; people say that if they are present when the meat is distributed, they can be sure of getting the proper share. The killing of the Bull of Childbearing automatically falls within this category of lineage sacrifices.

Among the LoWiili, where the clan sector is organized into a definite number of patrilineages, it is customary for the lineage that is making the sacrifice to invite the heads of other lineages in the local division of the patriclan to attend and accept a portion of the meat on behalf of their groups. Indeed, it is men from these other lineages who actually kill the Bull of Childbearing; and when an adultery sacrifice has to be made, the same kinsmen carry out the preliminary sacrifice on behalf of the lineage whose rights have been violated. The principle underlying this exchange of services is identical to that by which certain difficult funeral tasks are allotted to the other lineages in the same clan sector. At other times when sacrifices of a particularly serious nature are made to the ancestors, it is a "sister's son" who is asked to perform this preliminary oblation (*bun puru*, a thing of greeting). In this way the correct tone is set for the sacrifice proper. For the ancestors are too angry with their own agnatic descendants to be approached by them directly. The persons nearest to these descendants, outside the clan yet closely related by links of lateral kinship, are the sons of its female members. Such men clear the way by performing the preliminary sacrifice and are allotted the flesh of the beast they kill.

This partial rejection of the slaughtered animal bears some resemblance to piacular sacrifices in which the victim is simply thrown away. Such offerings are rare among the LoDagaa, for whom sacrifice is the usual way of consuming meat. The nearest approach to such a total rejection occurs when expiatory rites are performed at the Earth shrine to expiate a suicide in the parish. On such occasions the shrine is said "to have its hair shaved off" by being "swept" with a dog, which is then cast aside. However, even in this case the flesh was never in fact wasted, for the corpse of the victim could be taken away and eaten by the joking partners of the parish. In each situation some category of persons exists, members of a reciprocal lineage, the "sisters' sons," or the joking partners, to whom the rejected meat is not forbidden. Indeed, their entitlement to this flesh is a corollary as well as a reward of their cathartic services. What is dangerous to those in difficulties is safe for those who are in a position to offer ritual assistance, to "throw ashes," or to "pour water," to make "cool" that which is "hot."

The assistance of these partial outsiders may extend to killing the animal offered in the main sacrifice; more usually this is done by a classificatory "son" of the officiant. Among the LoDagaba, I have known a brother by a different mother hold the knife; but my information is not sufficient to show whether there are any standardized differences in this practice between the two communities.

GIVERS AND RECEIVERS

In discussing the worship of the ancestors, I have so far been able to treat the LoWiili and the LoDagaba as one. The central difference appears in the relationship between the donor and the recipient, a difference that can perhaps best be indicated by tabulating the data on the sacrifices to the ancestors in which I myself participated.[7]

The differences between the two communities that this table brings out are highly significant in terms of the general thesis put forward. If we set on one side the voluntary sacrifices, of which there were only two in all, one invocatory and one a thank offering, then out of ten

[7] I use the phrase "participated in" to indicate not only those sacrifices to the ancestors which I actually attended, but also those with which I was otherwise closely connected. I attended other sacrifices when blood offerings were made to a series of shrines, including the ancestors; but in the following table I have included only specific sacrifices to particular ancestral spirits.

Donor	Relationship of recipient	Reason underlying the obligation	Animal	Date
A. LoWiili				
1. Albaa	Fa	Farming	Cow	10. xii. 50
2. Bŏyiri	FaFaFa	Farming	Goat	22. ii. 51
3. Bŏyiri	FaFaFa (Fa)	Farming	Goat	14. ix. 52
4. Diiyir	FaFa	Farming	Sheep	14. vi. 51
5. Diiyir	Fa	Farming and grave-digging	Sheep	1. vii. 51
6. Gazeri	Fa	Inheritance (invocation)	Fowl	23. ii. 51
7. Gazeri	Full Br	Inheritance	Cow	3. iv. 51
8. Gazeri	FaFa	Inheritance	Cow	11. xii. 51
9. Kpaari	Fa	Wage labor	Fowls	various
10. Kulor	Fa (and sheep to FaFa)	Farming	Cow	19. xi. 52
11. Kwonyene	Fa	Inheritance (bridewealth)	Cow	4. viii. 51
B. LoDagaba				
1. Jerry	MoBr (same matriclan)	Inheritance	Cow	12. x. 52
2. Kanyuur	FaFaFa (same matriclan)	Farming	Cow	13. viii. 52
3. Nibe	Fa	Fulfillment of conditional promise about childbirth	Sheep	16. viii. 52
4. Timbume	MoBr (same matriclan)	Wage labor	Fowls	various
5. Turnyoghr	FaFa (same matriclan)	Farming	Cow and sheep	xii. 52

* I also have records of other sacrifices in which I did not participate; I list these below to show that they do not contradict the conclusions based upon Table 12.

LoWiili

Donor	Recipient
Bazio	Fa, FaFa
Tontol	Fa, FaFa
Milka	Fa, FaFa
Bŏyiri	Fa, FaFa
Gazeri	Fa
Dire	Fa
Kwonyene	Fa (fowl)

In addition, I was present at a divining session when Dapla, who had been sleeping badly, was told to kill a farming fowl to his father, and Ngmurko, whose child was ill, a hunting fowl to his father.

LoDagaba

Donor	Recipient
Dakpaala	Fa, FaFa (same matriclan)
Nibe	FaFa (same matriclan)

LoWiili sacrifices, half were to the father, and of the rest, one was to the full brother, two to the father's father, and two to more distant agnates.

The underlying reason for the sacrifices was that the donor had accumulated wealth with the help of his agnatic ancestors and had now to make a return prestation. The wealth had been accumulated by various means, by inheritance, grave-digging, farming, and wage labor. Four sacrifices were made by the inheritor to a recently dead holder with the express purpose of rendering the rest of the property safe to enjoy. Indeed, in a sense, it is obligatory for an heir to kill one of the animals he has inherited to the former holder; if he does not, the ancestor will demand it. As in the case of the offspring of the Cow of Breeding, which a man receives from his maternal uncle, acceptance of this livestock means that the recipient ought to make at least a partial return in the form of a sacrifice.

The significance of holder-heir relationship was especially clear in the sixth, seventh, and eighth cases listed in Table 12. Gazeri, a man in his late fifties, had inherited a considerable fortune from his older brother, who, before he died, declared repeatedly that he wanted his property to go to his sons rather than to his full brother. The animals slaughtered at these sacrifices were part of the inheritance offered by Gazeri explicitly to render the remainder of the property ritually safe ("cool") for himself, and to prevent the jealousy of the sons and the sister's sons from being translated into aggressive action.[8]

In six cases the sacrifice was attributed to farming (*kuur bagre,* hoe sacrifice). Either during the final funeral ceremony or when he begins to farm on his own, a man receives a hoe from his father; when the son is successful and accumulates wealth, then the father, if alive, gets the "father's leg," and if dead, a blood sacrifice.

Of the LoWiili sacrifices, two were made to the father's father. From reports of other sacrifices it appears to be a fairly general pattern that in the course of his lifetime a man makes a large offering, first to his father and then to his grandfather. The two sacrifices to more distant agnates were made by a lineage elder who had already made similar offerings to his less distant ascendants; gradually the cause of misfortune retreats further back in time as a man exhausts the nearer possibilities.

Although there are some circumstances in which it might be feasible, I have never heard of a LoWiili sacrificing to his mother's brother; when asked about this a man would say, "What have I received from

---

[8] Mention in one sacrifice of the sister's sons as possible claimants is a further indication of changes that appear to have occurred among the LoWiili.

him?" Indeed, you make no sacrifice to your father if he "gives" you nothing, "gives" here referring to whether or not you have acquired livestock through his help. Nor have I ever known any discussion of the matriclan relationships of giver and receiver; the whole activity is thought of in agnatic terms.

Among the LoDagaba the situation differed considerably. Of the sacrifices recorded in Table 12, two were made to the mother's brother, and the others were made to agnates; in two cases these patrilineal ancestors also belonged to the same matriclan as the donors, a matter that was the subject of much discussion. In only one of the five sacrifices was there no uterine tie between the donor and the recipient; this was a thank offering for the father, who had fulfilled a specific request made to him by his son. Nibe had made a conditional oath to his father's shrine, promising him a goat if he still proved capable of begetting children. Now at last his wife was pregnant. It is possible that even here the slaughtered animal was one of those the matrilineal heir left behind for the children of his mother's brother to use in such a situation, but I do not know whether this was so on this occasion.

Turning to the sacrifices of obligation among the LoDagaba, we find that the underlying reasons for these demand offerings are the same as among the LoWiili. A man accumulates wealth by farming, inheritance, bridewealth, wage labor, and other activities, and out of this he has to sacrifice to those who have contributed. But it is the contributors that differ. A man still gets his hoe from his father, and he also obtains bridewealth from the same source. Hence he has some obligation to sacrifice to him on these counts, and I have reports of cases when this has happened. For example, out of the bridewealth Dakpaala received for his eldest daughter, he bought a sheep to kill to his father's father, a member of the Some matriclan like himself, and offered the Bull of Childbearing to his father, who belonged to the Hienbe matriclan. But a man receives inherited wealth from his matriclansfolk, not from his father; and it is to them that his wealth will pass when he is dead. Hence it is between members of the same property-holding group that the major obligation to sacrifice is seen to exist.

An instance of one such sacrifice I attended was that in which the donor was a man called Jerry, an inhabitant of a neighboring settlement. A number of people around Tom had acquired Christian names as the result of the influence of the Roman Catholic mission at Nandom, but the possession of such a name did not always indicate a reluctance to participate in sacrifices to the ancestors. The pattern of religious experience here is eclectic, although total conversions of the kind demanded by the world religions are becoming increasingly frequent.

Jerry had inherited the livestock of his mother's brother and was also entitled to any livestock that was owed to this man at the time of his death. These uncollected debts consisted of the bridewealth cattle for the deceased's daughter, married to the headman, Nibe, who had not yet paid the second installment. During the course of 1952 the child of this marriage became ill, and Nibe went to consult a diviner. He was told that the child was ill because of the anger of the maternal grandfather at not having received the bridewealth cattle due to him; for, as an ancestor, he was entitled to the Bull of Childbearing. It is often the case that the sickness of children is interpreted as the result of a wrong done by the parents, whose sins are thus visited on their descendants. Because of Nibe's omission his wife returned with her child to her father's house. The husband was therefore forced to provide the cattle, not only to appease his dead father-in-law and thereby save his child, but also to persuade his wife to come back and live with him. He did provide the cattle, but Jerry, who was the heir, had to sacrifice the Bull of Childbearing immediately in order to appease his mother's brother. For although Jerry was not directly affected at the moment (unless there was some trouble that I did not hear about), the matriclan were to blame for not insisting upon payment of the bridewealth that the dead man jointly owned. Hence Jerry, too, might have suffered some misfortune had not the matter been repaired. And besides relieving the particular situation, the sacrifice also fulfilled part of the general obligation of the heir toward the dead holder. Thus behind this sacrifice lay several sorts of conflict: that between male affines in respect of their diverging interests in women and their children, that between husband and wife, and that between holder and heir. Although the son-in-law provided the sacrifice, the uterine heir was the actual donor.

In two other cases recorded in Table 12, the LoDagaba sacrificed to persons who belonged to the same matriclan and the same patriclan as the donor—in other words, to persons who were his duplicate clansmen. Owing to the rule of exogamy, a father cannot stand in a relationship of this kind to his son, but a grandfather can, and will do so if a patrilateral cross-cousin marriage has taken place.[9]

I attended an example of such a sacrifice among the Natshiele patriclan sector living in Tom.

Kanyãã had received a succession of sacrifices from the Some members of the patriclan, in particular from his grandson Nibe; it happened

---

[9] In his analysis of double clanship among the Ashanti, Rattray remarks upon this feature of cross-cousin marriage in such systems, but he attributes it to bilateral cross-cousin marriage; whereas in fact it is a function of one of its constituent components, namely, marriage to the father's sister's daughter ([1927] pp. 317 *et seq.*).

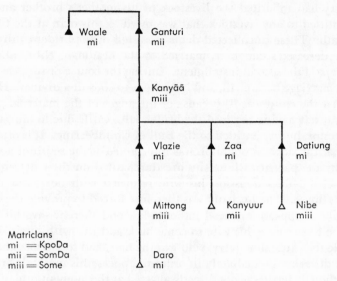

FIG. 14.—The genealogy of Ganturi's descendants.

that members of this matriclan were both more numerous and more wealthy than the rest of his descendants. Toward the middle of 1952 a diviner who had been consulted about some misfortune to a member of the patriclan declared that Ganturi was angry at having been neglected in this way. He always received the "father's leg" of any sacrifice made to his son, Kanyãã, but why should he forever eat meat belonging to another matriclan? Hence Kanyuur, as the senior SomDa in the patriclan sector, was selected to be the donor of the sacrifice. I was told that the next request would probably be from Waale, a member of the KpoDa matriclan, and the responsibility for meeting this would fall upon his duplicate clansman, Daro, who was very sick at the time.[10]

An important aspect of these sacrifices to duplicate kinsmen is that they fulfill a man's obligations to both his patriclan and his matriclan. I have spoken earlier of sacrifices to the ancestors as being an extension to the supernatural plane of the food-sharing that centers upon domestic groups. Just as the ancestors are offered a little of every gourdful of beer that is drunk, so, too, they have a claim upon any surplus of production over consumption.

This is true for the LoWiili. There the duty of a man to sacrifice an animal got by selling the produce of his fields can be seen as an extension of the obligation he has to offer anything he earns to his living

---

[10] In other contexts Waale was given as the son of Ganturi and father of Kanyãã, but he was still said to belong to the KpoDa matriclan.

father; for it is through his patrilineal forebears that he acquires land and a hoe, the basic productive resources and the tools to work them. Among the LoDagaba, however, the situation is more complex. A man is set up in life by his father, who not only brings him up, but also provides him with land, hoe, and a wife; but the rest of his possessions come from uterine sources. It is this latter fact that has the greater influence on the relationship between the givers and the receivers in the sacrificial situation.

The position is perhaps best summed up in the LoDagaba proverb: "Father and son eat together in life but not in death." The LoDagaba do sacrifice to their fathers, though not so commonly as the LoWiili; from them are inherited the main means of acquiring wealth, even if the wealth itself passes matrilineally. But a man has no general obligation to share his livestock with his father. Indeed, the LoDagaba often told me that a dead father could not demand an animal from his son. Should a diviner suggest this, the son would reply, "What did he give me? I've nothing I can kill to him." Thus the social relations between the living control, in a very direct manner, those that are thought to exist with the dead. Although sacrifices are made to the father, it is the dead members of the corporation in which wealth is vested who are usually seen as demanding property from their living descendants. For it is these persons who hold joint rights in the objects of sacrifice, that is, in the livestock themselves. Hence, say the LoDagaba, "Sacrifices to the ancestors always follow the matriclan" (*Sāākum bagre ma turi belo*).

I have translated *sāākum* here as "ancestor," whereas it also means "grandfather" and refers to all persons, living and dead, beyond the next senior generation; "fathers" (*sāāmine*) are deliberately excluded. But the saying does draw attention to the fact that a sacrifice to duplicate clansfolk unites the interests of patrilineal and matrilineal descent groups, interests that are inevitably divided in adjacent generations. Such a sacrifice plays precisely the same part in reverse as does transmission of property to the "heir in the house"; indeed, when the recipient of the sacrifice is of the alternate generation, the donor may be that very heir. In any case, he will have indirectly enjoyed what the ancestor left behind, both to his agnates and to his uterine kin.

The number of cases I have recorded in Table 12 is not large, but if we take into account as well both the general trend that these examples display and the statements of informants, the difference between the two communities is apparent; the obligation to sacrifice to the ancestors varies according to the lineality of the descent group in which the sacrificial objects are vested.

I have emphasized that the donor of a sacrifice is not always a member of the patrilineage. But the shrines of the ancestors can be approached only through their agnatic custodians. When Jerry sacrificed the cow to his maternal uncle, he sat on the rooftop of his mother's house, quite apart from the group of her agnates who were making the preliminary arrangements for the rite. When the officiant began the invocation, Jerry slipped quietly down the ladder and squatted behind the group sitting in front of the shrines.

This rule, that sisters' sons cannot approach the ancestors directly, also applies to slaves and women; for access to the shrines reflects status differences within the lineage.

Although women cannot approach the shrines directly, they do sometimes make offerings both to dead husbands and to their own patrilineal forebears. When Kpere, an aged LoWiili widow long past childbearing, wanted to make such a sacrifice to her husband, she approached the custodian of his shrine, who was his younger full brother and heir to his estate. This man was angry with Kpere because she had not accepted him as a leviratic husband, preferring to live in another set of rooms with her son and his wife. When she asked him to kill a goat to the shrine, he refused outright. So Kpere dragged the goat into the byre and tied it to a post, saying to the shrines, "This is yours." In this way the custodian was forced to kill the animal, lest the ancestors should wreak their vengeance upon him.

Women may also sacrifice to their own patrilineal ancestors. The wife of Baaluon of Kwõnyũkwõ was afflicted with a severe stomach complaint and unable to move. A diviner declared that although she had made money by selling beer, she had never sacrificed a fowl to her father, and that it was her agnatic ancestors who were causing her sickness. Her "brother" was called from Birifu to repair this matter. Since the shrines could not be carried this distance, the sacrifice was performed on a small pile of earth (*tiungser*) where the path leading to the woman's natal home was crossed by another track (*sortshera,* crossroads). Such a spot may also be used for domestic sacrifices to the Earth. The Earth and the ancestors merge together at several points in the conceptual scheme. Here, however, the offering was made specifically to the ancestors, and the same method is used when a man far from home is told by a diviner to make a sacrifice to his forebears.

I have been speaking here of cases when women indirectly offered sacrifices to the ancestors. Do they also receive offerings? Their shrines are aggregated to those of their patrilineal forebears, as well as to their husbands', so that they in fact partake of any sacrifice that is made. Among the LoDagaba it sometimes happens that misfortunes of members of both sexes are attributed to women in the uterine line, a matter that can be repaired by a sacrifice for the mother's stem (*ma per*). Although I was never present at any such occasion, I was given a few detailed accounts. Daakpala told me of a time when he had been warned to make such an offering. He first went to his mother's natal home, in the same settlement; he was then directed to his maternal grandmother's home, some six miles away; from there he was sent to her mother's house, at least twenty miles distant, across the River Volta; and finally to her mother's home, which turned out to be very near his own. There he got the residents to address the shrines and offer the sacrifice he provided; even so, this was done not to the shrine of the woman herself (his mother's mother's mother's mother), but to that of her elder brother. "The spirits of women," it was explained to me on another occasion, "cause little trouble."

PROCEDURE

The participants in a sacrifice squat on their haunches in front of the shrines, since to sit on a stool while making such an offering would be lacking in respect. The assistant takes a calabash of water and pours it over the shrines, saying, "Earth, take this cold water" (*Tan, de a kwõ 'baaro*), an act that cools the wrath of the ancestors. The same gesture is sometimes performed before a person sets out on a long journey, when it has the force of a conditional promise; if the traveler comes safely home, he should then make an offering to the shrine in question.

The Earth is always addressed first in any sacrifice, because it is said that all shrines rest upon the earth. Similarly, in sacrifices to any shrine, the names of the ancestors are also called, since it is from one's forebears that all sacrificial objects, or the means of obtaining them, have been inherited. The Earth and the ancestors thus enter into sacrifices of all kinds.

Having addressed the Earth, the officiant then calls the names of the ancestors, starting with the earliest. But this address is no formal recitation of a genealogy; the generation of any particular ancestor is not indicated, and the order, though basically lineal, branches laterally in a somewhat unsystematic way. Finally, the speaker calls the name of the particular ancestor to whom the sacrifice is being made. If it is a general sacrifice, such as a Bull of Childbearing, then the dead man is asked to accept the animal and take it to his own forebears.

The officiant addresses the ancestor upon the subject of the sacrifice, explaining why his descendants have come together and what help he can give them. Then a fowl is killed to "greet" the shrine. The donor has as yet only the diviner's word that his trouble is due to this particular cause. In order to confirm the verdict of the diviner and discover whether the ancestors will accept the oblation, a preliminary offering must first be made. The officiant grasps the fowl by the legs and thrusts it three times at the shrine, following the pattern of pretended gesture that is adopted in so many dealings with the dead. Holding back the head of the chicken with one hand, he slits the neck with a knife and allows the blood to drip upon the wooden figures. Some of the tail feathers are plucked out and stuck in the blood. The fowl is then thrown aside to see which way up it expires—on its back auspiciously, on its belly unfavorably.

If something is wrong, the main animal is not killed immediately; a diviner has first to be consulted to discover what error has been made. Often the officiant acts as his own diviner and, asking for another chicken to be killed, addresses the shrine, saying, "If it is for such and such a reason you refused the first, then accept this one." If this fowl dies in an auspicious way, then the ceremony goes on as usual.

The sacrificial animal is then dragged close to the shrine, while its legs are held by some of the young men present and sometimes tied with a rope; the assistant pours a gourd of water on its neck and slits its gullet, catching the blood as it gushes into a bowl. Then the animal itself is cut up and laid out on skins or leaves, ready to be distributed to those entitled to a share.

THE DISTRIBUTION OF THE MEAT

The way in which the meat is distributed depends to some extent upon the nature of the sacrifice to the ancestors, but basically it is the same as that employed in the distribution of the Cow of the Rooftop (Table 4, p. 174). One leg of the animal is allotted to the "fathers" and one to the "brothers"; as I explained in analyzing funeral prestations, each of these categories tends to be defined differently in the two communities. If the animal killed is a Bull of Childbearing, the left front leg (or "children's leg" in the case of the Cow of the Rooftop) is given to the patriclan "sisters" of the woman whose bridewealth bull this is, since it was they who "bore" the children. The fourth leg of the Cow of the Rooftop is allotted to the joking partners of the dead man's matriclan. It is consistent with the patrilineal basis of this system of ancestor worship that in sacrifices to the shrines this leg is taken by the "sister's sons," persons who play a cathartic role in relation to the ancestors just as the joking partners of the matriclan do in other contexts. However, the actual sons of female members of the ancestor's lineage are prevented from snatching this meat. Close sororilateral kinsmen share rather than seize; only more distant relatives, sons of women of other patrilineages, or in Tom of linked patriclan sectors, would act in this way.

This ban on "ritual stealing" by close "sister's sons" seemed to me more categorical among the LoDagaba than the LoWiili; indeed, among the former this leg was sometimes taken by the joking partners of the recipient's matriclan instead. My evidence relating to this question is not extensive, but the differences I have noted appear generally consistent with the different roles played by the sister's son in these two societies. Where the matrilineal relationship is given greater weight, especially in the holder-heir situation, the close sister's sons are no longer as free to render cathartic assistance, particularly when one of them is actually supplying the sacrifice.

Of the remainder of the flesh of the Bull of Childbearing, the fillet (*sie*) is given to the mother, another portion (*zige*) to the father's father, and the ribs (*jello*) to the person who has looked after the animal. Other parts go to the officiant and to the men who cut up the animal. In the case of a Bull of Childbearing only, the skin is set aside to be dried and made into a mat for a newborn child.

The portion allotted to the shrine itself is a part of the liver; this is the *nen tuo*, the "bitter flesh," which only senior men can eat. The liver is roasted on the spot and divided between the elders who have participated, except for a small corner, which is cut off and thrown on the shrine. At the time the animal is killed, some of the blood is poured over the ancestral figures, and the rest boiled in a pot, together with part of the guts. All this is consumed on the spot, whereas people take the other flesh back to their compounds.

THE ANCESTORS AS AGENTS OF SOCIAL CONTROL

In explaining the donor-recipient relationships in the two communities, I related the differences to variations in the system of property-holding groups. We saw how a person sacrificed to, and expected sacrifices from, other members of the group that held joint rights in the objects of sacrifice. But because of the turnover problem, these corporate groups are also differentiated in terms of holder and heir, a situation that has its full quota of tensions, centering particularly on the anticipated inheritance. On one level, the tension is resolved by the death of the holder, when the heir enters into full enjoyment of the estate. On the other hand, the corporate group is seen as consisting of both living and dead, so that the superordinate position of the holders is maintained, and in some ways enhanced, at death. The ancestors are not only fellow members of the corporate group, but also authority figures, who maintain the norms of social action and cause trouble if these are not obeyed. This section attempts to compare the position of the ancestors as agents of social control in the two communities and to relate their role to the distribution of authority among the living.

I have earlier mentioned the case of Diiyir, whose son's death was attributed to Diiyir's failure to provide his own father with any of the animals he had acquired by farming (Figure 13). This situation is typical of the LoWiili. A man has the power of life and death over his agnatic descendants not only when he is dead, but also while he is still alive, a power that is reinforced by his position as custodian of his own dead father's shrine. It is this *jus vita necisque* that gives a father's curse such potency.

One example of its use among the LoWiili occurred when Bõyiri's two sons Wulma and Kutshaan both wanted to marry the same girl. Kutshaan's mother stepped in and persuaded the girl to take her own son, and the other brother was so angry and disappointed that he ran off to the South. When Bõyiri first heard he had gone, he cursed his son (*o ngmena nuor yong*) for running off without saying anything. Later he was told about the boy's disappointment over the girl and wanted to withdraw his curse. He went to the ancestor shrines to make a retraction, but the fowl he killed fell unfavorably, showing that the ancestors would not agree. Meanwhile the boy got sick and died. His smock and sleeping mat were brought back from the South, but, much as he wanted to, Bõyiri could not hold a proper funeral for the lad without incurring mystical retribution. Since the boy had died an evil death, he had to bury these possessions of his as quickly and as quietly as possible. Such is the power of a father's curse, even when he wants to retract the words he has used.

From the LoWiili point of view, the power of the father is buttressed by his position as custodian of the ancestor shrines. From the sociologist's standpoint, the ancestors are themselves standardized projections of the father's role. The weight of their authority is related to his position as both holder and socializing agent. When these two roles are vested in different males, which is in effect the situation among the Lo-Dagaba, the power that each has over a person is partial. The tensions produced by these authority relationships are therefore differently distributed in the two communities, and this is directly reflected in the attribution of death, sickness, and other misfortunes to the ancestors (Table 12). Among the LoWiili, I encountered no instance when misfortune was attributed to the mother's ancestors. Consequently, I found no case of a man sacrificing to the shrines of his mother's patrilineage. Neither in his lifetime does the mother's brother constitute a major source of anxiety, nor is his curse greatly to be feared.

Among the LoDagaba the situation differs considerably, despite the many similarities in culture. The power of the mother's ancestors is illustrated in the circumstances surrounding the sacrifice that Jerry made to his maternal uncle; the sickness of the young child that was the immediate occasion for the sacrifice was caused by the anger of his mother's kin. When Timbume, a member of my staff, returned home from the Ashanti capital, Kumasi, he offered a fowl to the ancestors who had protected him on his journey; but it was at the shrine of his dead mother's brother, not his father, that the fowl was killed.

This power of the mother's ancestors arises from the authority held by the mother's brother during his lifetime. For unlike the LoWiili, here the maternal uncle occupies the role of holder. And ownership of wealth is associated with other powers, such as the right to sell a sister's son into slavery. Another example is the curse. Among the LoDagaba a man's curse is effective not only against his patrilineal descendants, but also against his sister's children. The use I heard most frequently quoted is to enforce patrilateral cross-cousin marriage. For example, when Turnyoghr's sister's daughter came to stay in his house as a nurse-maid (*biyaal*) to look after a young child, he intended her to marry his son. But she turned out to have a lazy disposition, and one day when she had been reprimanded for her slackness, she collected her shrine basket and stole back to her father's house. Turnyoghr merely uttered the words "You'll come after me" (*fu na bier ma*). The sentence is ambiguous; it could mean either "Some misfortune will result from this, and you'll come running back to ask my forgiveness" or, alternatively, "When I die you'll follow shortly after." In each case the outcome of the curse could be death.

Just as the ancestor worship of the LoDagaba reflects the greater tensions existing between a man and his mother's brother, so also it indicates a relatively freer relationship with the father. I recorded no instance of a sacrifice arising out of misfortune attributed to a dead father; the one sacrifice to the father that I attended was the result of a conditional oath, the circumstances of which I have briefly explained. The other sacrifices to patrilineal ancestors were all made to persons who were also members of the same matriclan, a category that of necessity excludes the father.

Thus, when the LoWiili say "the ancestors are angry" (*a kpime ziora*) they are speaking of their own agnatic forebears, and when the LoDagaba use a similar phrase (*a kpime zebra*) they may be referring either to the shrine of their mother's brother or to the shrines of duplicate clansmen. Both communities explain this situation in terms of the differences in the manner of inheritance, an explanation that our analysis fully supports. But the difference is not simply a matter of the projection of the authority roles of the living onto the dead. It is the type of authority that is important, the control of money and livestock. The heirs gain control of these goods only at the death of the holder, an event that is therefore hoped for as well as feared; when it comes, the death arouses joy as well as sadness, the inheritance brings guilt as well as pleasure. For all concerned accept hostile thoughts as a sign of complicity. The idea that the bereaved had a hand in the death that is being mourned pervades a number of the rites at a LoDagaa funeral. And it is the differences in the expectations of close kin that are reflected in the worship of the ancestors. In the main, it is those from whose death one benefits that one fears as ancestors.

There is one interesting aspect of the relationship of authority and ancestor worship that I have not yet discussed. Despite the tension that exists between LoWiili fathers and sons, I have heard little open comment about these difficulties among the junior generation themselves. On the other hand, the LoDagaba are constantly discussing the conflicts they have with their mother's brothers. However, on the supernatural plane the LoWiili father acts as a more hostile figure than the LoDagaba uncle. This reversal seems to be related to the fact that the mother's brother in the second group is not the straight counterpart of the father in the first. Among the LoDagaba it is the father (or grandfather) who is in charge of the household; the mother's brother lives elsewhere, and his absence gives freer rein to a discussion of the difficulties inhering in the relationship. Among the LoWiili the tensions with the father are considerable; but since he is head of the household, master of the shrines, controller of the food supply, upbringer as well as holder, the pressures, internal and external, against the expression of hostility are great, and the sons appear to suppress their objections, only to bring them out more sharply at his death. There is no similar impediment among the LoDagaba to the expression of hostility against the maternal uncle; he is not the upbringer, not a member of the household. His spirit is not so greatly feared, partly because his earthly authority is divided with the father and partly because he is a more ready target when alive.

ANCESTOR WORSHIP AND THE SPIRIT GUARDIAN

For most purposes, the actual congregation in the worship of the ancestors is limited to members of the patrilineage. Fellow patriclansmen outside this range do not participate in joint sacrifices to the ancestors; even the members of different lineages of a local clan sector worship separately at the shrines of their own founding ancestors. At one level, however, the cult of the spirit guardian (*siura, sigra*) does provide a focus for the wider descent group. Each clan has its spirit guardian, although linked clans may have the same one. But the altar is usually different for each local clan sector, a rocky hill situated near the settlement itself or some place of significance in the story of the clan's migrations. Like the belief in a totemic animal (*dume*), which is also sometimes spoken of as a spirit guardian, the concept is associated with the patrilineal descent group. There is some evidence that in earlier times children were periodically taken to the altar of the spirit guardian and initiated into its mysteries, which appear to have corresponded in certain ways to the External Boghar of the Tallensi. Today this altar is mainly associated with initiation into the Bagre society. In addition, a stone from the dwelling place of the spirit guardian is often kept at the foot of the ancestor shrines in the senior house of the lineage, and in some other byres as well; in this way all sacrifices to the ancestors are also sacrifices to the spirit guardian.

Apart from the spirit guardian of the patriclan, every individual has his own tutelary (*siura*). Each group has a selection of possible guardians available to its members, including the spirit guardian of the clan itself, individual ancestors, and usually the most important medicine shrines of the lineage. Three or four months after birth, a child is formally carried out of the compound and taken up on the roof; at this time, a diviner is often consulted to discover his spirit guardian, frequently an ancestor of the alternate generation. Some clan sectors perform this ceremony only when a child is initiated into the Bagre association; since membership in this secret society is not compulsory, not every child gets to know his tutelary. Others perform the ceremony when a child is sick.

At this level the institution of the spirit guardian serves to differentiate individuals one from another. But on the clan level it acts as a focus for cohesive sentiments, thus counterbalancing the fissile tendencies inherent in the worship of specific ancestors or groups of ancestors. Whereas the most inclusive congregation involved in a sacrifice to any particular ancestor is limited to the patrilineage, the cult of the spirit guardian emphasizes the whole range of clanship ties. Although the spirit guardians of the clans are not ancestors, they are, like totemic animals, intimately connected with them.

ANCESTOR WORSHIP IN THE WIDER SOCIAL SYSTEM

In his account of the Tallensi, Fortes has emphasized that the main focuses of Tallensi ritual,[11] in the sense of sacrifice and prayer, are the

[11] I have used the word "religion" in this limited sense and given "ritual" a wider meaning.

ancestors and the Earth. Ethnographic evidence suggests that this situation applies to most if not all of the Voltaic-speaking peoples,[12] although the Earth plays a less important part in the cosmological schema of the centralized states. In the widest terms, the worship of the ancestors provides a supernatural framework for the principle of unilineal descent, and the worship of the Earth for the principle of contiguity. It is perhaps true that in all societies in which descent and contiguity are of central importance in the recruitment and organization of social groups, they are given some ritual embodiment, of which the worship of the ancestors and the Earth represent two possible modalities. This ritualization of social organization is of particular importance in stateless societies; supernatural sanctions reinforce both the system of authority within the lineage and the jural sanctions operating between descent groups. The ancestral cult fulfills the first of these functions, the Earth cult the second.

Worship of the ancestors provides sanctions on relationships between members of the descent group in two ways: by giving supernatural support to the system of authority and by the threat of mystical retribution in life and in death. The existence of these spiritual supports means that, for the actor, the traditional norms of the society are handed down from on high, just as God gave to Moses the two tables of stone and to Joseph Smith the plates of gold. In this way social regulation is placed beyond the vagaries of human action; its validity is established by sanctions that no human agent can readily challenge, even though he may at times overlook them. The sociologist, on the other hand, interprets ancestor worship from the opposite standpoint and sees the norms of the society, and the system of authority itself, projected onto the supernatural plane.

Within the descent group, the supernatural sanctions of ancestor worship supplement the authority vested in its senior members. Punishment for breaches of the restrictions upon sexual access and for intragroup aggression lies in the hands of the ancestors. But in the case of theft within the lineage, or from neighboring groups with which it has friendly relations, where the delict is punished by the other members themselves, the power of the elders to deal with these and other offenses is buttressed by their control of the shrines, though this control is only absolute in the case of a man whose father is still alive.

12 See, for example, H. Labouret, Les Manding et leur langue (Paris, 1934) for the Mandingo; L. Tauxier, Nègres Gouro et Gagou (Paris, 1924) for the Southern Mande (or Mande-fu); Tauxier, Le Noir du Soudan (Paris, 1912) for the Bobo; Tait [1961] for the Konkomba; and Rattray [1932] for Northern Ghana generally.

ANCESTORS, AUTHORITY, AND INHERITANCE

One way of summarizing the main features of ancestor worship among the LoDagaa is to point out the similarities and differences with some other societies.

In terms of the variables I isolated at the beginning of this chapter, the LoDagaa system can be characterized as inclusive, individual, and unilineal. As in the case of the Tallensi, the distribution of authority in the lineage is linked with the computation of the genealogy and with officiation at sacrifices. The main difference with the Tallensi lies in the greater degree of individuality involved, since a shrine is created for each adult man during the course of the funeral ceremonies. His translation is thus automatic, and only in rare cases does it become the subject of conflicts among his descendants. Moreover, this means that lineage seniors do not control all approach to the ancestors. Even a younger son may have independent access to his dead father if he builds his own house, for he can take with him the provisional shrine; and, similarly, the shrine of the founding ancestor is not always found in the byre of the senior member of the lineage. Perhaps this situation reflects the relative lack of emphasis on the lineage head's authority over the group as a whole; the ability to obtain obedience to commands does not extend far beyond adjacent generations of close kin in domestic groups.

I emphasize these factors to point up the differences not only with the Tallensi of Ghana, but also with the Lugbara of the Congo-Uganda border. In his admirable study of their religion, Middleton distinguishes between sacrifices arising out of the process of "ghost invocation," when the dead are invoked to bring sickness upon the living, and those arising from "ghostly vengeance," when it is the dead themselves who initiate the illness. He concludes that among the Lugbara both types of sacrifice, which correspond to my invocatory and demand offerings, are usually a response to disputes over authority ([1960] pp. 211 *et seq.*).

At the level of the over-all lineage, there is little authority for the LoDagaa to quarrel about. At the domestic level, tension occurs between the generations, and this may lead to the use of curses and invocations against other members of the community. But although the ancestors certainly help in a general way to maintain the authority of the senior generations, it is uncommon to find them approached to cause sickness to others; there is a danger that such appeals may boomerang back upon the supplicant if there are any gaps in his moral defenses. Appeals are often made to medicine shrines for this purpose, but rarely to ancestors. Occasional sacrifices to the ancestors are usually expiatory in kind, a person's sickness being attributed to a neglected obligation to the dead, rather than to any invocation initiated by another living person.

The two main kinds of ancestor sacrifice among the LoDagaa are the regular performances that involve the maximal lineage as a whole, and the occasional ones, the sacrifices of affliction, that are performed at the behest of a diviner. The relationships between the diviner, the donor, the provider, the officiant, the sacrificer, and the congregation as a whole, all of them relationships between living persons, inevitably involve conflicts over the command of actions and of existing benefits and resources.[13] The actions that precede and follow a sacrifice illustrate the tensions arising out of the authority situation and the control of restricted resources. But the most striking evidence, and that which bears most directly upon the differences between the two communities, comes not from the relationships between the living participants, but from those between the living and the dead, between the human donor and the supernatural recipient of the material objects, the offering of which constitutes the focal point of the sacrifice.

A comparison of the donor-recipient relationship in the two communities shows that among the LoWiili the offerings in demand sacrifices are usually made to the father or grandfather, whereas among the LoDagaba they are made to uterine kin who may also be members of the same patriclan—that is, persons from whom the donor did receive, or could have received, the objects of sacrifice themselves.

As we have seen, these offerings to ancestral beings are not made simply out of the goodness of a man's heart. They are made not as gifts, but in fulfillment of obligations to those who expect offerings because they have helped to provide the living with earthly goods. This the dead do by various means, but mainly through inheritance. However, by transmitting property at their death, they do not relinquish all rights in the goods; for as ancestors they continue to belong to the same property-holding corporations that they belonged to in life and are entitled to share in the gains that accrue to their descendants.

Consequently, these living descendants always see themselves as in debt to the dead. This situation stems partly from the objective benefits that they have received, but also from the anticipation of such benefits by the heirs while the holders are still alive. Because the enjoyment of the property depends upon the death of the holder, the process of in-

---

13 See Nadel's dichotomy between *ca* and *crb* ([1957] pp. 114 *et seq.*).

heritance itself is regarded as dangerous for the heir. The danger derives from the fact that many deaths are attributed to human agents, and
those likely to be suspected, and to suspect themselves, are those who
stand to profit most. People who harbor hostility suspect themselves
of complicity in the death of a near kinsman, and hence they fear as
ancestors those from whose death they had most to gain. Half of the
sacrifices recorded in Table 12 were offered by the inheritor; all demand
sacrifices were offered to members of the descent group within which
the inheritance of wealth takes place. And the occasional sacrifices that
the LoDagaba make to their fathers are to be accounted for by the
division of authority roles in general—and by the holder-heir situation
in particular—between the father and the mother's brother, between
the patriclan and the matriclan. For the relationship here between corporate ownership and intergenerational authority is close and crucial.

CHAPTER XIX

Conclusions

This study has dealt with the mortuary institutions of the LoDagaa. True, there are institutions that I have not discussed, such as the Bagre society, which offers its initiates victory over death and then dashes these hopes to the ground. But I have covered the main areas of social life concerned with man's mortality—the funeral ceremonies, the system of inheritance, and the cluster of beliefs and practices that the people use to dismiss and enshrine their dead, and in particular their departed kin.

In studying the mortuary institutions of the LoDagaa, I have tried to examine the part these play in their total social life and to interpret the meanings of the various actions, both in the wider context of their other acts and beliefs and in relation to the theoretical interests of comparative sociology. But the central problem throughout has been the attempt to explain the differences found to exist between the two communities that I call the LoWiili and the LoDagaba. And the hypothesis upon which I have worked has been one put forward by the LoDagaa themselves: that many of the most important differences result from the inheritance system.

The first task was to isolate the differences, and in order to offset as far as possible the danger of selecting only the evidence that suited my thesis, I presented as comprehensive and detailed a treatment of funeral practices as my field notes would allow. The results of the attempt to specify in what respects customary behavior differed are summarized in Tables 13 and 14, the first of which records twenty-six differences in the funeral ceremonies themselves, and the second, eleven other cultural differences that were touched upon in the course of my account of these rites.

The problem the inquirer faces here resembles that involved in the analysis of the dialects of a language. Shifts of sound and meaning may be related to other cultural features, to questions of the differentiation of social groups or changes in technology. On the other hand, other

LoWiili	LoDagaba	Page
1.	Greater help given by sisters in a man's illness	49
2. The heirs are responsible for distributing some of the dead man's wealth at the funeral, hence different persons are sometimes involved		50, 157
3.	Tree-trunk drum only played at the funeral of a homicide	51
4.	More emphasis on threat by dead woman's lineage to remove corpse if bridewealth debts are not paid	52
5.	No paired burial groups; diffuse exchange of burial services	67
6. Reciprocal funeral groups based on patrilineages	Reciprocal funeral groups based on patriclan sectors	68, 74, 230
7. A dead grandfather propped on the byre door, not placed on the stand		79
8. Pots of cowries placed beside funeral stand of a rich man		83
9.	Funeral chants make reference to mother's patriclan	102
10. More use of *Dagaa* xylophone	More use of *Lo* xylophone, especially among LoSaala	102
11. Relics of clan sector kept in the byre of the last member to die	Relics of clan sector kept in the "big house" of the group	110
12.	Less emphasis on matriclan joking partnerships among the LoPiel, more among the LoSaala	123, 157
13. Grave marked out by grave-diggers	Grave marked out by Earth priest	143, 153
14.	Burials only occur when sun is low	143
15. Witches, including all who die on a certain day of the week, are buried in an old grave	Witches buried in river bank	152
16. Funeral contributions, the provision of animals, and the distribution of their meat all display greater agnatic emphasis among LoWiili and greater uterine emphasis among the LoDagaba		158 to 182
17. Whitewashing of widow often postponed until after cause of death is ascertained at the Diviners' Beer		186, 195
18.	More emphasis on duplicate kinship roles	187, 266
19. Agnates not questioned about debts during the ceremony in the room	Uterine kin not questioned about debts during the ceremony in the room	205
20.	Added rites for Bagre members at Diviners' Beer	218

TABLE 13 (*Continued*)

LoWiili	LoDagaba	Page
21.	Different distribution of beer in the ceremony in the room	253, 255
22.	No questions asked of "fellow slaves" during the ceremony in the room	257
23. Ancestor shrine taken into byre early in day	Ancestor shrine is taken in at end of day	259
24.	Members of matrilineal moiety may contribute "fathers'" money when the orphans are tested	261
25.	Matriclans operate in reciprocal groups	264
26.	Special rite for transmitting property to outside heir	259

TABLE 14.—CULTURAL DIFFERENCES BETWEEN THE LoWIILI AND THE LoDAGABA, APART FROM MORTUARY INSTITUTIONS*

LoWiili	LoDagaba	Page
1. Larger patriclan sectors, divided into specific number of lineages, i.e., "organized"	Smaller clan sectors without division into specific number of lineages, i.e., "unorganized"; more emphasis on linked patriclans	8, 68
2. Vukāle ceremony		57
3. Entrance to compound by ladder to roof	Entrance to compound through the byre	77
4.	Earlier fission of productive units and more use of "young men's plots"	97, 302
5.	More gambling in the past	130
6.	More "friendship"	138
7. More divinatory shrines to the "beings of the wild" (*kontome*)	More divinatory shrines to the "gods" (*ngmini*)	140, 212
8.	More gifts from father to son	205, 264
9. If mother's brother pays bridewealth for non-resident sister's son, children belong to his patriclan	Mother's brother pays the bridewealth for a man's second wife; children belong to her husband's patriclan	222
10.	More emphasis on FASIDA marriage	350
11.	Greater emphasis on "mother's stem"	405

* I have not listed here the differences in inheritance and ancestor worship discussed in Chapters XVI and XVIII (pp. 383, 397 *et seq.*) or those in slavery, witchcraft, and nuclear kin relationships treated later in this chapter (see also pp. 407, 408). The reader should also be reminded that among the LoDagaba the matrilineal subclan is exogamous; among the LoWiili only the matrilineage.

changes may result from the process of linguistic drift. We cannot assume, as some holistic approaches to comparative sociology have tended to do, that all variations in social action interlock one with another; nor yet can we accept an atomistic view that dogmatically asserts the opposite.

If we look at the situation from the standpoint of our hypothesis, the differences between these two communities can be divided into those directly connected with the differing modes of transmitting property, those indirectly connected, and those that have no apparent connection at all.

Of the twenty-six differences in the funeral ceremonies, eleven (3, 5, 7, 8, 11, 13, 14, 15, 17, 20, and 23) fall into this last category, and so do three (2, 3, and 7) out of the eleven other cultural differences. Indeed, not only am I unable to find any relationship with differences in inter-generational transmission, but I cannot discern a necessary connection with any other features of the social system. Two of the differences (Table 13: 15 and 17) point to an increased preoccupation among the LoWiili with anti-witchcraft measures, and these seem to have been introduced with the support of the late chief of Birifu, who was much concerned with matters of this kind. Other differences, such as the popularity of divining shrines (Table 14: 7), represent functional alternatives, choices among the available idioms of the whole region. In ritual matters the inadequacy of many of the procedures, as a means to the ends that the actors desire, gives them a gradual obsolescence, which leads to a change in the means employed; although mostly such changes simply involve a replacement of one shrine, oracle, prophet, diviner, or cargo cult by another of a similar kind.

As well as this process of substituting one feature for another, there is also a process of elaboration upon a common theme. For instance, people in Birifu understand quite well when told that the LoDagaba of Tom bury their dead when the sun is low, since it makes sense in terms of their own beliefs in the dangers that beset wandering souls at funerals. Equally, the LoDagaba find the LoWiili treatment of grand-fathers and rich men perfectly comprehensible, since it is simply an elaboration of a common method of distinguishing these roles.

Of the other differences in the funeral ceremonies of the two socie-ties, seven (2, 16, 19, 21, 22, 24, and 26) appear to be directly connected with the uterine transmission of property, and this is again reflected in the greater emphasis given to matriclan ties (18 and 25), to relationships with the mother's brother (9), and to the bond between a brother and the sister whose son will inherit (1 and 4). In addition, I have tried to explain yet another feature, the numerically smaller patrilineal groups among the LoDagaba (6), in terms of the greater emphasis laid upon the matriclan. And, finally, the use of *Lo* and *Dagaa* xylophones (10) is to be interpreted as an expression of the dominant cultural trends (Goody [1956a]). In one case, that of joking partnerships between clans (12), the differences appear to reflect the fact that double clanship offers a system of alternatives for some institutions.

A similar situation emerges from Table 14; of these other cultural differences, six have a direct connection with property (4, 5, 8, 9, 10, 11), and two (1 and 6) are connected with the size of patriclans mentioned above. But we are not simply interested in what proportion of cultural differences among the LoDagaa appear to be related to the transmission of property, but rather in the comparative importance of the features so related and the reasons behind the variations.

The burden of the analysis has been that these major differences can best be explained by taking property transmission as the independent variable. The basic variable is the fact that among the LoWiili all property is transmitted agnatically; whereas among the LoDagaba the productive resources—the immovable property—are passed on in the same way, but the consumer goods—the movable wealth, especially money and livestock—are inherited between uterine kin. Rights over women among the LoDagaba occupy an intermediary position, for they are acquired with bridewealth that is supplied by the father as well as by the mother's brother; and they are vested in those members of the patriclan who are also members of the holder's matriclan. The importance of persons who exactly duplicate the clan affiliations of the dead man crops up again in the inheritance of labor services for married sisters or daughters, as well as in the transmission of house timbers and of that special emblem of a man's masculinity, the bitter quiver.

Both the LoWiili and the LoDagaba have a system of double clanship, but the pattern of inheritance means that it is only among the latter that both patriclans and matriclans are corporate in the property-holding sense. By this I mean that whereas property, whether in land or in goods, is usually worked and held by single individuals or by small groups, the whole of the named unilineal descent group is spoken of as having joint rights. Nor is this simply a matter of words. For between members of the corporation in which wealth is vested, there is no debt in the full sense of the word. Loans between members should be repaid, but at death the obligation ceases to exist.

Just as the wealth-holding corporations are in one instance patrilineal, in the other matrilineal, so in the one case a man cannot continue to be in debt to his agnates, nor in the other to his uterine kin.

Not only the dead man's debts, but other differences in the ritual surrounding the settlement of his movable estate, his money, his wives, and his cattle, derive directly from this same fact. So, too, do differences in funeral contributions; where the matriclan is a property-holding corporation, there is greater stress on the contribution of its members to the funeral of one of their number. The major offerings are the animals slaughtered to the dead man's name. Among the LoDagaba, matriclan members have to supply a Cow of the Rooftop out of the wealth they corporately own, usually an animal belonging to the heir; and as a corollary they all share in the distribution of its flesh.

Like the funeral ceremonies, the practices and beliefs involved in the worship of the ancestors are very similar in the two communities, but again the variations are of considerable significance. In both societies a man has an individual wooden shrine carved for his father during the last of the funeral ceremonies; and the custodianship of this shrine, which is placed with those of other lineage members in the byre of the dead man's house, is transmitted, together with the house itself, in the agnatic line. But when we examine the sacrifices made to these shrines in situations of affliction, who kills to whom, we see that a man is directed to sacrifice to those ancestors who belonged to the same wealth-holding corporation, the group that holds and inherits rights in the objects of sacrifice themselves, the cows, the sheep, the chickens, and the goats. For in these demand offerings a man can only return by sacrifice what he has received. One major way he receives is by inheritance. These transactions place him under a heavy obligation to the ancestors, an obligation that he is always behindhand in fulfilling; so he is reminded of his duty by some affliction of supernatural origin that can be cured only by making an offering to repair the omission. It follows that such expiatory sacrifices are not seen as gifts. In the sense I have used the word, a gift can be made only to a member of a different wealth-holding corporation, a person who does not possess a joint interest, however limited, in the objects that comprise the gift. Sacrifices of affliction, on the other hand, are made in fulfillment of an obligation to a fellow member of the group, a man who has as much right to these objects as one does oneself. Among the LoWiili the donor of a demand sacrifice was always an agnate of the deceased, whereas among the LoDagaba he was usually a uterine kinsman.

Several other important institutions differ in ways that are connected with the whole problem of debt and its relationship to corporate descent groups. Two such institutions, mentioned in the course of this study, are witchcraft and slavery.

The concept of debt is related to the attacks of witches in the fol-

lowing manner. Among the LoDagaba it is said that if a witch attends
a coven and feeds on the human flesh provided by witches of other
matriclans, he or she will eventually be called upon to provide a victim
for the feast. The debt incurred must eventually be repaid. To bring
the soul of a person of another matriclan would be to incur another
debt to the matriclan of the victim, just as to kill a member of a descent
group by other means is visualized in terms of debt. Witches of the
victim's group would object to an outsider attacking one of their members, who are their own prey. So the witch is forced to take the soul of
one of his own matriclan, since this can be done without incurring a
debt, just like taking his wealth. As a consequence, it is the witches of
one's own matriclan who have especially to be feared. This was how
the LoDagaba viewed the connection between witchcraft and matriclanship. But with the LoWiili, on the other hand, there was no direct
connection; uterine kinsmen could be in debt one to another, and witchcraft was not specifically confined to the matriclan. As in the case of
the matrilineal Ashanti and the Agni to the South, the range of a witch's
activities among the LoDagaba is broadly defined by the boundaries of
the wealth-holding corporation. Although accusations are also made
between spouses, it is those standing in an actual, or potential, relationship of holder or heir to a person who are considered most likely to
bewitch him.

Formerly the concept of debt was also associated with the institution of slavery. To sell a fellow member of the parish into slavery was
an offense against the Earth in both communities. Or, rather, it was
and is an offense for the alienated person to return to live there without
performing certain sacrifices at the Earth shrine. His birthright has
been sold. Nevertheless, in times of hunger, people were sold into slavery
by their relatives, and indeed the act was often a welcome one; for to
reduce the numbers dependent upon a scanty food supply was to relieve
the suffering of both the seller and the sold. Among the LoWiili, *patria
potestas* obtained; a man had the power of selling an agnatic descendant,
a son, or better still, a dead brother's son. Among the LoDagaba, *avun-
culi potestas* prevailed. The father had no power to dispose of a son,
and were he to do so he would incur a debt to his wife's matriclan. The
power over life and death, to sell or to slay, was vested in the hands of
the maternal uncle.

Then, again, closely connected with the different systems of inheriting movable property are the various methods by which a man seeks
to ensure that at least a part of his wealth remains within the compound
in which he lives. Here I have called attention to the importance of
gifts between father and son, a procedure that should have the approval

of the close matrilineal kin concerned; otherwise they may deny all knowledge of the transaction when the man dies. I have also described a number of mechanisms, such as marriage to the father's sister's daughter, which serve to keep wealth within the compound by transmitting it not to the adjacent but to the alternate generation, from a man to his grandson, an agnatic descendant who is also a member of his own matriclan. This is the man who, in the absence of a full brother, constitutes the duplicate heir par excellence; although, since the sister's son is closer in strict genealogical reckoning, some division of the heritage is made. But, in any case, the grandson is heir to the sister's son, so that the return of the property to the house is only a matter of time.

Reference to these "circumventing mechanisms" brings us back to a question that we raised but did not answer. The problem is of general relevance to systems of uterine inheritance, but especially where the method of transmission runs contrary to, or is disharmonic with, the residential pattern. This happens in situations in which the domestic group is formed around an agnatic core, either a temporary one, as in matrilineal systems with virilocal residence and child return, or a permanent one, as in double descent systems with fixed patrilineal descent groups. The question is this: Why should a society continue with a particular mode of inheritance when it apparently spends so much of its energy in circumventing its provisions?

A frequent answer to this question is that these are transitional systems and the contradictions they display result from the partial survival of earlier forms of organization. Without intending to deny the existence of disparities of this kind (for societies are always undergoing changes that differentially affect the component parts), I would suggest that the persistence and distribution of these forms of behavior indicate that the answer lies elsewhere.

Earlier in this study I pointed out that in societies in which residence is agnatically based, uterine inheritance produces a flow of property between local units which, like the passage of women between exogamous groups, widens the whole area of significant social relationships, but between kin rather than between affines.

I do not mean to imply that either these transactions or these relationships are mutually exclusive. Among the LoDagaba, property transactions accompany marriage, and in the father's sister's daughter marriage may anticipate inheritance. Moreover, in such marriages, kinship and affinity are not of course exclusive; a cousin becomes one's wife and kinsfolk one's in-laws.

The LoDagaa are conscious of some of the advantages to be gained from the wide spread of extraclan ties, likening these to the creeping vines of the gourd. Moreover, transactions in goods and services tend to become reciprocal, to endure over time and to acquire a group reference. This was brought home to me when I was discussing with Doctaa (a member of the Tiedeme patriclan in Tom) the recent attempt by some of the neighboring Nambegle to abduct his son's wife and marry her to one of their lads. The scheme failed because in the end the young man refused to take the woman. He had previously been married to a Tiedeme girl, and he came to see Doctaa and told him, "It's your daughters I want, not your wives." Doctaa approved of this sentiment and said, "How could he have taken her? Those people are all the children of our sisters, our fathers' sisters, our lineage sisters; they are all from here, and all the cattle they have comes from our fathers."

Clearly this situation is reciprocal, since if Tiedeme women marry Nambegle men, then Tiedeme men will also marry Nambegle women; bridewealth will pass from group to group in one generation, and inherited property from one generation to the next. However, it is not reciprocal to the extent of leading to prescriptive exchange between any two groups, and many marriages take place with other patriclan sectors, thus establishing the kind of network that is well illustrated by the fact that Dakpaala's sacrifice to his mother's mother's mother's mother took him on a lengthy trek through the region. While this range of relationships is brought about mainly through the movements of women (since marriage is virilocal), Doctaa's remarks illustrate the point that the LoDagaba visualize these connections in terms of relationships to the children of sisters rather than to their husbands, to the receivers of wealth, and later the donors of sacrifices, rather than to the receivers of women and the givers of bridewealth. The reason is perhaps not hard to seek; marriage ties are easily severed, kinship not.

Moreover, the LoDagaba see these ties to kinsmen outside the local agnatic group as having a greater significance as channels of communication, because movable property is passed along them. But while conscious of certain of the advantages of this system of inheritance, they are also reluctant to see the property leave the compound. The creation of an "heir within the house" serves as a compromise; only part of the property is taken away, and at the same time the corporate nature of the matriclan is maintained. Nor is this entirely a fiction, in Maine's sense of the word. The system is not simply one of disguised agnatic inheritance, because, apart from the controlled passage of gifts between father and son, the other circumventing mechanisms still involve the transfer of property between members of the matriclan. Since both the matrilineal and the patrilineal clans are exogamous, transmission to sons, and usually to paternal half-siblings, is excluded. Looked at from the standpoint of the agnatic "house," movable property can be inherited only by members of the same or alternate generations. The latter, like the former, are "brothers" (*yeb*) of the deceased. But in systems of double clanship, particularly when associated with double inheritance, the equivalence of alternate generations acquires a more far-reaching character, comparable in some respects to that produced by the section systems of Australia. For where patrilateral cross-cousin marriage takes place, members of alternate generations belong to the same patriclan and to the same matriclan. And each generation is heir to the second ascending one above. The social system is like a layer cake, with every other tier having the same filling.

But even in the absence of specified kinship ties, the definition of the alternating generations within the house by matriclan membership takes on considerable importance in transmitting the objects that are always inherited by duplicate clanship, by the "heir in the house." I refer here to the widows, the farming services, and the house timbers. For if we take into account the possibility of inheriting not only between reciprocal matriclans, but also within the two moieties, Some and Da, it is clear that a man is almost bound to have a possible heir within his own compound.

The fundamental way in which even transmission within the "house" differs from agnatic inheritance is that it prevents the transfer of rights between adjacent generations who are residing together; it avoids saddling the father-son relationship with the problem of the anticipated inheritance, since movable property always remains vested in "fathers" and never passes to "sons."

I have also noted that there is a sense in which the LoWiili regard their own system in the same light. In contrast to patrilineal peoples to the east or Dagaa side, the LoWiili only permit the leviratic transfer of rights between members of the same or alternate generations; once rights in women are acquired by the "fathers," they continue to be vested in them and are never transferred to the "sons." That this is at least partially true of the tools and weapons needed to farm and hunt is seen in the elaborate ceremonies by which the "fathers" hand over these objects to the sons. At this time it is explained to them that although their own father is dead, the children will remain under the perpetual tutelage of their father's "brothers"; perpetual because the group is being continually recruited, either by equating alternate generations or else by linking the concept of "fatherhood" to the whole matriclan. It is by the generous permission of these seniors that the sons take over the land and equipment necessary to get themselves a living, and the whole ceremony stresses how this dependence must continue to be recognized throughout a man's life, by setting aside a portion of the farming surplus and a part of all animals killed, as well as by offering to perform filial tasks such as carrying heavy logs.

To some extent the rights of a LoWiili in the remainder of the movable property, rights that among the LoDagaba are inherited by a uterine heir, also continue to be held by a man's "brothers" after his death. They will hold an interest in bridewealth still to be received on behalf of the dead man's sisters; they will supervise the transactions that the children's marriages involve; and they will benefit yet more directly from the farm services supplied by their "sons-in-law."

Nevertheless, there is a critical difference here between the LoDagaba and the LoWiili. The former have no expectations from their fathers, except while they are alive; the latter, on the other hand, do inherit from them, though the rituals of transmission emphasize a man's continuing dependence upon the senior generation.

This discussion touches upon a further issue. At one level the central difference between these two communities turns upon the question of whether or not the descent groups are corporate; but the whole question of inheritance has a fundamental influence on interpersonal ties among close kin. Not only the major corporations of the society, but the minor ones, too, are affected—the kinsfolk who constitute the units of production, on the one hand, and the holders and the heirs, on the other. Among the LoWiili there is an almost complete overlap, and in most cases sons farm with their father until he dies. But among the LoDagaba the minimal wealth-holding units run counter to the productive ones, and sons tend to establish their own fields and granaries apart from their father, so that when he dies his heir will have no claim upon the wealth they have accumulated. Not only does the composition of the basic productive unit differ in the two communities, but also the pattern of labor services. For whereas the LoWiili farm for their in-laws as well as for their own and neighboring units of production, the LoDagaba are expected to farm for their mother's brothers in addition. Indeed, to the LoDagaa this is perhaps the crucial difference, because working on somebody's farm is the most concrete way of establishing a claim upon that person's resources. By farming for the father of his betrothed, a man establishes a claim to the daughter. By farming for his own father, a man obtains the right to the goods he needs for the bridewealth payments. By farming for his neighbors, he gets their help in meeting his obligations to farm for his in-laws after the marriage has taken place. In the same way, the LoDagaa see a general connection between farming for the mother's brother and laying a claim to his property.

The connection is neatly crystallized in the origin myth of the Lo-Dagaa, told to those initiated into the Bagre society, which "accounts for" many of the main features of LoDagaa culture as well as giving the order of the initiation proceedings.

The story runs as follows. Once an old man was hoeing in the heat of the sun while his sons were reclining nearby at the foot of a shady tree. As he was working away, the son of his sister chanced to pass that way and, seeing his uncle laboring there alone in the midday heat, said to him, "Here, old man, let me give you a hand. Sit down and rest yourself awhile."

The old man and his nephew continued to hoe together, while the sons lazed under the tree. When the work was done, the uncle turned to his companion and said, "When I die it's you that shall inherit my wealth, not those sons of mine."

Other versions of this tale are told outside the Bagre room, but all trace uterine inheritance to two interconnected features of the situation: the work a man puts in on his mother's brother's farm and the tension that exists between father and son.

Farming is regarded as the main source of wealth, though bride-wealth, inheritance, and hunting and other activities may also contribute to increase a man's estate. Thus, by assisting the mother's brother, a claim is established on the surplus product of the farm, his wealth. In practice, inheritance from the uncle is not dependent upon working on his farm. What is affected by these labor services is whether or not he provides the sister's son with the bridewealth for a wife.[1] In fact, in both communities the provision of bridewealth is tied to farming obligations. A man has no responsibility for finding the bridewealth for a son who has gone out to farm on his own. The difference is that among the LoWiili nowadays a man does not farm for his maternal uncle unless he is actually living with him. They then form part of the same productive unit, and the sister's son expects the mother's brother to produce the bridewealth for a wife. In this case, it seems, the children of such a marriage belong to the patriclan of the sister's son, as among the Lo-

[1] In my interim report on the area, I mentioned that among the LoDagaba the mother's brother not only provided the bridewealth for the second wife of his sister's son, but also received a proportion of the cowries from the marriage of his sister's daughter ([1956a] p. 50). This applies only to the LoPiel. It was suggested to me (in Zambor) that in this region the mother's brother's return for help with the marriage payments was either the bridewealth of the sister's daughter or else farming services from the sister's son. This correlation appears to hold; but, in any case, there is close connection between farming services, the provision of bridewealth, and the inheritance of the objects employed in marriage transactions—cowries, livestock, and women.

Dagaba; but if in any other circumstances a man used as bridewealth the goods he had acquired from such a source, the LoWiili would regard the offspring of the marriage as belonging to the donor's patriclan.

Although the myth finds the origin of and justification for uterine inheritance in farming services, I have remarked above that, as the system works in practice, it is not obligatory upon an heir to have helped his maternal uncle in this way. On the other hand, it is true that in those communities of the region that practice agnatic inheritance, no such help is given. Moreover, farming services have something to do with changes in the type of system people use. On the border between the areas where the agnatic and uterine inheritance of wealth prevail, there is often some intermarriage between nearby communities practicing different systems of inheritance, When an agnatically inheriting male marries a woman from an area where wealth is transmitted between uterine kin, then the offspring have a certain liberty to choose from whom they will inherit. Although my cases are not numerous, it seems that the choice of the uterine alternative is usually made by a man who has spent some time living with and working for his mother's brother in his youth. The main reasons for a man's taking up residence away from his natal home are either that he has quarreled with his agnates, or else that his mother has returned home with her children because her marriage has been dissolved by death or by divorce. In either of these situations the ambiguous claim of the sister's son is crystallized by his residing and farming with his mother's brother.

It is occurrences of this kind that may have such far-reaching effects; for a man who accepts uterine wealth in this way commits others as well as himself. "Things of the mother's stem are passed on in that line" (*ma per bume, mamine so*) is a maxim whose force is recognized even in the agnatically inheriting areas of this border country and one that is supported by ancestral sanctions. Property that has been inherited down a certain line should be passed on in the same manner. Indeed, by accepting uterine wealth a man lays open all of his property, however accumulated, to a claim by his matrilineal heirs. For whether or not his natal community recognize matriclans, he has automatically become a member of one through his father's marriage, and he has fully accepted the corporate implications by entering into his uncle's estate. So that even if his full sister makes an "agnatic" marriage, his more distant matriclansmen from his mother's settlement are unlikely to forget that he has enjoyed a portion of their corporate wealth.

I have sketched the process of change from agnatic to uterine inheritance of wealth because the problem of "origins," raised in the

LoDagaa myth, is relevant to the general theme; for although the evidence provided by these two communities has little to say about ultimate origins, it does help to clarify proximal ones, that is, the considerations that lead to small-scale changes. As a result of their father's marriage to a woman from a community with the matrilineal inheritance of wealth, a number of people in this border area are offered what often amounts to a choice. They may take up the uterine alternative for a variety of reasons: the uncle may be better off than the father; the mother may have returned to her natal home, taking her children with her; or a man may have quarreled with his father or proxy father. This last reason is the one that the LoDagaa themselves emphasize in the myth. It is because the sons are unwilling to work for their father that the sister's son is called in to help.

Whatever the role of conflict among close kin in the change-over from one system of inheritance to another, it is certainly true that such relationships differ considerably in the two communities. The kinship terminology is virtually the same, for distant as well as for close kin; in each society the same set of terms is used in the context of both matrilineal and patrilineal descent groups, giving rise to the phenomenon of duplicate kinship. But the relationships to which these terms refer are far from the same.

The most striking difference is certainly that between a man's relationships with his father and his mother's brother, the two closest male figures of the senior generation.[2] The situation among the groups with uterine inheritance was noted by the first European to visit the area, the French ethnologist Maurice Delafosse. Writing of the Birifor,[3] a people with a social organization similar in many ways to the LoDagaba, he claimed that the "nephew and heir" would sometimes kill the mother's brother "pour s'emparer de l'héritage" ([1908] p. 155). This statement, I believe, somewhat exaggerates the element of open conflict, as distinct from hidden tension, that marks this relationship—although it is true that a similar attitude is found in other nearby societies. Rattray records an Ashanti proverb that goes: "A sister's son is his mother's brother's enemy, waiting for him to die so that he may inherit" ([1929] p. 20). This proverb could well serve for the LoDagaba. A man

[2] I have treated these relationships in more detail in my paper "The Mother's Brother and the Sister's Son in West Africa" [1959a].

[3] Phonetically, this name appears to be the same as that of the main LoWiili settlement which, following the map spelling, I have written as Birifu. What past connections there were, I do not know; some of the Birifor claim to have migrated from the settlement of Birifu. But the Birifor practice uterine inheritance of movable property like the LoDagaba.

stands to gain property (and possibly wives) by his uncle's death, and the hostility between the two is often considerable.

Contrast this with the LoWiili situation, in which there is no holder-heir component in the relationship of a man with his mother's brother. The whole position is similar to that recorded by observers in many patrilineal societies, Junod for the BaThonga, Firth for the Tikopia, and Fortes for the Tallensi. The uncle's home provides a man with a temporary, and sometimes a permanent, refuge, should he need an alternative place to live. The relationship is relatively free and easy, certainly a far cry from that epitomized in the Ashanti proverb.

The father-son relationship provides a similar, though not so striking, contrast between the two communities. Among the LoWiili a man may talk of cutting off his sons without a penny if he is displeased with them—though the community would not in fact allow his threats to be carried out. Among the LoDagaba, threats of this sort would be pointless; the father is not the holder of a man's eventual heritage, nor is he the person that wields, even in theory, the power of life and death. He cannot sell his son into slavery, nor is his curse so greatly to be feared as among the LoWiili. Moreover, the son can farm on his own without difficulty and is not tied economically to his father in the same way. The father provides land, tools, and a wife; apart from this, any property he manages to pass to his son is an indication of a good personal relationship rather than of jural obligation.

As we have seen, these differences in the relationships between kin—between members of successive generations in particular and corporate descent groups in general—are also observable in the worship of the ancestors. A person does not simply make an offering to a dead man's shrine because of a general obligation between members of the same wealth-holding corporation; he does so because he sees the ancestor as an actual or potential trouble-maker, as liable to cause him great misfortune because the obligations are not fulfilled. Since this causal chain is a purely human invention, it seems reasonable to say that such attitudes are "projected" onto the manes. In one way, they derive from, and reinforce, authority relations that exist in life. On the other hand, the ancestors are the living in a more extreme form, more extreme still when intergenerational authority is undivided; for they not only possess a theoretical power of life and death, but are thought to use this power against their descendants.

Such magnification of the evil, and to some extent the good, characteristics of the dead "holders" is more than a matter of placing social control in supernatural hands, and hence past human questioning. Sacrifices that are demanded by the ancestors and result from affliction are usually made to near rather than to distant forebears; half the recorded sacrifices of this kind were offered by heirs, and the rest by other members of the group, or groups, within which property is inherited. A man sacrifices to those who have helped him prosper, but it is often their very death that has brought these benefits. Looked at against the background of the funeral rituals and the beliefs in mystical causes (the search of the former for the agent of death among close kin and the association of the latter with envy, resentment, and anticipated gain), the evidence seems to suggest that an important component in these sacrifices is the "guilt" that marks the relationship of the survivors with the dead "holders." The hostility of particular ancestors appears more pronounced when the holder-heir and other authority relationships are undivided. For in ancestor sacrifices, as in the funeral ceremonies, we see the results of splitting the locus of authority and the ownership of property between two sets of descent groups, and the particular importance in these contexts of duplicate clanship, of kinsfolk who belong both to the same patriclan and to the same matriclan.

Suggestive comparisons of the main differences in the relationships of close kin in "patrilineal" and "matrilineal" systems have been made by a number of writers. In the course of his critique of Freudian theories, "Sex and Repression in Savage Society," Malinowski put forward what he spoke of as a "somewhat crude formula," that "in the Oedipus complex, there is the repressed desire to kill the father and marry the mother, while in the matrilineal society of the Trobriands the wish is to marry the sister and to kill the maternal uncle" ([1927] pp. 80–81).

I have referred only in passing to differences in the relationships between men and women among the LoDagaa, and I can but briefly touch upon them here. The most vivid illustration I had was in a discussion that took place in the LoDagaba settlement of Kwõnyũkwõ, a parish that abuts on the northernmost boundary of Birifu. Several of us were gathered together drinking beer, and the conversation turned to the part played by women in economic activities. The elder upon whose rooftop we were sitting had provided the drink for a party of female helpers whom his sister's daughter had brought along to weed his groundnut farm. Among the LoWiili I have never seen women carrying out such work even within their own productive units, let alone for their maternal uncles. My LoWiili companions were bemoaning the lack of assistance they got from their womenfolk, to which the elder replied, "But at least you can get your wives to sell your produce in the market. Here, if we did that they would keep all the money. No, we have to get our sisters to do our marketing for us."

Two features of women's economic activities among the LoDagaba are brought out by the elder's remarks. First, women play a larger part in the production of crops. Second, sisters are considered more trustworthy with money than wives. The first difference is probably incidental, since in other nearby "patrilineal" areas (e.g., the DagaaWiili) females seem to help on the farms as much as they do among the Lo-Dagaba. But the belief in the greater trustworthiness of sisters was definitely connected by one of those present with the uterine inheritance of property. Although in both societies full siblings belong to the same wealth-holding corporation, among the LoDagaba the brother and sister are drawn more tightly together, partly because a man's heir is the son of his sister, not of his wife.

The trend of this discussion receives some confirmation from the differences listed in Tables 13 and 14. There we noted the larger part the LoDagaba sister plays when her brother falls sick (13 : 1), as well as the greater emphasis placed by "brothers" on the threat to bury their "sister" themselves if debts between affines are not settled (13 : 4). These differences, slight as they are, indicate the stronger brother-sister tie, and this in turn is supported by analyses of other societies where uterine inheritance prevails.

In its application to women, Malinowski's formula might be interpreted as supporting the hypothesis that "matrilineal" systems place a greater emphasis upon the sibling bond, and "patrilineal" ones upon the conjugal. But whereas the LoDagaba material stresses the fact that brother and sister are co-members of a wealth-holding corporation, Malinowski concentrates his attention primarily on sexual relationships. In this context, too, the formula needs some revision; I would rather summarize the difference by saying that in "matrilineal" societies the sexuality of sisters is more sacrosanct than that of wives.[4]

Malinowski's discussion of differences in the relationships that a man has with his father and his mother's brother is more in line with my own observations. But once again, engaged as he is in a polemic with Freudian theorists over the question of the universality of the Oedipus complex, he follows them in focusing too narrowly on sexuality as a source of intergenerational tension.

The question of these differences in father-son and mother's brother–sister's son relationships is taken up by Homans in a comparison of the "patrilineal" Tikopia and the "matrilineal" Trobriands ([1950] pp. 252 *et seq.*). Applying to this situation a method of approach that has developed largely from factory and small-group studies, he concludes that in both societies a man has respect for, and low social interaction with,

---

[4] This problem is discussed in more detail in my paper "A Comparative Approach to Incest and Adultery" [1956*b*].

the male of the older generation who is "his chief boss." The crucial factor is the locus of authority in the external system. As this shifts, the emotional relationships in the internal system rearrange themselves accordingly (*ibid.*, p. 258).

In Homans's analysis the independent variable is the locus of authority, later "jural authority" ([1955] p. 21), which is seen in terms of the work group. But in the LoDagaba situation such authority relationships are of two main kinds, those falling within the work and residence group, which are based upon local agnatic ties, and those within the main holder-heir situation, the wealth-holding group, which are based upon non-localized uterine ties.[5]

The division of jural authority at this level resembles what Malinowski referred to, again thinking largely of the control of sexuality, as the splitting of the Oedipus complex ([1927] p. 278). For among the Trobriands, in this respect a typical matrilineal system with virilocal residence, a boy lives with his father during his childhood and goes off to his maternal uncle when he grows up and marries. The father is the upbringer, and the mother's brother the holder; socialization is separated off from the holder-heir situation, and kinship authority is distributed between the two main figures of the parental generation. Only after marriage is the "work boss" the same person as the holder of one's future heritage.

Dual descent systems of the LoDagaba type—that is, systems in which both sets of unilineal descent group are corporate—have much in common with systems like that of the Trobriands, in which matrilineal descent groups are found in conjunction with virilocal marriage. But whereas among the Trobriands domestic (i.e., residential) authority is split between the father and the mother's brother on a temporal basis, among the LoDagaba the authority of the property holder is permanently divided between father and mother's brother, since fixed resources are transmitted to agnates, and movable property to uterine kin.

Although the importance of the holder-heir situation as a variable in the comparison of "patrilineal" and "matrilineal" systems was not fully brought out in these discussions by Malinowski and Homans,[6] the thesis is far from new. The close connection between inheritance and

---

[5] In an earlier publication, I have referred to this split as one between domestic authority and potestality, since it is the uterine kin who are vested with the power over life and death ([1959a] p. 87n.).

[6] On the other hand, this is excellently done in Homans's study *English Villagers of the Thirteenth Century.* Of course, inheritance plays quite a different part in peasant societies, and its role in medieval Europe had already been discussed by Maine, Vinogradoff, and others of the great school of legal historians; whereas in studies of factory organization, problems of ownership are often of peripheral importance.

ancestor worship, explicit in the recorded texts of Greece and Rome, was a theme brilliantly pursued by Fustel de Coulanges in *La Cité antique* [1864] and was taken up by Sir Henry Maine in *Early Law and Custom* [1883].[7] There was no doubt in the minds of these writers about how these two institutions were related. Referring to the Brahmanical codes of Bengal, Maine writes that "they display not only a close connection between ancestor-worship and inheritance, but a complete dependence of the last upon the first" (*ibid.*, p. 116). A transformation in ancestor worship, he maintains, led to changes in the law of inheritance.

While the close association between the two is confirmed by the LoDagaa material, the nexus of dependency has to be completely reversed. For it is differences in the mode of inheritance that appear to have led to changes in the propitiation of the ancestors. In this context we should rather take as our guides Xenophanes,[8] Feuerbach, Marx,[9] Tylor,[10] and a host of others, and treat religious practices and beliefs, in the restricted sense in which I use the phrase,[11] as the result rather than the cause. But although this hypothesis, that changes in ancestor worship have been caused by changes in the mode of inheritance, seems to be the best starting point for interpreting the LoDagaa material, it does not mean that it is correct in each and every case. What makes it acceptable here is the opinion of the actors themselves, the number and kind of differences between the two communities that make sense from this standpoint, and the actual mechanisms of social change that we have briefly sketched.

The caveat I enter with regard to the dependent variable, sacrifice to the ancestors, applies with equal force to the independent variable, inheritance. Although the LoDagaa evidence gives general support to Morgan's thesis that the changes from one system of descent groups to another took place "under the influence of property and inheritance" ([1877] pp. 355–56), I am not trying to imply that property relationships are the cause of all social change, either among the LoDagaa or elsewhere. The elucidation of these questions is a matter for sociological investigation, rather than political or religious conviction. The insistence

[7] Especially the chapter entitled "Ancestor Worship and Inheritance."

[8] "If oxen, horses and lions had hands to paint with and produced works as humans do, the horses would fashion the gods as horses, the oxen as oxen, and each would make images according to his own form" (Diels-Kranz [1956], Vol. I, fr. 15).

[9] "In direct contrast to German philosophy, which descends from heaven to earth, here we ascend from earth to heaven" (*German Ideology* [1845–46], translated by T. B. Bottomore [1956], p. 75).

[10] See Chapter 2.

[11] See Goody [1961*b*].

of Marx and Engels upon the importance of property relationships has sometimes been a greater handicap to those social scientists who have studiously avoided their approach than to those who have zealously adopted it.

Furthermore, in this study, the independent variable has not been property in the sense of technological achievement; the actual means and objects of production are roughly the same in all societies in the area, whether they have patrilineal or matrilineal descent groups, or both, or neither. Nor do differences in the level of productivity appear to be of any great significance here. What has appeared important in attempting to explain the main differences between the mortuary institutions of the two communities is the system of inheritance. In both communities double clanship exists; the same patrilineal and matrilineal clans are found in both places. It is the system of transmission of property from generation to generation that differs.

Of course the mode of inheritance exercises a considerable influence upon the organization of descent groups. Radcliffe-Brown ([1925*b*] p. 48) and Forde [1947, 1948] have both suggested that the existence of unlineal descent groups is connected with the transmission of continuing rights in material objects between generations. Whether or not this is so, the question of the corporateness of a descent group (that is, whether it acts as a group within which property is seen as held or inherited) is a factor of great importance in determining the part that the group plays in the total social system.

But the system of inheritance not only influences the organization of descent groups; it also plays an important part in the kind of relationships that exist between close kin. In analyzing the sources of tension in the Ashanti kinship system, Fortes has pointed out that "the critical element in the relationship of mother's brother to sister's son is the latter's status as the former's prospective heir ([1950] p. 272). It is this variable of the anticipated, and achieved, inheritance—the locus of the holder-heir relationship—that explains many of the differences in the communities that we have been considering. For variations in the relationships between close kin provide the link between the mode of inheritance and the pattern of sacrifices—the link between death, property, and the ancestors.

Bibliography

Adam, Leonhard. 1935. "Inheritance Law in Primitive Cultures," *Iowa Law Review*, 20:760–73.

Anthony, Sylvia. 1940. The Child's Discovery of Death. London: Kegan Paul.

Arensberg, Conrad M. 1937. The Irish Countryman. New York: Macmillan.

———. 1960. "The American Family in the Perspective of Other Cultures," in The Nation's Children, I, 50–75. New York: Columbia University Press.

Bastian, Adolph. 1860. Der Mensch in der Geschichte. 3 vols. Leipzig: Wigand.

Bendann, E. 1930. Death Customs. London: Kegan Paul.

Benedict, R. 1936. "Marital Property Rights in Bilateral Society," *Am. Anthrop.*, 38:368–73.

Bernardi, B. 1959. The Mugwe, a Failing Prophet. London: Oxford University Press.

Bleuler, E. 1930. Textbook of Psychiatry. Translated by A. A. Brill. New York: Macmillan.

Bohannan, L. 1952. "A Genealogical Charter," *Africa*, 22:301–15.

Bottomore, T. B., and Rubel, Maximilien (eds.). 1956. Karl Marx: Selected Writings in Sociology and Social Philosophy. Translated by T. B. Bottomore. London: Watts.

Bowdich, T. Edward. 1819. Mission from Cape Coast Castle to Ashantee. London: Murray.

Bowlby, John. 1960. "Grief and Mourning in Infancy and Early Childhood," in The Psychoanalytic Study of the Child, No. 15, pp. 9–52. London: Hogarth Press.

———. 1961. "Processes of Mourning," *Int. J. of Psychoanalysis*, 42:317–40.

Brough, John. 1959. "The Tripartite Ideology of the Indo-Europeans: An Experiment in Method," *Bull. Sch. Orient. and Afr. Stud.*, 22:69–85.

Busia, K. A. 1951. The Position of the Chief in the Modern Political System of Ashanti. London: Oxford University Press.

———. 1954. "The Ashanti of the Gold Coast," in African Worlds. Edited by D. Forde. London: Oxford University Press.

Chapple, E. D., and Coon, C. S. 1942. Principles of Anthropology. New York: Holt.

Cole, G. D. H. 1932. "Inheritance," in Encyclopedia of the Social Sciences, VIII, 35–43. New York: Macmillan.

Colson, E. 1955. "Ancestral Spirits and Social Structure Among the Plateau Tonga," *Int. Arch. Ethnog.*, 47:21–68.

Commons, John R. 1959. Legal Foundations of Capitalism. Madison: University of Wisconsin Press. (1st ed., Macmillan, 1924.)

Crawley, Ernest. 1932. The Mystic Rose. 4th ed. London: Watts. (1st ed. 1902.)

Crooke, W. 1908. "Ancestor Worship and the Cult of the Dead," in Encyclopaedia of Religion and Ethics. Edited by James Hastings. New York: Scribner's.

Delafosse, M. 1908. Les Frontières de la Côte d'Ivoire, de la Côte d'Or et du Soudan. Paris: Masson.

Diels, H., and Kranz, W. 1956. Die Fragmente der Vorsokratiker. 8th ed. Vol. I. Berlin: Weidmannsche.

Dieterlen, Germaine. 1951. Essai sur la religion bambara. Paris: Presses Universitaires.

Duncan-Jones, Arthur S. 1932. "The Burial of the Dead," in Liturgy and Worship, pp. 616–25. Edited by W. K. L. Clarke, London: Society for Promoting Christian Knowledge; New York: Macmillan.

Durkheim, Emile. 1933. On the Division of Labor in Society. Translated by G. Simpson. New York: Macmillan. (1st French ed. 1893.)

———. 1947. The Elementary Forms of the Religious Life. Translated by Joseph Ward Swain. Glencoe, Ill.: Free Press. (1st French ed. 1912; 1st English ed., translated by Swain, 1915.)

———, and Mauss, Marcel. 1901–2. "De quelques formes primitives de classification. Contribution à l'étude des représentations collectives," *L'Année sociologique*, Vol. 6: 1–72.

Eliade, M. 1958. Patterns in Comparative Religion. New York: Sheed and Ward. (Translation by Rosemary Sheed of Traité d'histoire des religions, Paris, Payot.)

Engels, Friedrich. 1942. The Origin of the Family, Private Property and the State in the Light of the Researches of Lewis H. Morgan. New York: International Publishers. (1st ed. 1884.)

Evans-Pritchard, E. E. 1933. "The Intellectualist (English) Interpretation of Magic," *Bull. Fac. Arts.*, 1:282–311. Cairo: University of Egypt.

———. 1940. The Nuer. Oxford: Clarendon Press.

———. 1956. Nuer Religion. Oxford: Clarendon Press.

Fauconnet, Paul. 1920. La Responsabilité. Étude de sociologie. Travaux de l'année sociologique. Paris: Alcan.

Feigl, H. 1958. "The 'Mental' and the 'Physical,' " in Concepts, Theories, and the Mind-Body Problem, pp. 370–497. Edited by H. Feigl, M. Scriven, and G. Maxwell. Minneapolis: University of Minnesota Press.

Festinger, L. 1957. A Theory of Cognitive Dissonance. Evanston, Ill.: Row, Peterson.

Field, M. J. 1948. Akim-Kotoku: An Oman of the Gold Coast. London: Crown Agents.

Firth, R. 1957. "A Note on Descent Groups in Polynesia," *Man*, 57:4–8.

Flügel, J. C. 1932. "Theories of Psycho-Analysis," in An Outline of Modern Knowledge. London: Gollancz.

———. 1948. The Psycho-Analytic Study of the Family. London: Hogarth Press. (1st ed. 1921.)

Forde, D. 1947. "The Anthropological Approach in Social Science," *Advanc. Sci.*, 4:213–24.

438 *Bibliography*

————. 1948. "The Integration of Anthropological Studies," *J. R. Anthrop. Inst.*, 78: 1–9.

————. 1958. The Context of Belief. Liverpool: Liverpool University Press.

————, and Jones, G. I. 1950. The Ibo and Ibibio-Speaking Peoples of South-Eastern Nigeria. London: Oxford University Press.

Fortes, Meyer. 1945. The Dynamics of Clanship Among the Tallensi. London: Oxford University Press.

————. 1949. The Web of Kinship Among the Tallensi. London: Oxford University Press.

————. 1950. "Kinship and Marriage Among the Ashanti," in African Systems of Kinship and Marriage. Edited by A. R. Radcliffe-Brown and D. Forde. London: Oxford University Press.

————. 1959. Oedipus and Job in West African Religion. Cambridge: Cambridge University Press.

Frazer, Sir James G. 1911. Taboo and the Perils of the Soul. The Golden Bough. 3d ed. London: Macmillan.

————. 1913–24. The Belief in Immortality and the Worship of the Dead. London: Macmillan. (Vol. I, 1913; Vol. II, 1922; Vol. III, 1924.)

————. 1918. Folk-Lore in the Old Testament. 3 vols. London: Macmillan.

————. 1933–36. The Fear of the Dead in Primitive Religion. London: Macmillan. (Vol. I, 1933; Vol. II, 1934; Vol. III, 1936.)

————. 1935. The Magic Art. The Golden Bough, Vol. II. 3d ed. New York: Macmillan.

Freud, Sigmund. 1952. Totem and Taboo. Translated by James Strachey. New York: Norton. (1st ed., Vienna, 1913; 1st English trans. by A. A. Brill, New York, 1918.)

Fromm, Erich. 1959. "The Oedipus Complex and the Oedipus Myth," in The Family: Its Function and Destiny, pp. 420–48. Edited by Ruth N. Anshen. New York: Harper.

Fusfield, Daniel B. 1957. "Economic Theory Misplaced: Livelihood in Primitive Society," in Trade and Market in the Early Empires. Edited by Karl Polanyi, Conrad M. Arensberg, and Harry W. Pearson. Glencoe, Ill.: Free Press.

Fustel de Coulanges, N. D. 1864. La Cité antique; étude sur le culte, le droit, les institutions de la Grèce et de Rome. Paris: Durand.

Gibson, G. D. 1956. "Double Descent and Its Correlates Among the Herero of Ngamiland," *Am. Anthrop.*, 58:109–39.

Gluckman, Max. 1937. "Mortuary Customs and the Belief in Survival After Death Among the South-Eastern Bantu," *Bantu Studies*, 11:117–36.

————. 1950. "Kinship and Marriage Among the Lozi of Northern Rhodesia and the Zulu of Natal," in African Systems of Kinship and Marriage, pp. 166–206. Edited by A. R. Radcliffe-Brown and D. Forde. London: Oxford University Press.

————. 1954. Rituals of Rebellion in South-East Africa. Manchester: Manchester University Press. (The Frazer Lecture, 1952.)

————. 1955. The Judicial Process Among the Barotse of Northern Rhodesia. Manchester: Manchester University Press.

Goodenough, Ward H. 1951. Property, Kin and Community on Truk. New Haven: Yale University Press. (Yale University Publications in Anthropology, No. 46.)

Goody, Jack. 1956a. The Social Organisation of the LoWiili. London: H.M. Stationery Office. (Colonial Office, Colonial Research Studies, No. 19.)

———. 1956b. "A Comparative Approach to Incest and Adultery," *Brit. J. Soc.,* 7:286–305.

———. 1957. "Fields of Social Control Among the LoDagaba," *J. R. Anthrop. Inst.,* 87:75–104.

———. 1958. "The Fission of Domestic Groups Among the LoDagaba," in The Developmental Cycle in Domestic Groups, pp. 53–91. Edited by Jack Goody. Cambridge: Cambridge University Press. (Cambridge Papers in Social Anthropology, No. 1.)

———. 1959a. "The Mother's Brother and the Sister's Son in West Africa," *J. R. Anthrop. Inst.,* 89:61–88.

———. 1959b. "Death and Social Control Among the LoDagaa," *Man,* 59: 134–38.

———. 1960. "Sociology and Ethnology Among the LoDagaa," *Man,* 60:55.

———. 1961a. "The Classification of Double Descent Systems," *Current Anthrop.,* 2:3–25.

———. 1961b. "Religion and Ritual: The Definitional Problem," *Brit. J. Soc.,* 12:142–64.

Gough, E. K. 1958. "Cults of the Dead Among the Nayars," *J. Amer. Folklore,* 71:446–78.

Gouldner, Alvin W. 1960. "The Norm of Reciprocity: A Preliminary Statement," *Am. Soc. Rev.,* 25:161–78.

Gray, R. F. 1953. "Positional Succession Among the Wambugwe," *Africa,* 23: 233–43.

Griaule, Marcel. 1948. "L'Alliance cathartique," *Africa,* 18:242–58.

de Haan, J. A. Bierens. n.d. Animal Psychology. London: Hutchinson's University Library.

Habakkuk, H. J. 1950. "Marriage Settlements in the Eighteenth Century," *Transactions of the Royal Historical Society,* 4th series, 32:15–30.

Hallowell, A. Irving. 1955. "The Nature and Function of Property as a Social Institution," in Culture and Experience, pp. 236–49. Philadelphia: University of Pennsylvania Press. (Originally published in the *Journal of Legal and Political Sociology* (1943), 1:115–38.)

Hartland, E. Sidney. 1924. Primitive Law. London: Methuen.

Hearn, W. E. 1885. The Theory of Legal Duties and Rights: An Introduction to Analytical Jurisprudence. Melbourne: Ferris.

Herskovits, Melville J. 1938. Dahomey: An Ancient West African Kingdom. 2 vols. New York: Augustin.

———. 1952. Economic Anthropology. New York: Knopf.

Hertz, Robert. 1960. "A Contribution to the Study of the Collective Representation of Death," in Death and the Right Hand, pp. 27–86. Translated by Rodney and Claudia Needham. Glencoe, Ill.: Free Press. (Translation of "Contribution à une étude sur la représentation collective de la mort," *L'Année sociologique* (1907), 10:48–137.)

———. 1960. "The Pre-Eminence of the Right Hand: A Study in Religious Polarity," in Death and the Right Hand, pp. 89–113. Translated by Rodney and Claudia Needham. Glencoe, Ill.: Free Press. (Translation of

"La prééminence de la main droite: étude sur la polarité religieuse," *Revue philosophique* (1909), 58:553–80.)

Hinsie, Leland E., and Shatzky, Jacob. 1940. Psychiatric Dictionary. New York: Oxford University Press.

Hocart, A. M. 1936. Kings and Councillors. Cairo: Barbey.

Hoebel, E. Adamson. 1942. "Fundamental Legal Concepts as Applied in the Study of Primitive Law," *Yale Law Journal,* 51:951–66.

Hogbin, H. I., and Wedgwood, C. H. 1953. "Local Grouping in Melanesia," *Oceania,* 23:241–76; 24: 58–76.

Hohfeld, Wesley N. 1923. Fundamental Legal Conceptions. New Haven: Yale University Press.

Holdsworth, W. S. 1923. A History of English Law, Vol. II. London: Methuen. (3d ed. rewritten.)

Holmes, G. A. 1957. The Estates of the Higher Nobility in XIV Century England. Cambridge: Cambridge University Press.

Homans, George Caspar. 1941. English Villagers of the Thirteenth Century. Cambridge, Mass.: Harvard University Press.

———. 1947. "Group Factors in Worker Productivity," in Readings in Social Psychology, pp. 448–60. Edited by T. M. Newcomb and E. L. Hartley. New York: Holt. (Reprinted from Chap. 4 in Fatigue of Workers: Its Relation to Industrial Production, New York, Committee on Work and Industry of the National Research Council, 1941.)

———. 1950. The Human Group. New York: Harcourt, Brace.

———, and Schneider, David M. 1955. Marriage, Authority, and Final Causes: A Study of Unilateral Cross-Cousin Marriage. Glencoe, Ill.: Free Press.

Hopen, C. E. 1958. The Pastoral Fulbe Family in Gwandu. London: Oxford University Press.

Hsu, F. L. K. 1948. Under the Ancestors' Shadow. New York: Columbia University Press.

Ihering, Rudolph von. 1875. Geist des römischen Rechts, Vol. II, Pt. 2. 3d ed. Leipzig: Breitkopf und Härtel. (1st ed. 1852–78.)

———. 1894. Entwicklungsgeschichte des römischen Rechts. Leipzig: Breitkopf & Härtel und Duncker & Humblot.

James, E. O. n.d. [1948?] The Beginnings of Religion. London: Hutchinson's University Library.

Jevons, F. B. 1902. An Introduction to the History of Religion. London: Methuen. (1st ed. 1896.)

John, Eric. 1960. Land Tenure in Early England. Leicester: Leicester University Press.

Jolliffe, J. E. A. 1933. Pre-Feudal England: The Jutes. London: Oxford University Press.

Jones, Ernest. 1917–19. "The Theory of Symbolism," *Brit. J. Psych.,* 9: 181–229.

Junod, H. A. 1927. The Life of a South African Tribe. 2 vols. 2d rev. ed. London: Macmillan.

Kahn-Freund, O. 1949. "Introduction," in The Institutions of Private Law and Their Social Functions, by K. Renner. London: Routledge and Kegan Paul.

Kephart, Calvin. 1938. Origin of the Conjugal Community (or Community Property Law), etc. Washington, D.C., privately printed.

Kluckhohn, C., and Dorothea Leighton. 1946. The Navaho. Cambridge, Mass.: Harvard University Press.

Kris, Ernst. 1948. "Prince Hal's Conflict," *The Psychoanalytic Quarterly*, 17: 487–506.

Labouret, Henri. 1920. "Mariage et polyandrie parmi les Dagari et les Oulé," *Rev. d'eth. et des trad. pop.*, 1:267–83.

——. 1931. Les Tribus du Rameau Lobi. Paris: Institut d'Ethnologie.

Leach, E. R. 1951. "The Structural Implications of Matrilateral Cross-Cousin Marriage," *J. R. Anthrop. Inst.*, 81:23–53.

Leites, N., and Bernaut, E. 1954. Rituals of Liquidation: Communists on Trial. Glencoe, Ill.: Free Press.

Le Play, M. F. 1874. La Réforme sociale en France. 5th ed. Paris: Plon. (1st ed. 1864.)

Letourneau, C. H. 1896. Property: Its Origin and Development. London: Walter Scott.

Lévi-Strauss, C. 1949. Les Structures élémentaires de la parenté. Paris: Presses Universitaires.

——. 1956. "The Family," in Man, Culture and Society. Edited by H. L. Shapiro. New York: Oxford University Press.

Lowie, R. H. 1928. "Incorporeal Property in Primitive Society," *Yale Law Journal*, 37:551–63.

——. 1948. Social Organization. New York: Rinehart.

Lubbock, Sir John. 1865. Prehistoric Times, as Illustrated by Ancient Remains, and the Manners and Customs of Modern Savages. London: Williams and Norgate.

——. 1902. The Origin of Civilisation and the Primitive Condition of Man. 6th ed. London: Longmans, Green. (1st ed. 1871.)

Maine, Sir Henry. 1875. Lectures on the Early History of Institutions. London: Murray.

——. 1883. Dissertations on Early Law and Custom. London: Murray.

Malinowski, Bronislaw. 1927. Sex and Repression in Savage Society. London: Routledge and Kegan Paul.

——. 1954. Magic, Science and Religion. New York: Doubleday. (Reprinted from *Science, Religion and Reality*, ed. Joseph Needham, London, Macmillan, 1925.)

Marris, Peter. 1958. Widows and Their Families. London: Kegan Paul.

Matson, J. N. 1953. "Testate Succession in Ashanti," *Africa*, 23:224–32.

Maybury-Lewis, David. 1960. "Parallel Descent and the Apinayé Anomaly," *Southwestern J. Anthrop.*, 16:191–216.

Meyerowitz, Eva L. 1951. The Sacred State of the Akan. London: Faber.

Middleton, John. 1960. Lugbara Religion: Ritual and Religion Among an East African People. London: Oxford University Press.

Morgan, Lewis H. 1877. Ancient Society. London: Macmillan.

Murphy, Gardner. 1959. "Discussion," Chap. 19, in The Meaning of Death. Edited by Herman Feifel. New York: McGraw-Hill.

Nadel, S. F. 1942. A Black Byzantium. London: Oxford University Press.

——. 1947. The Nuba. London: Oxford University Press.

——. 1950. "Dual Descent in the Nuba Hills," in African Systems of Kinship and Marriage. Edited by A. R. Radcliffe-Brown and D. Forde. London: Oxford University Press.

———. 1951. The Foundations of Social Anthropology. London: Cohen and West.

———. 1954. Nupe Religion. Glencoe, Ill.: Free Press.

———. 1957. The Theory of Social Structure. London: Cohen and West.

Neale, Walter C. 1957. "The Market in Theory and History," in Trade and Market in the Early Empires. Edited by Karl Polanyi, Conrad M. Arensberg, and Harry W. Pearson. Glencoe, Ill.: Free Press.

Needham, R. 1960. "The Left Hand of the Mugwe: An Analytical Note on the Structure of Meru Symbolism," Africa, 30:20–33.

Newcomb, Theodore M. 1950. Social Psychology. New York: Dryden Press.

Noyes, C. Reinold. 1936. The Institution of Property. New York: Longmans, Green.

Onians, Richard Broxton. 1954. The Origins of European Thought. 2d rev. ed. Cambridge: Cambridge University Press.

Opler, M. E. 1936. "An Interpretation of Ambivalence of Two American Indian Tribes," J. Soc. Psych., 7:82–116.

Parsons, Talcott. 1937. The Structure of Social Action. New York: McGraw-Hill.

Patai, Raphael. 1959. Sex and the Family in the Bible and the Middle East. New York: Doubleday.

Paulme, Denise. 1940. Organisation sociales des Dogon (Soudan français). Paris: Domat-Montchrestien. (Institut de droit comparé. Études de sociologie et d'ethnologie juridiques, 32.)

Peters, E. L. 1960. "The Proliferation of Lineage Segments in the Lineage of the Bedouin of Cyrenaica," J. R. Anthrop. Inst., 90:29–53.

Phillpotts, Bertha Surtees. 1913. Kindred and Clan in the Middle Ages and After. A Study in the Sociology of the Teutonic Races. Cambridge: Cambridge University Press. (Cambridge Archaeological and Ethnological Ser.)

Polanyi, Karl, Arensberg, Conrad M., and Pearson, Harry M. (eds.). 1957. Trade and Market in the Early Empires. Glencoe, Ill.: Free Press.

Radcliffe-Brown, A. R. 1929. "The Sociological Theory of Totemism," in Proceedings of the Fourth Pacific Science Congress, 3:295–309. Java.

———. 1948. The Andaman Islanders. Glencoe, Ill.: Free Press. (1st ed., Cambridge University Press, 1922; reprinted with additions, 1933; first American printing, 1948.)

———. 1952a. "Social Sanctions," in Structure and Function in Primitive Society, pp. 205–11. Glencoe, Ill.: Free Press. (Reprinted from Encyclopedia of the Social Sciences, XIII, 531–34, New York, Macmillan.)

———. 1952b. "Patrilineal and Matrilineal Succession," in Structure and Function in Primitive Society, pp. 32–48. Glencoe, Ill.: Free Press. (Reprinted from the Symposium on Intestate Succession, Iowa Law Review (1935), 20:286–303.)

———. 1952c. "Taboo," in Structure and Function in Primitive Society, pp. 133–52. Glencoe, Ill.: Free Press. (First published, Cambridge University Press, 1939.)

———. 1952d. "Religion and Society," in Structure and Function in Primitive Society, pp. 153–77. Glencoe, Ill.: Free Press. (Reprinted from J. R. Anthrop. Inst. (1945), 75:33–43.)

————, and Forde, D. (eds.). 1950. African Systems of Kinship and Marriage. London: Oxford University Press.

Radin, P. 1930. "Ancestor Worship," in Encyclopedia of the Social Sciences, II, 53–55. New York: Macmillan.

Rattray, R. S. 1927. Religion and Art in Ashanti. London: Oxford University Press.

————. 1929. Ashanti Law and Constitution. London: Oxford University Press.

————. 1932. Tribes of the Ashanti Hinterland. Oxford: Clarendon Press.

Richards, Audrey I. 1956. Chisungu: A Girl's Initiation Ceremony Among the Bemba of Northern Rhodesia. London: Faber.

Ridgeway, William. 1910. The Origin of Tragedy. Cambridge: Cambridge University Press.

Rivers, W. H. R. 1926. Psychology and Ethnology. London: Kegan Paul.

Robertson Smith, W. 1927. Lectures on the Religion of the Semites. 3d rev. ed. London: Black. (1st ed. 1889.)

Rose, H. J. 1930. "Ancient Italian Beliefs Concerning the Soul," *The Classical Quarterly*, 24: 129–35.

Ryle, G. 1949. The Concept of the Mind. London: Hutchinson's University Library.

Schnore, Leo F. 1958. "Social Morphology and Human Ecology," *Am. J. Soc.*, 63:620–34.

Southall, A. W. 1959. "A Note on Local Descent Groups," *Man*, 59:65–66.

Spencer, H. 1896. The Principles of Sociology. 3d rev. ed. New York: Appleton. (1st ed. 1875–76.)

Spiro, Melford. 1953. "A Typology of Functional Analysis," *Explorations*, 1: 89–94. Toronto.

Srinivas, M. N. 1952. Religion and Society Among the Coorgs of South India. Oxford: Clarendon Press.

Stenning, Derrick J. 1959. Savannah Nomads. London: Oxford University Press.

Steiner, F. 1954. "Notes on Comparative Economics," *Brit. J. Soc.*, 5: 118–29.

Stone, Lawrence. 1961. "Marriage Among the English Nobility in the 16th and 17th Centuries," *Comparative Studies in Society and History*, 3:182–206.

Tait, David. 1961. The Konkomba of Northern Ghana. London: Oxford University Press.

Togan, A. Z. V. 1939. "Ibn Fadlan's Reisebericht," *Abhandlungen für die Kunde des Morgenlandes*, 24:3. Leipzig.

Trimingham, J. S. 1959. Islam in West Africa. Oxford: Clarendon Press.

Turner, V. W. 1953. Lunda Rites and Ceremonies. Livingstone, Northern Rhodesia. (Occasional Papers of the Rhodes-Livingstone Museum, No. 10.)

Tylor, Edward B. 1865. Researches into the Early History of Mankind and the Development of Civilization. London: Murray.

————. 1866. "The Religion of Savages," *Fortnightly Review*, 4:71–86.

————. 1889. "On a Method of Investigating the Development of Institutions," *J. Anthrop. Inst.*, 18:245–69.

————. 1920. Primitive Culture. 6th ed. New York: Putnam's. (1st ed., London, Murray, 1871.)

Vedder, Heinrich. 1938. South-West Africa in Early Times. London: Oxford University Press.

Van Gennep, Arnold. 1960. The Rites of Passage. English translation, London: Routledge and Kegan Paul. (1st French ed. 1909.)

Vinogradoff, Sir Paul. 1920. Outlines of Historical Jurisprudence. Vol. I: Introduction—Tribal Law. London: Oxford University Press.

————. 1922. Outlines of Historical Jurisprudence. Vol. II: Jurisprudence of the Greek City. London: Oxford University Press.

————. 1926. "Succession," in Encyclopædia Britannica, XXVI, 2–5. 13th ed.

————. 1929. Roman Law in Medieval Europe. 2d ed. Oxford: Clarendon Press. (1st ed. 1909.)

Warner, W. Lloyd. 1937. A Black Civilization. New York: Harper.

————. 1959. The Living and the Dead: A Study of the Symbolic Life of Americans. New Haven: Yale University Press.

Whiting, John W. M., and Child, Irvin L. 1953. Child Training and Personality. New Haven: Yale University Press.

Wilson, Monica. 1951. Good Company: A Study of Nyakyusa Age-Villages. London: Oxford University Press.

————. 1954. "Nyakyusa Ritual and Symbolism," Am. Anthrop., 56:228–41.

————. 1957. Rituals of Kinship Among the Nyakyusa. London: Oxford University Press.

Worsley, P. M. 1955. "Totemism in a Changing Society," Am. Anthrop., 57: 851–61.

Zuckerman, S. 1932. The Social Life of Monkeys and Apes. London: Kegan Paul.

Index